Chicago Divided
The Making of a Black Mayor

Paul Kleppner

Northern Illinois University Press / DeKalb, Illinois

Library of Congress Cataloging in Publication Data

Kleppner, Paul.
    Chicago divided.

    Bibliography: p.
    Includes index.
    1. Washington, Harold, 1922– . 2. Chicago (Ill.)—
Mayors—Election. 3. Chicago (Ill.)—Politics and
government—1951– . 4. Chicago (Ill.)—Race
relations. I. Title.
F548.52.W36K54 1984   324.9773'11043   84-25531
ISBN 0-87580-106-4
ISBN 0-87580-532-9 (pbk.)

Table of Contents

Illustrations and Maps

Illustrations

Maps

Tables

Acknowledgments

■ This book will always remind me that the Princes of Serendip still ride across the landscape and sometimes intrude into our lives to alter our best-developed plans.

Seven months ago, I had no thought of writing this book. I was then busily at work on two other books, and well along in developing the research design for a third, none of which bear any resemblance to this one in subject matter, concept, or even style. Only now, armed with infallible hindsight, can I see that I moved through distinct stages on the way to the decision to write this book and to complete it before the others.

The first stage was initiated by Mark Posner and Robert Berman, lawyers for the U.S. Department of Justice, Civil Rights Division, Voting Rights Section. In September 1982, they asked me to "look at" the biracial aldermanic contests that had occurred in Chicago since 1975 and to testify to my findings in a federal suit challenging the city's recently redrawn ward map. The analysis was fascinating to me, because it revealed patterns of racial polarization so stark that they had no obvious counterparts except in the late-nineteenth-century South.

The next stage came in April 1983, when Jonathan Levine, Midwest Region Director, American Jewish Committee, asked me to prepare a "brief but thorough" research report describing the voting patterns of ethnic, racial, and religious groups in Chicago's recent mayoral election. That work reminded me of what I shouldn't have forgotten: citizens bring their memories with them to the polling places. The mixture of enthusiasm and bitterness that marked Chicago's 1983 electoral season can't be comprehended except in light of that simple maxim. Still, even when the research report was completed and released, in August 1983, I had no intention of writing this book. In fact, I was anxious to dedicate whatever time I could snatch from my administrative responsibilities to other projects.

The third and decisive stage in the process was due to the intervention and quiet but persuasive persistence of Mary Livingston, Director of the Northern Illinois University Press. She read the research report and asked whether I planned "to do anything more" with it. Her questions and suggestions were stimulating. And she prodded me further by sending the report to an anonymous referee, whose evaluation was positive and whose suggestions for expansion largely reinforced the notions that Mary's queries had led me to develop. Finally, in early September 1983, at the end of a pleasant luncheon session with Mary and my colleague Bruce Lincoln—probably as we were finishing our second bottle of wine—I agreed "to fill in the holes" in the research report and deliver a book manuscript to the NIU Press within a few months.

Of course, by the time I made that commitment, Wilson Goode had won the Democratic mayoral nomination in Philadelphia, and Jesse Jackson was on the verge of announcing his candidacy for the Democratic presidential nomination. Thus, questions bearing on the political mobilization and cohesiveness of the country's black citizens had relevance that went well beyond Chicago. That consideration appealed to my analytic interests as a social scientist and to my concerns as a citizen.

To all those who nudged or prodded me through these stages, I owe considerable gratitude. I especially want to acknowledge the American Jewish Committee, Chicago Chapter, both for funding the earlier research report and for the support and encouragement its professional staff provided through the phases of that work.

Once I turned to the task of writing this book, I made two other significant decisions. First, at Mary Livingston's urging, I decided to simplify the presentation of statistical information. Second, I decided that I had to do much more than flesh out the original research report. Completing that document was a useful, and perhaps a necessary, heuristic exercise, but its mode of argument and even its organizational framework no longer remained appropriate. I judged that it was better to begin virtually *de novo*, and so I did.

I was able to translate these decisions into the pages that follow because I could avail myself of the skills and commitment of an extremely able research staff. Deepack Kumar, Elizabeth Johnson, Loomis Mayfield, and Nadeem Mazhar handled the data-processing tasks and, as usual, worked well beyond the normal call of duty. So did Stephen Baker, who initially directed and supervised their activities and also gave invaluable counsel concerning the analysis. When

Steve left to join the Department of Political Science, University of Texas at Arlington, Kevin Himmelberger took over the supervisory duties and continues to perform them ably and with abundant good humor. Thomas Butcher and Mark Pullinger provided invaluable assistance in tracking down legal citations and newspaper reports.

At one stage or another in the process, I incurred still other debts that are a pleasure to acknowledge. The Board of Election Commissioners of the City of Chicago provided precinct voting and registration data in machine-readable form, and the speedy cooperation of the data-processing staff of that office was especially important. The Census Data Laboratory, Social Science Research Institute, Northern Illinois University, provided block-level census data for Chicago; and the programming staff of the Institute's Center for Governmental Studies developed the software to aggregate the block data to match the city's precinct boundaries at each election.

Nick Panagakis, Market Shares Corporation, was generous in allowing me access to the Channel 2 News exit polls from the primary and general elections; he also shared other poll reports with me and answered my questions concerning the technical standards he had used to design and conduct the surveys. Bill Gammel, Roper Center for Public Opinion Research, intervened to speed the process of cleaning and reformatting the WMAQ-TV (NBC) exit polls to assure their timely availability. Peggy Einnehmer, NBC News, provided copies of staff reports on the results of those election-day polls and information concerning technical standards. Juan Andrade and Wilfredo Nieves, both of the Midwest Voter Registration Education Project, supplied copies of their own analysis of the MVREP exit poll among Hispanics and made the original data available for secondary analysis.

The staffs of the Chicago Municipal Reference Library and Founders Library, Northern Illinois University, were invariably and enthusiastically helpful. I received unusual help in searching for graphic materials to illustrate this book. Mamie Grady, Art Section, the Chicago Public Library, provided items from her personal collection of campaign materials. Howard I. Finberg, photo/graphics editor of the *Chicago Tribune*, interrupted his busy schedule, answered my questions, and cooperated with my requests. And Barry Stark, of the Art/Photo Department of Northern Illinois University, skillfully solved the problem of making reproducible photographs from videotapes.

My colleagues at the Social Science Research Institute contributed to this enterprise by quietly tolerating my preoccupation and patiently listening to my seemingly endless ramblings about Chicago politics and politicians. Even more importantly, however, they encouraged my commitment through the example of their own productivity. And one of them, Kevin McKeough, made a special contribution. He shared with me his firsthand knowledge of Chicago, its people, and its politics, and thereby enhanced my understanding and, especially, my appreciation of the city and of its political folkways.

I must also acknowledge the enduring contribution of three administrators: William R. Monat, President of Northern Illinois University; John E. LaTourette, Vice President and Provost; and James D. Norris, Dean of the College of Liberal Arts and Sciences. It was because of their decisive leadership and research commitment that the Social Science Research Institute was established. They have worked tirelessly, and sometimes thanklessly, in behalf of the research mission of the university.

This book could not have been begun, let alone completed, without the assistance, support, and encouragement that I received from all of these quarters. But there remains an even greater debt. It is to the black citizens of Chicago, to the leaders of their community and social organizations, and to Harold Washington. Together, they had the courage to make the political revolution that I have only chronicled. It may still be true, as Alderman Paddy Bauler observed in 1955, that "Chicago ain't ready for reform"; but ready or not, "Heeeere's Harold"! His election has made Chicago politics more lively than it has been in decades. Even more importantly, it has restored the democratic process to the city's government and, for the first time in generations, offered meaningful hope to its minorities. It is those developments, and not simply buildings, programs, and the appearance of orderly procedures, that promise to make "the great city of Chicago" even greater.

Chicago Divided
The Making of a Black Mayor

1. Politics Chicago Style
The Turning Point

Why did they do this to me? *Richard J. Daley (6 April 1968)*

■ Friday, 5 April 1968, should have been a day of happiness and celebration for Mayor Richard J. Daley, his family, his friends, and his political dependents. It was the thirteenth anniversary of his first election as mayor of Chicago.

If events had unfolded routinely, Mayor Daley would have begun the day, as he had since childhood, by attending mass at the Church of the Nativity of Our Lord, where he had been baptized and married, just around the corner from his home in Bridgeport. After mass, his limousine would have made the short drive to City Hall, about four miles northeast. Between Bridgeport and the Loop, the city's downtown business district, the car would have used the Dan Ryan Expressway, following a route that crossed the Stevenson and Eisenhower Expressways and passed an exit to the Circle Campus of the University of Illinois. As the Dan Ryan neared the Loop and blended into the Kennedy Expressway, which leads to O'Hare Airport, the world's busiest jetway, the limousine would have exited into the business district and made its way northward to City Hall. On this leg of the journey, it would have passed some of the 125 new office and apartment buildings whose construction had redefined the city's skyline.

The expressways, the campus, the new buildings, and most of O'Hare, which Daley always called "O'Hara," were among the achievements of his first three terms as mayor. But His Honor probably would not have noticed any of this scenery, since during the drive he usually read the city's two morning newspapers. On this day, he might have expected to read editorials congratulating him on his anniversary and extolling his record of accomplishments. He might also have been thinking how to respond, later in the day, when City Hall reporters added their voices to the swelling chorus of praise. Normally, the mayor would have accepted their compliments in a matter-of-fact fashion, using the occasion to express yet once more his ardent love affair with "the great people of the great City of Chicago." But this time perhaps he might respond more expansively, for this anniversary day climaxed an especially good year. Just twelve months earlier he had polled the support of nearly three fourths of the city's voters and had been reelected to his fourth term by his largest margin of victory so far. Moreover, while 1967 saw rioting, burning, and looting in Atlanta, Cincinnati, Detroit, Newark, Tampa, and nearly 145 other cities, his "positive, constructive programs" saved Chicago from a similar fate. It was no wonder that Mayor Daley, in a newspaper interview in early January, had looked back on 1967 as a year to savor, as one might a vintage wine.[1]

Of course we shall never know what Mayor Daley *would have* said to the press corps that afternoon, because Chicagoans were not to remember that day, the Friday of Passion Week in the Catholic liturgical cycle, as the thirteenth anniversary of his first election as mayor. Instead they would remember the stunning news of the assassination of a man who had won the Nobel Peace Prize. The script for Daley's day of celebration had been rewritten the night before in Memphis, Tennessee, when a sniper's bullet ended the life of the Reverend Martin Luther King, Jr. For Daley, his city, and its people, Passion Friday became a day of agony.

The news of Dr. King's death reached Mayor Daley on Thursday evening, while he was attending a dinner of the Chicago Medical Society in the Drake Hotel, at the northern end of Michigan Avenue's "Magnificent Mile." As he sat through the remainder of the program, the mayor's thoughts may have turned to his earlier dealings with the civil rights leader. He may have remembered Dr. King's 1965 march on City Hall to protest segregated conditions in Chicago's schools; or he may have recalled 1966, when Dr. King focused on housing conditions and demanded that the city government make open housing a reality. On these occasions, Daley had shown the minister how the game was played—Chicago style. He had deftly identified himself with the struggle against poverty and discrimination, proclaiming that "your goals are our goals," even while he denied that segregation existed in Chicago and successfully resisted any substantive change in the city's housing and school policies.[2]

Still other recollections of 1966 may have come to the mayor's mind that evening. He may have thought of August, when Dr. King led his marches for open housing into Gage Park and Marquette

Park on the Southwest Side, and into Cragin, on the Northwest Side. The white residents of these neighborhoods reacted with fury: Dr. King was hit by a stone, and the Catholic priests and nuns marching with him were cursed and spat upon by their coreligionists. Large squads of police were needed to extricate the nonviolent marchers from the mobs of violent resisters.

And Daley must have thought about what had been, to that point, the worst period of his public life, the second week of July in 1966. The trouble began on Tuesday, just two days after Dr. King's address to a crowd of 40,000 at Soldier Field, the city's lakefront stadium. Despite an oppressive heat wave, the firemen in the Lawndale area had reacted to the falling water pressure by turning off the hydrants that black children used to cool themselves off. Tempers flared in the 100-degree heat, and rioting soon broke out. Policemen called to restore order were fired on by snipers from the windows and roofs of the public housing projects, and the city's West Side soon was in flames. Three days of shooting and looting ensued, and 4,200 National Guardsmen were needed to restore order to the riot area.

Many white Chicagoans, including the mayor, associated the riot with Dr. King's activities and his calls for civil disobedience. On the morning of the third day of rioting, Daley appeared on television and articulated the connection: "I think you can't charge it directly to Dr. Martin Luther King, but surely some of his people who came in here and have been talking for the past year of violence—they are on his staff. They are responsible in great measure for the instruction that has been given, for the training of these youngsters." But later that day, meeting with King and other black leaders, Daley disavowed any claim that civil rights activities had been responsible and accepted a suggestion that the firemen turn the hydrants back on and equip them with spray nozzles. Indeed, Daley eagerly jumped on that suggestion; it was a program, and he liked programs. City Hall joined forces with the Fire Department and the Chicago Park District to attach sprinklers to hundreds of hydrants and to truck in portable swimming pools. The mayor's enthusiasm for this "wet-the-black" program prompted one civil rights worker to observe: "I think they're hoping we'll all grow gills and swim away."[3]

"They" had not yet swum away, and Mayor Daley must have surmised, as he left the Drake that evening, that his own hopes for racial peace in Chicago also died on the balcony of that motel in Memphis. His intelligence sources in the black communities—the Democratic precinct captains and policemen who worked or lived there—soon confirmed his darkest fears. Throughout that night they transmitted to City Hall their sense of the feelings that were building in the ghetto, feelings of disbelief and numbness that quickly gave way to outrage.

As Thursday turned to Friday, an eerie calm seemed to settle on the city. Behind that facade, tensions were building on both sides of the racial divide. The sickening despair that blacks first felt when they heard the news was turning to anger, and whites were becoming increasingly fearful that the outrage of the ghetto would be directed against their communities. Mayor Daley did what he could to defuse the time bomb before it exploded. He ordered the American flag to be flown at half-staff above all municipal buildings, and he scheduled a memorial service in City Council chambers for Friday morning.

Daley addressed the Council service, and the radio and television audience beyond its chambers, praising Martin Luther King as "a dedicated and courageous American who commanded the respect of the people of the world." But even as the mayor was urging his listeners to "soften the grief of Dr. King's family and associates by demonstrating that his life was not in vain," the crowds were gathering on the city's West Side.[4] Black schoolchildren, boycotting classes out of respect to Dr. King, were coming together to mourn his death. Once they had assembled in Garfield Park, their collective anguish rapidly turned to anger. The crowd of schoolchildren became a mob, moving out of the park into West Madison Street, smashing windows and snatching merchandise. By mid-afternoon they began to burn down their own community.

The first fire alarm from the West Side riot area was reported at 3:49 P.M. A second was received within a minute. Then there was another, and another, and 594 more within the next twenty-three hours. They came so fast that the city's chief fire alarm operator, Daniel Sullivan, couldn't log them all. "You can't tell where the fires are," he told reporters. "They're walking west and burning as they go."

Before the city's Passion Week had ended, 162 buildings had been destroyed by fire; 268 buildings and homes had been looted; 2,931 persons had been arrested; 500 people had been injured, and 9—all blacks—had been killed. To restore order, 12,000 army troops, 7,000 National Guardsmen, and half of the city's 12,000-man police force had served on riot duty. And the damage that had been done to race relations in the city was beyond arithmetic calculation.[5]

As he did so often, Mayor Daley voiced the feelings of those white Chicagoans who could not understand this apparently senseless violence. On Saturday, during his first inspection of the still smoldering West Side, he wondered aloud, "Why did they do this to me?" Why, he seemed to be asking, when he had done so much for them, did blacks repay his benevolence with such ingratitude? Again, on Palm Sunday, after a forty-five-minute helicopter flight over the ravaged area, the mayor expressed incomprehension: "I never believed that this would happen here." He had done too much, he was suggesting; he

1. Aerial view of 3300 block of riot-torn West Madison Street, 7 April 1968. (*Chicago Tribune.*)

had too many programs for this to have occurred. "No city has as many programs as Chicago," he added later, as if to underscore his disbelief.[6]

Daley's state of shock wore off by mid-week, and by Holy Saturday the riot area seemed to be under control. The mayor left the city to spend a peaceful Easter weekend at his estate in Grand Beach, Michigan. By the time he returned to City Hall on Easter Monday, his initial incomprehension had hardened into resentment and anger. "The pendulum has gone too far," he had concluded. "Now I'm goin' out and make a statement about this and everybody is goin' to understand what we mean."[7]

No one could have mistaken what Mayor Daley said and meant at his news conference on that day. He began by naming a nine-member committee to investigate all aspects of the riot. Then he criticized the police and the administration of the public schools for conditions that he characterized as "indescribable" on the day the rioting began. "The beating of girls, the slashing of teachers, and the general turmoil and the payoffs and the extortions. . . . Principals tell us what's happening and they are told to forget it." Those who opposed school integration had long believed as much, and now the statements of the city's chief executive gave credence to the rumors and fears. In denouncing disorder and danger in the schools, however, Daley was only warming to his task. His real targets that morning were those individuals who had participated in the riots. The mayor said that he had ordered the police "to shoot to kill any arsonist or anyone with a Molotov cocktail in his hand, . . . to shoot to maim or cripple anyone looting any store," and to use MACE, a chemical deterrent, to "detain youngsters" involved in arson or looting. Lest anyone misunderstand, or think that he had only recently converted to this brand of vigilante justice, Daley added that he had issued similar orders before the riot. "I assumed [the] superintendent would issue instructions to shoot arsonists on sight and to maim the looters, . . . [and] I was disappointed to know that every policeman out on the beat was supposed to use his own decision." There would be no similar disappointments in the future, Daley assured the press, because he had conferred with Superintendent of Police James B. Conlisk that morning and reissued the orders.[8]

The negative reaction to Mayor Daley's "shoot to kill" statement was instantaneous and massive. The mayor and his press spokesmen spent the better part of the next two days explaining "what I really said." On Tuesday night, following his speech at a dinner of the Western Railway Club, Daley told a reporter that his order had "been completely misunderstood. Everyone has blown this thing out of proportion." On Wednesday he read a carefully drafted statement to the City Council to clarify his earlier declaration: "It is the established policy of the Chicago Police Department—fully supported by the administration—that only minimum force necessary be used by policemen in carrying out their duties." But whenever "minimum force necessary cannot prevent or deter" arsonists and looters, such persons "cannot be given permissive rights" to engage in criminal action. "We cannot resign ourselves to the proposition that civil protest must lead to death and devastation—to the abandonment of the law that is fundamental for the preservation of the rights of all people and their freedom."[9]

Daley's "shoot to kill" pronouncement was no doubt an instinctive reaction, prompted by temper mixed with a sense that his benevolence had been betrayed. As a lawyer he knew that the statutes of the state of Illinois imposed stringent restrictions on the use of deadly force by police and that Conlisk could not legally issue the order as the mayor commanded. While Daley's statement was bad law, it expressed the anxieties and fears of most white Chicagoans, and it proved to be good politics.

The dramatic events of April 1968 serve to bring Chicago's problem of race relations into clear focus. On the one side, there were the

2. Looters in action on the 400 block of West Division Street, 6 April 1968. (Chicago Historical Society, ICHi-03621. Photograph by T. Kneebone.)

hopes and rising expectations of the city's blacks. Hopes for better schools, better housing, better jobs—in short, for opportunities that most white Chicagoans had long taken for granted. The marches, demonstrations, and protests of the mid-1960s had awakened these yearnings as never before. They had conditioned younger blacks, especially, to expect improvement, for if it could come in Alabama and Mississippi, the citadels of southern segregation, why not in Chicago?

On the other side, there were white Chicagoans, especially those who lived in or near racially changing neighborhoods, or who had moved from those areas to more distant residences. They hoped at least to conserve what they had for themselves, while expecting improved schools, housing, and better jobs for their children. They saw the civil rights movement, with its demands for integrated schools and housing, as a threat to these aspirations.

In the middle, there was the city government, personified to black and white Chicagoans alike by His Honor Richard J. Daley. The mayor became the focal point and symbol for the city's racial tensions because, for all practical purposes and for a generation of Chicagoans, he *was* the city government. Through his control over the city's dominant political party, he surmounted the limitations the city charter placed on the mayor's authority. As chairman-mayor, he ruled the city, controlling its taxing and spending policies, dispensing jobs, initiating programs, and always striving, according to his own lights, "to make this great city even greater."

For all his vision of Chicago's future and his sense of its past, Daley could not understand the aspirations of its black residents. He had given them programs; he had dispensed patronage to black politicians; he had built housing projects in their communities; he had even selected some blacks to serve on the Board of Education and the Chicago Housing Authority. What more could they want? Daley could not have answered that question, even if he had bothered to ask it. Self-determination and control over one's own destiny ultimately involve abstract principles, and Daley thought and spoke best in the language of concrete programs. "It's easy to criticize," he said so often, implying that his critics had no constructive "programs" to suggest as alternatives to his own. From his point of view, black leaders offered no positive alternatives, none at least that failed to involve integrated housing and schools, the right of blacks to choose their own political leadership, and the opportunities to advance the interests of the black community politically. The mayor simply did not regard programs with those objectives as constructive.

In the final analysis, Mayor Daley responded the way he did to the events of April 1968 because he viewed black Chicagoans as subjects of his regime rather than as citizens of the city. His paternalistic attitude, which justified the continued imposition of white leadership in areas where whites had become small minorities of the population, collided with an awakening self-consciousness among blacks. This collision in turn spawned the political revolution through which Daley's heirs lost control of the city government.

This book tells the story of that political upheaval, how it developed, how it was accomplished, and whose votes brought it to pass. If this were a fictional account, we would see the movement for black redemption arising phoenix-like from the ashes and rubble of the West Side conflagration. Black consciousness would have been aroused immediately and would have turned toward political action to secure for black citizens a larger and more equitable share of the Chicago version of the American dream. But reality is not only frequently stranger than fiction; it always develops more slowly. Daley was again reelected, in 1971 and 1975, outpolling his opposition within the black areas of the city on both occasions. And his successors, Mayors Michael Bilandic and Jane Byrne, proved to be no more sensitive to the aspirations of the city's growing black population than Daley had been.

On 12 April 1983, fifteen years and eight days after the assassination of Martin Luther King, blacks finally asserted their rights as citizens of Chicago. They came alive politically and took control of the executive branch of their city's government. This dramatic event—the election of Chicago's first black mayor—is the focal point of the city's political revolution and of this book.

Dramatic events capture headlines, and Chicago's recent mayoral election attracted unprecedented coverage by the national media: reports of campaign events were aired on the networks' evening news shows, and stories and feature articles appeared on the pages of nationally distributed news magazines, opinion journals, and newspapers. But a dramatic event such as this is often only the tip of the proverbial iceberg, the climax of a larger, longer, and perhaps less dramatic process.

So it is with Chicago's 1983 election. The out-of-town journalists who reported the campaign were at once appalled, fascinated, and mystified by its tenor. Politics Chicago style, vintage 1983, seemed to them to be a throwback to the politics of the Deep South pre-1964, or even earlier. These visitors wondered aloud how two decades of progress and enlightenment in race relations could have bypassed Chicago, or at least had so little lasting impact. Had they known enough of the history of the city's politics and of the political cultures of its major population groups, they would have understood better why that electoral battle took the shape it did and what the struggle meant to the people of Chicago.

This study of the 1983 election provides this necessary historical context. It begins with a panoramic view of the city's population shifts and its political changes over the past century, looking especially at the ethnic composition of the city's population and at the ways in which the distinctive mixture of groups worked to shape party strategies and voting coalitions. Next, it presents a closer view of the changes in racial composition that have occurred since 1940 and shows how the increased size and residential expansion of the black community generated new social tensions and political issues. It then turns to an analysis of electoral politics during the Daley years (1955–1976) and links the growing racial tension to the change that occurred by the mid-1970s in the mayor's (and the Machine's) sources of voting support. Changes in voting patterns continued during the Bilandic-Byrne years (1977–1983); and while the faces, names, and incidents differed, that six-year interregnum was but another installment in Chicago's longest-running saga—the politics of race. The story reaches its climax with the events of 1982–1983: the voter-registration drive in the black community, the heated primary contest, and the sulfurous general election. The final chapter appraises the longer-term and broader significance of Chicago's electoral drama of 1983.

The rationale underpinning this historical approach is simple enough. We can understand current events only by locating them within the framework that shapes their character and gives them meaning. While it is true that people make their own history, it is equally true that they do so under circumstances and conditions and with memories inherited from the past.

Some final notes of explanation are in order. The description and analysis that follow are built upon an extensive empirical foundation. The building blocks are an analysis of voting returns for city, county, state, and national offices at the ward level since the 1870s and at the precinct level since 1970, as well as a large body of evidence from public opinion polls, including secondary analyses of the 1983 election-day exit polls. Only a small portion of the statistical results appears on these pages, and I have tried to present the information in a way that is easy to understand, usually confining it to simple percentages. For those who want explanations of the techniques and fancier statistics, the notes draw attention to the appropriate literature and to papers and reports in which I have used and discussed more complex statistical operations and models.

The use of public opinion polls as a source of evidence also requires some discussion. Over the past two decades, polling has become as routine a part of electioneering as door-to-door canvassing was in an earlier period. Candidates for major offices regularly hire pollsters to determine what subjects most concern the public, to aid them in shaping and targeting their campaign appeals, and to track their standing among the voters.[10] Not content with reporting the activities and statements of the candidates, media outlets now create their own campaign "news" by commissioning preelection polls, presenting their findings, and speculating on what they mean. As a result, the horse-race aspect of contemporary campaigns—who's ahead this week?—receives far greater publicity than the policy dimensions.[11]

By the end of a campaign, the public has endured a barrage of poll findings, but it still faces one final survey—the election-day exit poll. These are usually commissioned by the major television networks (or their local affiliates) to give their analysts a diagnostic tool that allows them to describe and interpret the reported voting preferences of particular groups. Contrary to popular impression, however, television analysts do not base their early predictions of the outcome on these election-day polls. They use voting returns from selected and demographically "key" precincts for that purpose, with the results of the exit polls serving only as a baseline for comparison.

As polls have become more prominent in campaigns, the public has grown increasingly skeptical of them. Some candidates and campaign managers, including those who use polls, also harbor doubts. This distrust partially reflects the ill-founded belief that polls create a bandwagon effect and thus become self-fulfilling prophecies.[12] Paradoxically, however, the more serious basis for doubt is a widespread belief that polls do not reliably measure the public's preferences. Unfortunately, there is no single and simple answer to questions concerning the accuracy of public opinion polls. Each survey has to be evaluated individually, paying special attention to the design of the sample and the wording of the questions—the major sources of invalidating bias. Generally, however, if credible procedures are used to design and conduct the survey, then its results are a reliable gauge of public opinion on those questions at the time they were asked.[13] Those results do not, however, indicate how the public will react to later events. In other words, polls measure current opinion, but they do not predict its future state.

Of course, since predicting the outcome of an election is precisely what most interests the candidates, the media, and even the voters, there is a nearly irresistible tendency to construe "who's ahead at the moment" as meaning "who's ultimately going to win." If the election returns then don't square with the preelection soundings, observers routinely decry the polls, typically without noticing the actual source of error—the use of static information to predict the outcome of a future event.

Discrepancies between preelection polls and voting returns can be due to a number of factors that do not reflect negatively on the credibility of the polling process. Last-minute campaign developments may push undecided citizens toward a single candidate and/or lead others to switch from their previous choices. In these cases, polls taken earlier can't be faulted for failing to detect reactions to events that hadn't yet occurred. Another type of discrepancy arises from the simple fact that there are no "undecided" responses on election day, at least among those who vote, whereas preelection reports are usually based on all respondents, including those who haven't yet made up their minds. Thus, what seems to be a dramatic jump— from, say, 8 percent in the final preelection poll to 25 percent among those who vote—may result from nothing more than "dropping" the undecideds.[14]

Still another source of discrepancy is unique to political polling. Pollsters can easily develop samples that accurately represent the general population or even the voting-age population of some jurisdictions. But political polling is especially concerned with the opinion of those who are most likely to vote, and pollsters have to factor some turnout estimate into their results. Typically, they use each group's past record of turnout as the baseline for projections. If the involved groups turn out at much greater (or lower) rates than they had historically, the poll results will miss the mark. What is inaccurate in such cases is not the poll itself but the factors used to weight the responses from particular groups into an overall result.

This analysis of Chicago politics steers clear of these potential sources of discrepancy and misinterpretation. The preelection polls that are referenced were conducted by organizations with solid reputations and, more to the point, with excellent records for accurately measuring public opinion in Chicago. Thus, it is highly unlikely that their procedures were technically faulty, and that is especially so since several polling agencies independently developed similar results. Moreover, my use of these preelection polls is appropriately limited to presenting a picture of what the public, and especially the candidates, knew of public opinion *at the time of each survey.* I have developed descriptions of trends in public opinion by explicitly comparing separate preelection polls taken at different times, and I have not attempted to use the results from one poll to describe opinion at some future point. Finally, my detailed analysis of the patterns of voting support and motivation relies on the election-day exit polls, whose overall results square remarkably well with the actual voting returns.[15]

2. Population Diversity and Political Change, 1870–1970

Having seen it, I urgently desire never to see it again. It is inhabited by savages . . . and its air is dirt. *Rudyard Kipling (1889)*

■ Chicago is not a genteel and sophisticated city. It does not pretend to be the "Athens of America," the country's center of high culture and quiet refinement. Even its boosters describe it in Carl Sandburg's pithy but unglamorous phrases as the "hog butcher to the world," the city of "the big shoulders."

For most of its past, Chicago was a city of stockyards and smokestacks, where the pungent odors of slaughterhouses and manufacturing plants mixed together to foul the air. Except for its attractive lakefront, it was an ugly and depressing place, a city of densely populated and aging neighborhoods interspersed with unsightly industrial developments. And its civic image always matched its physical appearance. Chicago gained a reputation as a sprawling and lusty town, inhabited by tough and brawling people, a place where public corruption outstripped civic virtue. Other cities were recognized for the accomplishments of their respected social, religious, and political leaders, but Alphonse Capone became the personification of Chicago's civic image and the St. Valentine's Day Massacre its best-known event. In the popular imagination, criminal violence became an integral part of the city's broader reputation for toughness and corruption.

More than a thousand gangland assassinations (practically all unsolved) and countless newspaper exposés of payoffs and crooked deals involving local officials inured most Chicagoans to crime and corruption. Even the cold-blooded murder of an alderman in 1963, which would have led to a public clamor in other places, merited only fleeting attention and cynical indifference from the city's tough, uncultured, and parochial population. "The feeling is that if he's an alderman, he's a crook, and if he's a crook, then that's their business." Rather than becoming defensive, some Chicagoans took perverse pride in their city's unsavory reputation. "Chicago is unique," one reformer remarked almost boastfully. "It is the only completely corrupt city in America."[1]

Studies of Chicago politics have generally reflected and contributed to this negative image. For the most part they have dealt with the unseemly—graft, corruption, the buying and selling of public officials and services—and have glossed over the relationship between the city's politics and its social groups. They have depicted colorful personalities, attacked the evils of bossism, or described what the aldermen took from the city, while paying scant attention to the larger question of what the masses of Chicagoans got from participating in the political process. This neglect has yielded a one-dimensional view of the city's past that limits understanding of its political present.

Population Growth

■ Chicago has always been a city of immigrants and neighborhoods. But the same description applies to Boston, Cleveland, Philadelphia, Pittsburgh, Milwaukee, New York, and other cities, which grew in size during the second half of the nineteenth century by recruiting labor forces from Europe. And immigrants who came to all of these places established their own ethnic neighborhoods and networks of social relations. Chicago's pattern of population growth and settlement was simply part of the common experience of burgeoning industrial cities.[2]

A wide variety of immigrant groups came to these cities, and each of them ended the century with a more heterogeneous population than it had one hundred, or even fifty, years earlier. Each city differed from the others in the number and comparative sizes of its immigrant settlements, and Chicago differed from the rest in yet another respect. Chicago's population included a wide range of reasonably sized immigrant groups, but none of them came close to constituting a majority. No other single fact of the city's social demography played so important a role in shaping its politics.

Chicago grew from a moderately sized city of about 300,000 in 1870 to a major urban center of nearly 1.7 million by 1900. The foreign-stock component must have accounted for most of this explosive growth, since the net increase in the number of Chicagoans who were native born of native-born parents was only about 203,000 (Table 1).[3] Over the next three decades, the city's population

Table 1. Components of Chicago's Population, 1870–1970 (in 000s)

| | | White | | Black |
	Total	Native Stock[1]	Foreign Stock[2]	
1870[3]	298	150	144	3
1880[3]	503	291	204	6
1890	1,099	230	855	14
1900	1,698	353	1,315	30
1910	2,185	447	1,693	44
1920	2,701	645	1,946	109
1930	3,376	968	2,174	233
1940[4]	3,394	1,036	2,082	277
1950	3,620	1,499	1,611	492
1960	3,550	1,428	1,277	812
1970	3,362	1,180	958	1,102
Components as Percentages of Total Population				
1890		20.9	77.7	1.2
1900		20.7	77.4	1.7
1910		20.4	77.5	2.0
1920		23.9	72.0	4.0
1930		28.6	64.4	6.9
1950		41.4	44.5	13.5
1960		40.2	35.9	22.8
1970		35.0	28.4	32.7

[1] Native-born of native-born parents.

[2] Foreign-born and native-born of foreign-born parents.

[3] In 1870 and 1880, the census reported only the numbers of foreign-born residents.

[4] In 1940, the census did not report the separate nativity categories, and the figures used here are estimates derived by applying the known 1930 ratios to the total white population reported for 1940.

almost doubled again, with about half of the increase deriving from gains among the foreign-stock, and another third from among the native-stock, whites. Thereafter, through 1970, there was little change in the size of the city's population: it grew by about 7 percent over the 1930 to 1950 period and then declined by about the same proportion over the next twenty years.

As early as 1890, and probably even earlier, Chicago was an "immigrant city," with its foreign-stock component making up over three quarters of the total population. The proportionate size of the foreign-stock category did not change much through the 1910 census. It dropped slightly by 1920 and then began a fairly linear decay, reflecting the combined effects of a slowdown in immigration and the census practice of classifying as native stock those whose grandparents were foreign born.

At least through the 1930s, Chicago's white ethnics comprised a clear majority of its population (Table 2).[4] If they had united in sup-

Table 2. Ethnic Categories as Percentages of Total Population [1]

	German and Irish	British Stock [2]	Norway and Sweden	Southern and Eastern Europe
1890	45.6	9.9	8.6	9.7
1900	38.5	9.5	8.6	15.1
1910	32.3	7.1	7.5	22.6
1920	23.0	5.3	6.1	28.0
1930	16.9	5.3	5.7	22.2
1950	9.8	3.2	3.2	17.3
1960	6.9	2.4	2.0	13.8
1970	3.8	1.4	1.1	10.5

[1] Each category includes the foreign-born and native-born of foreign-born parents.
[2] England, Scotland, Wales, and English Canada.

port of a single party or candidate, they could have dominated elections. But the city's foreign-stock population was never homogeneous; many of its subgroups were at war with each other. And no immigrant group was ever large enough to control electoral politics, either by itself or in combination with a likely ally (see Table 2). The best possibility of control by a simple coalition of two groups occurred toward the end of the nineteenth century, when German and Irish immigrants made up about 45 percent of the city's population.

The composition of Chicago's ethnic population has changed considerably over the past century. Northern and western European groups made up a majority through 1900, and a plurality as late as 1910. The sources of immigration shifted in the early years of the century, and by 1920, groups from southern and eastern Europe outranked the German and Irish tandem and were only slightly smaller than the combined total of all the older immigrant groups. The 1920 census was also the last time that the Germans ranked as the city's largest immigrant group, a place they had held since 1890. By 1930, the Poles moved into first place and have held the lead through 1970.

Even this picture doesn't tell the full story of Chicago's diversity. Ethnic-group labels often conceal great internal differences. Knowing that a person is Irish, for example, does not reveal much about the individual's social and political views. In this case, it is necessary to know whether "Irish" is an adjective modifying Catholic or Protestant. Similar sorts of distinctions must be made within other ethnic categories. Chicago's Germans were divided among Catholics, Lutherans, Jews, anticlericals, and Protestants. The Polish category in the census included Catholics, Jews, and a smaller number of secularist and anticlerical Poles, who formed the core support for the Polish National Alliance in the city. Even religious groups were divided internally. Among Jews, for example, the older Germans tended to be more liberal in religious practice than the newly arrived eastern Europeans.[5]

How diverse was Chicago's population? Unfortunately, since the Census Bureau frequently changed its reporting categories and conducted very few counts of religious membership, we can't develop a consistent series of measures covering the past century. However, we can answer the question for a shorter period of time by using data for racial and ethnic groups in combination with the religious information available from 1890 to 1930.[6] At the beginning of that period, if we had randomly selected pairs of individuals from Chicago's population, each pair would have differed on 43 percent of these racial, ethnic, and religious characteristics. By 1930, they would have differed on a slightly larger 48 percent.[7] How high was that level of difference? There is no absolute standard, but it compares quite well with what was measured thirty years later, when the population should have been generally more diverse. For example, in 1960, randomly selected pairs of Illinois residents differed on only 50 percent of their social characteristics, and the inhabitants of no state differed on more than 55 percent. Put another way, only eleven *states* in the country had a higher level of population diversity in 1960 than the *city* of Chicago had in the years between 1890 and 1930.[8]

Party Development

■ Its polyglot population conditioned Chicago's political practices and political structure. If parties and candidates wanted to win elections, they had to avoid presenting themselves as the exclusive representatives of the tangible or symbolic interests of any single group, or even handful of groups. Party managers had to aim their appeals at a wide variety of groups, to reach beyond their core supporters and mobilize a heterogeneous coalition of voters. They had to balance interests, to smooth social conflicts, and to develop a common front to rally all of the party's potential supporters. That task is always difficult, but especially so when the population is growing rapidly and its ethnic composition is in a state of flux.

Through the end of the nineteenth century, in most of the North and the Midwest, ethnic and religious conflicts underlay party battles.[9] Chicago's party managers responded to these larger political currents by developing a local coalitional politics that pivoted on ethnic and religious self-consciousness. The heterogeneity of the city's population and the structure of its government combined to complicate their task. To construct inclusive and broad coalitions, the managers of citywide parties had to work with the leaders of the city's ethnic neighborhoods and accept these leaders as co-partners in the enterprise. The result was a brand of politics in which each party's coalition was composed of ethnically identifiable, and often personality-oriented, factions.

As long as elections were tightly contested affairs, with neither party regularly assured of victory, these factional coalitions usually held together. When one party became dominant, however, its coalition tended to splinter, with the separate factions warring against each other for a larger share of the spoils. To hold these tendencies toward open factionalism in check, party managers needed mechanisms of centralized control. They needed some means to assure the nomination of the candidates they designated and to control their behavior once in office. Controlling mechanisms of this type were not likely without the prior development of a political party capable of "institutionalizing a particular pattern of [popular loyalties and] preferences, and in the process, . . . [organizing] other plausible lines of cleavage out of politics."[10] Such a party would, of course, exhibit the characteristics that we usually associate with a political machine; it would be capable of operating as a political institution through which party managers could rule the city.

Through the 1920s, however, Chicago's parties were not institutions of that type; they lacked the required degrees of integration and control. Well before then, reformers had routinely denounced "bosses" and spoke often and negatively of "the Machine." When they used these terms, however, they were referring to the network "of parochial loyalties and individual payoffs" that linked politicians to voters. When reformers assumed that these connections summed to a political institution capable of ruling the city, they mistakenly identified the character of the political bonds between leaders and followers—the style of politics—with its structure.[11]

Turn-of-the-century reformers imputed wider influence to ward leaders than the latter typically did or could exercise. As with most American cities, Chicago's government was a highly decentralized affair. The city's first charter in 1837 provided for the annual election of two aldermen from each ward. The charter of 1851 increased the length of the term to two years, and an ordinance in 1869 stipulated that the aldermen from each ward would serve nonconcurrent terms. As the city grew in population and expanded physically, the number of wards and aldermen increased, but the manner of their selection remained the same. Each alderman was nominated by a party convention at the ward level and elected (or defeated) by a ward constituency.

Beginning in 1912, reform groups in Chicago advocated a redistricting of the city's ward boundaries to provide greater representation for the faster growing peripheral areas of the city. They also sought to reduce the size of the council by requiring single-member districts, to lengthen the term of office, and to eliminate partisanship in the selection process. The Municipal Voters League led the agitation and was mainly responsible for the reorganization of 1921, which created the system that is still in force. The reorganization increased the number of wards from 35 to 50, reduced the number of aldermen to a single representative from each ward, and lengthened the term to four years. It also provided for the nonpartisan election of aldermen, with the elections to be held in February and the two leading candidates facing each other in an April runoff, if no contender received a majority of the vote. However, because the February elections coincided with the party primaries for mayor, and the runoffs with the mayoral general election, aldermanic contests were never wholly separated from partisan influences.[12]

None of these changes, however, altered the principle of territorial representation. Chicago's aldermen have always been nominated and elected from wards, and their success at the polls has depended on their ability to deliver services and benefits (both tangible and symbolic) to their constituents. Territorial representation insulated aldermen from outside control, so that in office they could serve as ambassadors from their communities to the larger political world of the city. However, ward representation complicated the task for the leaders of the citywide party: since they lacked influence over the nominating process even before 1921, they could not control the behavior of elected aldermen. Secure in their own wards, aldermen were free to reject the preferences of their party's leaders. They could form voting alliances in the council with other aldermen, work out the necessary trade-offs, and obtain jobs and benefits for their constituents and dependents. To secure the legislation they wanted, mayors had to negotiate with, or buy off, the council's factional voting blocs. These processes worked to strengthen ward organizations, while preventing the development of citywide parties capable of performing as political machines.[13]

Territorial representation had another important consequence— it encouraged groups to become politically active even when they were relatively small components of the citywide population. Predominant strength within a ward provided the group with an opportunity to secure political representation and recognition by electing one of its members to the city council. This possibility encouraged the early development of ethnic-group political consciousness and then helped to maintain and reinforce it.[14]

Political Changes

■ Decentralized systems of representation impede but do not prevent the development of centralized party control. Even the obstacles that territorial representation presents can be overcome under the appropriate political conditions—conditions that simply did not exist in Chicago through the late 1920s.

In late-nineteenth-century Chicago, neither major party could develop and sustain a majority coalition. Elections at this time were generally hard fought and closely contested affairs, with candidates only rarely polling as much as 55 percent of the vote. Between 1876 and 1896, each major party carried the city in three of the six presidential elections, although the Democrats did slightly better in mayoral contests, winning seven of the eleven held before 1893. In five of these seven victories, however, the Democratic candidate was the same person, Carter H. Harrison I.

Harrison's five elections as mayor of Chicago testified to his personal popularity and not to the strength and durability of a Democratic party coalition. Politics turned on matters that touched the concerns of the city's ethnic and religious groups, such as prohibition ordinances, Sunday-closing laws, and attempts to outlaw the use of any language other than English in the parochial schools. Harrison was attuned to ethnic-group sensitivities, and his ability to campaign in several languages evoked a strong bond of psychological rapport between him and some ethnic groups that usually gave only lukewarm support to Democratic candidates. The strength of his personal appeal became clear when he ran as an Independent Democrat in opposition to the party's regular nominee in 1891. Two years earlier, as the party's endorsed candidate, Harrison had polled 55 percent of the vote. His independent candidacy in 1891 split that vote nearly in half: Harrison received 26 percent to 29 percent for the party's nominee.[15]

Although the activities associated with the World's Fair somewhat delayed its impact, the depression that began in early 1893 took its toll in Chicago by the end of the year. As in other northern cities, support for Democratic candidates declined; and by 1896, the Republicans carried the city for William McKinley, with 57 percent of the vote. Between 1900 and 1928, Republican candidates were victorious in the city in all but one of the eight presidential elections. The lone exception came in 1912, when Theodore Roosevelt, a Republican turned Progressive, carried Chicago with 37 percent of the vote.

In city elections the pattern was quite different, with the Democrats winning seven of the twelve mayoral contests between 1895 and 1927. In most of these elections, personality rather than party strength was the critical factor underlying Democratic success. Carter H. Harrison II was the Democratic candidate in five of the seven Democratic victories, and like his father, he had unusually wide appeal among the city's ethnic groups.[16] But his personal appeal did not automatically translate into Democratic *party* success: the Democrats had a majority in the City Council for only four of Harrison's twelve years as mayor. Indeed, split-party outcomes became characteristic of city elections in the early twentieth century. The mayor and the City Council majority were of the same party for only nine of the twenty years between 1900 and the end of partisan aldermanic elections in 1920.[17] Lacking dependable electoral majorities, party organizations were unable to exert sustained control over the distribution of city resources. And without that leverage, party managers were unable to develop effective mechanisms to control access to office or the behavior of elected officials.

These conditions changed dramatically in the 1930s. Between 1928 and 1936, the Democrats assumed complete control of all the governmental agencies of the city of Chicago, with the Republicans hanging on to only a handful of judgeships and five county commissioners from suburban Cook County. This Democratic takeover was not a flash-in-the-pan phenomenon: no Republican has served as mayor of Chicago since William Hale Thompson ended his term in 1931, and only once since then (in 1956) has the Republican party been able to carry the city for its presidential nominee. But until about 1955, the Republicans still remained a viable force in city politics. Between 1939 and 1955, Republican candidates averaged a 44 percent share of the vote in the five mayoral elections, polling over 40 percent in each one of them. Moreover, Republicans won 24 percent of the 250 ostensibly nonpartisan aldermanic contests in these five elections. In mayoral elections between 1959 and 1975, however, the five Republican candidates averaged only 30 percent of the vote, with only one of them (in 1963) receiving as much as 40 percent—and he was a former and prominent Democrat. Republicans fared even more poorly in the coinciding aldermanic elections, winning only 9 percent of those contests between 1959 and 1975.[18] The political developments of the 1930s made the Democrats the city's majority party, but it was only during the Daley Administrations that the Democrats became its hegemonic party, its ruling institution.

The emergence of a Democratic majority in the city resulted from a combination of national and local factors. The Great Depression, the New Deal, and the national swing against the Republicans coincided with and reinforced the party-building efforts of the city's local leaders, especially those of Anton Cermak.

Cermak, a Bohemian and a non-Catholic, proved to be an ethnic politician *par excellence*. Well before the depression struck, he had built an ethnic coalition broader than any the city had seen previously. The Harrisons, father and son, had earlier shown the potential of a broadly based ethnic coalition, but their special appeal had largely been limited to German Lutherans and other non-Catholic Germans who normally voted against the "Catholic party"—the

Democrats. Among the city's newer immigrant groups, the Harrisons did have considerable popularity with Bohemians and Poles, but those groups were Democratic regardless. Cermak appealed to a broader range of these newer immigrant groups, especially to those southern and eastern Europeans who were repelled by Irish control of the Democratic party. Cermak's Democratic party became a coalition of the city's newer minority groups.[19]

The key to the development of this ethnic coalition was Cermak's identification with the drive to end prohibition. To achieve this identification, he used his position as secretary of the United Societies for Local Self-Government, an interethnic pressure group that by 1919 was made up of some 1,087 separate ethnic organizations representing over 250,000 people. Cermak knew (and four referenda between 1919 and 1930 gave additional evidence) that the city's newer immigrant groups, as well as many of its older ones, were strongly opposed to prohibition. More than any other single question, it cut across ethnic cleavages and united the foreign-stock elements of the city's population. Immigrants saw prohibition as "something willfully and maliciously foisted upon them" by native-stock groups. Repeal of prohibition became a symbolic issue to immigrants, a question of the recognition of their ethnic rights.[20]

Cermak was first elected to the City Council in 1909, and he remained an elected officeholder until his assassination in 1933. He won his first citywide office in 1912, but he began the process of rebuilding the Democratic party organization in earnest after his election in 1922 as member and president of the Cook County Board of Commissioners. He was reelected president of the County Board in 1926 and again in 1930; and for each contest he set up a referendum on prohibition, so that the man and the issue remained linked.

Unlike the Harrisons, Cermak consciously worked to convert his personal popularity into a durable *party* coalition. He used his position on the County Board to build an organization by skillfully distributing patronage and using the Board's control over licenses and franchises to develop alliances with leaders of the city's ethnic factions. He allied himself, for example, with Moe and Ike Rosenberg and Jacob Arvey of the heavily Jewish 24th Ward on the city's West Side, adjacent to Cermak's own 22d Ward. He cemented his connections with the Germans on the near North Side by forging alliances with Alderman Mathias (Paddy) Bauler, from the 43rd Ward, and with Charles Weber, the ward committeeman from the 45th Ward.[21]

While Cermak worked to recruit the newer immigrant groups into the party's voting coalition, he did not write off either its Irish constituency or all of its Irish leadership. He was not anti-Irish in general, but he did wage a battle against a particular group of Irish leaders in the party. His Irish opponents were those who came from the more affluent Irish neighborhoods, the group that the Bridgeport Irish described as the "bicycle Irish who made your ass sore." It was this group of Irish leaders who deprecatingly referred to Cermak as "Pushcart Tony" and who refused to slate him for mayor in 1923, choosing one of their own instead. Furious at this rebuff, Cermak vowed to "fuck those Irish someday." To get even, while satisfying his own ambitions, he skillfully exploited factional divisions among the Irish. Those conflicts reflected differences in outlook between middle- and working-class groups, and it had already taken on the overtones of a clan war, as battles among the Irish almost inevitably do. Cermak found his allies among the leaders from the "pigshit Irish" neighborhoods, as the uptown Irish derisively described them. He formed alliances with the representatives from the working-class communities, with Patrick A. Nash, the committeeman from the 28th Ward on the city's near West Side, and with Joseph B. McDonough, the committeeman from the 13th Ward on the Southwest Side.[22]

With these alliances in place, Cermak was able to take practical control of the party in 1928, following the death of George Brennan, the chairman of the Democratic Central Committee of Cook County. Cermak blocked Michael Igoe (Irish, 5th Ward), Brennan's designated successor, from becoming chairman and took the position himself. He gave up the party chairmanship after he became mayor and installed his own candidate, Patrick A. Nash. With his election as mayor of Chicago in April 1931, Cermak had even greater patronage and power at his disposal.

At least from 1928 until his death in March 1933, Cermak was the dominant force in the local Democratic party. Unlike any of his predecessors, Cermak ruled the party with an iron hand. He aimed at building a centralized organization, one through which party control over the city could be institutionalized. He used patronage to cement his alliances with the leaders of the city's newer immigrant groups and to reward his supporters from the working-class Irish areas, among whom was a then relatively obscure aspirant from Bridgeport, Richard J. Daley.

Cermak was a stronger leader than any the Democrats had seen previously, but his control was not absolute. It relied on an intricate network of alliances with still powerful ward leaders. And while he had outflanked his patrician foes among the Irish, they still had control over their wards and considerable voting strength on the Democratic Central Committee. Displeased with Cermak's ascendency, they awaited an opportunity to reclaim control of "their" party. Cermak's assassination gave them an opening, and factional struggle within the party broke out anew.

That struggle immediately focused on succession to the mayoralty. The contest pitted several groups of South Side and West Side Irish against each other, but it did not lead to a reassertion of control over the party by the "bicycle Irish" faction. Patrick Nash rejected the leading factional candidates and, after a brief interim mayoralty, secured the election by the City Council of Edward J. Kelly, chief engineer of the Metropolitan Sanitary District and a native of Bridgeport. The Kelly-Nash combine enjoyed the support of Cermak's factional allies, and it was initially opposed by the middle-class Irish leaders. But the Kelly-Nash partnership envisioned an open party, and from the outset they pursued a policy of dealing with their party opponents by cutting them in on a share of the spoils. They did not assert control over the party as much as they bought off their factional enemies with a generous dispensation of patronage and contracts. As a result, power began to devolve again to the factional leaders in the Central Committee and the City Council. The slippage was clear as early as 1941, when Jacob Arvey, chairman of the Council's powerful Finance Committee and a Kelly-Nash ally, resigned his aldermanic seat to go off to war in the Illinois National Guard. Unable to replace Arvey with one of their own supporters, Kelly and Nash had to acquiesce to the selection of John Duffy, the leader of the opposition forces in the Council.[23]

Despite his rhetoric and the self-serving complaints of his opponents, Kelly was no more forceful as the city's chief executive than he and Nash were as party leaders. Prohibition had been repealed, but mob violence did not seem to abate; the newspapers screamed of police corruption; and prostitution was so rampant that even the rector of the fashionable Fourth Presbyterian Church complained to the mayor of being openly propositioned during his evening strolls on North Michigan Avenue. Taxes were high; the delivery of city services was deteriorating; the city's finances were in shambles; and a study by the National Education Association revealed widespread corruption in the city's school system. Instead of addressing these problems, Mayor Kelly spent increasing amounts of time away from the city, nursing his health at a fashionable resort.[24]

When Nash died in 1943, Kelly also assumed the chairmanship of the party, thus exposing himself to even more criticism. As the problems multiplied and citizen ire grew, Duffy and his allies, in late 1945, moved to ease Kelly out of the chairmanship, a move the mayor did not resist. Kelly designated as his successor Jacob Arvey, who had returned from military service, and the Duffy group, dubbed "the Irish Turkeys of Beverly" by Arvey, agreed rather than risk a battle that might needlessly weaken the party prior to the 1946 elections.

Kelly ended his fourteen years as mayor in virtual disgrace, and

Duffy didn't think the time was ripe to mount a coup to seize control of the party. If the legacy of Kelly's tenure was to be a Democratic defeat in 1947, Duffy wanted no share of the blame. But he wanted to be in a position to pick up the pieces after the anticipated debacle. Therefore, at the December 1946 slating session, he was content to join with other disgruntled committeemen in refusing to reslate Kelly for mayor and in allowing Arvey to suggest an alternative.

Arvey's choice, and the party's endorsed candidate, was Martin H. Kennelly, a native of Bridgeport who had made a fortune in the moving and storage business. Although a lifelong Democrat, Kennelly had not been active in party affairs, but he had been a public critic of Mayor Kelly. In 1939 he had managed the campaign of his good friend, State's Attorney Thomas Courtney, against Kelly in the primary. He had served on numerous civic committees, had been productive in raising money for the American Red Cross, and was so generally well respected that he was endorsed by more than one thousand business and civic leaders, most of whom were Republicans.[25]

The designation of Kennelly was one of the moves that earned Arvey his reputation as a political genius. By choosing someone without ties to any of the Irish factions, he avoided another outbreak of that internecine strife. At the same time, Kennelly was an Irishman and a Bridgeporter and appealed to those elements of the party's constituency. Since he had an image as a reformer and had been a critic of Kelly, he was not saddled with the burden of defending fourteen years of ineptness and corruption. Kennelly's selection by Arvey was a master political stroke, and Arvey was widely credited with winning the election and saving the mayoralty for the Democrats in 1947.

Once in office, however, Kennelly's lack of political experience had other consequences. He was uninformed, naive, and indecisive—"the most inept man I ever met," as Arvey later put it. Derided as "Snow White" by many of the Democratic regulars, and as "Fartin' Martin" by the vulgar Alderman Bauler, Kennelly simply ceded power to the City Council, and the aldermen ran the city.[26]

Mayor Kennelly was equally indifferent to party affairs. While his slating and election had postponed the next stage of the ongoing struggle for control of the Democratic organization, the battle soon resumed. As it had after Cermak's death, the contest for power within the party pitted the leaders of the more affluent Irish wards against those from the working-class Irish neighborhoods, especially the Bridgeport group. By the time this phase of the battle was finally joined, the Bridgeport Irish had a new and experienced leader, Richard J. Daley. Daley had held office as state representative, senator, state revenue director, and clerk of Cook County, and for most of the period between 1934 and 1949 he had functioned as chief deputy comptroller of the county. That apparently unexciting position was his most important: it enabled him to develop a thorough knowledge of budgeting, payrolls, and the operation of the patronage system at the county level. And, in January 1947, with Arvey's quiet assent, Daley had ousted Alderman Hugh Connelly as committeeman of the 11th Ward, a position that gave Daley his membership on the Democratic Central Committee.

The struggle for control over the party resumed overtly when Arvey resigned after the defeat of the Democratic county ticket in the 1950 elections. The Central Committee chose a caretaker, Joseph L. Gill, to preside during the presidential election year, and throughout the interim the power brokers maneuvered for advantage. The edge eventually went to Daley, who was elected chairman of the Democratic Central Committee of Cook County on 21 July 1953. From that position Daley secured his own slating for mayor of Chicago in December 1954. His accession to the mayoralty was not uncontested, however. Kennelly did not bow out quietly, and a Polish Democrat, Benjamin Adamowski, made it a three-way primary race. But Daley won the contest, as he did the general election against the Republican candidate, Robert Merriam; and in April 1955, he began the first of his six terms as mayor of Chicago.

What Cermak had begun, Daley completed. Under Daley's leadership the Democratic party became a tightly integrated, highly centralized organization. It became a political institution through which the chairman-mayor ruled the city of Chicago.[27]

Party Coalitions

■ In late-nineteenth-century Chicago, as elsewhere, the Democrats drew strong support from Catholic voters, whatever their ethnic background. The Irish were their strongest and most assertive supporters, of course; but Democrats also enlisted the votes of German, Polish, and Bohemian Catholics. The party also enjoyed some lingering support among native-stock groups, especially from Episcopalians and the more Calvinistic of the Presbyterians and Baptists. Other native-stock groups, particularly the Methodists and the Irish Protestants, the anticlericals among the Germans, Poles, and Bohemians, and a heavy majority of the Norwegians and Swedes, supported the Republicans. The German Lutherans were something of a swing group, reacting negatively to the Republicans when that party pushed prohibition or became identified with assaults on German culture but reacting just as negatively when the Democrats appeared to be a "Catholic party."

By the beginning of the new century, however, Democratic voting among the party's traditional support groups had fallen off somewhat. More critically, the party's identification with the depression of the 1890s and the unsettling candidacy of William Jennings Bryan in 1896 limited its attractiveness to newly arriving immigrants. Moreover, the class character of the Bryan crusade had led most of the party's better-off native-stock supporters to abandon it. And, since the Irish quickly moved into that leadership vacuum, the Democrats increasingly took on the tone and character of an Irish and Catholic party.[28] The frequent candidacies of Carter H. Harrison II temporarily muted the electoral effects of the leadership change, but Irish predominance at the ward level slowed recruitment among the growing pool of southern and eastern European immigrant voters.[29]

Religious conflict in Chicago was virulent, public, and often partisan throughout the early decades of the century. The public battles mobilized Catholic voters in support of the Democratic party, while retarding the movement of other immigrant-stock voters into the Democratic ranks. Cermak bridged this religious divide. His identification with the anti-prohibition sentiment resonated positively with the values of most of the city's Catholic population, and so did his Democratic partisanship. His immigrant, non-Catholic, non-Irish background, combined with his assertive attacks on native-stock cultural imperialism, contributed to his popularity among the city's new and non-Catholic immigrant population. The depression of the 1930s sharpened and reinforced the cleavage lines that underpinned Cermak's coalition of minorities.

The city's black voters, however, were conspicuously absent from Cermak's coalition of minorities. Northern blacks were traditionally Republican, and in Chicago, their Republicanism was stronger than elsewhere, principally because of the efforts of William Hale Thompson. Early in his career, Thompson had served as alderman from the 2d Ward, a predominantly black neighborhood on the South Side. He secured patronage appointments for black leaders and recreational facilities for the ward's population, and he articulated antisegregationist views. As the size of the black population grew, black voters became an increasingly important and visible support group within the Republican coalition.[30]

Democratic leaders, at least prior to Cermak, made no serious efforts to recruit black support. On the contrary, they often engaged in race baiting. In 1927, for example, the Irish leaders of the Democratic party realized how important black support was to Thompson's bid to return to the mayor's office, but they were also aware that they had little chance to attract black voters; and so they used the situation to mobilize their white supporters. They sent calliopes through the streets playing "Bye, Bye, Blackbird," and they distributed cartoons showing a trainload of blacks, piloted by Thompson, coming up from Georgia: "This train will start for Chicago, April 6, if

Thompson is elected." The tactic may have attracted some white voters to the Democrats, but it certainly solidified black support for Thompson: he received over 90 percent of the vote in black areas in 1927.[31]

Cermak was more sensitive than his Irish predecessors. Even before he became mayor, he worked to develop relations with black leaders. In 1927, while other Democrats played on white fears that blacks would take over the city, Cermak appointed the publisher of a black newspaper to a County Commission post. In the mayor's office, Cermak used a heavier hand to "persuade" black leaders to switch their allegiance to the Democrats. He cracked down on vice in black neighborhoods, filling the jails with large numbers of black arrestees, and he discharged large numbers of black jobholders. He designed these actions to show black leaders that they could continue to deliver services and benefits to their constituents only if they accommodated to the new political reality and aligned themselves with his Democratic party.[32]

The depression and the New Deal provided another push in the same direction. Black businesses were especially hard hit by the economic collapse, with their bankruptcies running at a much higher rate than for similar white businesses in the city. And while 18 percent of the city's overall population found itself on relief during the depression, the proportions were consistently much higher in the heavily black areas, reaching a peak of 89 percent in the Douglas community.[33] Since a national Democratic administration organized relief efforts, and a local Democratic organization distributed relief and controlled all patronage, it became increasingly important for black leaders to switch their allegiance.

That change did not come quickly, and it did not come at all for some black leaders. But William L. Dawson, an alderman and a key black leader, made the switch during Kelly's mayoralty. With access to Democratic patronage, Dawson built a strong party organization in his own ward (the 2d) and dispatched followers to other black areas on the South Side to serve as Democratic precinct captains. The building of Dawson's black sub-machine was a gradual process, but eventually it came to involve five wards (2d, 3rd, 4th, 6th, and 20th), which routinely returned very large Democratic majorities.[34]

Chicago's politics of ethnic accommodation was a pragmatic response by party managers to the diversity of its population. With the city's heterogeneous population and its ongoing shifts in composition, successful coalition building required avoiding exclusiveness. To be sure, not all party managers were equally adept at the task, and at times one party or another took on the aura of an exclusive organization. But if the goal was not always realized, it was nevertheless the objective that most party leaders worked to achieve.

This mode of politics was a response to existing conditions, and its successful practice depended on those conditions rather than on the numerical superiority of any single voting group. As the city's population became less diverse in politically important ways, as one group approached majority status, this brand of accommodationist politics became increasingly less viable.

3. Racial Change and Group Conflict

Our concern is that a little bit of integration is like being a little bit pregnant—there ain't no such thing. *Bogan Area mother (1977)*

■ On the eve of World War II, a visitor to Chicago might have walked through its downtown business district, shopped in Marshall Field's, dined at the renowned Pump Room of the Ambassador East, and toured most of its neighborhoods without encountering a single black person. In those days fewer than one of every twelve residents of the city was black, and few of those ventured beyond their own neighborhoods. Forty years later, the odds against such a possibility were much longer; by that time, more than one of every three Chicagoans was black.

This dramatic change in the city's racial makeup has been the overriding fact of its economic, social, and political life since World War II. The rapid influx of a large number of blacks created demands for living space, better schools, and more jobs. But when blacks pressed these claims for their share of the American dream, many of the city's white residents mobilized, organized, and resisted. The conflict that ensued between black Chicago and white Chicago, two cities separate and unequal, was always vituperative and sometimes violent. And when the battle spilled into politics, as it inevitably had to, it threatened to fragment the Democratic party, the city's ruling institution.

Racial Change
■ No modern Paul Revere lit warning beacons and rode through the neighborhoods shouting the alarm. Even the newspapers played

down the blacks' arrival, none of them exclaiming hysterically, as they had four decades earlier, that "Darkies from Dixie" were swarming to the city.[1] White Chicagoans didn't need formal notice; they could see what was happening, as block after block of their neighborhoods "fell." At the meetings of their PTAs and neighborhood improvement associations, they discussed a future turned ominous now that "the blacks are coming."

The change was sudden (Table 3).[2] Lured by a postwar boom in construction and manufacturing, blacks flocked to Chicago from the Upper South, from the Border States, from the Deep South, and from other northern cities. The combination of migration and natural population growth almost tripled the size of Chicago's black population between 1940 and 1960 and then increased it by nearly another 50 percent during the next twenty years. As blacks poured into the city, and out of their old residential enclaves, whites began their inexorable exodus. Propelled at first by postwar affluence, the movement to the suburbs started slowly; it accelerated by the early 1950s, as the pace of racial change quickened, and by 1980 the city had lost over 1.8 million white residents.[3] In less than forty years, this two-way movement changed Chicago from a city where nine of every ten inhabitants were white to one where whites are a minority of its total population.

As their numbers increased, blacks pushed beyond their core residential area on the near South Side and occupied sections of the city that previously had been white (Map 1).[4] The Cottage Grove Avenue and Fifty-fifth Street boundaries, "defended" successfully for a generation, fell in the 1950s, as blacks moved outward in several directions. They moved east into Hyde Park and Kenwood, south into Woodlawn, Park Manor, and Chatham, and southwest into Englewood, reaching a new Maginot Line at Ashland Avenue. In the 1960s and 1970s, even that barrier was breached all the way from Fifty-fifth to Eighty-seventh Streets. Western Avenue became the new western boundary of black settlement, and its southern edge extended all the way to the city limits. While this southward expansion was in process, the small black community on the West Side was also growing rapidly. Beginning in the 1950s, blacks pushed into the formerly Jewish area of Lawndale, reached the western limits of the city abutting Cicero and Oak Park, and turned north through Garfield Park and Austin to North Avenue.

Because Chicago has two housing markets, one for each race, expanding the supply of housing available to blacks required transferring property from the white to the black housing market. These transfers occurred on a block-by-block basis, through "invasion" and "succession" at the margins of the existing black residential areas. As a result, the physical expansion of black settlements followed the

Table 3. Racial Components of Chicago's Population, 1940–1980

| | Population (in 000s) | | | Percent of Total Population | |
	Total	White	Black	White	Black
1940	3,394	3,118	277	91.8	8.1
1950	3,620	3,111	492	85.9	13.5
1960	3,550	2,705	812	76.1	22.8
1970	3,362	2,181	1,102	64.8	32.7
1980[1]	3,005	1,299	1,187	43.2	39.5

[1] White and black Hispanics are included in the total population but are not counted under the racial categories.

paths of least resistance, usually into adjacent middle- and upper-income sections, since their residents could more easily afford to move to other parts of the city or into the suburbs. Much of this movement was encouraged and hastened by the panic peddling and block-busting tactics of some real estate agents and brokers. Whenever a black "jumped" across one of the well-known dividing lines, the real estate operators saw "the green light. Then it's open season. . . . We don't care if the whites run all the way to Hong Kong as long as they run. . . . It's good business for us when they're frightened."[5]

Not all of the city's whites were frightened; and even when they were, many could not afford to run or were unwilling to do so. Some whites accepted integration and used their community organizations to deter panic peddling and to maintain a numerical balance between white residents and incoming blacks. Lower-income whites were limited in their choices of housing areas and simply couldn't afford to move. Besides, many were lifelong residents, deeply involved in the social life of their neighborhoods and with strong sentimental attachments to them. For them, moving away involved emotional as well as financial distress.[6]

Frightened but resolute, these groups were determined to hold the line against the black advance. Through improvement and property owners' associations, neighborhood and parish groups, and block clubs, they tried to counter panic peddling and to resist integration of their neighborhoods and schools. They also used their associations to watch out over one another lest someone burst the dam by "selling out" to a black family. When all else failed, some resisters turned to more direct action, involving fires and bombs as their main weapons and gang and mob harassment as their supporting tactics. Almost three quarters of the approximately 500 racial incidents in Chicago between 1945 and 1950 had to do with housing. In

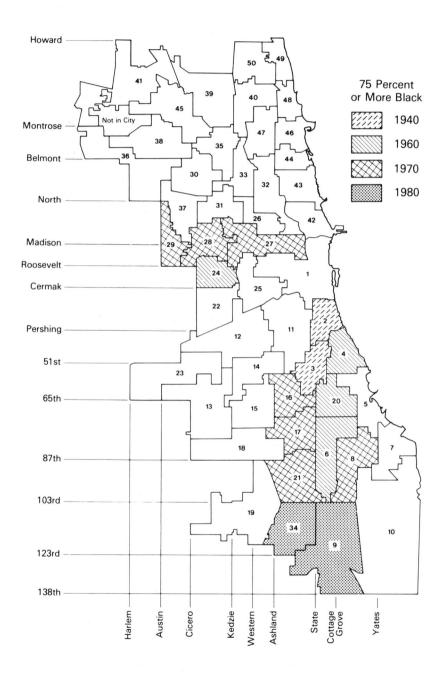

MAP 1
GROWTH OF CHICAGO'S BLACK POPULATION

75 Percent
or More Black

▨	1940
▨	1960
▨	1970
▨	1980

1956 and 1957 alone, there were 115 attacks by whites on blacks or their property, including major incidents in Calumet Park and Trumbull Park in the southeastern part of the city.[7]

No one familiar with Chicago's history of race relations was surprised at the intensity and tenacity of its white resisters. It was also no surprise that violence came hand in glove with racial change. Thirty years earlier, the first large influx of blacks had sparked the same reactions, and the violence of that era had indelibly marked the two Chicagos that did battle with each other after World War II.

As late as 1900, there were only about 30,000 blacks in Chicago, and they made up less than 2 percent of the total population. About half of them lived on the South Side in what was known as the Black Belt, a narrow strip of land about four blocks wide, stretching from the downtown business district as far south as Thirty-ninth Street. Despite this concentration, and a few smaller enclaves elsewhere, blacks were relatively well distributed throughout the city. Only a quarter of the black population lived in precincts that were over 50 percent black, and almost a third were in areas that were 95 percent white. Even a decade later, in 1910, Italian immigrants were more highly segregated from native whites than were blacks.[8]

Between 1900 and 1910, the black population became slightly more concentrated, although still not more than a dozen blocks on the South Side were exclusively black. But whenever blacks filtered beyond the limits of the Black Belt, anxious whites resisted. When the small cluster of blacks on its eastern edge began to move into Hyde Park after 1900, the area's affluent white residents became fearful of a black "invasion." In 1908 they organized an Improvement Protective Club to guarantee that "the districts which are now white . . . remain white. There will be no compromise."[9] Through a variety of tactics, including a boycott of merchants who sold goods to blacks living in white neighborhoods, the Club succeeded, and the rest of Hyde Park remained white for the next forty years. Similar reactions occurred in other neighborhoods whenever blacks first attempted to move there: Neighbors protested, tried to buy the property, and sometimes resorted to violence to drive out the invaders. Often these efforts were successful; but when they failed, most whites moved out, leaving behind a predominantly black neighborhood.

The early shaping of Chicago's physical ghetto, then, was not the result of voluntary clustering by blacks. It was primarily the product of white hostility. When more and more blacks began to arrive in the city, they would have no choice but to settle in the well-defined black areas. Property owners in the Black Belt also encouraged this, because they found it profitable and more peaceful to force out white tenants and convert previously mixed areas into all-black ones.

The sudden influx of a large number of blacks from the rural

South—over 50,000 between 1915 and 1920—swelled Chicago's Black Belt and accelerated the earlier trend toward residential segregation. The Black Belt expanded somewhat, and a few new neighborhoods emerged beyond its confines. For the most part, however, housing was provided for the incoming population by converting mixed neighborhoods within the black enclave into exclusively black areas. In 1910, no blacks were living in census tracts that were as much as 75 percent black; by 1920, over 35 percent of them lived in such areas. Only 7 percent resided in tracts that were 95 percent white, a sharp change from 1898, when 31 percent of the blacks had lived among mostly white neighbors.[10]

The migration of the late 1910s had some other consequences. Self-help activities expanded within the black community to serve a larger and more concentrated population, and the migration experience created a sense of racial consciousness among blacks that produced a new type of militancy. But its most critical effect was on the attitudes of the white community. The prospect of more blacks competing for houses and jobs threatened the Irish and the Poles living to the west of the Black Belt and the old-stock groups living to its south and east. They reacted by trying to tighten the color bar in housing, schools, and public accommodations; and some resorted to terrorism. The sporadic racial violence of the prewar years gave way to guerilla warfare. Neighborhood improvement societies bombed black houses, and the politically connected white athletic clubs attacked blacks on the streets. By the beginning of 1919, the city was on the brink of a full-scale racial war.

That war erupted on a hot Sunday afternoon, 27 July 1919, when a black youth swam across the invisible line that separated blacks from whites on the Twenty-ninth Street beach. Blacks claimed that the youth was stoned by a group of white boys and then drowned during the ensuing argument between the white and black bathers. When the beach police ignored these charges and refused to arrest any of the whites, the black crowd attacked a group of white men. Rumors of a general race war swept through the South Side, and the riot was on.

For the next six days, the South Side was a racial battlefield. White gangs attacked blacks as they left their workplaces; they pulled blacks from streetcars and kicked and beat them; and they raided black neighborhoods, firing into some houses from their automobiles and setting fire to others. Black mobs retaliated by attacking whites who worked in the Black Belt. By the time peace was restored on the following Saturday, 23 blacks and 15 whites had died, and 342 blacks and 178 whites had been injured. The larger casualty, however, was the future of race relations in the city.[11]

The race riot of 1919 hardened attitudes on both sides of the racial divide. It added strength to the pressures originating within the black community to strive for self-sufficiency. By creating new demands for services and institutions within the Black Belt, the migration had reinforced the argument for a self-contained black community. The riot added to the pressure, because during it blacks saw that "you could not buy a loaf of bread or a bottle of milk, because the white people, who own or control 99% of all business places, closed their doors and left the Negroes to sink or swim." The drive for separatism, the building of a "black metropolis," became a practical and necessary response to implacable white hostility. Blacks built an institutional ghetto, because whites had first created and confined them to a physical ghetto.[12]

On the other side, the riot experience led whites to develop a more effective mechanism to segregate blacks, while providing themselves with a new rationale for explaining their actions. In November 1919, the Kenwood and Hyde Park Property Owners' Association inaugurated a year of "ruthless campaigning" to keep blacks out of the area east of Cottage Grove Avenue. Among other actions, they began publication of a newspaper, the *Property Owners' Journal*, to spread their ideas. The *Journal* popularized the view that blacks destroyed property values and argued that every white property owner "has the right to defend his property to the utmost of his ability, with every means at his disposal." A few weeks later, the *Journal* summarized its case in more earthy terms: "Niggers are undesirable neighbors and entirely irresponsible and vicious." By the mid-1920s, the Property Owners' Association devised a potent weapon—the racially restrictive covenant—to combat the danger.[13]

Agreements among property owners within certain districts not to sell or rent their property to blacks proved to be a highly effective device to control the spread of the black community. The Chicago Real Estate Board and the Chicago Title and Trust Company cooperated with the associations of neighborhood property owners to enforce these restrictive covenants. By 1930, three fourths of all the residential property in the city was bound by them, with the proportion reaching 95 percent in some white areas on the fringes of the ghetto.[14]

Through the use of restrictive covenants, individual prejudice became a deeply embedded institutional racism. Of course few white Chicagoans saw and explained the situation in those terms, because the riot experience encouraged another and more satisfying explanation. The riot, they argued, proved the need for more, not less, racial segregation. While admitting the "possible justice" of the black demands for integration, the *Chicago Tribune* pointed to the fact that "the races are not living in harmony. . . . How long will it be before segregation will be the only means of preventing murders?"

One white minister gave his answer: "I believe in segregating the blacks for their own good as well as the good of the whites."[15]

Segregation, wherever possible, now and forever, became white Chicago's answer to its black "problem."[16] In its neighborhoods, in its schools, in its parks and amusement halls, and on its beaches and playgrounds, blacks and whites were to be kept apart. In a predominantly white city, run by white politicians responsive to white constituents, separate inevitably meant unequal. But most whites persuaded themselves that blacks would willingly pay that price because it was for their own good, to prevent racial violence. In this final twist of reasoning, segregation became an act of white benevolence.

The fear of renewed racial violence permeated the thinking and policies of Chicago's white leaders after 1919. Race relations became an exercise in riot prevention, and news of disturbances elsewhere invariably led to a flurry of local activity aimed at avoiding another bloodbath like that in 1919. The Harlem riot in New York in 1943 galvanized the city's civic leaders, and both whites and blacks urged Mayor Kelly to appoint a committee to study ways of preventing a similar outbreak in Chicago. The mayor set up his Committee on Race Relations, which concentrated its efforts on that task throughout the summer. When the summer ended without major incidents, the Committee turned its attention to the larger task of searching for the causes and cures of racial tension. Early in 1944, it sponsored the Mayor's Conference on Race Relations to explore the underlying sources of the city's troubled race relations.

The Mayor's Conference didn't contribute anything original to the analysis of the causes of racial tension, but it showed how large the gap was between the attitudes of black and white civic leaders. Whites spoke of the need for "tangible" actions to improve conditions in the ghetto, reduce tensions among the black population, and diminish the likelihood of a riot. But since moving too far, too fast would only excite anxiety among the white population, they counseled "goodwill," "education," and "gradualism," while opposing immediate and drastic measures to change the status of blacks. The black speakers derided "gradualism," a slogan they had heard for too long, and called for action now: "We will not wait, but we are pressing hard to integrate the Negro into all phases of life in this and other communities."[17]

The two groups of leaders attended the same conference and addressed the same topics; but they did not communicate with each other, as much as they spoke past each other. They came from different worlds, from different Chicagos. Whites had not experienced the grinding physical and psychological oppression of the ghetto and couldn't understand it; blacks understood it too well and would endure it no longer. To whites, riot control was the prime objective; to blacks, full integration was the immediate goal. There was the difficulty: blacks saw integration as the solution, and whites saw it as the problem.

It was into this Chicago, a city with a long history of racial hostility and violence, that blacks poured after World War II. They came seeking a better life, and what they found was a city in which remarkably little had been done to improve race relations in thirty years. Blacks were still unable to acquire housing beyond the ghetto, and within it they remained cut off from the economic and social life of the larger city. Although many of the city's white ethnic colonies had dissolved or developed new forms in the suburbs, the black ghetto "remained much as it had been—cohesive, restrictive, and largely impoverished."[18] Still unchanged, too, was the implacable white hostility that had shaped and limited the black ghetto from its inception. The very segregation that blacks saw as oppressive, the tough and resolute white populace still regarded as the city's standing and benevolent solution to its black "problem." In a city whose white population remembered so much, and learned so little, from its past experiences, renewed racial conflict was virtually inevitable.

Arenas of Conflict

■ The increase in the black population after World War II raised the levels of racial tension in Chicago. Blacks were unable to acquire housing in white areas, and the ghetto could not expand very much to accommodate the incoming population. Although the number of blacks nearly doubled during the 1940s, the Black Belt was only slightly larger in 1950 than at the end of World War I. As black piled upon black, the city's most densely populated area became even more crowded, and living conditions deteriorated further. "In this black man-heap there is no such thing as a vacancy," one black complained in 1949, "though outside there are twenty square miles of vacant land labelled 'white.'"[19] Other blacks, realizing that they were confined to an increasingly impoverished ghetto and surrounded by a hostile white population, shared that sense of resentment. They wondered why the country's recently ended crusade for democracy abroad had not extended to Chicago. From about the mid-1940s, a growing number of white Chicagoans asked the same question and involved themselves in the task of improving race relations. Their efforts centered on ending the contradiction between the ideal of democracy and the practice of segregation.

In Chicago and other northern cities, concerned whites and resentful blacks joined forces after the war to attack discriminatory practices. From the vantage point of the 1980s, some of those practices—e.g., restricting blacks to the balconies of movie theaters—

may seem only minor irritants; but they were continual reminders to blacks that whites regarded them as inferiors. Dismantling the network of discriminatory practices was slow going; for example, as late as the early 1960s, some of Chicago's public beaches remained off limits to blacks.

Casual and voluntary social contact with blacks was not what most excited white Chicagoans. Their passions were stirred by the prospect of blacks' moving into their neighborhoods and sending their children to the same schools as white children. On some matters, white Chicagoans might compromise, if only reluctantly; on housing and schools, they would fight to the bitter end, rejecting even pallid suggestions for "a little bit of integration."

Chicago suffered no shortage of racial issues in the years following World War II, but housing and schools were the key arenas of combat. These issues touched the lives of large numbers of people and aroused strong emotions, and each was a complex matter. The housing question, for example, involved legal challenges to the use of restrictive covenants, the actions of the city's Real Estate Board, its lending institutions and insurance companies, and the activities of its politically connected private developers. The school issue was partially a problem of finances, and it was linked to the larger set of relationships between the city and state governments. Untangling the several aspects of these issues is too broad a task to tackle here. Instead, I will look at the public agencies that exercised responsibility in these policy areas—the Chicago Housing Authority and the Chicago Board of Education; and I will concentrate on those actions that directly affected the mass public and aroused its emotions. This focus captures only part of the story, but it is the part with the most direct bearing on the city's electoral politics.

The involvement of the CHA and Board of Education with the integration issue has been a long-running drama, acted out at a slow-motion, nearly surrealistic pace. Since the stories span three decades and involve mayors from Kennelly to Washington, an overview of what the agencies did (or didn't do), and when they did it, is useful. This should offer insight into how and why the CHA and the Board of Education became focal points of the city's racial conflict, while providing necessary background for the political analysis that follows.

The Chicago Housing Authority

■ Through a combination of legal and extra-legal techniques, white Chicagoans had closed most of the private housing market to blacks. With the development of public housing programs, however, residential segregation faced a new threat. It was a challenge to which the city's white populace was quick to respond.

The National Housing Act of 1937 was the federal government's first large-scale involvement in public housing. It encouraged local communities to create agencies to build and manage low-income housing, but it did not aim at increasing the total housing supply: a slum unit was to be torn down for every new unit of housing constructed. Public housing took on a larger role when plans were developed for the period after World War II. To forestall a possible depression after the war, urban redevelopment schemes called for making federal subsidies available to private developers for rebuilding the blighted areas of the nation's cities. Public housing appeared in these plans as "relocation housing," a means of providing quarters for people displaced by private development or by public improvement projects. Public housing also was thought of as a quick solution to the pressing problem of providing low-cost accommodations for the returning war veterans.

This mixture of aims attracted support from a broad coalition in Congress and led to the passage of the Housing Act of 1949. Title I of that measure provided federal subsidies for private redevelopment of blighted land; Title III amended the Housing Act of 1937 by authorizing loans and subsidies for 810,000 units of low-rent housing to be built in six years and to be managed by local authorities. The scheme for allocating these units opened the way for the construction of as many as 40,000 new units of public housing in Chicago.

Even that impressive number fell far short of the city's immediate needs. By the late 1940s, Chicago's 50-year-old housing problem had become a housing crisis, the city's "number one problem and emergency," according to Mayor Kennelly. There were nearly 1.2 million families in the city, but the best estimate put the available housing supply well short of a million units. Another quarter of the city's population lived in substandard housing, mostly in the twenty-two square miles of slums that lay in a half circle extending about five miles from the Loop.[20]

Anticipating federal legislation, the CHA began to develop a plan to address the crisis. On the very day that Congress passed the Housing Act, 8 July 1949, the Authority presented Mayor Kennelly with its proposal for building 40,000 units of low-rent public housing during the next six years. During the first two years of the program, 21,000 units were to be started, with 12,000 getting under way within twelve months. About two fifths of the units were to be constructed on vacant land and the rest in redeveloped slum areas. One week after the CHA gave the mayor its proposal, the City Council approved it and authorized an application to the Public Housing Administration for funds to cover the costs of site selection and planning. All that remained now was to select the sites for the first year's program, have them approved by the City Council, secure the Public

Housing Administration's acceptance of the whole plan, and begin construction.

It all seemed simple enough, and the supporters of public housing were optimistic that the remaining steps would go smoothly. As it turned out, their optimism was ill-founded. July 1949 was the high point of their success; it was all downhill after that.

The CHA staff worked on the problem of site selection for several months, and in late November, the commissioners presented their choices to the City Council. The package contained seven sites and provided for about 10,000 units of housing, about half to be built on vacant land. In early March 1950, Alderman William J. Lancaster, chairman of the Housing Committee, reported his committee's rejection of the CHA package. While the Council set up a subcommittee to negotiate a solution with the Authority, Lancaster and Alderman John J. Duffy, chairman of the Finance Committee and Kennelly's floor leader in the Council, put together their own list of sites.

The Duffy-Lancaster compromise, as it became known, involved fifteen sites, eight of which were on vacant land. But 10,500 of the 12,000 units targeted for the first year were to be constructed on the slum sites. The plan provided for relocation housing for about 2,000 families, while displacing about 12,500 families, all blacks. The construction called for by the "compromise" plan promised to add a total of forty-seven units to the city's housing supply. When the CHA staff and commissioners suggested more relocation housing for persons displaced by the slum construction, Duffy and Lancaster added another feature to their plan. They proposed building the new housing units before tearing down the old ones, constructing them in stages in the alleys, cross streets, and other open spaces of the slum sites. By building in stages and making the new projects very tall buildings, the scheme avoided the need for interim housing. More importantly, it also avoided having to move the slum dwellers out of their existing districts and into white communities.

Despite the objections of their staff, the CHA commissioners reluctantly voted to accept the "compromise," believing some public housing to be better than no public housing at all. In August 1950, the City Council voted its support for the Duffy-Lancaster plan. The Public Housing Administration approved in November 1951, and Chicago launched its large-scale public housing program. When it did, public housing became yet another mechanism for containing the black population within its ghetto.

The heart of the matter was whether to build public housing on slum sites or on vacant land. This wasn't a question of space but of people—black, lower-class people. By far the largest group of slum dwellers were blacks, while most of the vacant land was in lower-middle-class white neighborhoods on the South and Northwest Sides

of the city. Building projects on slum sites would stabilize and perpetuate racial separation; building them on vacant land would move
blacks into white neighborhoods and erode some of the racially segregated residential patterns. Like it or not, the housing problem and
race issue were inseparable.[21]

White Chicagoans didn't like that link, and they had already shown
their willingness to resist the use of public housing as a tool for integration. To house returning veterans, the CHA planned several
biracial projects in white areas. In December 1946, when the Authority moved carefully selected tenants into a project on the near
South Side, mobs of whites hurled stones and shouted profanities at
the black veterans. After two weeks of living under siege, the black
families left, and Airport Homes remained a white project. The following year, August 1947, even larger mobs of whites attacked black
families moving into the Fernwood Project, on the far Southwest
Side. It took six months and a standing force of police to establish
the blacks safely in the project. In early 1948, with these events
fresh in his memory, Mayor Kennelly reacted to peaceful demonstrations by irate whites and rejected the CHA's list of vacant sites
for relocation housing.[22]

By mid-1949, with the CHA planning to launch its first large-scale
public housing program, site selection became an even more burning issue. When it did, the city's whites were not without ways to
inform, arouse, and organize public opinion in defense of their neighborhoods. There were eighty-two community newspapers in Chicago, reaching about a million readers weekly, and some 200 neighborhood improvement associations, most of which belonged to one
or more of a dozen federations. The improvement associations, led
usually by local merchants, real estate men, and bankers, were dedicated to "maintaining property values" in their areas. Homeowners
were usually indifferent to the activities of these associations, except when some issue of particular interest arose. And no issue was
of greater interest to white homeowners than keeping "undesirable
people"—especially blacks—out of their neighborhoods. By 1949,
opposing integration had become the main business of most of the
neighborhood improvement associations.[23]

As the City Council considered the package of sites recommended
by the CHA, the neighborhood and district improvement associations labored "to get the property owners stirred up to put the pressure on the aldermen."[24] They bused angry homeowners to the Housing Committee hearings and packed the gallery, and their leaders
testified and presented petitions opposing public housing sites in
white areas. Mayor Kennelly and the City Council bowed to this
aroused opinion and adopted a public housing program designed to
keep blacks in the ghetto.

That outcome was never really in doubt. Many aldermen shared their constituents' beliefs that blacks were undesirable neighbors. Still others feared riots and violence if the CHA moved blacks into white areas. Besides, the black community exerted no counterpressure. Some black leaders wanted to preserve the cohesiveness of the Black Belt and opposed apparent efforts to scatter blacks to the outskirts. Higher-income blacks, whose class outlooks proved stronger than their racial identifications, joined with influential black politicians and "remained silent and mute on this housing tragedy."[25]

The decisions made in 1949 and 1950 reflected the past experiences and current fears of the city's civic and political leaders. In turn, these early decisions shaped the future of public housing in Chicago. Forty-nine of the fifty-one sites approved by the City Council for five later programs, between 1955 and 1966, were in black areas. By 1968, the CHA was operating fifty-four family projects; and more than 99 percent of its family units were located "in areas which are or soon will be substantially all Negro."[26]

Public housing Chicago style meant high-rise projects, "slum castles in the air," intended to keep blacks where whites thought they belonged. The largest, and a symbol of the rest, is Robert Taylor Homes, named after the black who chaired the CHA during the 1949–1950 controversy. Taylor consists of twenty-eight buildings, extending from Pershing Road (Thirty-ninth Street) to Fifty-fourth Place, a distance of nearly two miles, and filling the space between the Rock Island embankment and State Street, a block east. Each building rises sixteen stories above the ground and houses about 1,000 people, making the total population of the Taylor project larger than many cities in Illinois. Its inadequate play space for children; frequently broken elevators; unsafe hallways, stairwells, and entrance areas; and generally dingy and overcrowded conditions, also make Taylor "a vertical mausoleum for the hopes . . . of those who dwell" there.[27]

In later years, site selection continued to be the central issue in public housing, but, at least through 1966, it did not become the public *cause célèbre* that it had in 1949–1950. That was not because public concern diminished but because the CHA adopted a different set of tactics. In 1949–1950, the commissioners had sent their package of sites to the City Council without first discussing it with key aldermen. Thereafter, they avoided that boner by informally submitting their selections to the alderman in whose ward the site was located. Aldermen invariably vetoed sites in white areas because the CHA's 90 percent black waiting list and occupancy rate would bring a black population into their wards. Between 1955 and 1966, for example, the CHA had tentatively recommended forty-one sites in white areas, but only two of these survived pre-clearance and were

3. One of the high rises of Robert Taylor Homes on the near South Side. (Photograph by Paul Kleppner, 30 June 1984.)

approved by the City Council. In contrast, the aldermen approved forty-nine of the sixty-two recommended sites in black areas. The pre-clearance veto effectively confined public housing to the ghetto, while avoiding acrimonious public debate over the choice of sites.[28]

By the mid-1960s, black Chicagoans were not as quiescent as their leaders had been in the early 1950s. In August 1966, a group of black public-housing tenants, aided by the American Civil Liberties Union, filed suit in U.S. District Court charging that the CHA's tenant assignment and site selection procedures violated their constitutionally guaranteed civil rights. The case was argued before U.S. District Judge Richard Austin, whom Mayor Richard J. Daley had handpicked to run for governor in 1956.

If Daley and the aldermen expected Austin to repay past political debts, they were badly mistaken. On 10 February 1969, after the parties amassed thousands of pages of affidavits, depositions, and exhibits, Judge Austin found compelling evidence of racial discrimination in the CHA's procedures for assigning tenants and selecting sites. He issued an injunction prohibiting these practices and gave the parties thirty days to formulate a plan to eliminate the abuses and remedy their past effects.[29]

When the thirty days stretched into five months without agreement, Austin, on 1 July 1969, entered his own judgment order for relief. He ordered the CHA to construct 75 percent of its future housing units in predominantly white areas and to make no more than half of these units available to the residents of the immediate neighborhoods. The order expressly prohibited the "pre-clearance procedure" and was made binding on the members of the City Council. Finally, and ironically as it turned out, Judge Austin ordered the CHA to "use its best efforts to increase the supply of [housing units] as rapidly as possible."[30]

Within the relatively short period of five months, Judge Austin dropped two bombs on the network of practices designed to protect white residential areas from invasion by blacks. Moreover, his Memorandum Opinion expressly rejected the reasoning that had been used since 1919 to justify residential segregation. Noting that CHA officials had admitted to using racial quotas in assigning tenants, Austin argued that "the 'history of tension, threats of violence and violence' urged in justification by CHA cannot excuse a governmentally established policy of racial segregation."[31] Henceforth, he ordered, neither fear of riot nor aldermanic veto was to deter the onward march toward integrated public housing.

If Judge Austin expected immediate compliance with his orders, he had yet to learn how the game was played Chicago style. For the next eight years, until Austin's death in February 1977, Mayor Daley educated him. The strategy was simple: profess good intentions and raise side issues; appeal some court orders, agree to others, then ignore the agreements; and stall as long as possible between each step.

Neither the CHA nor the city appealed Austin's finding of racial discrimination or his judgment order, so the Authority should have moved quickly to select the sites. When nearly a year elapsed and no sites had been submitted to the City Council, plaintiffs' lawyers began making inquiries to determine whether the commissioners were using their "best efforts" to comply with Austin's judgment order. The CHA responded that it did not intend to submit sites to the City Council prior to the city's mayoral election, scheduled for April 1971. To spur the CHA to act, Austin conferred informally with the parties in chambers on five occasions between 2 June and 20 July 1970. At the fifth conference, Judge Austin entered a judgment order modifying the "best efforts" provision of his earlier order. He now ordered the CHA to select sites and submit them to the Chicago Plan Commission by 20 August 1970 and to the City Council within thirty days after that date. The CHA immediately moved to vacate Austin's newest order. When that motion was denied on 13 August, the Authority appealed; and the order was stayed during the appeal.

On 16 December 1970, the Court of Appeals affirmed Austin's order. When the court denied later motions for a rehearing and for a stay of the order, the city announced its intention to appeal to the U.S. Supreme Court. In the meantime, Judge Austin established 5 March 1971 as the new deadline for the CHA to submit its list of sites to the Plan Commission. When the Supreme Court adjourned on Friday, 5 March, without hearing the city's appeal, the CHA was finally compelled to transmit its list of 275 proposed sites in white communities to the Plan Commission. The locations now became public knowledge, and the firestorm of protest commenced.[32]

"FIRST HITLER NOW AUSTIN" read the placard carried by one of the many groups of whites who took to the streets over the weekend to denounce the court order. Since the City Council still had to approve the sites and acquire the land, protestors besieged the aldermen's ward offices to let them know the feelings of their constituents. Most of them got the hint quickly. As Alderman-elect Edward Vrdolyak assured his 10th Ward constituents: "I don't think we have a need for low-cost public housing here. People shouldn't be alarmed because nothing can happen without City Council approval."[33]

But how would the City Council vote? Austin had made his July 1969 order binding on the aldermen. Would they obey the federal court or flaunt the law? On Monday, 8 March, the city's law-and-order chief executive gave the answer. Mayor Daley denounced the CHA's plans to build low-rise public housing on sites in white areas: "The public housing proposal . . . is . . . detrimental to all the people of Chicago. In my opinion, these units should not be built." To no one's great shock, the mayor's opinion became the verdict of the aldermen. At its Wednesday meeting, the City Council voted against suspending its rules to permit immediate consideration of the CHA site plan and referred it instead to the Rules Committee, a favorite burying ground for unpopular measures. Later that day, Daley promised to announce his own plan to put public housing "in neighborhoods where people want it." The mayor didn't need to add that his plan would involve no construction of new family units in white areas.[34]

There is no doubt that Daley and the aldermen reflected the views of most Chicagoans. For several days after the council meeting, the *Chicago Sun-Times* conducted street-corner interviews on the question of CHA site selection. The returns indicated that among blacks "the principal issue [was] the need for more and better low-income housing, regardless of where it is." The white respondents registered a "substantial" margin for Daley's position, favored neighborhood control of CHA locations, and "none thought [public] housing should be located near them." As the *Chicago Defender*, the city's major black newspaper, had remarked earlier: "Everybody likes black folk but no one wants to live near them."[35] As far as the city and the CHA were concerned, whites wouldn't have to worry about that possibility.

With the CHA's package of recommended sites languishing in the Rules Committee, the city faced a cutoff of federal funds for low-income housing. To avoid that, in May 1971, the city and the Department of Housing and Urban Development (HUD) agreed to a letter of intent requiring the city to acquire suitable sites according to a specific timetable. Needless to say, the city ignored the schedule, and in a sharply worded opinion filed in October 1971, Judge Austin castigated Mayor Daley. "It is an anomaly," he wrote, "that the 'law and order' chief executive of this city should challenge and defy the federal law." Despite his rebuke to the mayor and his injunction against HUD's release of further funds, the City Council still refused to hold any hearings or to acquire any sites. Finally, in response to a supplemental complaint that named the mayor and the aldermen as defendants, Austin ruled that the provision of Illinois law requiring City Council approval of land acquisition by the CHA "shall not be applicable to CHA's actions . . . taken for the purpose of providing [housing units]."[36] When the Court of Appeals upheld this ruling, one roadblock on the path of integrated public housing was ostensibly removed.

From the time of Austin's 1969 ruling until September 1974, no construction was begun for public housing in white areas. Thereafter, the city and the CHA moved at "less than turtle-like speed," constructing only sixty-six units in the next three years, while the CHA's waiting list grew to include 11,200 families. By early 1978, black neighborhoods faced a housing shortage of "cataclysmic proportions," and the Chicago Urban League, the NAACP, Operation PUSH, and other civil rights groups asked for a modification of the Austin order to allow some new construction in black areas.[37]

In May 1979, the Federal District Court modified the decade-old Austin ruling and ordered the CHA to use $100 million in funds available from HUD to construct 1,337 units of family housing and to locate at least 400 of them in white areas. The city's newly elected mayor, Jane Byrne, announced with considerable fanfare a scattered-site housing program to comply with the court order. The city's prompt announcement of plans to implement a court order on public housing was unusual and led to some hope that a new era had dawned in Chicago.

But nothing had really changed. Within a year, the lawyers were back in court to charge that the CHA had made no progress and to ask U.S. District Judge John Powers Crowley to strip the Authority of responsibility for the program and give it to a court-appointed receiver. Crowley refused the request, but he criticized the CHA for dragging its feet and gave the commissioners six months to make a "substantial start" toward full compliance with his earlier order.[38]

Mayor Byrne then backed away from her scattered-site program, announcing that she would ask the District Court for permission to scrap it and use the remaining funds to maintain the existing units. "Why build another $100 million worth of units when it is practically impossible to operate what you have? There would be literally no money to operate those new buildings."[39] Why, indeed, especially when the new construction was targeted for sites in sensitive, and politically important, white areas?

Byrne wasn't able to scrap the 1979 plan formally, but her sensitivity to pressures from white areas meant that progress remained as slow as ever. When the Southwest Side Parish and Neighborhood Federation and the Lithuanian Homeowners Association objected in 1982 to two proposed sites in Marquette Park, Byrne was reported to be sympathetic and willing "to help all she can." Her help took the form of asking the CHA commissioners to sell the sites, a move the Authority attempted but the court blocked. By the end of Byrne's term, only 44 percent of the 400 family units the court had designated for white areas were built or under construction, while over 70 percent of the units targeted for black areas were completed or in progress.[40]

In April 1983, after nearly seventeen years of litigation, the lawyers again returned to Federal District Court to argue that the CHA had made "insufficient progress." As Roman Pucinski had prophesied in 1969, Austin's order "dealt the death knell to public housing [in Chicago]."[41] The city's political leaders had simply decided that no new public housing was better than even "a little bit" of integrated public housing.

The Chicago Board of Education

■ The struggle for integrated public education was as long, bitter, and unsuccessful as the battle for integrated housing. Over the years, the school struggle focused on a variety of specific questions of policy and practice. But underlying the details, and shaping the battle lines, was a basic and uncompromisable conflict over objectives. To blacks, the school question involved "the right of black school children to a desegregated school system." To the Board of Education, the central problem was stopping the flight of whites from the city. The Board's policy statements implied that much as early as 1964, and it removed any doubt when it presented its 1967 integration plan:

> Anyone who carefully analyzes the block-by-block neighborhood patterns of Negro immigration and white flight cannot help but see the handwriting on the wall for Chicago. . . . The immediate short range goal must be to anchor the whites that still remain in the city. To do this requires that school authorities quickly achieve and maintain stable racial attendance proportions in changing fringe areas. . . .
>
> Working class whites who are often just one step ahead of the rolling ghetto are less secure economically and socially than their middle class counterparts. The Negro is perceived as a threat and appears to jeopardize their tenuous economic security and social status. We . . . propose . . . that Negro enrollments in the schools in these changing sections of the city be limited and fixed immediately.[42]

Of course throughout the conflict, the Board of Education routinely admitted the general desirability of integration. But when the time to act arrived, that general goal did not compete seriously with the concrete objective of racial stabilization.

As with the housing issue, the school battle arose from the postwar growth in the size of the black population. It began in 1961, when a member of the Board of Education, the Chicago Urban League, and the NAACP all questioned whether schools in white areas were underutilized while those in black areas were overcrowded. A group of black parents also filed suit in Federal District Court, charging that district boundaries had been gerrymandered to create all-black schools. This complaint was withdrawn in 1963, when the Board of Education agreed to appoint a panel of experts to study the school system and to develop a desegregation plan. But even before settling the suit, the Board acted to reduce overcrowding. It approved a voluntary transfer plan allowing students whose parents paid the transportation costs to move from overcrowded schools to selected schools with underused classrooms, and it bought 150 trailers to be used as mobile classrooms. By 1972, the Board had 1,352 mobile classrooms in use, mostly for black schools.[43]

At this early stage of the struggle, the focal point of controversy was Benjamin Willis, the general superintendent of schools, whose tenure dated to the Kennelly Administration. Willis was autocratic, arrogant, unyielding, and unwilling even to acknowledge the fact of

4. Mobile classrooms at Henderson Elementary School, 19 January 1982. There were still 320 mobile units being used as classrooms at 58 schools in 1982. (*Chicago Tribune.*)

segregation. His preference for using mobile classrooms, "Willis Wagons" as they became known, led some blacks to suspect him of racism. That impression grew stronger in 1963, when Willis cut back on the number of receiving schools involved in the permissive transfer plan, forcing black parents to get a court order requiring him to carry out the full plan. Rather than comply, he resigned, but the Board refused to accept his resignation and instead simply rescinded the transfer plan.

From this point, Willis's dismissal became the central demand of civil rights groups. They sent complaints of discrimination to the U.S. Office of Education, filed lawsuits, organized school boycotts, and staged demonstrations, including marches in July and August 1965 outside Mayor Daley's home in Bridgeport. Throughout all of this, neither Willis nor Daley budged. Civil rights leaders looked forward to the expiration of Willis's contract at the end of August 1965, especially since an informal newspaper poll of Board members indicated that a majority opposed renewing it. However, a few days after the newspaper reported its poll, three Board members with ties to Daley changed their minds and voted to extend the contract until Willis reached retirement age in December 1966. Civil rights groups "felt that the slap in the face we got with the reappointment of Willis came directly from the mayor."[44]

While the anti-Willis agitation was going on, the panel of experts appointed to settle the 1961 lawsuit issued its report (in March 1964). It found that the city's public schools were segregated and that "quality education is not available in Chicago to the [black] children who are in greatest need of it." The panel recommended integration of teachers and liberal transfers of students, and the Board of Education accepted the recommendations "in principle" but took no action to implement them. Eight months later, a second major report on the condition of Chicago's schools was submitted to the Board. This one, a report on curriculum, administration, and neighborhood school policy, had been commissioned three years earlier, over the objections of Superintendent Willis. The report recommended integrating the schools and decentralizing the administration, but Willis simply ignored its recommendations.[45]

In September 1965, responding to complaints filed by a coalition of civil rights groups, the U.S. Commissioner of Education froze $30 million in federal aid to Chicago schools. Within five days, Mayor Daley negotiated a release of the funds in return for a commitment by the Board of Education to review its enrollment policies. Two years later, after the review had been completed, the new superintendent, James Redmond, presented a plan calling for a number of desegregation programs, including magnet schools, educational parks, financial incentives to teachers working with black children in the inner city, altered attendance boundaries, and pupil busing. The Board unanimously approved the document "in principle," and the following December, Redmond proposed to begin implementing it by busing about 1,000 black children from two Chicago neighborhoods—South Shore and Austin—to predominantly white schools in South Chicago and Belmont-Cragin. By an eight-to-two vote, the Board agreed to set aside the funds for the busing scheme.

The public outcry was nearly instantaneous. White parents and neighborhood groups denounced the limited use of "forced busing." They quickly elicited support from locally elected politicians, especially the aldermen and state legislators from South Chicago, Belmont-Cragin, and similar white neighborhoods. The local politicians attended anti-busing rallies, spoke against the proposals at public hearings of the Board, and introduced resolutions in the City Council and the state legislature. Congressman Roman Pucinski, a member of the House Committee on Labor and Education and a prominent figure in the Chicago Democratic organization, also joined the anti-busing phalanx. When Pucinski identified busing as a measure that "may ultimately lead to the kind of blockbusting that has destroyed many of Chicago's finest communities," it was reasonably clear that the Democratic Machine had no interest in defending the Redmond plan. Mayor Daley's public statements removed any lingering doubts on that score. Daley was reluctant to become involved in the issue, and he defended the Board's autonomy. At the same time he said that "any program today should have the maximum participation by the people in the neighborhoods"; and, "if the majority of the people don't want a certain thing, who in government has the right to set themselves up above the majority?" Moreover, he described himself as being old-fashioned enough to believe that children should be "home for lunch," which was not very likely to occur if they were bused to school. On balance, Daley's statements clearly tilted in favor of the neighborhood-school groups and probably served to encourage their resistance.[46]

In the face of this public clamor, the Board of Education saw that the plan would not achieve its objective. The Board member who later cast a decisive vote, Cyrus Adams III, complained that "if plans intended to retain middle-class people in the city are going to drive a larger number of the middle-class people out of the city, they don't make sense." On 28 February 1968, the Board registered its agreement: it voted nine to one to reject Redmond's plan for South Shore, and by a five-to-five vote the members failed to approve a compulsory busing plan for Austin.[47]

The Board made a critical decision by rejecting Redmond's original plan and substituting voluntary for compulsory busing. Leaving pupil placement entirely to the discretion of parents meant perpetuating neighborhood attendance patterns, which were highly segregated ones, and sacrificing the black community's right to an integrated school system. Moreover, the controversy involved in making the decision preoccupied the Board and took the steam out of later efforts to implement the comprehensive aspects of Redmond's plan. Only one magnet school, for example, was built prior to Redmond's resignation in 1975. Thus, while the Board chose racial stabilization over racial integration, in the long run it managed to achieve neither objective; and the exodus of whites from the city and its public schools continued unabated (Table 4).[48]

The next phase of the struggle began in April 1976, when the Illinois Board of Education told the city that its schools did not meet the state's rules for racial balance and threatened an eventual cutoff of state and federal funds. To avoid losing half of its $1.2 billion budget, the Chicago Board of Education passed a resolution the following January committing itself to comply fully with the state's guidelines. Joseph P. Hannon, Redmond's successor as general superintendent, then took steps to implement the resolution. He announced that a citizens' committee would be set up to develop a comprehensive desegregation plan, and he unveiled a limited desegregation program as an interim measure. Students of different races were to meet by means of closed-circuit television; later they were to travel

Table 4. Racial Categories as Percentages of Total Enrollment in Chicago's Public Schools

	White	Black	Other[1]
1950	62.1	36.1	1.8
1960	55.2	42.1	2.7
1966	46.6	50.9	2.5
1970	34.6	54.8	10.6
1976	24.9	59.4	15.6
1980	18.6	60.8	18.5
1983	16.3	60.7	22.9

[1] For 1970 and after, Hispanics are by far the largest group in this category.

in small vans for classes at academic centers; and, finally, they would work together in special projects at non-school facilities.

Although approving Hannon's interim scheme, several Board members expressed doubts. One called it "antiseptic integration"; and another, wondering whether it would use "black and white or color TV," said it was "difficult to think in terms of beginning desegregation via television." Henry McGee, a black member of the Board of Education, was more blunt: "If I were the parent of a black child, I'd be insulted. . . . This is a gimmick, and I think we ought to stop playing around with this desegregation business and get down to doing something that is real and solid." But even integration through television went too far for some white parents from Southwest Side neighborhoods. As one infuriated mother expressed it, "we are not going to accept any kind of plan, and that's it."[49]

For four months, Hannon and the Board wrestled with the problem of setting up the citizens' committee, which was called the City-wide Advisory Committee (CWAC). It finally began its deliberations in early May 1977, but a few weeks later the busing issue erupted again. Still under pressure from the state board, Hannon suggested an update of the permissive transfer program that had begun in 1963. Since that program had never recruited many participants, the superintendent proposed to make it more attractive by providing the voluntary transfer students with free bus transportation. By removing the burden of the added transportation costs from their parents, Hannon hoped to attract as many as 2,200 student volunteers.

The news of Hannon's plan ignited the white communities on the Southwest Side. Parents from Bogan, one of the white high schools slated to receive black students, attended the meeting of the Board of Education in early June to protest the superintendent's plan. They intended, they told the Board members, "to keep our students in an all-white school in an all-white neighborhood," and they promised to resist integration "with parent power." In fact, their first re-

5. Bogan High School parents protesting the Board of Education's busing and teacher-transfer plans outside the Southwest Side school in June 1977. (*Chicago Tribune.*)

sistance effort used student power: they called a one-day boycott of classes in June, which was reported to be about 95 percent effective.[50]

During the summer, the opposition became more determined. The Bogan Community Council voted to boycott on the first day of classes and every Friday in September until the Board postponed the transfer plan. The Southwest Side Civic Federation called for a three-year moratorium on the plan. Voluntary busing became so controversial an issue that seven of the city's eight television stations refused to accept a commercial featuring Ernie Banks, a former Chicago Cubs baseball star, urging parents to cooperate with the plan.[51]

Those who spoke on behalf of the white community organizations left no doubt why they opposed Hannon's plan. "Let the educated blacks educate their own, and teach them how to be clean," said the chairperson of Mothers for Neighborhood Schools, American Style. One mother from the Bogan area likened "a little bit of integration [to] being a little bit pregnant," and another wore blackface to a meeting of the Board of Education "to get them to pay attention to us." To the resisters, compromise was out of the question; it was an all-or-nothing battle. Mrs. Betty Bonow, a delegate to the recent Boston convention of the National Association of Neighborhood Schools, summed up their attitude: "I learned two words in Boston. One is resist and the other is never."[52]

"Operation Resist," as one of the protesting mothers called it, received tacit encouragement from the city's chief executive. After meeting in June with representatives of the Bogan Community council, Mayor Michael Bilandic observed that he didn't "think that busing achieves any major purposes. . . . Do we want to educate or integrate? Could you do both of them? What's the cost benefit?" By August he went further and promised a group of Southwest Side residents that he'd use his influence to get the Board to accept a three-year moratorium.[53]

Hannon and the Board held firm, however, and on the opening day of classes only a few minor incidents occurred, leading to the arrests of several of the irate white mothers on charges of disorderly conduct. The Bogan boycott was about 80 percent effective on opening day, but it petered out over the next two weeks. By mid-September, the Board announced that a grand total of 650 pupils had transferred from overcrowded schools; and by mid-October the number had grown to 1,003, still far below the original goal of 2,180.[54]

During this furor over the voluntary transfer plan, the Citywide Advisory Committee was at work developing its general desegregation plan. There was never any real doubt that the CWAC would recommend a voluntary plan, but there was a question about whether its plan would also include a mandatory backup scheme if the voluntary provisions failed to achieve their goals. The CWAC initially voted to include some mandatory reassignment; then, two days later, it confused matters by refusing to table a resolution calling for an entirely voluntary program. The next week, the desegregation project manager for the Board of Education, Edward A. Welling, Jr., presented a package of twelve desegregation programs and included a provision for mandatory backup. Finally, in late December 1977, the CWAC endorsed Welling's twelve programs and provided that the Board of Education could decide to make participation in any program mandatory for the next school year if that program failed to meet its assigned goal by March of the preceding year.[55]

After the citizens' panel formally presented its plan in January 1978, the next move was up to Hannon and the Board of Education. Even the ambiguous clause allowing (but not requiring) mandatory pupil transfer if all else failed upset the neighborhood groups, and Hannon indicated that he would weigh their concern along with the proposals of the CWAC as he developed a final plan to submit to the Board. He was aware, he said, that any type of mandatory action "would exacerbate the movement of middle-class [white] people out of the city" and defeat the prime and persisting objective of Board policy. He promised that he would recommend "strictly a voluntary plan."[56]

Hannon kept his promise. "Access to Excellence," as he named his five-year plan, aimed at drawing over 200,000 students into integrated programs, including magnet schools, academic interest centers, and advanced placement classes. In these respects, it was basically similar to the twelve-point scheme that Welling had presented in November. The key difference was that Hannon's plan contained no mention of a mandatory backup provision. As he emphasized repeatedly in his briefing of the press, "its cornerstone is voluntary participation. . . . No student will be required to participate in any program implemented under this plan. . . . Only students who choose to participate in a program will be involved."[57]

On 18 April 1978, the Board of Education, by a six-to-five vote, defeated a last-ditch attempt to include mandatory action as part of the plan, and then it approved Hannon's proposal by a six-to-four margin. As it had a decade earlier, in dealing with Redmond's plan, the Board opted for voluntary approaches because its chief objective was still racial stabilization and not racial integration.

If Hannon's plan did not go far enough to satisfy civil rights groups, it went too far to please the white resisters. In mid-June 1978, the Education Councils of Bogan and Hubbard High Schools on the Southwest Side announced their opposition. As they had from the outset, the white parents again "took a stand for neighborhood schools for neighborhood children." And on the opening day of classes, the white mothers made their stand in the streets. They held their children out of classes, picketed, threw eggs, and shouted epithets at the incoming black children. Not even arrests for disorderly conduct discouraged their protest. "I am a mother in action," one of the leaders declared. "I know the life of my neighborhood is being threatened and I must stand up and fight for it."[58]

Hannon publicly interpreted the events in the best light possible, claiming that it was "probably the finest opening day in Chicago public schools in the last decade." The demonstrations and egg-throwing incidents, he claimed, were not typical of the Southwest Side, an area which Hannon said suffered from an "unfair stigma." The superintendent applauded the initial success of his plan, playing down the fact that only 17,371 pupils, about 3 percent of the students in Chicago public schools, applied for "Access to Excellence" programs. Blacks and civil rights groups judged the program more harshly. It was "the Hannon Hustle," according to one community newspaper. Although "all its fancy footwork" is difficult to follow, "when you're done dancing you're left several steps behind where you started."[59]

HEW's Office of Civil Rights (OCR) also took a dim view of the progress made under "Access to Excellence." In April 1979, OCR rejected Chicago's application for 1980 funds under the Emergency School Aid Act, charging willful segregation of students over the past thirty-five years. The OCR report explicitly rejected the Board of Education's claim that segregation of pupils was simply a reflection of segregated housing patterns. The report pointed to the location of new schools, the use of mobile classrooms, changes in attendance boundaries and feeder patterns, and other specific acts as evidence that the Board had deliberately "contained black students in segregated black schools, while protecting white students in racially identifiable white schools." In response to Hannon's claim that no larger amount of integration was possible, OCR in late August released its own feasibility study, which called for busing 114,000 students.[60]

Hannon and the Board denied the charges of deliberate segregation, but Mayor Jane Byrne cut the ground from under these claims of innocence in early August. She publicly conceded that the existing racial segregation was the result of practices in the past. That's the way the public had wanted it then, she said, but now "times have changed." However, when OCR's feasibility study was released later that month, it was the mayor who changed her mind: "It is not acceptable to bus 114,000 students. . . . Nothing's going to be done to upset people's lives. . . . I think the neighborhood school system should definitely be preserved."[61]

Other political leaders joined the chorus denouncing the call for massive and involuntary busing. Alderman Roman Pucinski (41st Ward) claimed that "there is not an iota of truth that the Board of Education creates segregation through official actions. Chicago is not guilty of deliberate segregation." To William O. Lipinski (23rd Ward), chairman of the City Council's Education Committee, nothing less than "the survival of the City of Chicago" was at stake. The OCR plan was "absolutely ridiculous," he said; it would simply increase "white flight."[62]

Faced with these dire predictions, yet still under pressure from OCR, Hannon developed a new version of his plan. "Access II" was an expanded voluntary transfer plan that included a new pupil assignment policy, but one which guaranteed, Hannon emphasized, that no students were to be told to which schools they had to transfer. The Board quickly approved the revision, held its collective breath, and awaited HEW's verdict. On 21 September, HEW Secretary Patricia Roberts Harris rejected "Access II," and on 29 October, she sent the case to the Justice Department, urging it to file a civil rights action.

While Chicago's civil rights leaders were still applauding HEW's action, the Board of Education's chronic financial problems reached the crisis stage. With the system nearing bankruptcy, Hannon, who had been given a new four-year contract in mid-September, abruptly resigned on 28 November 1979. While the Board struggled to regain some semblance of financial stability, Attorney General Benjamin Civiletti moved slowly on the issue of a civil rights action.

When Hannon resigned, the Board, ignoring the claims of the black deputy superintendent and the protests of the black community, selected a white woman, Angeline Caruso, as acting superintendent. The larger change, however, was the creation of a Chicago School Finance Authority, which Governor James Thompson had recommended in early January 1980. Henceforth, the five-member Finance Authority, not the Board of Education or the general superintendent, would control the budget. In May 1980, Byrne, acting under the legislation that created the Finance Authority, named an entirely new Board of Education, which included five blacks. The new Board immediately opened negotiations with the Justice Department on the pending civil rights charge. Four months later, in September 1980, the Board and the Justice Department signed and filed with U.S. District Judge Milton I. Shadur a consent decree in which the Board promised a comprehensive desegregation effort, while admitting no liability for official segregation. Now the Justice Department would learn what Dr. King and others had discovered earlier: Chicago officials have their own unique ways of "interpreting" such agreements.

The Board hired a team of outside experts to develop yet another desegregation plan. News leaks concerning the experts' suggestions fueled white opposition and led Board officials to make public statements assuaging anxieties. The Board's chief desegregation consultant assured the public that mandatory busing would not be a central feature of the plan and that "every option will be exhausted to enable public school children to walk to school." When the rumor spread that the plan would bar white enrollment of over 60 percent in any elementary school, the white neighborhoods again displayed their anger. Angeline Caruso publicly argued for a higher figure and said that "if the objective is to get all the white children out of the system, this [60 percent maximum] will do it." The plan that the consultants recommended included that maximum and involved the reassignment of 41,706 students through mandatory busing and boundary changes. At a secret meeting of the Board in late March 1981, six of the eleven members apparently approved the recommendations. However, by early April, when the plan was formally unveiled, the maximum on white enrollment was actually set at 65 percent.[63]

Neither the experts' recommendations nor the version that the Board proposed had a chance. Both lacked support in the white neighborhoods. The local PTA and education council meetings in early April were packed with angry parents opposing the desegregation plan and pledging to "picket and boycott and do all that radical stuff, for as long as it takes" to defeat the scheme. And the city's political leaders were just as adamant in their opposition. Only hours after the Board had revealed its details, Mayor Byrne condemned the plan as "childish," "silly," and too expensive. Ignoring her 1979 admission that past practices by the Board had encouraged segregation, Byrne now said that it was understandable that many schools remained entirely white because whites attend "their neighborhood schools. . . . I think it's silly for them to get on a bus. Why should we tell them to go to schools where they can't walk?" Besides, she added, "the whole thing is moot, because the Board of Education doesn't have the money to do this." Three days later, in a letter to Reverend Kenneth Smith, the black president of the Board, the mayor underscored what had always been the key point for the city's chief executives: "Any desegregation plan that would further erode our tax base must be judged irresponsible and, ultimately, unacceptable."[64]

As the firestorm of protest continued through the next week, the mayor noted, prophetically as it turned out, that the busing issue might be settled when the new administration in Washington took action. "President Reagan is against busing, and it's his Justice Department," she observed. Five aldermen drew up a resolution assailing the plan, and fifteen more quickly joined them. The governor announced that no state funds were available to pay for implementing the plan. Most critically, the mayor continued to imply a link between the desegregation plan and her continued opposition to the property tax increase that the Board said it needed to balance its budget.[65]

Finally, the Board cracked under the pressure and began to move away from the desegregation plan that it had approved earlier. On 11 April, the newly appointed general superintendent, Ruth Love, a black, indicated that she favored some modifications in the plan. Four days later, by a six-to-five vote, with all five blacks in opposition, the Board voted to drop the mandatory busing and student reassignment portions of the desegregation plan and to raise the maximum limit on white enrollment to 70 percent. The revised plan that the Board of Education submitted to Judge Shadur, in January 1982, once again stressed voluntary desegregation.

Now Shadur had to determine whether the plan complied with the terms of the 1980 consent decree. Civil rights groups denounced the plan for not providing enough integration; groups from the white neighborhoods on the Southwest Side condemned it for moving too far in that direction. In February 1982, the Justice Department filed a brief with Judge Shadur, indicating that the voluntary plan "is constitutional and consistent with the consent decree." The chief of the Justice Department's Civil Rights Division, testifying in April before a House Judiciary subcommittee, cited Chicago's program as "a model for the nation," and an outstanding example of the Reagan Administration's approach to school desegregation. After listening to those claims, then-Congressman Harold Washington said he "thought [he] was in Disneyland it was so unreal."[66]

Judge Shadur's opinion, issued on 6 January 1983, found the Board of Education's voluntary desegregation plan "constitutionally acceptable." Shadur recognized that the plan's definition of a desegregated school would leave nearly 60 percent of the system's schools virtually all minority; however, he argued, that was no reason "to damn the plan with . . . faint praise. For the facts are that this aspect of the plan is not only adequate to pass constitutional muster but—vital to public acceptance and support—reasoned and reasonable." In November 1983, the Board's special attorney, Robert Howard, announced that the plan's goal of at least 30 percent minority enrollment had been achieved in all Chicago public schools. It was "deeply satisfying to pass this landmark," Howard added, "particularly when you consider that it was achieved with a minimum of public turmoil." By this standard, and despite the fact that most public school students still attend classes in predominantly black or Hispanic facilities, the Chicago school system was officially "desegregated."[67]

Several themes run through these long and sorry sagas of the black community's frustrated quests for meaningful integration in public housing and public education. First, the primary goal of Chicago's policy on public housing and education was racial stabilization, stopping white flight from the city by containing blacks within the ghetto, an objective that precluded meaningful integration. Second, the city's white political leaders—mayors, aldermen, CHA commissioners, and Board of Education members—seemed especially sensitive to the articulated interests and fears of the white populace. Whether the public clamor shaped their decisions or simply reinforced their own personal preferences, the effect was the same—a set of decisions that consistently sacrificed the rights and interests of the city's blacks. Third, although there were notable exceptions, the city's black political leaders, and especially its elected politicians, were not equally sensitive to the needs of the black populace. Until very recent years, they often joined with their white colleagues to support measures that limited the housing and educational opportunities of their black constituents. Finally, the white resistance groups were well organized and highly active, while the black community lacked an equally well-developed set of grass-roots institutions through which to apply counterpressure. The Chicago Urban League, the NAACP, and the leaders of religious groups made the argument for integration, but they had no ability to arouse the black populace or to translate their concern into votes. As early as 1950, Mayor Kennelly, who was never accused of being especially astute politically, spotted the difference. Told that eighty-nine ministers had testified in behalf of the CHA's original housing program, the mayor retorted that they "are just ministers. They are not property owners."[68] Since elected officials were in the business of getting votes, the mayor seemed to imply that they should be attentive to the opinions of those who were most likely to be moved to political action. Later political leaders shared Kennelly's outlook.

These struggles, or for that matter those for integration of the police and fire departments, were not one-shot battles. They were not contested strenuously, resolved by compromise, and then forgotten. They were acrimonious, protracted, and never amicably settled. Historically conditioned racial animosities prompted them in the first place, and each battle then heightened racial tensions and solidified feelings of racial hostility.

This dominating context of ongoing racial combat gave larger meaning to particular events, some of which seemed quite small when viewed independently. This explains why both blacks and whites came to attach such importance to membership on the CHA and the Board of Education and the seemingly outsized uproars that greeted some appointments. This racial context allows us to understand the reactions of political leaders and to identify the targets of their appeals for voting support. Finally, and most important, the existence of a racially charged context helps explain why a biracial contest for mayor of Chicago had to become a battle between the races. No third parties, whether reporters or politicians, had to "inject" race into the campaign; it was there, as it had been for nearly forty years, in the open, simply waiting to be mobilized at the polls. No candidate could escape it or overcome the deep feelings held by voters of the opposite race, because none could instantly wipe out these memories of past experiences.

4. Race, Ethnicity, and Electoral Politics

The Daley Years, 1955–1976

Power is dangerous unless you have humility. *Richard J. Daley*

■ On Tuesday evening, 5 April 1955, a crowd gathered at the candidate's headquarters in the old Morrison Hotel on Madison Street. While an earlier straw poll had shown their candidate trailing, they came expecting a victory and cheered boisterously as workers posted each batch of returns. They soon had reason to celebrate: at 8:58 P.M., the opposition candidate conceded the election. Tumultuous cheers greeted this news, and the band added to the din with its loud rendition of "Happy Days Are Here Again." Suddenly the musicians stopped playing, and the cheers began to die down; then, as if on signal, the band burst into a lusty version of "Chicago." The next mayor of Chicago, the self-proclaimed "kid from the stockyards," was striding into the room to claim his triumph.

Surrounded by his family, the mayor-elect looked over the throng of jubilant party workers, smiled, waved, and acknowledged their cheers. He thanked his family, his party, and the voters of Chicago for this moment of victory and assured his listeners that he would work to build a better city. Then, speaking softly as he gazed into the glaring lights and flashing bulbs, he concluded with a promise: "As Mayor of Chicago, I shall embrace charity, love mercy, and walk humbly with my God."[1]

Fifteen days later, at a ceremony in the chambers of the City Council, Richard J. Daley took the oath of office for the first time. He was to repeat that act five more times before his reign over the city ended on 20 December 1976, twenty-two years to the day since his first slating for mayor by the Central Committee of the Democratic party.

6. Newly inaugurated Mayor Richard J. Daley being congratulated by Judge Abraham Lincoln Marovitz (center), who administered the oath of office, and former Mayor Martin Kennelly, 20 April 1955. (*Chicago Tribune.*)

Presidents came and went—Eisenhower, Kennedy, Johnson, Nixon, and Ford—while Daley remained ensconced on the fifth floor of City Hall. His mayoralty was the longest in the city's history, lasting twenty-one years and eight months. During that time, "his Chicago" became a modern metropolis, a city of expressways and skyscrapers, a center of international commerce and finance.

Yet in other respects his city did not change at all. On the day of Daley's death, as it had been on the day of his birth seventy-four years earlier, Chicago was a city of ethnic neighborhoods, with almost fixed boundaries separating its various nationalities. Some groups moved from their old locales into newer communities farther away from the center of the city; and economic differences appeared within each group, separating the upwardly mobile from those who hadn't done so well. But still the old ethnic clannishness and sense of cultural identification remained strong; so, too, did the feeling of antipathy to the city's rapidly growing black population. Race relations in Chicago continued to be shaped by bitter memories of past experiences.

The boom after World War II in the number of blacks opened a new phase in the battle between black and white Chicagoans for access to neighborhoods, schools, and jobs. This black migration combined with the outflow of whites to the suburbs to alter the terms of the city's coalitional politics. When these two dimensions of what whites saw as the "black problem" became linked, as they inevitably had to, the relationship between the city's blacks and its white political leaders changed significantly. That change began in the Daley years, underwent a long gestation period, and culminated in the 1983 election of Chicago's first black mayor.

The Biracial Coalition, 1955–1967

■ In the relatively short span of three decades, the human arithmetic underlying Chicago's electoral politics changed drastically (Table 5).[2] Between 1950 and 1980, Chicago experienced a net gain of 413,478 blacks of voting age and a net loss of over 1 million white voters. Whites fell from over three quarters to just under half of the city's electorate, while the black share of the voting-age population nearly tripled.

The implications of this change were not visible during the 1950s. At that point, blacks were a highly mobilized and reliable part of the Democratic Machine's biracial coalition. Indeed, it is one of the ironies of his career, and of the city's history, that strong support among black voters played a crucial role in Richard J. Daley's early mayoral victories.

Daley's first contested race for mayor came in the form of a three-way primary in February 1955. The Democratic slatemakers had refused to endorse the incumbent mayor, Martin Kennelly, and instead bestowed their collective blessing on Daley. But Kennelly, who had already announced his intention to seek a third term, refused to quit the race. He told reporters that he had been dumped because he refused to yield to the Machine's pressure to change the leadership of the Civil Service Commission and to abandon his system of centralized city purchasing. The Machine's "'draft' of Daley was phoney," he charged. "The question [now] is whether the people of Chicago will rule, or whether the city will be ruled by the willful, wanton inner-

Table 5. Racial Composition of Chicago's Voting-Age Population, 1940–1980

| | Numbers (in 000s) | | | Percent of Total | | |
	White	Black	Hispanic	White	Black	Hispanic
1940	2,205	191	—	86.6	7.9	—
1950	2,236	345	—	79.7	13.3	—
1960	1,850	471	—	71.7	20.2	—
1970	1,513	576	—	63.1	27.1	—
1980	946	758	252	48.3	38.7	12.8

circle of political bosses at the Morrison Hotel."[3] To give the Democratic voters of the city a choice, Kennelly declared that he would run against Daley in the primary.

Another contestant had declared his intention to run for mayor in November. Benjamin Adamowski had been Kennelly's corporation counsel until resigning in disgust in 1950. Although admitting that Kennelly was personally honest, Adamowski argued "that he was morally dishonest, because he let the boys at Democratic headquarters use him as a front." Adamowski had anticipated Kennelly's rebuff by the slatemakers; and he expected the mayor to withdraw after that, making the primary a straight contest between himself and the Machine candidate. When Kennelly refused to follow the script, Adamowski still decided to stay in the race.[4]

Daley won the three-way primary, polling 49 percent of the vote cast; Kennelly came in second, and Adamowski was a distant third. Kennelly carried the white ethnic wards on the Northwest Side, and Daley had a plurality in the South Side's more populous white ethnic areas. But because Adamowski also ran well in both of these areas, Daley's overall plurality was a slim 5,270 votes. Daley and Kennelly battled to a virtual draw in the six Lake Shore wards, with Kennelly winning by a margin of only 56 votes out of nearly 75,000 cast. The key to Daley's victory was his strength in a cluster of wards that Len O'Connor later dubbed the "Automatic Eleven," the five predominantly black wards of Congressman Dawson's sub-machine on the South Side and six wards running from the Loop through the West Side of the city. In these eleven wards, Daley outpolled Kennelly by 96,876 votes, which amounted to 95 percent of his citywide plurality.[5]

Table 6 offers a view of Daley's strength in each area of the city in the 1955 primary and in the general elections from 1955 through 1967. The measure used in the table is not the one conventionally employed as an indicator of political popularity. However, the more common measure—the percentage of the total vote cast—can be misleading: a candidate's (or party's) percentage of the vote cast can remain roughly unchanged from one election to another, while the number of voters participating drops (or increases) sharply. We

Table 6. Percentage of the Voting-Age Population Supporting Daley, 1955–1967

	1955P	1955G	1959G	1963G	1967G
Automatic Eleven	27.7	39.8	38.8	37.9	37.9
Dawson Five	25.9	36.2	35.2	38.6	36.0
West Side	29.5	43.3	42.3	37.3	39.8
White Ethnic	16.0	37.8	40.4	28.0	39.2
Northwest Side	12.6	30.3	35.4	24.0	34.0
South Side	17.7	41.1	45.1	31.7	44.3
Lake Shore	12.2	22.9	25.1	24.8	29.6
Rest of city	11.0	24.2	30.1	28.0	39.0
Total for Daley citywide	16.2	31.1	34.2	29.8	37.6
Total turnout citywide	33.0	56.6	47.7	53.5	51.5

G = General election for mayor (partisan contest).

P = Primary election for Democratic mayoral nomination.

would miss this sign of changing appeal if we looked only at the conventional measure. To avoid that problem, we can measure popularity in a different way. Instead of dividing each candidate's vote by the total vote cast, we can divide it by the size of the total voting-age population. This gives us a measure of group mobilization which simultaneously takes into account the direction of the group's support and its turnout rate.[6]

What is most noticeable in Table 6 is the comparatively high rate of pro-Daley mobilization in the Automatic Eleven in the 1955 primary. It was only in those wards that Daley ran above his citywide level. The West Side wards, which then still held a majority of white voters, gave Daley a slightly higher level of support than the heavily black wards on the South Side. Even so, the Dawson wards alone accounted for 45 percent of his citywide margin over Kennelly. Daley's narrow victory in the 1955 primary clearly depended on the high turnout and strong support he received from the voting population of the Automatic Eleven.

The general election campaign in 1955 was not an anticlimactic affair. Robert Merriam was an alderman from the Hyde Park area, and he was well known to be a Democrat, although running on the Republican ticket for mayor. He had the endorsement of three of the city's four major newspapers, an army of enthusiastic volunteers, and a reformer's zeal to do battle against the Machine. But Daley had the precinct captains, and he won the election with 55 percent of the vote cast.[7]

The pattern of support in the general election didn't differ much from the primary, although the turnout was generally higher, and the vote was divided between only two candidates. Pro-Daley mobilization was larger in the white ethnic wards than it had been in the primary, but Daley still lost the Northwest Side and had only a 6,327-vote plurality overall. That margin was offset by Merriam's edge of 8,687 votes in the Lake Shore wards. Again, it was in the Automatic Eleven that Daley won the election. Their mobilization was high and decisively imbalanced in Daley's favor, giving him a plurality of 129,442 votes. That was larger than his citywide edge, and Dawson's wards alone accounted for nearly 40 percent of his victory margin.

Daley was nominated and elected mayor in 1955 not because he had overwhelming, or even well-distributed, support across the entire city. His winning percentage was lower than all but one of the Democratic candidates for mayor since 1931.[8] Moreover, he was not the choice of most voters in the northern sections of the city, whether on the Lake Shore or in the ethnic communities on the Northwest Side. He carried seven of the eight South Side ethnic wards, but his margins were decisive only in his home ward, the 11th, and in the adjoining 14th. In both contests, his citywide victories resulted from solid support in Dawson's wards and in the six West Side wards, which were still white but with rapidly increasing numbers of black voters.[9]

Daley did not face another serious electoral challenge until 1963, when Adamowski ran for mayor under the Republican banner. Adamowski's appeal to the city's Eastern European ethnic voters, especially the Poles, posed a serious problem for Daley and the Machine. And Daley had other reasons to be apprehensive about the outcome in 1963. Three years earlier, Adamowski, as state's attorney, had uncovered a major police scandal, involving a ring of burglars operating out of the Summerdale Police District. Eventually, eight of the accused policemen were convicted, and five served time in jail. Second, several of the Daley stalwarts among the ward committeemen had died since 1955, and their successors were still unproven in the high art of piling up massive majorities for the slated candidate. Third, Daley had financed his programs and building activities by engineering increases in the real estate tax, and the business community and the city's homeowners were becoming increasingly disillusioned. The Marshall Field newspapers, the *Chicago Sun-Times* and *Chicago Daily News*, hit the mayor especially hard for fattening the city payroll at the expense of the small homeowner. Finally, the links between criminal activities and the city's politicians were again in the headlines. Sam Giancana, the reputed crime syndicate boss, shuffled three of his frontmen into and out of the 1st Ward aldermanic seat in the space of a few weeks. And two days after the February aldermanic elections, one of Daley's figurehead ward bosses, Benjamin Lewis, a black alderman from the 24th Ward, was found murdered. His body was discovered in his ward headquarters, handcuffed to his chair, cigarette burns on his arms and legs, and three bullets in the back of his head.[10]

However, corruption, taxes, criminal activities, and Adamowski's ethnic appeal weren't enough to catapult him to victory in 1963. Daley again had the precinct captains, and he was reelected to his third term with 56 percent of the vote cast. The patterns of support and opposition to the Machine were essentially the same as in the 1955 primary. The Automatic Eleven once again turned the tide, giving Daley a plurality slightly larger than his citywide margin, with the Dawson wards alone contributing half of his total plurality. In the areas that his opponents carried in the 1955 primary, Daley made inroads only in the six Lake Shore wards, carrying them by a margin of 22,992 votes. But he ran well behind Adamowski in the white ethnic areas, even losing six of the eight wards on the South Side.[11]

We can summarize these voting patterns by looking at all five contested elections in which Daley was involved between 1955 and 1967 (see Table 6).[12] First, the levels of pro-Daley mobilization in the Automatic Eleven remained pretty consistent after the 1955 primary. Even the changing racial composition of the West Side wards failed to affect their support for the Machine. Second, the Lake Shore wards, which were among the most affluent in the city, were never enthusiastic supporters of Daley. He carried them against Adamowski in 1963, and against weak Republican challengers in 1959 and 1967, but he was never able to mobilize the support of as much as a third of their voters. Finally, the South Side white ethnic communities were generally more supportive of Machine candidates than were those on the Northwest Side, but neither area was entirely dependable, as evidenced by Adamowski's success in both in 1963. It was only when Daley faced nominal opposition, in 1959 and 1967, that he was able to carry both areas and to attract a well-mobilized white ethnic vote. Even then, however, white ethnic voters were simply components of a larger coalition, and hardly as yet its dominant elements, since their contribution to Daley's citywide vote even in those landslide years was never more than 2 percentage points larger than their share of the city's voting-age population.

Surely, neither Daley nor any other candidate could have won city elections during the 1950s and 1960s without decent support in the white ethnic wards, since they held just under a third of the voters. Running competitive races in these areas, winning or losing by small margins, however, was not the same as dominating them. Through 1967, at least, Daley and other Machine candidates could be content simply to be competitive among white ethnic voters, because they could count on large majorities in the black wards of the South Side and in the racially changing wards of the West Side. In other words, black voters were indispensable cogs in the electoral wheels of the Daley Machine.[13]

It is not arresting to discover that the Machine's voting strength was concentrated in the poorer wards of the inner city, while the white ethnic areas resisted its control. With the exception of a few of the working-class white enclaves on the South Side, including Daley's own ward, the income and education levels of the white ethnic wards ranked them above the city's median. For the most part, their residents were not likely to depend on the Machine for public employment or for other tangible incentives. The willingness of the voters in these areas to support Kennelly in 1955, and then to switch to the ethnic candidacy of Adamowski eight years later, provides evidence of their electoral volatility, of the Machine's lack of control over them.

We typically expect political machines to be strongest among voters with low incomes and low levels of education. Those are the citizens who most need, and are interested in, the direct benefits that a political machine has to offer, especially city jobs. Moreover, it is only through their electoral commitment to the dominant political organization that such voters have any leverage to secure adequate levels of city services for themselves. In Chicago, at least through the 1960s, this reciprocal relationship—votes in return for jobs and services—seemed to operate and to make a vital contribution to the Daley Machine's continued dominance over electoral politics.[14]

The real significance of the relationship, however, lay in the constraints it imposed on the black community and its political representatives. Since the primary goal of political activity was maintaining the Democratic Machine, issues and appeals that threatened it had to be avoided. No issues were more potentially divisive than race questions, especially those dealing with discriminatory practices. If they became election issues, public rallying points, it would be difficult for the Machine to maintain its biracial coalition. The Machine's maintenance requirements, in other words, simply defined the black community's concern for racial fairness out of electoral politics. However, by serving the interests of the Machine and avoiding such questions, black politicians denied their constituents opportunities to use politics as a vehicle for the public expression of their racial grievances. Thus, the white leaders of the Democratic Machine, by establishing the terms and limits of their political expression, denied autonomy to the city's black community. Blacks became separate and unequal partners in the Machine's coalition—subjects, not citizens, of their city.[15]

The character of this colonial and imperialistic relationship, in which the black areas were treated as exploitable and subordinate partners, was not always so evident. As long as William Dawson was active, there were some appearances of parity, although never autonomy. After Dawson switched to the Democrats in 1939, he built the black sub-machine in the South Side. Operating from his own ward, the 2d, and using his access to Machine patronage, he sent his workers into the adjacent wards to organize for the Democratic party. By 1955, Dawson had installed his own lieutenants as ward committeemen in the 3rd, 4th, and 5th wards. When one of his loyalists became ward committeeman in the 6th Ward in 1956, he effectively controlled a five-ward suborganization within the Democratic Machine. As Dawson extended his control, and as the majorities his wards piled up for Machine candidates increased, his influence within the party grew. By the early 1950s, he was one of the inner circle of committeemen who ran the affairs of the County Central Committee through its executive committee.[16]

But Daley's centralized direction of party affairs eclipsed the influence of the executive committee and the ward committeemen. He made the decisions, allocated the benefits, and distributed the patronage. Dawson retained control over his five wards, a control that depended as much on personal loyalties as patronage, but one that brought him no extra clout with a chairman-mayor who believed that "there can be no organizations with The Organization."[17] Jobs and projects still flowed into the black wards, but they came as Daley decided, not as Dawson demanded.

The difference was more subtle than one might suppose, since Daley's and Dawson's views really didn't diverge that much. Each operated according to his own set of values, but their objectives overlapped sufficiently to allow ample room for compromise and accommodation. Dawson was not a militant crusader, insisting upon the immediate integration of blacks into the larger economic and social life of the city. He pursued more limited, pragmatic, welfare ends, seeking to gild the ghetto rather than break it up. That goal dovetailed neatly with the Machine's need to keep the race question out of electoral politics.[18]

Given this limited goal, the reciprocal relationship worked reasonably well for Dawson. He had access to patronage, although never to an appropriate share of managerial, supervisory, and leadership positions in the city government; and he was able to squelch challenges and maintain control within his fiefdom. In the process, Dawson's sub-machine effectively defined race interests out of electoral politics.[19]

In the black areas outside Dawson's bailiwick, the relationship between the Machine and black voters operated differently. On the West Side, and even initially in the middle-class black enclaves on the

South Side, the Machine exerted its control directly, without any intermediary playing a conciliatory role. As wards turned black, either the old white leadership remained in charge, often ruling as absentee barons, or Daley handpicked blacks to serve as frontmen for the Machine. Either way, the aldermen and ward committeemen functioned as viceroys of the Machine, posted to the neighborhoods to keep the black residents dutiful on election day and docile every day. This brand of "plantation politics" subordinated the concerns of the black community to the interests of the Machine.[20]

Rumblings of discontent began to appear in the 1960s, as some blacks questioned the accommodating postures of the older, more moderate leadership of their community. While the civil rights movement of that decade focused largely on voting rights and the desegregation of public accommodations in the South, it served to make blacks generally more aware of their racial identity and more sensitive to discrimination. Many Chicago blacks probably perceived the difference between themselves and their southern brethren to be one of degree rather than of kind. Blacks were legally enfranchised in Chicago, but the operation of the Daley Machine effectively excluded them from meaningful influence over the political institutions and public agencies whose decisions directly affected their lives. Since influence through the normal electoral channels was foreclosed, Chicago's blacks, like their southern counterparts, resorted to marches and demonstrations. But public gatherings in support of desegregated schools and open housing, meetings with the mayor, and Martin Luther King's marches through the white ethnic areas on the South and Northwest Sides produced no solutions, only outpourings of white animosity. As Dr. King commented after his march through Marquette Park: "The people of Mississippi ought to come to Chicago to learn how to hate."[21]

The demonstrations and marches had lasting significance, however. From them emerged a cadre of younger, better educated, more militant blacks, who saw the value of developing voluntary associations at the grass roots of their communities. Unlike the Machine's blacks, many of this generation of leaders pursued racial ends rather than welfare objectives, and they contributed time and energy without expectation of tangible gain. They also led the first political challenges to Dawson's paternalism and Daley's colonialism. This took the form of a spurt of political activity in the 1963 aldermanic elections. Independent black candidates ran against Machine loyalists in seven South and West Side wards, although only one was elected. Three years later, two black independents defeated endorsed candidates in races for the state senate, and in 1967, two anti-Machine blacks were elected to the City Council.[22]

These independent candidacies, however, were not part of a coordinated and sustained uprising against the Machine. They were highly personalized and disjointed efforts. Some who stood originally as independents were later co-opted by the Machine. Others remained outside the Machine but were unable to develop their personalized organizations into a broader movement. Still, the campaigns were valuable. Those who participated in them gained practical experience, and some learned the importance of maintaining their organizations intact after the election. Perhaps most importantly, they served as signals of a developing rebelliousness and cast the first shadow of doubt, however faint, on the notion that the Machine was unbeatable.[23]

Black Demobilization, 1968–1976

■ The geographic patterns of support, and the Machine's electoral base, changed considerably in the 1970s. The Automatic Eleven no longer routinely returned large majorities for Daley or other slated candidates. Instead, the white ethnic wards emerged as the core and indispensable areas of Machine strength. The information in Table 7 allows us to focus on the two key areas involved in the change and to see what happened in each of them between 1963 and 1975.[24]

The change had two dimensions. First, after 1963, Daley solidified his support in the white ethnic areas. Adamowski had carried both the Northwest and South Side ethnic wards in 1963, mobilizing 35 percent of their combined electorate and outpolling Daley by over 47,000 votes. Thereafter, Daley never again lost either area, and his margins of victory grew with each election. In 1967 he defeated his Republican opponent by slightly better than a 2-to-1 margin; he increased that to 2.5-to-1 in 1971, and 3-to-1 over his nearest rival in the four-way Democratic primary in 1975.[25]

Second, Daley's voting support waned in the black wards. Better than a third of the voting-age population in the black wards had supported Daley in 1963 and 1967, and he defeated his opponents there by huge margins in both years: by 5 to 1 and by 7 to 1, respectively. The first signs of black demobilization appeared in 1971. Although the city's overall turnout rate didn't change much between 1967 and 1971, turnout for the Machine candidate in the black wards fell by nearly 7 percentage points, and Daley's margin over his Republican opponent dropped to a comparatively modest 2.4 to 1. The slide accelerated over the next four years, as the Machine's mobilization level shrunk by another 13 percentage points. As a result, in 1975 Daley outscored his closest rival by only 1.5 to 1, and his three opponents combined to mobilize 17 percent of the electorate in the black wards and outpolled the mayor by 6,508 votes.

In the early Daley years, the Machine's formula for victory in-

Table 7. Percentage of the Voting-Age Population Supporting Daley, 1963–1975

	1963G	1967G	1971G	1975P
Black Wards [1]	37.5	36.6	30.0	16.3
Dawson Five	38.6	36.0	29.8	19.1
Other South Side	27.4	31.4	27.2	14.7
West Side	47.6	38.8	35.1	17.6
White Ethnic	28.0	39.2	43.2	30.6
Northwest Side	24.0	34.0	39.0	24.1
South Side	31.7	44.3	47.3	37.3
Total for Daley citywide	29.8	37.6	35.1	22.1
Total turnout citywide	53.5	51.5	50.1	38.3

G = General election for mayor (partisan contest).

P = Primary election for Democratic mayoral nomination.

[1] The black majority wards: 1963 and 1967, n = 9; 1971, n = 15; 1975, n = 19.

volved running competitive races in the white ethnic and Lake Shore wards, while piling up large majorities in the West Side and South Side black wards. The Machine's strongest support at that time came from exactly where traditional textbook accounts claim it should have—the inner-city wards, among low-income, poorly educated voters. By the early 1970s, however, the Machine's electoral center of gravity had shifted away from the inner city, and its strongest support came from white ethnic voters, in areas with above-average income and education levels. In 1971, for the first time since Kennelly's day, a Machine candidate won by a wider margin in the white ethnic wards than in the black wards. In the 1975 primary, the white ethnic wards accounted for 45 percent of Daley's citywide vote, although they held only about a third of the city's voting-age population.

One other election helps to illuminate the process of change—the 1972 contest for state's attorney of Cook County. That office was always important to the Machine for practical and symbolic reasons. Political opponents, such as Adamowski, had used the office to investigate charges of corruption and vote fraud, and those inquiries usually proved embarrassing to the mayor and his party colleagues. Being able to elect an ally to the county's chief legal office eliminated the possibility of untimely investigations. It also gave access to more job patronage and came to symbolize the Machine's domination over local affairs.

The incumbent state's attorney in 1972 was Edward V. Hanrahan, until then a Machine loyalist. As U.S. Attorney for Northern Illinois, Hanrahan had gained publicity for prosecuting crime syndicate figures, and he was Daley's handpicked choice to retain the important office of state's attorney in 1968. Like Daley, Hanrahan had an explosive temper, feuded incessantly with reporters, and preached a tough law-and-order gospel, which in the context of the times meant cracking down on blacks.

After his election in 1968, Hanrahan had declared war on the young black street gangs and the Black Panther party, and he created a special unit within his office to combat their activities. At 4 A.M. on 4 December 1969, Hanrahan's gang unit, armed with a search warrant, raided a West Side flat occupied by Black Panthers. The unit was looking for unregistered guns. When the raid was over, it had the guns, Panther leaders Fred Hampton and Mark Clark were shot to death, and four others were wounded. Hanrahan claimed that his men had been fired upon by the Panthers and had returned fire only in self-defense. Reporters investigating the scene uncovered no evidence of the gun battle that Hanrahan's men vividly described. An investigation by a federal grand jury found that the police had apparently opened fire with little provocation and later had misrepresented the physical evidence to whitewash their conduct.[26]

The Hanrahan raid was a more wanton and gross abuse of the civil rights of blacks than even the Daley Machine normally tolerated. Hanrahan at once became a loathsome symbol within the black community, a living reminder of how lightly white leaders valued black lives and of how cavalierly and unapologetically they violated the civil and human rights of black citizens. It was small consolation to blacks that Hanrahan was indicted for allegedly obstructing justice in the investigation of the killings. And it was galling to them that the Democratic slatemakers in early December 1971 endorsed him for reelection.

But as Hanrahan's legal difficulties mounted, even Daley backed away. Two weeks after he had been routinely reslated, Hanrahan was unceremoniously dumped in favor of Raymond Berg, a judge in the city's traffic court. But Hanrahan was pugnacious, if nothing else, and he decided to seek the nomination for state's attorney in the March 1972 primary. The third candidate in the race was Donald Page Moore, an independent from the wealthy suburb of Barrington.[27]

Hanrahan was anathema in the black community but a law-and-order hero to the city's white ethnic voters. Berg had the Machine's formal endorsement, but many of the precinct captains were unenthusiastic, probably because they were overwhelmed by evidence of Hanrahan's grass-roots support. Moore appealed to the city's white liberals, who have never been as numerous as they are noisy, and he campaigned extensively and energetically in black areas, promising to be a "tough but *fair*" state's attorney. He opened a large campaign headquarters in the middle-class area of the South Side, and he even

Table 8. The Race for State's Attorney, 1972[1]

	Primary Election			General Election	
	Hanrahan	**Moore**	**Berg**[2]	**Hanrahan (D)**	**Carey (R)**
Black Wards	4.0	9.5	11.4	19.7	30.1
Dawson Five	3.7	8.1	11.8	19.9	27.3
Other South Side	4.0	13.2	12.3	17.4	40.0
West Side	4.5	5.3	9.3	23.1	17.7
White Ethnic	19.6	5.5	11.6	40.6	28.8
Northwest Side	17.8	5.8	8.8	40.5	30.6
South Side	21.4	5.2	13.4	40.6	27.0
Lake Shore	8.6	11.8	8.7	23.3	35.1
Rest of city	10.4	5.1	10.2	28.5	17.6
Total for candidate citywide	12.1	7.7	11.4	31.4	28.3

[1] Entries are percentages of the voting-age population.

[2] Slated candidate.

ventured into the public housing projects, the most tightly controlled precincts in the ghetto.[28]

The results of the primary and the general election in November gave further evidence of the drift away from the Machine in the black wards and the growing political clout of the white ethnic areas (Table 8). Despite the heated rhetoric from the candidates for state's attorney and a spirited contest for the Democratic nomination for governor, the primary did not arouse much voter enthusiasm: only 31 percent of the city's voting-age population, and only a quarter of its black voters, cast ballots. The total vote cast in the black wards was 29,062 votes lower than the number of ballots cast for Daley in the 1971 general election for mayor, and 3,027 fewer than he received in his uncontested primary in 1959, when the number of blacks of voting age was considerably smaller. The blacks who did vote gave a slim edge to Berg, although the middle-class black wards on the South Side narrowly favored Moore. Hanrahan won the primary in the white ethnic wards, where he piled up a plurality nearly four times the size of his citywide margin. Over 50 percent of his total vote came from the city's white ethnic communities.

However, the white ethnic areas were *not* rebelling against the Machine by delivering their vote to Hanrahan. Instead, they were opting for one of their own, a candidate who spoke their language and gave voice to their fears and hatreds. He was not the slated candidate, to be sure; but he had until recently been a Machine stalwart, and he had not campaigned against the Machine. The white ethnic areas' high mobilization for Hanrahan showed how important they had become to the city's electoral arithmetic. Cohesive and mobilized, they could deliver an important nomination to the candidate of their choice. This was a message that Democratic slatemakers could ignore in the future only at considerable risk.

The November general election delivered another message to the leaders of the Machine: there was a limit to the loyalties of the city's black voters. Most of the blacks who voted were willing to do the unthinkable, i.e., vote for a Republican candidate, rather than support Hanrahan. Bernard Carey, the Republican nominee, carried Dawson's wards by a plurality of just under 15,000 votes, and he won the other black wards on the South Side by over 53,000 votes. Only the "plantation provinces" on the West Side delivered for the Machine. Hanrahan's overall mobilization percentage in the black wards squared well with the judgment of one of the city's leading political strategists, Don Rose: "The Organization owns a lock on a solid 20 percent of the black vote. This is the vote the Machine would deliver for a George Wallace against Martin Luther King."[29]

The 1972 race for state's attorney was not really a sudden turning point; rather, it was a dramatic incident involved in a longer process. The euphoria of the moment led some to exaggerate the significance of the event, to claim that "there's no more ghetto vote for [the Machine]. Things won't ever be the same."[30] The fact was, however, that the Machine had still mobilized its hardcore supporters for Hanrahan; overall black turnout still lagged well behind that in the white ethnic areas, and, most tellingly, things were much the same again in 1975.

In 1975, twenty years after his first contested primary, Daley again faced a battle for the Democratic nomination. Three challengers sought to deny him a sixth term as mayor: Edward Hanrahan, the former state's attorney who had lost his bid for a seat in Congress in 1974; Richard Newhouse, a black state senator; and William Singer, a Lake Shore liberal who had won a special election for alderman in 1969 and had been returned to the City Council in the regular elections in 1971.

Apart from his growing troubles with the leaders of the city's black community, "The Greatest Mayor Chicago Ever Had" brought a powerful set of liabilities with him into the 1975 campaign. His health and age were question marks. On 6 May 1974, Daley had suffered a minor stroke, and a month later he underwent surgery to remove blockage in the left carotid artery, which carries blood to the brain. He remained out of public view through the summer, while convalescing at his estate in Grand Beach, Michigan. When he returned to City Hall on 3 September, the day after Labor Day, the mayor appeared twenty-five pounds slimmer than before the stroke;

there was no sign of a speech impediment, and he was about as alert as ever and able to handle his normal workload. He responded to reporters' questions by indicating that no medical reasons prevented him from seeking another term. But rumors concerning the seriousness of his condition had been rife throughout the summer, and some still wondered whether a seventy-three-year-old stroke victim could recover to the point of being able to withstand the daily pressures of running a complex city like Chicago.[31]

There were also signs of discontent within the Machine. The younger aldermen especially resented the mayor's total control over the Council. Beginning in December 1972 and extending through the early months of 1973, a group of Machine regulars, led by Alderman Edward R. Vrdolyak, held a series of "secret" meetings at the Sherman House prior to sessions of the City Council. They complained about the dictatorial way in which Alderman Thomas Keane (31st Ward), chairman of the powerful Finance Committee and the mayor's floor leader, controlled Council business. "We vote for Keane, but he doesn't vote for us," one of the dissidents complained, adding that Keane refused even to caucus with "his own aldermen" on ordinances and actions coming before the Council. The so-called "coffee club rebels," who numbered as many as twenty-three party regulars, wanted assurances of the administration's support for legislation they proposed and regular meetings with Keane prior to Council sessions. Keane arrogantly brushed off the brewing rebellion: "They don't bother me," he said. But Daley was more sensitive to the danger of the secret meetings and worked behind the scenes to arrange an accommodation. By late February, another attempt to hold a secret meeting fizzled, as only nine of the twenty-four aldermen invited bothered to attend. The uprising was an ominous sign, however, and Daley knew that it was directed at him as much as at Keane. He knew also, as Vrdolyak had said, that he and Keane weren't "going to be around forever" and that when they went, the leaders of the dissidents expected the Council to reassert its authority.[32]

Another police scandal and a series of indictments and convictions of Machine loyalists added to the mayor's discomfort in 1973 and 1974. The city's traffic chief and eighteen vice detectives serving under him were convicted in 1973 on federal charges of extorting protection money from tavern owners and nightclub operators. Before the investigation ended a year later, forty-five policemen and two district commanders had been implicated. To salvage what was left of the department's reputation, Daley was eventually forced to dump Conlisk and replace him with James Rochford as police superintendent.[33]

The convictions of several of Daley's close political associates dulled the luster of his administration even more. The county clerk,

Edward J. Barrett, fell in 1973, when he was convicted of soliciting and receiving payoffs from the company supplying voting machines to the county. Through the early months of 1974, the U.S. attorney, James Thompson, earned his reputation as "the toughest gun we've had around here since Al Capone."[34] On 21 February the federal grand jury indicted Earl Bush, Daley's press secretary for eighteen years prior to his resignation the preceding August. Bush was charged with mail fraud and extortion in connection with his secret owner-ship of a firm that since 1962 had held an exclusive contract with the city for all advertising and display promotions at O'Hare Air-port. Six weeks later, on 5 April, the grand jury indicted Alderman Paul Wigoda (49th Ward), a protégé of Keane and a member of the City Council's Committee on Building and Zoning. Wigoda was charged with extortion and income tax evasion relating to a payoff he had received for the 1969 rezoning of the former Edgewater Golf Club in his ward. The next week (10 April), Matthew Danaher, clerk of the Cook County Circuit Court, a former alderman, and a protégé of Daley, was indicted on charges of conspiracy and tax evasion growing out of a real estate development deal. And Thompson hooked an even bigger fish the following month. On 2 May the federal grand jury indicted Keane on charges of mail fraud and conspiracy related to his using political connections to buy parcels of tax-delinquent property and to resell them at great profit to agencies of the city government.[35]

His Honor, always so prompt in proclaiming the guilt of black pro-testers and student demonstrators, withheld public comment in the cases of his close political associates. Even when Bush, Keane, and Wigoda were convicted in October 1974, the mayor refrained from criticizing their illegal actions. The Machine rallies around its own and makes no apologies, for only the weak admit mistakes and ask forgiveness. Of the guilty verdict in Keane's case, Daley said, "It's an unfortunate thing. . . . Keane is one of the outstanding municipal authorities in the country. And he's done a good job." Alderman Vito Marzullo, another of the Machine's law-and-order zealots, was more blunt: "I think it's a Goddamn shame. He's innocent." Even the con-victed Keane displayed no remorse. Asked by a reporter whether he was sorry, Keane sneered and responded: "Sorry? What's there to be sorry about?"[36]

Daley himself was not named in any of the indictments, and there was no suspicion that he had been directly involved in any way in the illegal activities. Still, as Alderman Singer implied, the mayor was not without guilt. "Keane's part of the system; he is what the system is all about. The mayor had to be held responsible in these convictions." Most Chicagoans probably thought Singer's claim went too far, but there was evidence of the public's growing disenchantment with Daley's style of government. In June 1973, even before the rash of indictments, slightly more than half of the respondents in a public opinion poll expressed "no confidence" in their local public officials. And 47 percent opposed another term for Daley, with only 41 percent supporting the idea.[37]

Perhaps the poll captured public reaction to an event that had occurred earlier in the year, which illustrated Daley's "arrogance of total power," as Hanrahan later termed it.[38] The *Chicago Tribune* revealed in February that the mayor had ordered the transfer of city insurance policies to Heil and Heil in Evanston, a firm with which his son, John Patrick Daley, was associated. Estimates of the commissions on the premiums ran as high as $500,000. Daley first denied that he had influenced the decision, but his claims contradicted the statements of the city controller, David Stahl, who had told reporters earlier that "Heil and Heil was referred to me by the mayor." Asked why Daley picked that firm, Stahl replied, "You'll have to ask the mayor. I don't know his motives."[39]

When reporters asked the mayor, he again denied any undue influence. A few days later, however, Daley spoke more bluntly to a meeting of the Cook County Democratic Central Committee. He told the party leaders that he would make no apologies: "What kind of world are we living in," he asked, if a man "can't put his arms around his sons?" He stormed, "If I can't help my sons, then they can kiss my ass."[40] The mayor's listeners, dutiful as always, jumped to their feet and applauded. The committeemen understood this touching profession of fatherly concern. It was their city, their party, to be exploited now and later to be passed on to their sons, just as they had received it as a patrimony from their fathers. That was simply the way it was in Chicago; and Daley and the party leaders believed that neither reporters nor the public had any right to question the way it was.

Finally, the mayor was in trouble with some of his white ethnic constituents. Daley was pushing the construction of a $1 billion Crosstown Expressway, an L-shaped, twenty-two-mile highway to link the six other major expressways and shorten the travel time between O'Hare and Midway airports. The venture threatened to uproot thousands of homeowners and small businessmen along its route. The problem was that these were mainly in the white ethnic neighborhoods on the Northwest and Southwest Sides. Daley's archrival within the party, Governor Dan Walker, redeemed his 1972 campaign pledge to oppose the Crosstown and blocked the mayor's efforts to secure the necessary federal funding. So Daley ended up with the worst of both worlds: he was unable to deliver the new contracts and jobs, and his plan had aroused the fury of the prospective dispossessed.[41]

In all of these matters, Daley displayed a nearly total disdain for public opinion. He expressed sympathy for the families of his convicted associates, but he made no mention of the harm caused to the citizenry by their betrayal of the public trust. He snapped at reporters who had the effrontery to expect the city's chief executive to explain his seeming indifference to this public corruption or his use of public funds to enrich a firm with which his son was associated. "To hell with the press," he snarled at one point, angered with reporters who had forgotten that their proper place was to relate his accomplishments, not to probe and question his actions.[42]

Neither health problems, police scandals, corruption, upset over the Crosstown, nor even Daley's arrogance deterred Chicagoans from their habit of voting for The Greatest Mayor Chicago Ever Had. His Honor polled 58 percent of the vote and easily defeated his three rivals in the February primary. Six weeks later, on 1 April, he polled 80 percent and crushed yet another Republican sacrificial lamb.

The primary results are revealing on two counts. They show how the Machine's coalition had changed since Daley's first victory in 1955. Yet they also reveal how weak and vulnerable the Machine had become at the electoral level.

Fortunately, from 1975 on, we can use more exact methods and more precise data to examine the patterns of voting support. Precinct-level voting returns can be used in combination with block-level census information reporting the number of whites, blacks, and Hispanics of voting age.[43] By matching the census blocks to precinct boundaries, we can make use of regression procedures to estimate the voting preference of each group.[44] Moreover, since Chicago has nearly 3,000 precincts, the estimates can be calculated for distinct areas of the city and even particular wards. That is important since there are good reasons to suspect that the voting behavior of some groups differed from one part of the city to another. The whites in the Lake Shore wards, for example, probably didn't vote at the same rates for particular candidates as whites in the wards on the South Side.[45]

This approach is superior to the ward-level analyses reported in Tables 6 and 7. To be sure, given Chicago's residential patterns, its wards are reasonably homogeneous racially, and the figures reported in those tables offer very strong clues. However, they are not as exact as the information derived from regression procedures. For example, we can't be sure that blacks who lived in solidly black areas voted in the same ways as those who lived in other environments. Moreover, since even "relatively homogeneous" wards (or even precincts) contain other types of voters, we can't be sure how much each group's behavior contributed to the observed result, unless we make some arbitrary guesses about their turnout rates. But since there are reasons to expect differences in group turnout rates, and since those are of considerable importance, there is no sound basis for making the necessary assumptions. The regression procedures outlined here use all of the precinct information and can produce sound estimates of group preference and abstention rates.

Table 9 allows us to see how blacks, whites, and Hispanics divided their support in 1975 and to compare the citywide estimates of group preference with estimates calculated for particular areas of the city. First, Daley mobilized only a shade more than 22 percent of the city's electorate, a smaller proportion than in any of his contested elections since 1955. In fact, pro-Daley mobilization was only slightly higher in 1975 than it had been in his four uncontested primaries between 1959 and 1971, and his total count was nearly 20,000 votes below the total he had received in 1959.[46] An even clearer sign of the Machine's electoral vulnerability, however, is shown by the fact that better than three fifths of the city's voting-age population didn't bother to participate. In other words, there was a large pool of un-mobilized voters who might be aroused to oppose the Machine in the future.

Second, there is considerable contrast between the patterns of white and black voting. Daley ran well among white voters, outpolling Singer by almost 2 to 1 citywide. Among the whites in the ethnic areas, he beat Singer by 3 to 1 overall and by better than 4 to 1 on the South Side. In contrast, while Daley won a plurality of the black vote and beat Singer by over 2 to 1 on the West Side, nearly two thirds of the blacks simply didn't vote at all.

Daley had won his first primary and the hard-fought general election in 1963 by piling up huge majorities in the black wards in the inner city. In 1975, most of the mayor's primary vote, 64 percent, came from white voters, who made up slightly more than half of the city's voting-age population. White ethnic voters were especially tolerant of the Machine's corruption and arrogance and unwilling to be dissuaded even by the furor over the Crosstown. The Machine had developed a new formula for victory: high mobilization and cohesive support from both of the city's white ethnic areas and demobilization of the uncontrollable majority of its black electorate. That change in electoral strategy was enormously significant, both for what it revealed and for the ways in which it shaped the policy reactions of Daley and his successors.

The growing significance of race issues underpinned this change in the Machine's coalition. On questions of integrated housing, education, and public employment, and on issues of police-community relations, Daley invariably articulated the feelings of his fellow white ethnics. As conflict over these matters became public and increasingly important, white ethnic voters saw the mayor and his Machine as defenders of their values and interests, as the last hope for

Table 9. The 1975 Democratic Mayoral Primary: Regression Estimates of Group Voting Behavior [1]

	Daley	Singer	Newhouse	Hanrahan	Nonvote
Citywide [2]					
Blacks	16.7	10.4	6.3	0.6	65.8
Whites	29.1	15.3	1.1	3.0	51.4
Hispanics	19.6	2.6	0.8	1.7	75.0
Blacks					
Dawson wards	19.9	11.1	6.5	0.8	61.5
Other South Side	14.3	10.9	7.2	0.6	66.9
West Side	17.2	7.5	5.0	0.6	69.5
White Ethnics	34.3	10.7	1.1	4.0	49.7
Northwest Side	27.1	11.9	0.7	4.1	56.0
South Side	42.8	9.2	1.7	3.9	42.2
Total citywide	22.1	11.2	3.0	1.9	61.6

[1] Entries are percentages of voting-age population, and rows sum to 100 percent, except for rounding error.

[2] Developed by weighting the estimate of each group's behavior within eight subareas of the city.

continued white control. Since large numbers of blacks perceived matters in the same way, their enthusiasm for Daley waned.

As white ethnic support solidified, the Machine came to be sustained by a new type of reciprocal relationship. The traditional connection, involving the exchange of jobs and services in return for votes, was useless in cementing the voting loyalties of those who were generally better educated and more prosperous than the average. In return for their ballots, the Machine offered instead its guarantee of continued white dominance over the city's culture-transmitting agencies, especially its schools, its neighborhoods, and its police. Patronage and city contracts remained important to the committeemen and aldermen from these wards, but the Machine's defense of white racial interests was the glue that bound their voters to the Machine.

The same actions that attracted support from white ethnic voters repelled blacks. Daley's troubles with the city's black community began to surface in the early 1960s. By backing Willis in the school desegregation controversy, criticizing Dr. King, denying the existence of segregation in housing and education, and issuing his infamous "shoot to kill" order, Daley displayed what many blacks regarded as insensitivity and indifference to their concerns and interests. His refusal to renounce Hanrahan was viewed as another, even more potent, symbol of contemptuous disregard for black lives. The mayor's statements and behavior involved more than mere symbolism; on a series of substantive matters, Daley defended white interests against those of his black constituents.

Despite evidence that black children were confined to segregated and inferior schools, Daley publicly resisted the suggested remedies. He defended the weak palliatives offered by the Board of Education and, in no uncertain terms, lent his voice to the clamor against busing as a means of integration.[47]

He was no less committed to a defense of white interests on the issue of integrated housing. In March 1971, when the city had exhausted the appeal process, and the CHA was compelled to release its list of 275 sites for public housing in white areas, Daley quickly condemned the choices. Because they were "detrimental to all the people of Chicago," he said, "these units should not be built." For once his elusive press secretary did not have to explain what the mayor's statement meant—both blacks and whites got the message. The white community organizations were relieved that Daley, then in the midst of a reelection campaign, had forthrightly taken their side. Blacks correctly saw that he referred only to detrimental effects for white people, and some denounced his claim as "the most bigoted statement he has ever made," an example of his "paternalistic, plantation thinking, which attempts to placate whites, at the expense of black citizens." The mayor's appeal to white fears may have been poor ethics and bad law, but it attracted support from white ethnic voters and proved to be good politics.[48]

Daley's adamant defense of discriminatory hiring and promotion practices by the Chicago Police Department also won support in the city's white ethnic communities. In the 1960s, the proportion of blacks among police personnel roughly equalled their share of the population, although they were still underrepresented among sworn officers and sergeants. In the wake of the riots, and despite the increasing size of the black population in the city, the proportion of blacks in the police department dropped. The Law Enforcement Assistance Administration, the Civil Rights Division of the Justice Department, and the Office of Revenue Sharing tried to persuade the mayor to remedy the problem through negotiation. Daley refused to budge, however, arguing that since the police department didn't discriminate, there was nothing to negotiate. In November 1974, U.S. District Judge Prentice H. Marshall ordered the city to correct the abuses, and the next month another federal court impounded the city's federal revenue-sharing funds until it took corrective action. Still Daley stalled; he repudiated an interim hiring agreement, launched a legal counterattack on several fronts, and risked the loss of the federal funds. After a year of inaction, Judge Marshall, referring to the "arrogant, contemptuous" behavior "of the city defendants," imposed mandatory hiring quotas. "The quota system is totally un-American," Daley exploded. "We'll continue to fight this as long as we're around." But faced with the loss of $95 million in federal funds, Daley, a month later, simultaneously announced the city's reluctant compliance and its stubborn determination to appeal Marshall's decision.[49]

The conduct of the Chicago Police Department was the focus of another public controversy between Daley and the black community in the early 1970s. This time the attack came from a Machine loyalist, Congressman Ralph Metcalfe. As an alderman for fifteen years, Metcalfe had dutifully supported the Machine, and he was rewarded with a promotion to Congress in 1970 after Dawson's death. There he joined the Congressional Black Caucus, something Dawson had never done, and on his weekend trips back to Chicago he became increasingly aware of and concerned with the high rate of crime in the black community.

At first, Metcalfe put the responsibility on his own community, and in late 1971 he organized a Third Ward Committee on Crime Prevention to encourage residents to report crimes to the police and to appear in court as witnesses. When the effort produced no significant results, Metcalfe concluded that blacks "had no respect for the police," because they had so often been routinely victimized by them. The Chicago Urban League told Metcalfe that an average of seventy-eight cases of police brutality occurred every month in the black community. That statistic took on personal meaning after two friends of the congressman, both black dentists, were brutalized by Chicago policemen. Even then, Metcalfe confined his complaints to private meetings with Police Superintendent James Conlisk. But when police practices remained unchanged after that, and Metcalfe's constituents continued to report instances of harassment and brutality, the congressman went public.[50]

In April 1972, Metcalfe blasted Daley's police department. "The police abuse black people verbally and physically," he charged. "The police call blacks 'nigger.' They have no respect for our women. They say they're all whores, and they even abuse them in front of their children." Metcalfe didn't stop with a verbal tirade. He formed a new organization, the Concerned Citizens for Police Reform, and he confronted Daley and Conlisk with a set of demands, including more black police officers and sergeants and an end to aggressive riot-control task-force operations in the black community. Saying that "our patience has come to an end," Metcalfe insisted that the city satisfy his demands by the end of May.[51]

Almost overnight, Congressman Metcalfe, who had long been regarded as Daley's man in the black community, became a leader and a symbol of opposition to the mayor. He attracted widespread support, from the West Side as well as the South Side, from Hispanics as well as blacks, from conservative ministers as well as community activists. The black representatives in Springfield prepared a resolution criticizing the Chicago police force and demanding that Daley accept Metcalfe's invitation to come "to the black community and see the problem first hand." Two black aldermen broke with the mayor and backed Metcalfe's claims of police brutality. Some doubted Metcalfe's motives and questioned his conversion, but he silenced his critics by responding that "it's never too late to be black."[52]

Of course Daley refused to admit that the police were guilty of brutality, and he refused to attend a meeting with Metcalfe in the South Side black community. However, he did send Conlisk to a series of community meetings to hear and try to respond to complaints about police practices. And the mayor called a public meeting for 5 June in the City Council chamber to tell citizens what he had decided. He promised that the charges of brutality would be investigated, not by civilians from the neighborhoods but by members of the city's Commission on Human Relations. Daley's appointees, in other words, would investigate complaints against Daley's police. Blacks charged that the result would be what it always was in Daley's Chicago— "One big whitewash."[53]

The controversy was an important incident in the process of the changing relationship between Daley and the black community. It was one thing to be criticized by black activists, but it was quite another for the mayor's longtime frontman to turn against the Machine. Betrayal of that sort called for retribution, and the mayor didn't hesitate to act. City building and fire inspectors suddenly discovered code violations at Metcalfe's 3rd Ward headquarters; his patronage jobs were reassigned to other committeemen; and his usual quota of summer jobs with the Chicago Park District was cut to zero. While Daley denied that any of this was his doing and claimed that he wasn't out "to get" Metcalfe, the mayor was following the oldest maxim of Chicago politics: Don't get mad, get even. However, Daley didn't succeed at getting even. Metcalfe stood his ground, and each new attack by the Machine simply enhanced his stature in the black community. Even the 1976 effort to deny him renomination for Congress was a glaring failure, with Daley's handpicked candidate polling only 28 percent of the vote. As a result, Metcalfe's apostasy delivered a message to the black community. He bucks the mayor, as one veteran Machine black put it, "and he *doesn't* get his balls chopped off for it."[54] In time, blacks would heed the significance of that message, apply it on a broader front, and achieve their own political emancipation.

Conditions in 1975 were not yet ripe for that development. There were still "organizations and coalitions" to build, and divisions within the black community to heal.[55] Until those tasks were accomplished, until blacks could tap a network of existing community organizations and mobilize them to defend black values and interests, their electoral threat to the Machine was potential rather than real. Not even the presence of a black candidate in the mayoral race could arouse and mobilize the black electorate in 1975. State Senator Richard Newhouse garnered the support of a meager 6 percent of the black electorate, running third behind both Daley and Singer.

If blacks felt aggrieved by the practices of the Machine, why the lack of enthusiasm for a candidate from their own community? Two reasons account for the result. First, few opinion leaders among Chicago's blacks thought that Newhouse could win the primary. Most blacks, as well as most whites, were still convinced that the Machine was invincible, especially when The Greatest Mayor Chicago Ever Had headed its ticket. Consequently, no legion of volunteers emerged at the grass-roots level to offset the work of the precinct captains and to enable Newhouse to expand his appeal beyond his narrow base among middle-class blacks. Newhouse spoke of his campaign as "a real crusade," and civil rights workers from other cities came to Chicago to aid the cause. But no contagion swept the local black community, as it would eight years later, and Newhouse failed to carry a single black ward.[56]

Second, Newhouse was unable to bridge the divisions within the black community and combine all of its parts into a unified effort. Black opinion leaders remained split. The *Chicago Defender* endorsed Daley, while the publishers of the smaller community newspapers agreed in late January to back Newhouse.[57] The Reverend Jesse Jackson, head of Operation PUSH, equivocated, first suggesting that blacks should form a coalition to back Singer but later endorsing Newhouse and rejecting the idea of a coalition, saying that "there are just too many of us to fit into somebody else's car because now we've got the biggest car in town."[58] Congressman Metcalfe, who declined to make the run himself on the grounds of inadequate financial support for a black candidate, endorsed Singer as the best hope to defeat Daley. Saying that he would not support a candidate "just because of his blackness," Metcalfe singled out Newhouse's votes against the Equal Rights Amendment and the Regional Transportation Authority as reasons for choosing Singer.[59] Other black independents also supported Singer, and the Committee for a Black Mayor, an ad hoc group of black businessmen and politicians, rated both Newhouse and Singer as qualified. Refusing to choose between them, the Committee expressed its regret that "there is no moving together between Newhouse and Singer," freed its members to work for either candidate, and declared its own intention to concentrate on electing independent black aldermen.[60]

Superficially, this lack of cohesive support for Newhouse might be charged off to personal rivalries and personality conflicts. Newhouse was a relatively recent migrant to Chicago, having arrived only in 1958, and he did seem to cultivate the image of a loner among black officeholders. No doubt some black leaders resented his early decision to run, and others vocally objected to his later refusal to withdraw in the face of defections to Singer. He surely won no converts among the latter group with his claim that "electing Singer would be switching from one plantation to another."[61]

However, the failure of the Newhouse campaign to unify and mobilize the black community ultimately had little to do with any of the candidate's real or imagined shortcomings. Chicago's blacks were simply not yet ready in 1975 to nominate and elect a black mayor. Having experienced decades of political helplessness, they had not yet come to believe that they had the capacity to alter their own lot. This collective self-doubt translated into indecision and tepid involvement at the leadership level and into low mobilization for Newhouse among the black electorate.

Senator Newhouse did not defeat Daley for the nomination, but his efforts were important nevertheless. His own assessment, given three weeks before the primary, was generally on target:

> I think my campaign is already successful. It's been a way for people who never felt they had any power [to] feel they are politically important.
> That's what I set out to accomplish. . . . Daley isn't afraid of Singer. He's afraid of waking up and finding out that a couple of hundred thousand blacks have left the machine's ranks. I think we've accomplished that.[62]

Newhouse erred only in his belief that Daley feared demobilization of the black electorate. Since the riots of the mid-1960s, the Machine had willfully traded low turnout among blacks for high mobilization and cohesive support among the city's white ethnic voters.[63] The acrimonious conflicts between Daley and the black community over integrated housing, schools, public employment, and police practices disillusioned black voters, but they had positive effects among the city's white ethnics. By shelving, ignoring, and rejecting the claims of blacks for equal access to the larger economic, political, and social life of the city, Daley's postures and actions signalled the Machine's commitment to defending white values and interests. In turn, Chicago's whites, especially those in the ethnic enclaves on the Northwest and South Sides, dutifully repaid their political debt on election days by turning out at higher rates and by voting more cohesively than before for Machine candidates. In the process, the Machine developed a new—and predominantly white—voting coalition, one which was glued together by a shared set of racial values and a common opposition to black political autonomy.

Typically, whenever tensions arise among groups within a political party's coalition, it tries to quiet the conflict by working out compromises that avoid antagonizing either side. Conditions in Chicago, however, required the leaders of the Democratic Machine to come down squarely and unmistakably on the side of their white ethnic supporters. Since the Machine depended on their voting support, the continuing movement of whites from the city threatened its electoral control. To stem that outflow, the Machine defended white ethnic values openly and assertively and brought its actions into line with its promises. The politics of the Board of Education, the police superintendency, and the Chicago Housing Authority have to be interpreted within that context. The Machine defended continued white control of these agencies to reassure its white ethnic supporters, slow their out-migration, and solidify its last dependable base of voting support. Chicago's white ethnics, unlike those in other northern cities, had no need for a backlash vote because Daley's Democratic party institutionalized white cultural dominance.

Since at least the mid-1960s, race has been the dominant fact of Chicago's electoral politics. It was the issue that bound white voters to the Machine, requiring them to develop an extraordinary tolerance of public corruption and arrogance. It was the issue that prevented middle-class blacks on the South Side and white ethnics on the Northwest Side from uniting to challenge the increasingly dominant leadership of the South Side whites. It was, in short, the issue that enabled Chicago's Democratic party to maintain itself as the city's ruling institution.

5. Race, Ethnicity, and Electoral Politics
From Bilandic to Byrne, 1976–1982

To be in Chicago for Richard Daley's funeral is to understand, in a way, what it was like in China when Chairman Mao died. *Haynes Johnson,* **Washington Post**

■ Shortly after 2:16 P.M., on Monday, 20 December 1976, assignment editors at Chicago's newspapers and television stations noticed a sudden flurry of activity on the emergency radio frequencies used by the police and fire departments. They couldn't make sense of the garbled messages they heard, but they knew something extraordinary was happening at 900 North Michigan Avenue, the address to which the police and fire commanders were dispatching their personnel. Whatever it was had the earmarks of a big story, so the editors sent their reporters and camera crews.

When the media personnel arrived, they found the area around the 900 Building jammed with police cars and fire ambulances. A crowd of onlookers was beginning to gather, attracted to the scene by the wailing sirens and flurry of activity outside the building. Within a short time, several doctors arrived, sped over in squad cars from Northwestern Memorial Hospital. The physician in charge of the Chicago Health Department's medical service reached the scene a little later, accompanied by Dr. Robert Vanecko, Mayor Daley's son-in-law. The police then blocked off Walton Street to Michigan Avenue, ordered a paramedic to drive one of the ambulances to the building's loading dock, and put up wooden barricades to keep the press and public at a distance from the freight entrance in the alley.

Inside the 900 Building, in the second-floor office of Dr. Thomas Coogan, the activity was even more frantic. Four paramedics and six physicians, including the anesthesiologist and the thoracic surgeon from Northwestern Memorial, injected medications and applied electrical shocks to stimulate their patient's heart into some degree of activity. Nothing worked; there were no responses, no signs of life. They tried over and over again. Finally, at about 3:40 P.M., one hour and twenty-five minutes after the first emergency call, they conceded that nothing more could be done.

The paramedics placed the body on a stretcher, covered it with a blanket, and used the freight elevator to take it to the ambulance parked at the building's loading dock. Led by two squad cars with their revolving lights on and sirens growling, the ambulance left the alley and went east on Walton Street to Michigan Avenue, where it turned right and headed south. It drove past the historic Water Tower and the Wrigley Building, through the Loop and the black neighborhood to the south, and then into the far South Side of the city. At Thirty-fifth Street the ambulance headed west for about a mile, passing old Comiskey Park, home of the Chicago White Sox. It turned off Thirty-fifth Street at Lowe Avenue and slowly made its way up the block on which its passenger had been born and had lived all his life. On this bone-chilling Monday of Christmas week, Richard J. Daley, The Greatest Mayor Chicago Ever Had, came home to Bridgeport for the last time.[1]

The news of Daley's death shocked most Chicagoans. True, he was seventy-four. He had suffered a stroke just two years earlier, and his health had been an unspoken issue in his successful bid for a sixth term. Yet, somehow, the thought of Chicago without Richard J. Daley had a stunning effect. For over twenty-one years, to Chicagoans and outsiders alike, he personified the city. In the government of his Chicago, "he was Hennessey, Fennesey, and all the other Irishmen in McNamara's Band."[2] So completely had he become identified with the city, and it with him, that it was often said, only partially in jest, that an entire generation of Chicago's youngsters grew up thinking that "Mayor" was his first name. Now, suddenly, he was gone, and things would surely change in his beloved city.

For most mortals, the numbness induced by a sudden loss through death wears off slowly. But Chicago's aldermen are not most mortals, and their planning for the interregnum was already well advanced by 22 December, when they assembled at the Church of the Nativity of Our Lord to attend the funeral mass for their deceased chairman-mayor. The vice president of the United States, the president-elect, cabinet officers, senators, governors, and mayors, as well as the city's civic, religious, and social leaders, came that morning to pay final homage to "a prince of politics." As they heard Chicago's Catholic archbishop, John Cardinal Cody, commend "his body to be committed to the earth from which it was made," they, too, must have wondered what the city and its politics would be like without Daley.[3]

The aldermen could have told them what they planned for the post-Daley years. Much would change, of course. The positions of chairman of the Democratic Central Committee of Cook County and mayor of Chicago would be divided, the relations between the mayor and the City Council would be different, new faces and names would become prominent in the Council, and frustrated power seekers would be more willing and likely to challenge the decisions made by the inner circle of the Council or the Central Committee. Yet in the most important way of all, nothing would change. The city's blacks would still be treated as subjects of the regime, while the Machine assertively defended the interests of its white constituents. Race would remain the issue binding the Machine together—the dominant fact of the city's politics.

The Bilandic Interlude

■ After 20 December 1976, no one was in a position to exercise the unquestioned power that Daley had for so long. The committeemen who dumped Kennelly in 1955 thought they were ridding themselves of a threat and asserting their control; but they soon learned the truth of Alderman Paddy Bauler's prophetic, if inelegant, election-night assessment: "Keane and them fellas—Jake Arvey, Joe Gill—may think they are gonna run things. Well, . . . they're gonna run nothin'. They ain't found it out yet, but Daley's the dog with the big nuts, now that we got him elected. You wait and see; that's how it is going to be."[4]

By holding the positions of chairman of the party and mayor of the city at the same time, Daley was able to exert more control than any of his predecessors. Because he recognized that potential, he had reneged on his promise to resign the chairmanship after the 1955 general election "to devote my full time and attention to the duties of the mayor's office." Through the combination of the two offices, Daley united city and party government and made the Machine into the institution that ruled Chicago. However, even this combination was no guarantee by itself of the type of power that he came to wield. A less ambitious, less calculating, and less attentive person may not have made this combination into what Daley did. His drive for power, his command of the operations of the city government, and especially his constant attentiveness to even the minute details of the workings of the patronage system made a difference. "For God's sake," one alderman exclaimed, leaving Daley's office, "you'd wonder how he could run the city, keeping all the shit about how many jobs you've got in his head."[5] Daley not only knew how many jobs each committeeman had, he kept track of how well their wards performed on election days and how loyally their aldermen supported his programs; and he adjusted the allocation of patronage accordingly.

When Daley first took office as mayor, the party organization resembled a feudal structure. Each ward organization was an independent entity, something of a fiefdom, ruled in the name of the party by its committeeman, its local baron who was also a voting member of the Central Committee that directed the party organization.[6] The feudal analogy remained appropriate throughout the Daley years, but the character of the lord-vassal connection changed significantly.

In Kennelly's day, and even in the Kelly and Cermak eras, the committeemen enjoyed the independence that came from a relationship of mutual need. By developing sources of popular and financial support outside the Machine, first among the labor unions and later in the business and financial communities, Daley changed that relationship. Many of the committeemen, especially those who came to office during his mayoralty, found that they needed him more than he needed them. He was the sole dispenser of jobs and other tangible benefits, and the ability of most of the committeemen to "grease" their own ward organizations depended on his continuing goodwill. Daley was no weak King John, to be pushed around by a feisty bunch of barons; he was more like Richard the Conqueror, co-opting and outmaneuvering some opponents, simply outliving others, and all the while using his power to dispense patronage and city business to cement loyalty and enhance his own power. In his dual capacity as chairman-mayor, as Alderman Charles Weber had surmised in 1955, "This Daley—he's . . . one tough sonofabitch."[7]

Daley built the organization he inherited into an institution that ruled the city but one that still depended uniquely on his own active control. With its linchpin now removed, could the vaunted Machine continue to perform as efficiently and decisively as it had under Daley's direction?

When the question was posed in these terms (as it most often was), political analysts missed the crucial point. Even before Daley's death, the Machine's electoral support had waned noticeably. It couldn't deliver the nomination for state's attorney to Berg in 1972; it lost several aldermanic and state legislative contests to white and black independents; and Daley was not able to deny a congressional renomination to Metcalfe in 1976. More important, the mayor had attracted less support in his own 1975 primary than in any of his previous contests, and the vulnerability of the Machine either to countermobilization by the city's blacks or to a split between its white ethnic supporters was especially apparent.

Academic analysts, columnists, and reporters often glossed over these signs of electoral weakness because they looked only at winners and losers and listened too uncritically to the boasts of the Machine's stalwarts. Many of the latter were colorful personalities, and their tales of services rendered and loyalties repaid by voters often beguiled inquirers. The published stories and analyses that resulted then contributed further to the notion that the Machine was invincible. By the early 1970s, there was as much myth as reality in this notion, but the popular image of control and invincibility continued to serve the Machine well. It helped fend off some serious challengers, while making it virtually impossible for more daring ones to raise adequate funds or enlist enough volunteers to wage effective campaigns.[8]

Since Daley's presence contributed mightily to the myth of the Machine's invincibility, his death focused attention, although often for the wrong reasons, on its vulnerability. The maneuvers and decisions that followed his passing added to the doubts, while increasing the likelihood that dissatisfied Machine loyalists would challenge the succession arrangements.

The day after Daley's funeral, Alderman Wilson Frost (34th Ward), the City Council's president pro tem and a black, told a press conference that the statutes and case law of the state made him the acting mayor of the city. Minutes afterward, Frank Sullivan, the late mayor's press secretary, challenged Frost's claim, saying that there was no acting mayor until the City Council elected one. Later in the day, William Quinlan, the city's corporation counsel, held his own press conference to reaffirm Sullivan's view and to point out that Kenneth Sain, who held the appointed title of deputy mayor, was the chief administrator of the city. Quinlan even questioned whether Frost remained president pro tem, arguing that the post existed only during brief absences of the mayor or at the mayor's request. In the meantime, most of the other black aldermen and black community leaders lobbied the white aldermen for the necessary votes to elect Frost. Their efforts were futile, of course; the leaders of the Machine did not intend to have a black serve as the city's chief executive, no matter how proven his loyalty. They intended to slam "the doors of the mayor's office in [Frost's] face as though he were a yardboy at the big house."[9]

Even as black leaders argued for Frost's election, the newspapers reported the outline of the succession arrangements. Alderman Michael Bilandic, from Daley's own 11th Ward and chairman of the Finance Committee, was to become acting mayor, with Alderman Edward Vrdolyak (10th Ward) taking over as president pro tem and Alderman Edward Burke (14th Ward) remaining in charge of the committee overseeing the police and fire departments. On 28 December, the City Council confirmed the arrangements, placated Frost by naming him to succeed Bilandic as chairman of the Finance Committee, and gave the newly created and symbolic position of vice-mayor to the dean of the Polish aldermanic delegation.[10]

Besides being a snub to blacks, Bilandic's designation as acting mayor was significant for other reasons. The choice of a Croatian symbolized declining Irish control and bestowed status benefit on the eastern European ethnics. That he was the alderman from Daley's ward signified the continuing dominance of the white leadership from the South Side, while representing yet another rebuff to the Poles on the Northwest Side. By picking the relatively obscure Bilandic, who was not even a member of the party's Central Committee, the aldermen clearly signalled their intention to prevent the emergence of another all-powerful leader. Bilandic's dependence on the party and the ward committeemen meant that he would not have the iron-fisted control over the city government that Daley had. The Council's "Young Turks," especially Vrdolyak and Burke, would at last have their opportunity to gain more power.[11]

When he was selected acting mayor, Bilandic assured the Council and the public that he would *not* be a candidate in the special mayoral election which Illinois law required the city to conduct within six months of the death of an incumbent mayor. Once in office, however, Bilandic qualified his earlier promise and indicated that he would not turn down a draft by the Democratic Machine. That was probably what many Machine regulars had in mind all along, of course; and by late January 1977, "party sources" accurately prophesied that "the 'Bilandic draft' appeared unstoppable."[12]

The leaders of two groups in the party's voting coalition, Poles and blacks, were dissatisfied with the succession arrangements and with the prospect of Bilandic's being slated for the nomination in the special primary on 19 April. Alderman Roman Pucinski (41st Ward), assuming the role of spokesman for the Polish dissidents, quickly announced his intention to seek the nomination. Pucinski, a ward committeeman and Machine loyalist, was a former congressman and a vocal defender of the integrity of white neighborhoods. His party ties, especially among the precinct captains on the Northwest Side, his ethnic identification, name recognition, and commitment to the cause of white cultural dominance made him a potentially formidable challenger.[13] His decision to contest the primary, after having been turned down by the party's slatemakers, did not represent an attempt to dismantle the Machine as a ruling institution, however. He ran as a candidate within the Machine, as the symbolic representative of the city's largest white ethnic group, a group seeking what it saw as its rightful but long-deferred place in the sun.

The succession arrangements also sparked dissent within the black community. By ignoring Frost's claims and selecting Bilandic, Daley's heirs again made clear the second-class status they assigned to blacks. The way the snub was accomplished indicated indifference as to how black voters might respond. Low turnout among the black electorate had reduced both the importance of its support and the danger of its opposition to the Machine. "Whites in power," Don Rose observed, "can basically write off the black vote. They don't need it, they don't want it. In fact, they snicker about black committeemen not being able to deliver the vote from their wards."[14]

Early in his tenure as acting mayor, Bilandic showed blacks that he planned to carry forward Daley's approach to race relations. In January 1977, the Court of Appeals upheld Judge Prentice Marshall's earlier decision that the hiring and promotion policies of the Chicago Police Department discriminated against minorities. Those policies violated civil rights statutes, although the court argued that there was no violation of constitutional rights involved since the plaintiffs had not shown an intent to discriminate. Bilandic seized the loophole, claiming that "no intent to discriminate is no discrimination," and he announced the city's plan to appeal the ruling to the U.S. Supreme Court. By early February Bilandic backed away from the planned appeal, but he found a new target in the efforts by federal attorneys to negotiate a consent decree in a case involving charges of discrimination in hiring and promotion by the Chicago Fire Department. By denying the existence of discrimination in the city's police and fire departments, Bilandic told the city's blacks, even the Machine's most faithful black lieutenants, that nothing of significance had changed for them.[15]

So, black leaders began to search for their own mayoral candidate. Two ad hoc search groups, with some overlapping membership, were in operation by early January, and by the middle of the month they agreed on their top choice, State Senator Harold Washington. The facade of unity broke down two days later, when Congressman Metcalfe announced that he could not support Washington. Publicly, Metcalfe implied that Washington's 1972 conviction on charges of having failed to file income tax returns made him unacceptable as a candidate. Others suggested that the congressman's opposition was due to Washington's refusal to support Metcalfe in the 1976 primary fight against Erwin France. Still others suspected that Metcalfe was in the process of working out a deal with Bilandic to get back into the Machine's good graces.[16] Whatever Metcalfe's motives, his opposition led Washington to announce his withdrawal. At that point, the unity effort was in shambles, with no prominent black opponent willing to make the race.

One week after Washington's withdrawal, the black search groups, operating as the Committee for the Election of a Black Mayor, held a press conference to announce the selection of Robert Tucker, a lawyer and general counsel for Operation PUSH, as their candidate for

mayor. While Metcalfe and the Reverend Jesse Jackson assured reporters that Tucker had agreed to run, the candidate himself did not
attend the press conference and had not been taking phone calls for
several days. On 28 January, the day before Tucker's name was put
forth as the candidate of the black community, another black attorney, Ellis Reid, announced his candidacy. Then, on 19 February,
Washington got back into the contest, announcing that he would file
for the primary "as a people's candidate."[17]

When he reentered the race, Washington became the focal point of
the black community's political effort. Gus Savage, who published a
chain of community newspapers and had organized one of the ad
hoc search groups, served as Washington's campaign manager. Savage and Renault Robinson, director of the Afro-American Patrol-
men's League, worked at the grass-roots level and established a network of political organizations in several of the black wards, which
persisted beyond the campaign. Charles Hayes, the black international vice president of the Amalgamated Meat Cutters Union, orchestrated endorsements by twenty labor unions representing over
100,000 workers. Moreover, Washington, who said that "he was not
running as a black candidate," consciously sought support from
white voters. He enlisted Warren Bacon, a black executive of Inland
Steel and a former member of the school board, to chair a citywide
Interethnic Citizens' Committee, and he secured the endorsement of
the Independent Voters of Illinois, which was the local branch of the
ADA and one of Chicago's two independent political organizations.[18]

While Washington was clearly the major black challenger, his entry into the contest did not unite the entire black community. Tucker
withdrew, but Reid stayed in the race, charging throughout that
Washington was "just holding the door open for Singer in 1979."
Metcalfe withheld his support of Washington, and Jesse Jackson
gave his blessing only late in the campaign, after considerable public (and probably even more private) prodding. Another group
of dissident black Republicans and Democrats, calling themselves
"Bridgebuilders," endorsed Roman Pucinski. Only one black alderman, David Rhodes (24th Ward), broke with the Machine to back
Washington. Several black committeemen and even more precinct
captains, unable to sell Bilandic to their constituents, pushed Reid.
Finally, when it served a useful public relations purpose, the Machine trotted out other groups of blacks, especially ministers, to sing
the praises of the acting mayor.[19]

The divisions that marked the black community weren't just the
results of personality conflicts and rivalries among ambitious leaders; they grew from the very nature of the Machine's relationship to
the city's blacks. For the most part, black politicians were "captives
of the Machine," depending on it for patronage, clout in their wards,

and even electoral support.[20] Since they were responsible to the leaders of the Machine, who put them in office and kept them there, and not to their black constituents, they performed loyally, supporting slated candidates in the precincts and voting as instructed in the City Council, even when their behavior ran counter to the racial interests of their community. Because they needed the Machine more than its leaders needed them, the relationship institutionalized the Machine's control over its "plantation provinces" and guaranteed the subordination of the racial interests of the black community.

Washington's candidacy now endangered this relationship. Machine blacks were not afraid that Washington would win the primary, but they did fear that a big vote would lead to the organization of a permanent "resistance movement" among blacks. Such a movement would hold black politicians accountable to their communities; and the Machine blacks, whose positions and power came "from 'The Man' downtown," correctly perceived that as a threat.[21] They defended themselves by attacking Washington's campaign for political autonomy, even though by doing so they also defended the Machine's continued control over the black community.

In spite of these factors, and even with the entry of Hanrahan and other fringe candidates, the primary did not spark much enthusiasm. Many viewed it simply as a struggle for control among Machine stalwarts, with none of the major contestants offering to dismantle the city's ruling institution. In a televised debate, Pucinski and Washington spoke of eliminating the patronage system, but their conversions were too recent and opportune to be convincing. Washington staked out something of a reformist posture, calling for the ouster of Police Superintendent James Rochford and attacking Bilandic for injecting politics into the city's schools and for failing to provide leadership. But his image as a reformer was clouded by his own past legal problems and what he saw as the local media's preoccupation with them. At the end of the campaign, he complained that "the press has been nipping at me. They should stop nipping at my heels and should be concerned with the issues."[22]

Bilandic, who at best was an unexciting campaigner, waged his battle in the style of his late mentor. He avoided debates with his challengers, limited his appearances to party gatherings, and held court in City Hall for representatives of business, civic, and labor groups to announce their endorsements. While the acting mayor presided over these staged public relations events, his real campaign was being waged in the precincts by the Machine's patronage army. These activities and the Machine's image of invincibility were Bilandic's major strengths. By mid-March, the *Chicago Tribune*'s poll showed Bilandic with a wide lead over Pucinski, his closest challenger, with more than half of the acting mayor's supporters indicating that the party's endorsement was a "very important" factor in making their choice. But the more revealing finding was that regardless of their own preference, 91.5 percent of all the respondents *expected* Bilandic to win.[23]

The results of the primary showed that the Machine's image was stronger than its performance (Table 10).[24] Since the ward committeemen wanted a heavy pro-Bilandic turnout to help affirm the Machine's strength and discourage future challenges, the precinct captains worked their turfs more feverishly than they had in 1975, when Daley's name headed the ticket. On election day, 46 percent of the voters reported having been contacted by a party worker. Despite their best efforts, however, Bilandic mobilized only 18 percent of the city's voting-age population, the poorest showing by a slated mayoral candidate since 1955.[25]

The Machine's support among blacks continued to decline, but Bilandic still won the votes of a majority of blacks who participated. Washington won less white support than Newhouse had in 1975, but he ran better among blacks, although still mobilizing less than 10 percent of the city's black voting-age population. Washington was strongest on the South Side, especially among the middle-class blacks outside the old Dawson bailiwicks, but Bilandic outpolled him by better than 2 to 1 among blacks on the West Side. The most significant indicator, however, was the generally low level of black participation, with only slightly more than 27 percent of the voting-age blacks bothering to vote. This represented a 6.7 percentage point decline in turnout since 1975, or almost twice the rate of the white decline. As in 1975, not even the presence of a candidate from their own community aroused the enthusiasm of black voters.[26]

The most ominous sign for the Machine was that the two areas of white ethnic concentration moved in opposite directions for the first time since 1963. Pucinski won among the white ethnics on the Northwest Side, but his was not an "ethnic-based challenge," as Adamowski's had been in 1963. The alderman's electoral strength was limited to his home area, approximating a "friends and neighbors" effect, while Poles and other white ethnics on the South Side preferred Bilandic by a wide margin. Strong support among the South Side's white ethnics and their high turnout (55.3 percent compared to 46.6 percent on the Northwest Side) combined to give Bilandic an overall plurality among the whites in the two areas. But it was a slim edge, only 9,279 votes, and one which underscored the tenuous nature of the Machine's continued hegemony.[27] It could guarantee delivery of the nomination to its slated choice only if the city's white ethnics were highly mobilized *and* cohesive. If they split their votes, then the outcome of a contested primary could be decided by other voters. This potential danger became a reality in the 1979 primary.

Table 10. The 1977 Democratic Mayoral Primary: Regression Estimates of Group Voting Behavior [1]

	Pucinski	Bilandic	Hanrahan	Washington	Nonvote
Citywide [2]					
Blacks	3.2	14.0	0.3	9.8	72.5
Whites	20.2	21.6	2.4	0.4	55.1
Hispanics	5.0	18.2	0.4	0.1	76.1
Blacks					
Dawson wards	3.7	15.3	0.4	9.4	71.0
Other South Side	2.8	11.3	0.3	11.3	74.1
West Side	3.6	15.5	0.3	7.4	73.1
White Ethnics	23.3	25.0	2.8	0.1	48.6
Northwest Side	29.8	16.4	2.5	0.2	53.3
South Side	16.7	35.2	3.2	0.1	44.6
Total citywide	11.5	18.0	1.4	3.8	65.1

[1] Entries are percentages of voting-age population, and rows sum to 100 percent, except for rounding error.

[2] Developed by weighting the estimates for each group within eight subareas of the city.

Once the formality of the general election was completed on 7 June, Michael Bilandic became mayor of the city of Chicago. As most Chicagoans expected, things were to change under his leadership. Most notably, Bilandic was unable to dominate city and party affairs as Daley had.

Daley was able to direct the affairs of the City Council because he controlled the party. Aldermen who went along with the administration got along, while the uncooperative were denied patronage, city business, and the Machine's endorsement. To be sure that the Council operated smoothly, Daley held meetings (prior to its regular sessions) with his floor leader, first Alderman Thomas Keane and later Bilandic himself, each of whom was also chairman of the Finance Committee. The fate of all pending legislation was decided at these preliminary meetings, and important ordinances were sent to the Finance Committee to guarantee that things went as planned.

From the outset, a larger number of aldermen participated in Bilandic's pre-Council meetings, the regulars being Wilson Frost (34th Ward), who was the mayor's floor leader and chairman of the Finance Committee, Edward Burke (14th Ward), Vito Marzullo (25th Ward), and Edward Vrdolyak (10th Ward). Soon other Machine aldermen began clamoring for access to the planning sessions, where they knew the important decisions were made. By early 1978 a group of about ten usually loyal aldermen, dubbed the "Reluctant Rebels" by reporters, began holding their own caucuses and introducing legislation without the prior approval of the mayor and his inner circle. Faced with the possibility of an open split, Bilandic yielded and invited the Council's eighteen committee chairmen to meet with him as a "legislative cabinet" prior to Council sessions. He also agreed to direct ordinances to the committee concerned with the affected area of government, rather than assigning all important ordinances to the Finance Committee.

This decision loosened Bilandic's control over the Council and reduced the importance of Frost's position. But the move was not intended solely "as a slap at Wilson [Frost]"; it was an attempt to give a larger number of Machine loyalists greater influence over the operation of the city government and to prevent the emergence of any single center of power within the Council.[28] Why did Bilandic agree to reduce his own power? Pucinski provided the answer; hailing the move as "a masterful stroke," Pucinski noted that it improved Bilandic's chances of being reslated by the Democratic party for the 1979 mayoral election.[29] Lacking Daley's power base within the Machine, this mayor, unlike his powerful mentor, simply needed the committeemen much more than they needed him.

While the relations among the mayor, the Council, and the Machine changed in the post-Daley era, race relations remained essentially the same. Under its new leadership, the Machine and the city government it controlled were as defensive of white cultural dominance as they had been during the Daley years.

During the summer of 1977, white ethnic communities protested the Board of Education's plan to pay transportation costs for students who voluntarily transferred to other schools, thereby improving the system's racial balance. Bilandic's statements regarding this issue left no doubt that he sympathized with the white ethnic groups. He questioned the value of busing, resisted requests from Machine blacks to endorse the program, and tried unsuccessfully to persuade the Board of Education to postpone its implementation. Black leaders denounced his "vague and mealy-mouthed comments," which they claimed had the effect of putting "the prestige of his office behind the howling segregationist mob."[30]

In the midst of the city's long-running battle over school integration, Bilandic's appointments to the Board of Education proved to be another source of conflict with the black community. By naming two whites to five-year terms on the Board in the late spring of 1977, the mayor administered "another slap in the face to the black community." Realizing that the terms of three more Board members expired in the spring of 1978, black leaders pressed Bilandic to appoint more blacks. They argued that a Board of Education whose membership was 64 percent white was unrepresentative of a school system in which whites were less than a quarter of the students. Bilandic ignored their arguments and a petition campaign organized by Operation PUSH and reappointed the incumbents, two whites and one black, leaving the racial balance of the Board unchanged.[31]

While Bilandic displayed his insensitivity to blacks on integration issues, the leaders of the Machine indicated their intention to maintain political control over the black community. By opposing Washington's 1978 bid for reelection to the state senate they tried to punish him for challenging Bilandic. And Washington only narrowly defeated what he described as "one of the worst combinations of lowbrow politicians that I have ever dealt with in all my years in politics." When Congressman Metcalfe died shortly before the 1978 general election, the ten committeemen whose wards comprised his congressional district, including nine blacks, took their cue from the Machine in naming his replacement. Ignoring the jeers of hundreds of blacks attending the party meeting, they chose Alderman Bennett Stewart, "a supine party loyalist."[32]

By these and other actions, the mayor and the Machine gave evidence that Daley's brand of "plantation politics" was alive and well in post-Daley Chicago. The city's ruling institution continued to subordinate the interests of its black subjects to those of its white supporters. By defending white values, it hoped to attract those who had voted for Pucinski or Hanrahan in the 1977 primary and to maintain its hegemonic control over the city through the high and cohesive mobilization of its white ethnics. As long as the black community was politically fragmented, with many of its politicians more attentive to the Machine's demands than to the racial interests of their constituents, and as long as black voter turnout remained low, there was no great electoral risk in that racial strategy.

Throughout 1978 the Machine's electoral arithmetic seemed to be on target. Bilandic's willingness to drop plans for the northern leg of the Crosstown Expressway and his opposition to Concorde landings at O'Hare showed responsiveness to the white communities on the Northwest Side, while his $100 million low-interest home mortgage plan benefited aspiring homeowners in most white areas of the city.[33] The mayor even refurbished his image by getting married and by participating in long-distance running events. By the end of 1978 there seemed no reason to doubt predictions that Bilandic was "an absolute certainty" for renomination and reelection in 1979.[34] There was no way to foresee at that point how Jane Byrne, bad weather, and the ire of the black community would combine to derail Bilandic's reelection express.

Jane Byrne and the Machine—Act One

■ On 27 February 1979, for the first time since Cermak's day, the Machine failed to deliver the mayoral nomination to its slated choice.

With nearly 100,000 more voters participating than in the 1977 primary, former Chicago Commissioner of Consumer Sales, Weights, and Measures Jane Byrne defeated Bilandic for the nomination by the slim margin of 16,775 votes. Five weeks later she buried her Republican opponent and became the first female mayor in Chicago's history.

The city's professional independents and its anti-Machine blacks hailed the victory as the end of bossism. But Alderman Vito Marzullo, the Machine's *pater familias*, knew the truth. "Everything will be all right," he said after the primary. "She's coming back. No one walks alone in this world."[35]

Byrne's background and experience should have given the Machine's opponents reason to pause before jumping on her bandwagon. Raised in Sauganash, an affluent and nearly cloistered community on the city's Northwest Side (39th Ward), she was the second-oldest of six children born to William and Katherine Burke. Although not wealthy, the Burkes were financially comfortable, and their children enjoyed the advantages that came from being part of the "fur-coat Irish" set. Jane Burke attended Catholic elementary and secondary schools; took her undergraduate degree at Barat College, a woman's school in the wealthy suburb of Lake Forest on Chicago's North Shore; and made her formal debut at the Presentation Ball, the Irish elite's answer to the WASPs' Cotillion. On New Year's Eve 1956, she married William Byrne, a Notre Dame graduate then doing a stint as a Marine Corps pilot, whom she had met when they were both undergraduates. When her husband died in a plane crash on 31 May 1959, she found herself with a seventeen-month-old daughter to care for but without job experience or marketable skills. During the trying months that followed, she was able to rely on the psychological support of her closely knit family and on its ample financial resources.

Jane Byrne's first involvement in politics, working in the Kennedy campaign in 1960, apparently came about without any thought of her launching a political career. After the election she returned to school to take education courses at the Chicago campus of the University of Illinois, which then was still located at Navy Pier. What happened next, how she became connected with Mayor Daley, is in some dispute. In any event, in 1965 she was hired by the city's Head Start program, and shortly thereafter she moved to the personnel department of the Chicago Commission on Urban Opportunity (CCUO), the city's central agency in the War on Poverty. Because CCUO's personnel office was the link between the Machine and federally funded jobs, she saw how Daley's system of rewards and punishments worked. The committeemen and precinct captains who were loyal and delivered the votes got the jobs, and those who didn't, got the axe. Since she functioned as one of his political operatives, Daley periodically met with her to ask about personnel matters. Finally, on 4 March 1968, His Honor called her into his office and announced that she was to be the city's next commissioner of consumer sales, weights, and measures.[36]

Daley's sponsorship wasn't limited to Byrne's appointment as head of a city department. He named her to his "All Chicago" reelection committee in 1967, and she became the first woman to be involved in the smaller planning group of that 2,000-member committee. That marked her as a "comer" in the party, while giving her both practical insight into the organization of a Machine-style campaign and exposure at ward meetings and rallies. In 1972, when Robert Strauss, the new chairman of the Democratic National Committee, offered Daley the chairmanship of the powerful Resolutions Committee of the national party, the mayor suggested Jane Byrne for the position. Three years later Daley stunned a Democratic party rally by casually announcing that "Janie Byrnes" (as he always mistakenly called her) was appointed co-chairman of the Democratic Central Committee of Cook County, sharing the position with none other than the mayor himself. "Jane had moved to the top of the mountain, sharing the throne with the king."[37]

Of course, no one was naive enough to think she also shared Daley's power. Still, her rise through the hierarchy of Chicago politics was unprecedented and unexplained. No one knew why Daley chose to sponsor her for city and party positions, and even she never knew why he decided to name her to head the Consumer Sales Department and then allowed her to grab headlines and expand her department's power. Some critics of the administration, like Alderman Leon Depres (5th Ward), thought of her only as "Daley's token woman." The Machine regulars, on the other hand, resented her, because she was forced on them without having worked a precinct or having been elected to a city or party office. The regulars tolerated her because Daley told them to; but she hadn't paid her dues, and they never accepted her.[38]

Jane Byrne ran the Consumer Sales Department competently, aggressively, and without scandal. She converted a little-known department into one that actively and honestly regulated condominium conversions, phosphates in detergents, bait-and-switch advertising, unit pricing, toy safety, and meat grading, among other areas. She fired inspectors who were on the take, dismissed incompetent employees, and fought industry lobbyists and the aldermen they bought, while expanding her department's role and power and making good news for the administration. At a time when the newspapers were headlining the indictments and convictions of Daley's trusted associates, at least his commissioner of consumer sales, "Janie Byrnes," listened to the complaints of citizens and acted on their behalf, even earning praise in the process from consumer advocate Ralph Nader.[39]

To City Hall insiders and party regulars, Jane Byrne was an enigma. She issued frequent press releases, held press conferences and kept her department squarely in public view, while most department heads avoided the press and coveted secrecy. She ran a clean department, firing lax employees even when they were valued precinct workers. Their committeemen complained to His Honor about that "crazy broad running things at Weights and Measures," but he backed his commissioner.[40] And when her office drafted new ordinances to protect consumer interests, Daley saw to it that the City Council rubber-stamped them. Jane Byrne obviously enjoyed the mayor's favor, and in Daley's Chicago, there simply was no greater clout than Daley. However, she had no other power base, no other claim to the support of the regulars, and when Daley died, her clout died too.

Within a week of Daley's funeral, George Dunne, the new party chairman, dumped her as co-chairman and left the post unfilled. The role of women in the party was to be changed, Dunne said, but there was still a place for her in politics, "perhaps putting on women's card parties, fashion shows, luncheons, dinners, and the like." The new acting mayor, also a Daley protégé, was no less anxious to curb her influence and penchant for grabbing headlines. Jane Byrne knew that her clout was gone. "That's politics," she said. "I can't have it the way I had it because the mayor is gone."[41]

Within a year, however, she would fight back and garner more publicity than ever. Jane Byrne's break with Bilandic came in November 1977, five months after he approved a request for a fare increase by the city's cab companies. Chicago had two cab companies, Checker and Yellow, both of which were wholly owned divisions of Checker Motors Corporation of Kalamazoo, Michigan; and since 1959 they had been regulated by city ordinance. This ordinance limited the number of cab medallions, giving these two companies a virtual monopoly. It also denied fare increases unless the taxi firms could show that their profits had fallen below 14 percent. This was easy enough to do, since their parent company manufactured their cabs and, through other subsidiaries, the firms sold each other fuel and cars. This cozy arrangement worked well for the cab companies as long as the public vehicle commissioner, the official charged with regulating the taxi fleet, didn't ask too many hard questions about their bookkeeping practices. However, in 1975, when a cab with faulty brakes struck and killed several children, the operations of the cab companies attracted considerable publicity; and Daley began to inquire into the way the office of the public vehicle commissioner was being run. He quickly discovered that federal investigators were looking into the commissioner's financial dealings with the taxi firms. In January 1976, to avoid yet another scandal, Daley transferred responsibility for regulating the taxi companies to his commissioner of consumer sales.[42]

Jane Byrne plunged into the taxi mess with her usual energy, requiring safety inspections of the cabs, eye exams and uniforms for the drivers, and tighter regulations for taxi registration. When the companies and the drivers resisted, she berated them to the press, knowing that their political clout was no match for hers. In May 1976, in the midst of this wave of negative publicity concerning their operations, the cab companies requested a fare increase, despite a pending lawsuit brought by Alderman Edward Burke alleging that they falsified figures to obtain a rate increase in 1974. There was no public action on the request until 7 July 1977, when the City Council approved an 11.7 percent increase and made it effective immediately.

Why did the Council approve such an increase? According to Byrne's account, Mayor Bilandic "greased" the way. He met with the president of the parent Checker Corporation, who had also enlisted the support of Alderman Edward Vrdolyak, accepted the company's figures without serious question, and steered the increase through Burke's suddenly cooperative subcommittee and the Council. Byrne, who was involved in the meeting, objected to the company's accounting practices and questioned the legality of the mayor's action, but her protests were simply ignored. After this first meeting, Byrne began writing her now famous "taxigate" memo, and on 19 July she had the memo notarized and filed it away for future use.[43]

In the meantime, she told her version of the events to investigators from the Federal Trade Commission who had been inquiring (since early 1973) into Checker's monopoly. Byrne also leaked the details to two newspaper reporters but swore both to secrecy, requiring them to dig up independent confirmation of her story. When the FTC investigation bogged down, Byrne began to go public with her story. In a press interview on Friday, 11 November 1977, she expressed doubts concerning the cost figures that the cab companies had used to justify the fare increase, saying there were inconsistencies in them and that Bilandic was aware of that. Alderman Burke gave the Machine's response. Over the weekend he appeared on a local television program to point out that Byrne had not questioned the figures at the earlier Council hearings and that she should be fired if she had withheld information. He also indicated that he would move in the Council to strip her office of the authority to supervise the taxi industry.

The exchange between Byrne and Burke hardly aroused public excitement. But on 15 November, WBBM-TV contacted Bilandic's press secretary, Celesta Jurkovitch, told her of their intention to broad-

7. Mayor Bilandic appearing on the WBBM-TV 10 P.M. news to answer charges in the taxi-fare-increase case, 15 November 1977. News anchors Bill Kurtis and Walter Jacobson are shown with the mayor. (*Chicago Tribune.*)

cast damaging details of the story, and invited the mayor to appear on the 10 P.M. news to respond. The conflict escalated that night, as Bilandic, following his sober and dull response to the charges, began to realize that Byrne was using the media to make him look like a crook.[44]

While Bilandic was in Washington on a scheduled trip for the next three days, the local media, and especially the *Chicago Daily News*, announced new revelations, including the full text of Byrne's notarized memo. At the suggestion of the *News*, Byrne took a lie detector test on 17 November to prove her veracity. And when Bilandic returned to Chicago on Saturday, 19 November, he also arranged for and took a lie detector test. On Monday morning, 21 November, Bilandic told a City Hall press conference that he had passed the lie detector test and that Commissioner Jane Byrne was fired. Sharon Gist, a black female and a "safe" party regular, was Chicago's new commissioner of consumer sales, weights, and measures.[45]

Jane Byrne was now out—out of her party position, out of favor with the Machine's new leaders, and out of City Hall. But she was not out of the news or out of favor with the public. Whether she was in a store, in a restaurant, or simply walking on the street, people came up to her and told her they were with her. Slowly, perhaps, but surely, the idea dawned: she should run for mayor herself. On 24

April 1978, only five weeks after her marriage to Jay McMullen and ten months before the Democratic primary, Byrne announced her candidacy.

She was encouraged to run, she said, "by citizens from all walks of life, including many foot soldiers in the regular Democratic organization." Calling Mayor Bilandic's record one of "deceptions, intrigues, secret meetings to concoct illegal schemes, evasions, and falsehoods," Byrne presented herself as an alternative to what she described as a "cabal of evil men [that] has fastened itself onto the government of the City of Chicago." Asked to name the "evil men," she said that "the mayor must toady to the committeemen," only later singling out Burke and Vrdolyak for criticism because of their roles in the taxi case.[46]

Byrne's declaration didn't cause alarm or panic among the Machine regulars. When asked by reporters how "Mayor McMullen" would sound, Bilandic sneered, "For Peoria or Kansas City?" Vito Marzullo dismissed her as "just another runner"; George Dunne said she "has no significant support that I can see"; and Vrdolyak observed that "she's going through a very difficult time in her life." Other Machine insiders were more blunt, calling her a "'menopausal bitch' who was going through her change of life in public."[47]

Her candidacy would be a nuisance, an irritant, but none of the party leaders saw it then as a serious threat to Bilandic's reelection. The city's political commentators and reporters, as usual, shared that conviction. Byrne had no organization, no loyal legion of precinct captains, little money, and by primary day the taxi case would be only a vague memory. They correctly assessed Byrne's campaign liabilities, but they erred in predicting the outcome. But then, neither political pundits nor party regulars could have foreseen how the events of the coming winter would arouse public discontent and crystallize support for her challenge to Bilandic.

In the flush of that discontent and in the later euphoria of Byrne's victory, many read into her challenge more than was ever there. Hers was never an anti-Machine candidacy. In her own way, Byrne saw herself as a Machine insider, a protégé and admirer of The Greatest Mayor Chicago Ever Had. She attacked Bilandic and the "cabal of evil men" because they had betrayed Daley's legacy by scuttling his programs and shutting out his loyal supporters. The problem was not the Machine's system of control; it was the leaders temporarily in charge of it. Oust those men from power, she implied in announcing her candidacy, and the city government would be restored to the greatness it knew under Daley.[48]

Through the next ten months, that remained the central theme of her appeal. She appeared at the party's slating session in December, attacked Bilandic for shunting aside the late mayor's loyalists, and asked the committee to endorse her for the mayoral nomination. At campaign rallies she spoke often of Daley, of their mutual admiration, and of the great government Chicago had when he was alive. Her television commercials presented her as Daley's "rightful heir," and one of them used a recording of the late mayor's voice to dramatize her claim. She presented herself, in short, as an insider who had been pushed aside by crass and conniving usurpers and who was now seeking to reclaim her rightful position and to restore the government to what it was under Daley.[49]

The Bilandic-Byrne struggle was not a contest between a Machine incumbent and an anti-Machine challenger committed to dismantling it. Both were Daley protégés, political creations of the Machine, dedicated to its preservation. Why then did the city's liberal establishment and the anti-Machine blacks support Byrne? The answer is simple: at that point, Byrne was the only alternative to Bilandic. Earlier in the election season, neither the liberals, the blacks, nor even ambitious Machine stalwarts thought there was any realistic chance of defeating Bilandic. Machine support and his own public relations blitz convinced everyone but Byrne that a challenge was futile. When circumstances changed and Bilandic became vulnerable, she was left as the only game in town for those seeking to express their discontent with Bilandic on election day.

Through the autumn and into the early weeks of the winter, the Byrne campaign sparked little excitement. As expected, she was rebuffed by the committeemen in early December, and she had little prospect of raising sufficient funds to counter the efforts of the Machine's precinct captains. But then the weather turned cold, and so did Bilandic's prospects.

The winter of 1978–1979 was more severe than most Chicagoans had ever experienced. The snow began to fall in late November; there were two more snowstorms during the first week of December; and another major storm hit to open the second week of the month. By Christmas, the total snowfall amounted to just over twenty-one inches, compared with the city's normal forty inches for an entire winter. And the worst was yet to come. January witnessed two paralyzing snowstorms and a nearly unbroken streak of sub-zero temperatures that virtually immobilized the city. The storm that began on New Year's Eve dumped fifteen inches on the city, and the strong winds accompanying it produced heavy drifting, which closed airports and roads and snarled commuter traffic. Then on Friday, 12 January, just as the city was recovering, the snow started falling again. This time, another sixteen inches piled up, and the thirty-mile-an-hour winds cut visibility and produced more drifting problems. With the temperatures almost constantly below zero, removing snow was like "moving cement."[50]

8. One of the many side streets made impassable by the snowstorms: Melrose Street between Broadway and Halsted on the mid—North Side, 16 January 1979. (*Chicago Tribune.*)

For most of the month, "the city that works" simply didn't work. The Chicago Transit Authority's buses ran hours late, if at all; the commuter trains from the suburbs broke down, as switches froze and rails snapped. Passengers waited hours in the freezing cold for buses or trains that often never came or that broke down before getting to their destinations. The major streets and expressways were thick with snow, and streets in the neighborhoods were simply impassable. O'Hare Airport, the world's busiest, was closed time and time again, snarling nationwide air traffic for weeks.

After the New Year's Eve storm, Mayor Bilandic made the rounds of the television studios, assuring viewers that everything was under control. The city had over 600 workers, including many from departments other than Streets and Sanitation, working to remove the snow and getting things back to normal. The 300,000 commuters who experienced rush-hour delays and breakdowns for most of the next ten days must have wondered how the mayor defined "normal." They wouldn't bother to inquire after the second storm, because then even CTA officials admitted that the mass transit system had become "a rolling disaster."[51]

Following the mid-January storm, Bilandic made more television appearances. He assured viewers that things were under control at O'Hare, and that the city would again win the award for having the best airport, as it had the previous year. As he spoke, the stations played their recent videotapes of the conditions at O'Hare, showing people sleeping on chairs, on suitcases, and on the floors, and the baggage area piled portal to portal with unclaimed luggage.

If the mayor damaged his credibility with his claims about conditions at O'Hare, he destroyed it by announcing his plan for clearing snow from the streets. Over 1,000 pieces of equipment and 2,500 workers, he said, had cleared Board of Education and Park District lots so that people could move their cars from the streets to the cleared lots, thus allowing the city's plows to open the side streets. Then two days later he announced that some people were defying the administration by not moving their cars from the streets. But when a team of *Chicago Tribune* reporters checked the designated lots, they found that many had not been cleared at all. Bilandic became a laughingstock almost overnight.[52]

Throughout January, streets in the neighborhoods remained impassable, bus and train service was undependable, and anger built against the mayor who kept telling his fellow Chicagoans that everything was under control. As far as they could see, nothing seemed to be under Bilandic's control. The mayor reorganized his snow command in response to public criticism, but then reporters discovered that his top appointee had close connections with the crime syndicate. At about the same time, the newspapers revealed that a year earlier the city had secretly awarded a lucrative consulting contract to former deputy mayor Kenneth Sain to develop a new snow removal plan. What Sain produced was little more than a rewrite of an earlier city report. Citizens wondered why the city paid Sain $90,000 to tell it to keep the main streets plowed, and why his plan said nothing about how to deal with a major snowstorm.[53]

Mass transit service remained a problem throughout the month, as service delays and equipment breakdowns exhausted the patience of riders. Then, at the end of January, CTA officials implemented a solution. Without advance warning, they simply closed six of the seven inner city stops on the Lake Street line, which runs west from the Loop through the West Side, and four of the five close-in stations on the Dan Ryan line, which runs south from the Loop to Ninety-fifth Street on the far South Side. Closing these stations during morning and afternoon rush hours, CTA officials argued, affected only 20 percent of the some 100,000 daily users of the two lines, while improving the service available to the others. That innocuous claim ignored the fact that all of the stops being closed were in the black community and that only white suburban commuters would receive better service. On the Lake Street line, for example, to provide more dependable service to largely white Oak Park, the stops in the black communities of Austin and Garfield Park were closed, and no alternative service was available to those areas. While denying charges of racism, CTA officials seemed indifferent to the effects of their action on the blacks who depended on mass transit to get to and from jobs and schools daily. After four days of protests and the threat of a civil rights suit, the CTA reopened the stations, but the closings had again shown blacks that their interests and well being were of little concern. "This city works," one black leader observed, "for some people only."[54]

Through the cold days of January and February, Byrne used the winter conditions to pound away at her hapless opponent. She told snowbound Chicagoans that if Daley were still mayor, the streets would be cleared, and the city would be back to normal. Her television commercials reminded them that Daley regarded her as "one of the most competent women I've ever known." The snow and the administration's inept attempts to cope with it converted her nuisance candidacy into a serious threat. "When I began," she reflected on election day, "I had to prove everything. When the snow came down, all my accusations came true. I didn't have to prove it any more."[55] And the news of Sain's consulting contract vividly added point to her central theme: Bilandic's rule meant government by clout and cronyism and scant concern for the neighborhoods.

For Bilandic the news from the precincts wasn't good. People were tired of snow-clogged streets and late-running buses and trains, and their mood was turning ugly. Night after night, the television news shows presented Byrne, wearing her plain blue wool coat, standing in a snow bank with the flakes still falling about her, telling voters that Bilandic was to blame for the mess. Her campaign was still poorly financed and badly organized, but it was gaining momentum by the day. To stop Byrne, Bilandic had to rouse his loyal precinct workers to even greater activity, to stimulate their enthusiasm and stir their passions, a task that was difficult for a candidate with a personality "as exciting as soggy melba toast."[56]

On the anniversary of the St. Valentine's Day Massacre, Bilandic addressed a traditional preelection rally of precinct captains in the ballroom of the Bismarck Hotel. He exhorted them to help him win the primary, telling them that history had many examples of "courageous people standing up to vicious onslaughts, and that is no different from what is taking place today." Leaving nothing to their imaginations, the mayor went on to compare the "vicious onslaughts" against his administration with the crucifixion of Christ, the mass murders of Jews, the takeover of Eastern European countries (especially Poland), the enslavement of blacks, and the oppression of Latin America. "It is our turn to be in the trenches, to stay on the firing line, to see if we are made of the same stuff as the early Christians, the determined Jews, the proud Poles, the blacks and the Latin-Americans." He expressed his certainty that the precinct captains, the "unsung heroes," were made of the right stuff. "I'm proud to be your friend. I'll stand side by side with you, shoulder to shoulder, and face any task, fight any foe, solve any problem, and go from here to hell and back for you."[57] When his comments were reported in the papers the next day, Bilandic became the object of widespread ridicule and derision. The reports of his outlandish comparisons of himself with Christ and the persecuted Jews made him a public fool.

But myths die hard, and the myth of the Machine's invincibility still captivated the local media. Byrne may have had the snow, the mayor's inept performance and foolish rhetoric, but Bilandic had media endorsements, money, and, above all, the Machine. Spokesmen for the Machine, while admitting some signs of discontent with Bilandic, reported no evidence of "aggressive support for Byrne," and they confidently predicted victory. "Citywide it will be better than 2 to 1," Alderman Vrdolyak claimed. "In the last week, we [the Democratic Machine] are good for 20 points."[58]

The public opinion polls told another story. A week before the election, the WLS-TV (Channel 7) poll showed Bilandic clinging only to a 6-point lead, with 12 percent undecided. The WBBM-TV poll (Channel 2), which tabulated those who "leaned toward one candidate or another" along with those who had decided, gave Byrne a 12-point lead. Even a straw poll conducted by the mayor's political operatives showed him doing no better than running even with Byrne. What at the outset had been expected to be a Bilandic landslide was clearly going to be a close race. Still, the media expected the election-day activity of the precinct captains to make the difference.[59]

Faced with evidence of his waning popularity in the polls, and with the committeemen reporting "some real anger around" the precincts, Bilandic switched tactics during the last days of the campaign. Speaking to the final preelection rally of precinct captains, he admitted mistakes in handling the city's snow cleanup and pledged to do better next winter. "Bilandic Promises a Better Snow Job," the *Chicago Sun-Times* headlined its report of his speech, and many Chicagoans thought his election eve penitence marked the beginning of that effort. Even his decision to spend $2 million for washing the residential streets and for bulk-trash pickups on the Saturday before the election couldn't convince them that what Bilandic professed to be a "new commitment" to services in the neighborhoods was anything but a cynical ploy. The mayor's last-minute breastbeating was no match for Chicagoans' memories of how his inept management magnified the winter's hardships. Then there was the news of Sain's sweetheart deal, and that "proved beyond a shadow of a doubt that a little cabal gets everything," as Jane Byrne had charged. "And when you're standing on an L platform in the snow waiting for a train, you don't forget that."[60]

Bilandic's bad fortune continued through election day. The day dawned as a harbinger of spring—clear, bright, and with a warming breeze—the sort of sunshiny day that encouraged a good turnout, just what the Machine didn't want. "That crazy broad's got everything going for her, even sun," one of the fearful precinct captains muttered.[61] She also had the voters and their memories of recent experiences going for her. When the ballots were counted, Jane Byrne was the Democratic nominee for mayor of Chicago.

At the time, conventional wisdom regarded Byrne's victory as a fluke, a reaction to the snowstorms, the paralysis of the city, and Bilandic's fumbling performance, rather than a product of the Machine's inherent weakness among the city's electorate. The weather conditions and the media's focus on them highlighted Bilandic's ineptness as an administrator and the Machine's arrogant and nearly contemptuous disdain for public opinion, while giving the underfinanced Byrne campaign invaluable publicity. Because they had ignored what "Daley always told these guys, just keep the streets clean and the buses moving and you can steal anything you want," the leaders of the Machine made it possible for Byrne to mobilize a combination of discontented voters.[62] However, Byrne did not manufacture her voting coalition of whole cloth; she built on the dissatisfaction that had become evident in earlier elections.

Byrne outpolled Bilandic by about 21,000 votes among the white voters in the liberal Lake Shore wards and by about 13,000 among the white ethnics on the Northwest Side (Table 11).[63] Bilandic more than made up that gap with his strong support among the South Side's white ethnics, and he ran ahead of Byrne by a wide margin among Hispanic voters. Black voters made the difference for Byrne. While Bilandic held a slim edge among blacks on the West Side, Byrne captured the black vote on the South Side and piled up a 45,000-vote lead citywide among blacks. Overall, 36.1 percent of the votes cast for Byrne came from blacks, and since they were the only one of the city's three major groups among whom she had an edge, they were obviously crucial to her victory.

Black support for Byrne was clearly a reaction to the Machine's continuing exploitation of the black community and Bilandic's efforts to appeal to white ethnic voters through his stances against integration. Dissatisfaction with the Machine was not a new sentiment among blacks, although it was no doubt crystallized and heightened by the CTA closings in late January. Unlike 1975 and 1977, however, black anti-Machine voters concentrated their voting efforts on a single candidate, in part because they had no other alternatives but also because Byrne carefully cultivated their support. For months she had been attending block-club meetings and church services, appearing at community celebrations and on the black-oriented radio stations. From the middle-class black precincts on

Table 11. The 1979 Democratic Mayoral Primary: Regression Estimates of Group Voting Behavior [1]

	Bilandic	Byrne	Nonvote
Citywide [2]			
Blacks	14.2	20.3	65.4
Whites	24.7	24.2	51.0
Hispanics	14.0	4.2	81.6
Blacks			
Dawson wards	14.7	20.4	64.8
Other South Side	12.1	23.7	64.0
West Side	16.0	15.1	68.8
White Ethnics	28.9	24.5	46.4
Northwest Side	21.9	26.4	51.6
South Side	36.9	22.3	40.6
Total citywide	18.6	19.5	61.8

[1] Entries are percentages of voting-age population, and rows sum to 100 percent, except for rounding error.

[2] Developed by weighting the estimates for each group within eight subareas of the city.

the far South Side to the integrated areas of Hyde Park to the human warehouses of the Robert Taylor Homes, she campaigned for black support and implicitly identified her candidacy with the black quest for political autonomy. There was, she reported a week before the election, a new sophistication among black voters. In the past the Machine bought black votes with cash or chickens, but now she detected that blacks were saying "we're going to eat their chicken and eat their sweet potato pie, but they can't tell us who to vote for." [64]

Byrne's support among black voters was one of the keys to her victory. While the commitment of blacks to the Machine had waned earlier, their performance in 1979 marked the first occurrence (probably since 1943) of blacks' not giving at least a plurality to the slated candidate for mayor. Although this was no small accomplishment, Byrne's candidacy hardly sparked a great deal of fervor among blacks. Black turnout increased by about 7 percentage points over 1977, but that only brought it to about the same level as 1975. Besides, it is hard to argue that an overall turnout rate of 34.5 percent signals widespread enthusiasm.

Byrne's accomplishment in carrying the black vote would not have produced a victory, however, had it not been for a second key development—the split in the white vote. In that respect, what happened in 1979 was nearly a repeat of 1977. In both primaries, the slated candidate had a healthy margin among the white ethnics on the South Side, while losing on the Northwest Side. Since Bilandic lost the white ethnic vote on the Northwest Side by a smaller margin in 1979 than he had two years earlier, he outpolled Byrne among the voters in the two areas combined by about 4.4 percentage points. Of course, if he had carried the white ethnics in both areas, he would have more than offset Byrne's margin among blacks.

Finally, there was a third possible key to the outcome—the behavior of the city's Hispanic voters. Most of the Hispanics who cast ballots marked them for Bilandic, but only 18.3 percent of the age-eligible Hispanics voted. Had Hispanic turnout been 15 points higher, or roughly equal to the black turnout rate, and had the vote division remained about the same, Bilandic would have netted enough additional votes to counter both the white split and Byrne's lead among blacks. That did not occur, of course, and there is no credible reason to suppose that Bilandic and the Machine missed any opportunities to mobilize their Hispanic supporters.[65]

When the estimates of group voting behavior for 1979 (see Table 11) are compared with those for 1975 and 1977 (see Tables 9 and 10), they suggest that Byrne's victory was not quite the fluke that it appeared to be. Her candidacy appealed to strains of discontent that existed before the snows—the ongoing antipathy to the Machine among white liberals along the Lake Shore, the resentment harbored by the Northwest Side ethnics over the leadership monopoly of the South Siders, and the growing disaffection of the city's blacks. She appealed to these groups by focusing on Bilandic and assailing him as the leader of a "cabal of evil men" who were arrogantly insensitive to the needs of the neighborhoods. At the same time, because she was not an outsider to the Machine and because she identified herself with Daley's image and evoked memories of what the city had been like when he was in charge, she reassured white ethnics that she posed no threat to their continued control of their neighborhoods and schools. Therefore, they felt free to choose between the white contenders without fear of jeopardizing their cultural dominance.

Since the mid-1960s, the Machine had depended on high mobilization and cohesive support among white ethnic voters. But it could not mobilize that type of support unless the rivalries and antagonisms between the voters and leaders of the two areas were muted by their shared perception of a threat to white cultural dominance. Without that stimulus, white ethnic voters might divide their support, or their mobilization rates might lag, and the Machine could not guarantee victory for its chosen candidate. Pucinski's candidacy in 1977 underscored this potential danger, and Byrne's challenge transformed it into a real occurrence. She built her winning coalition by capitalizing on the inherent vulnerability of the Machine among the city's voters.

Jane Byrne and the Machine—Act Two

■ In the weeks between the primary and the inauguration, Byrne was treated as a conquering heroine. Wherever she went, cab drivers honked and people greeted her with victory signs. The whole city basked in the warm afterglow of her triumph, as it took to its collective heart the petite but gutsy woman in the blue cloth coat who had accomplished what lesser mortals feared even to try.

Expectations ran high on 16 April, as Jane Byrne, swearing to administer her charge justly and wisely, took over the duties and powers of the mayor of Chicago. She was no starry-eyed liberal—even her liberal supporters knew that—but she had denounced the leaders of the city's ruling institution, singling out especially Vrdolyak and Burke, and she had promised a new order, an end to the "closed, corrupt system" of Machine dominance. She had spoken of decency and fairness in government, of the concerns of the neighborhoods and of their people. She had quietly given signals to the independent aldermen, suggesting that her election was a victory for their brand of politics. And she had the regulars on the ropes, reeling from the shock of their defeat in the primary and knowing that she owed them nothing.[66]

But the high hopes of the city were soon dashed. The leaders of the Machine were willing to come to terms. "Politics," Alderman Burke suddenly noticed, "is an art of accommodation," and soon Byrne and the regulars were "marching to the same drummer."[67] It wasn't apparent at first, of course, because publicly she continued the attack against the "evil cabal." However, what she did proved to be more revealing than what she said. She ignored the urgings of the independent aldermen and remained on the sidelines as the City Council reorganized, allowing Vrdolyak and the regulars to exert control by locking in all the committee chairmanships.

Perhaps "she was overwhelmed by the job and unprepared to govern," as Don Rose later said.[68] Or, perhaps, she instinctively recognized the tenuous character of her electoral coalition and realized the impossibility of transforming it into a governing coalition. The votes of Lake Shore liberals, blacks, and Northwest Side white ethnics put her into office, but those groups shared only their common dislike of Bilandic. Now that he was gone, how could Byrne keep her patchwork coalition together? Her major constituent groups had contradictory notions of what should be done and essentially conflicting interests. Placating one would antagonize the others; the coalition would unravel, and the mayor would be caught in the middle, appearing powerless and ineffective. As mayor of Chicago, she did not intend to become another Michael Bilandic, an object of public derision; she intended to be a chief executive in the mold of The Greatest Mayor Chicago Ever Had.

While she had served in Mayor Daley's administration, Byrne did not seem to understand fully how he had fashioned his system of governance, or on what it depended. The mayors who preceded Daley, lacking control over the party organization, found their governmental powers limited by their political need to pacify the committeemen, who often were little concerned with or interested in citywide problems. Because Daley combined political and governmental power in his own hands, he was able to use each of his two offices to strengthen the powers of the other. The Machine was the central institution in Daley's system of governance because it enabled him to control the administrative, legislative, and judicial branches of the city government, and to limit the ambitions and powers of other politicians. The smooth functioning of the Machine, in turn, depended on harmonizing the interests of its three constituent elements—the ward committeemen, the city bureaucracy, and the business/banking/labor communities. The Machine's power did not depend on their cooperation, but its capacity to govern the city was in jeopardy without it.[69]

Early in her administration Byrne still sounded like an anti-Machine politician. She continued to denounce the leaders of the Machine, especially former Bilandic supporters, who, she said, sacrificed the interests of the city for their own personal ends. At the same time, she quietly behaved like a Machine politician, threatening reluctant Machine regulars with the loss of their patronage and prerogatives. And this two-sided approach paid dividends. The ward politicians remained on the defensive, anxiously seeking an accommodation, while her public behavior made headlines, pleased her electoral coalition, and conveyed an impression of movement and change to the populace.

The appearance was illusory. Byrne never intended, and never initiated, any radical departures in public policy; she planned a return to Daley's policies. She never intended to dismantle the Machine; she planned to subordinate it, to control it, to rule the city through it as Daley had for so long. Of course Byrne made the customary disclaimer, saying that as mayor "I hope to keep myself busy with city government and I don't want to concern myself with politics." But wasn't it the favorite maxim of Daley himself that "good government is good politics and good politics is good government"?[70] As her mentor had, Byrne saw the two as inseparable; and, following his practice, she began her administration with a commitment to improve the quality of the city's public services. That approach had some additional advantages. It demonstrated her responsiveness, since it was, after all, the breakdown of those services that had aroused public discontent with Bilandic. It allowed her to concentrate on a tried and proven tactic she was familiar with, rather than

risking some new policy thrust that surely would splinter her fragile voting coalition. Finally, it provided an explanation for an attack
on the bureaucracy, the branch of city government that she most
feared and distrusted.

During the campaign, Byrne spoke of shaking up the bureaucracy,
making it more sensitive and responsive to the citizenry. To blacks,
that meant, among other things, a new police superintendent; an action to which Byrne explicitly committed herself. To the white ethnic neighborhoods, it implied a pledge to upgrade services. To Byrne,
it involved an opportunity to dismiss the bureaucrats whom she saw
as Bilandic's allies and friends, and whom she felt could not be trusted.
Within a year after becoming mayor, she replaced nearly all the
major department heads with her own appointees. But Daley and
Bilandic, for the most part, had staffed the top level of city departments with professionals, limiting patronage appointees to the second and lower levels of the bureaucracy. When Byrne dismissed the
trained professionals, often replacing them with persons whose
prime qualification was loyalty to her, she impaired the efficiency of
the city departments and disrupted an important aspect of Daley's
system. By leaving the departments in the hands of appointees unfamiliar with past policies and unprepared to develop new ones, she
reduced the independence and power of the bureaucracy.

The purge of the top level of the bureaucracy, and declining morale
at its lower levels, made the city government increasingly dependent
on control and direction from the mayor's office. But Byrne had no
way of taking advantage of this new set of conditions; it was difficult
enough to keep track from one day to the next of who worked for the
office of the mayor. In her first year she appointed two former news-
papermen, who had no administrative experience, as top aides and
then removed them; one comptroller resigned, and she fired another;
she hired and fired a budget director; and she went through three
press secretaries, ending up with her husband, who lacked both administrative experience and discretion.

The mayor's revolving-door approach to staffing her office became
an object of public ridicule. Some of her deposed aides joined in the
laughter, claiming that they lacked trust and confidence in her. She
always fired back, of course, and her elliptical and often untruthful
statements simply compounded the problem. So did her daily, and
sometimes hourly, shoot-from-the-lip press conferences, the "gang-
bangs" that City Hall reporters enjoyed almost as much as the mayor.
"The city that works" had become a shambles under Bilandic; now
under Byrne it was becoming a circus.[71]

The larger part of the problem was not how the public saw these
comings and goings, but their effect on the city government. High
administrative turnover prevented Byrne from creating a strong

policy-formulating and decision-making mechanism at the top of the city government. But without such an apparatus, no centralized planning was possible, and the bureaucracy continued to drift into inertia, looking in vain for direction from the mayor's office. Moreover, the mayor herself was reduced to making ad hoc decisions, often on the spur of the moment, without much thought of how they related to each other or to any larger plan.

Uncertain of the policy direction of the Byrne Administration, unfamiliar with the new faces in the bureaucracy, and unsure of their own status in the mayor's still undefined scheme of things, the banking, business, and labor constituencies also drifted into a stance of anxious waiting. They saw that Byrne was dismantling Daley's old system of relationships among political, governmental, and private interests, but they didn't know what plan she had in mind for a new order to replace it. Neither, of course, did she; Byrne simply had no comprehensive plan for building a new system of governance.

As governmental disarray and bureaucratic drift continued, the labor groups, especially, became upset. Several of them had endorsed Byrne during the campaign because she had promised written contracts to the public employees' unions. But now she seemed to be stalling, trying to perpetuate the old system of handshake deals, which left work rules and disciplinary procedures undefined and job security tenuous. By the end of Byrne's first year as mayor, the old cooperation between labor and the city government ended in a series of strikes that suspended city services and embittered the relationship between the mayor and the unions.

Chicago Transit Authority workers struck on 17 December 1979, when negotiations broke down over the CTA's changes in the cost-of-living formula and its use of part-time employees. The rapid transit workers and the bus drivers had been working without a contract since the beginning of the month, and Byrne had responded to the possibility of a strike by saying that she could have "10,000 women" ready to drive the buses and that strikers could be replaced by the unemployed. When the strike began, she accused the union leaders of reneging on an earlier (8 December) agreement to continue negotiating but again claimed that contingency plans had been developed to cope with the work stoppage. No one, and especially not the 700,000 Chicagoans left without public transportation, could figure out what those plans were. Two days later, in a joint press conference with the chairman of the CTA, the mayor called the strikers "greedy" and signalled her rejection of the latest union offer. She explained her decision by referring again to her claim that the unions had broken an earlier agreement not to strike, adding, "If a dog bites you once, it's his fault. If it bites you twice, it's your fault." She wasn't going to give in, she said on another occasion, because "if I did, there would be a strike every year." In the end, of course, she did give in, but only after earning a reputation as a "strike breaker and union buster."[72]

On the day the CTA strike began, the Chicago Firefighters Union, whose members had failed to authorize a work stoppage a year earlier, voted 4 to 1 to call a strike if Byrne refused to enter into contract negotiations. The two sides postured and talked for nearly two months after that; then, on 8 February 1980, the day that her chief negotiator presented what he described as the city's "last and final offer," Byrne appeared on an early morning radio program and warned that "there would be firings immediately" if a strike began. The union connected the two statements and accused the mayor of trying to "antagonize and provoke" the firemen.[73] If that was her intention, she succeeded: the firefighters went out on strike on St. Valentine's Day.

Byrne was furious. "Anyone who doesn't report to work . . . will never again work for the Chicago Fire Department. Never!" And the city immediately sought a restraining order, as it had in the CTA strike. Four days later, Byrne called a press conference to denounce "the terroristic tactics of roving goon squads," claiming that since "firemen who want to live up to their oaths are coming back . . . in increasing numbers," there was "adequate manpower to provide protection and services in all areas of the city." Most of the city's firehouses were still open, she added falsely. But to reassure citizens, the mayor announced that the city would enlist new recruits "to fill permanent vacancies created by dismissals caused by those on strike." The city, she said, would never resume negotiations with the union. "There aren't any negotiations. We're going to allow the commissioner to run the fire department of the City of Chicago."[74]

It was the campaign all over again: Byrne fighting the entrenched powers, and the public apparently rallying behind its feisty mayor. WBBM-TV (Channel 2) reported the results of a survey of public opinion, showing that 71 percent of the city's residents opposed the firemen's strike. The mayor held firm: twenty-three days after they walked out, and with the president of their union in jail for violation of a court order to end the strike, the firemen voted to return to work. The city agreed to drop charges against the union president, to reemploy the strikers, although not granting the total amnesty the union wanted, and to negotiate the remaining differences. The mayor won the battle with the firefighters, but her victory further alienated the city's labor constituency.[75]

Sandwiched between the CTA strike in December and the firemen's strike in February, the Chicago Teachers Union engaged in a work stoppage. In November 1979, in the face of yet another financial crisis in the school system, Superintendent Joseph Hannon had abruptly resigned. On his final day as superintendent, Hannon warned against a City Hall takeover of the school system, saying "it cannot become the 51st ward." Byrne immediately attacked, charging that Hannon had lied about the real size of the school system's deficit. With Hannon's resignation and the public controversy about the deficit, the patchwork alliance of city government, the financial community, and the school administration, which had kept the system's finances afloat and the schools open, fell apart.[76]

As the crisis deepened in December and early January, the Board of Education, the mayor, the governor, legislative leaders, and bankers worked to develop a bail-out scheme to keep the schools open. Their efforts eventually produced a plan that provided an infusion of additional funds, required cuts in the school system's current budget, created an oversight authority to control future budgets, and authorized the mayor to replace any or all of the members of the Board of Education by the end of April. In the interim, as the Board, the union, and the mayor battled over the shape and size of the budget cuts, the system ran out of cash, and the teachers experienced payless paydays.

On 24 January 1980, the mayor announced a plan to allow the teachers to receive partial pay in return for $60 million in budget cuts, and her press secretary (and husband) told reporters that "there is no way she is going to let the schools close. That is absolutely unacceptable." On Monday, 28 January, the work stoppage began, and one week later, the teachers, by a 3-to-1 margin, formally authorized a strike to prevent the job and pay losses required by the $60 million budget reduction. Byrne lashed out at the teachers for their greed, claiming that "the immediate cause of the crisis is the refusal of the Chicago Teachers Union to live up to the commitment made by [its president]." Then she aided the union by undermining the Board of Education's attempt to keep the schools open. "I wouldn't send my child," she said, "if the teachers aren't going to be there." Two weeks after it began, the work stoppage ended, with the union winning back about half the jobs and programs it sought to restore. And the mayor won the ire of both the teachers and the parents of the city's public school students.[77]

In her battles against the CTA workers, the firemen, and the teachers, Byrne depicted herself as the lonely warrior defending the city's financial integrity against the clout of the greedy union bosses. That portrayal made good headlines, and it may have won some fleeting popular approval; but it caused alarm among the bankers and businessmen. She spoke of staggering city deficits and began to criticize not only Bilandic but Daley for the financial mess she inherited. The financial community panicked. The city's bond ratings dropped twice, and analysts blamed the city's sagging credit rating on the confrontations, confusion, and chaos stirred up by its mayor. It was proving "really bad for the [city] government to have a person in the mayor's office who is . . . a nutcake."[78]

Because she had permanently weakened the bureaucracy, Byrne was not able to use it as Daley had to counter the influence of the ward politicians. Her attacks on the unions, the chaos that strained relations with the financial and business communities, and her rebuff to blacks, all lessened her chances to enlist these constituencies against the current leaders of the Machine. In the end, she was left with nowhere else to turn for support but to the "evil cabal," to the very persons whom she had denounced during the campaign.

That alliance was neither accidental nor the product of desperation on the mayor's part. As consumer sales commissioner, Byrne had been primarily a political aide to Mayor Daley and not a bureaucrat. Her talents and instincts were political, not administrative, and as mayor it was almost inevitable that she would turn to the politicians with whom she was familiar and to the political practices with which she had experience. Moreover, given her ambitions and the circumstances that existed, it was also almost inevitable that she would turn to politicians like Vrdolyak and Burke, the dominant figures among the so-called "Young Turks" on the council. While both were party regulars, neither had close political associations with Mayor Daley, his family, or his circle of political intimates. Both were intensely ambitious men, willing to battle for a larger share of power, as their earlier roles in the "coffee club" rebellion against Daley and Keane indicated. Their political and personal drives meshed with Byrne's need for allies as she pursued her goal of becoming another Mayor Daley.[79]

The immediate obstacle to Byrne's ambition was another Daley— State Senator Richard M. Daley, the eldest son and presumed political heir of The Greatest Mayor Chicago Ever Had. The Chicago media, and some of the city's politicians, were fascinated by the idea of a Daley Dynasty, with Richie as the anointed and groomed successor to his father. His Honor's untimely death postponed the passing of the scepter, but many assumed that Bilandic was chosen simply to keep the mayor's chair warm for the inevitable coming of another Daley. There was even some speculation when Byrne announced her candidacy that she was simply a stalking-horse for Richie. That was the wildest of rumors, of course, and it gained even fleeting credibility only because most of the media treated the mayoralty as Richie Daley's patrimony, wondering only when and how he would move to lay claim to it.

All of the reports, rumors, and speculation fueled Byrne's ample paranoia; she became convinced that Richard M. Daley would challenge her bid for reelection in 1983. Given that belief, it was logical that she would forge an alliance with those party regulars who had interests of their own in checking Daley's political power, and just as logical that they would exploit her ambition and political vulnerability to pursue their own objectives. The quid pro quo relationship gave Byrne leverage with the Machine, while allowing Vrdolyak and Burke to maintain and even expand the power they had begun to acquire during the Bilandic interlude.

The conflict between Byrne and Daley quickly took on the appearance of an Irish blood feud, but there was a great deal more at stake than personal ambitions. Their rivalry became the focal point of a larger battle between contending factions of Chicago's Democratic Machine. The issue involved in that struggle was whether the ward committeemen would control the Machine, or whether it would dominate them, as it had for so long under Mayor Daley. Since the Machine was the city's ruling institution, the power of the ward committeemen to control the city was also at stake.

To be sure, the battle lines were not tidy; they rarely are in factional struggles. Personal loyalties and ongoing feuds produced some unlikely allies on both sides. There were also lingering traces of older conflicts—the resentment the North Siders and the eastern Europeans felt toward the South Siders and the Irish. Moreover, since most of the committeemen were habitual followers, content to go along with any lead in return for continued status, patronage, and clout, their interests became identified with a few prominent personalities. As a result, the media presented the struggle largely in personal terms, concentrating on its leading figures and ignoring its structural aspect.

The structural dimension was the more important of the two for the city government and the citizens of Chicago. By virtue of their backgrounds and the requirements for their continued success, Chicago's ward committeemen have always been parochial creatures, subordinating public needs and citywide concerns to their own private interests and the needs of their wards. Because Daley had controlled the party and professionalized the top level of the bureaucracy, he had limited the ward committeemen's influence over public policy. During Daley's Administrations, his definition of the public interest took precedence over the private interests of the ward committeemen and the parochial needs of their wards. Under Mayor Bilandic, who didn't control the party as Daley had, the ward committeemen began to reassert their influence, but the bureaucracy still operated as a counter to their control over city policy. Mayor Byrne cleaned out the professional bureaucrats, alienated most of the elements of the makeshift coalition that had elected her, and relied on the ward politicians to govern the city. In the process, their private interests and parochial concerns came to dominate public policy at the expense of the city's public needs.[80]

The opposition faction was not a group of reforming politicians set on dismantling the Machine. Some were old guard regulars, politically indebted to the late mayor and still dependent on the support of his loyalists. Others, like Cook County Assessor Thomas Hynes (19th Ward) and Congressman Daniel Rostenkowski (32d Ward), had political involvements beyond their ward bases and were dissatisfied with a new system that subordinated their interests to the demands of the parochial ward chieftains. These groups of regulars challenged the Machine, not to destroy it but to take it over and to restore Mayor Daley's system of governance.

The fight for control burst into public view within six months of Byrne's becoming mayor. Presidential politics was the sideshow providing the occasion for the first round of the battle between Byrne and Daley. In late October 1979, when Byrne held a fund raiser with President Jimmy Carter as the featured speaker, she told the audience that "if the convention were tonight, I would vote . . . to renominate our present leader for four more years." Two weeks later, Byrne endorsed Senator Edward M. Kennedy for president. She then quickly engineered a Kennedy endorsement by the Democratic Central Committee of Cook County, berated Senator Daley for not going along, and moved to show her power by firing or demoting about twenty of his 11th Ward precinct captains.[81]

Daley fought back. On 19 November he announced that he would seek the Democratic nomination for state's attorney, the only county office then held by a Republican. The decision was a surprise, since observers had expected him to run for clerk of the circuit court, an office loaded with patronage jobs. Instead, he chose the higher profile state's attorney's office, which would put him in a position to oversee Byrne's activities and possibly serve as a springboard for a run against her in the next mayoral election. By running for state's attorney, Daley also avoided challenging an incumbent Democrat, thus showing his continued loyalty to the party's traditions.

Byrne did not miss the significance of Daley's announcement, and she spent the next several days searching for a candidate to oppose his try for the nomination. Alderman Edward Burke finally announced that he would seek the nomination, "but only with the endorsement of the Democratic party." Byrne and Vrdolyak attended to that detail, and on 29 December the Central Committee endorsed Burke. Despite arm-twisting by Byrne and her allies, and even after Daley asked that his name be withdrawn, seven committeemen voted "present" and two prominent figures, Assessor Hynes and former Lieutenant Governor Neil Hartigan, stayed away from the session.

As Burke acknowledged in accepting the endorsement, there was "divisiveness in the party, but this party is bigger than one man or one woman."[82]

Unfortunately for Burke, the party wasn't bigger than Jane Byrne. The strikes by CTA employees, the teachers, and the firemen focused anti-Byrne feeling, and Daley rode the crest of that sentiment. "There are a lot of people out there who hate her guts," a Northwest Side Democratic committeeman said. "They think a vote for Daley is a vote against Byrne. She is killing [Burke]." Things were so bad that some of the twenty-eight Democratic committeemen who were facing challenges began to pass out Daley literature, and even more voiced resentment of Byrne for forcing them into a battle between two regular Democrats. During the final weekend of the campaign, Burke spent his effort denying that he was Byrne's candidate. "Elect me, not Byrne," he desperately pleaded with voters.[83]

Not many voters heeded his plea. Daley buried Burke in the city, defeating him in every geographic area and among all the major voting groups except Hispanics (Table 12). And to everyone's surprise, Daley even ran ahead in the suburbs. The easy victory weakened Byrne's prestige and further fueled speculation that Daley would run for mayor in 1983. In his victory speech, Daley referred to Byrne's harsh attacks on his candidacy and the Daley name. "No one can destroy a name," he said. "No one can destroy a family . . . yours or mine. And no one can destroy a spirit."[84]

Daley ran for state's attorney against the Byrne-Vrdolyak-Burke faction to increase his power within the Machine, not to overthrow it. Once the primary votes were counted, he expected to "start hearing from the ward committeemen." Those messages came quickly, starting with County Democratic Chairman George Dunne, who said "the voters have spoken and we accept their wisdom." Even Byrne indicated her backing, saying, "I'd support any Democrat" who won the primary.[85]

Daley's campaign strategists weren't anxious for Byrne's support, thinking she was a political liability. If voters perceived her moving toward Daley, it might cut his appeal among independents and blacks, whose support he needed in the general election against the incumbent Republican, Bernard Carey. Taping a radio interview two days after the primary, Daley voiced concern that close ties with Byrne would politicize his campaign and the office. While welcoming the support of the "Regular Democratic Organization," he minimized the significance of Byrne's backing. "She's one person. I'm not just looking for the support of one person. I'm looking for the support of many people."[86]

Byrne did not take the bait right away; she remained on the sidelines through the early stages of the Daley-Carey contest. In mid-

Table 12. The Race for State's Attorney, 1980: Regression Estimates of Group Voting Behavior[1]

	Primary Election			General Election		
	Daley	Burke	Nonvote	Daley (D)	Carey (R)	Nonvote
Citywide[2]						
Blacks	11.9	8.3	79.3	38.2	14.2	47.2
Whites	22.2	12.2	65.4	38.5	31.0	30.3
Hispanics	5.2	10.1	83.9	19.6	0.6	79.1
Blacks						
Dawson wards	13.7	8.7	77.5	42.2	13.0	44.7
Other South Side	13.4	7.6	78.9	37.0	17.6	45.3
West Side	8.2	7.6	84.1	35.8	9.5	54.6
White Ethnics	25.2	13.2	61.5	39.7	29.8	30.3
Northwest Side	18.3	12.8	68.8	32.6	33.6	33.6
South Side	33.3	13.6	53.0	47.8	25.5	26.5
Total citywide	14.9	9.8	75.1	32.5	20.0	47.4

[1] Entries are percentages of voting-age population, and rows sum to 100 percent, except for rounding error.

[2] Developed by weighting the estimates for each group within eight subareas of the city.

September, she finally entered the fray with a vengeance. She reacted strongly and publicly to the fact that she and several of her allies among the committeemen had not been invited to a Daley fund-raising dinner featuring Rosalyn Carter. The Daley campaign has "become a campaign of hate," she said, adding that "most of the men he had disinvited had carried Mayor Daley in their wards. . . . They were some of the men who were the closest and greatest advisers to him [Mayor Daley]. . . . [While] most of the people he's working with did everything they could to destroy his father." Still, she vowed she would support Daley because "we're all Democrats." William Daley, the candidate's brother and campaign manager, interpreted the outburst differently. "Mayor Byrne has stated that she's going to stay out of the state's attorney's race," he said. "Apparently, she has changed her mind."[87]

Actually, she hadn't changed her mind at all: she had wanted to see Daley defeated from the outset. Most of the county's voters were aware of that. In an early October poll, 70 percent said that they thought Byrne wanted Daley to lose. The ward committeemen had even fewer doubts, since she and her allies encouraged them to make only a tepid effort on Daley's behalf. The defection rate among the committeemen was so high—only about ten of the fifty were in Daley's corner—that his campaign bypassed the regular Democratic organizations in the wards and set up its own campaign groups.

When the Daley camp aired these charges publicly, the tension escalated.[88]

The mayor's husband and press secretary, Jay McMullen, denied that Byrne was working against Daley. "That's a very sick, paranoid charge," he claimed. "I don't know what's going on in his [Daley's] mind, but there's a nest of wooly caterpillars in there somewhere. . . . Maybe he should see a psychiatrist to find out what's wrong." But three pro-Byrne black committeemen announced that they were thinking of supporting Carey, and this simply added credence to Daley's charges.[89]

In late October, Byrne "just got jammed up and couldn't fit" into her schedule the first of two traditional preelection rallies of precinct captains. Daley attended the meeting at the Bismarck Hotel, gave a dull and unenthusiastically received speech, and shrugged off questions from reporters about Byrne's boycott. The following day, 22 October, Byrne ended the charade and formally withdrew her earlier endorsement of Daley, accusing him of condoning the use of the inspection powers of the city building department to discourage racial minorities from living in his 11th Ward. Referring to him as "the so-called Democratic candidate" for state's attorney, Byrne charged that "documented evidence" showed him to be "against all true Democrats, the poor, the blacks, and the Latinos who helped elect me mayor." She could no longer in "good conscience" pretend to endorse such a candidate, even though he had "begged" for her support behind the scenes as "part of his phoney pretense that he is an independent candidate."[90]

Whether by design or by accident, Byrne's charges hit Daley where he was vulnerable—with independents and black voters. The claim that he was secretly plotting with the committeemen dulled the image of professionalism that he had carefully cultivated to attract independent voters. The allegation of racism threatened his appeal among blacks, whose support Daley needed in large numbers to offset Carey's anticipated margin in the suburbs. To repair the damage among both constituencies, Daley struck back in his speech at the final rally of precinct captains. He accused Byrne of teaming up with the Republican Carey to orchestrate a campaign of "McCarthyism" against him. They have used "the technique of the Big Lie . . . [spewing] out a stream of innuendos, smears, and false charges." Why had they formed this alliance? "They need each other," he answered. Carey needs Byrne to get reelected, and Byrne needs Carey because in eight years he has failed to prosecute a single corrupt public official. After this election, Daley asked, "will there be anybody in a position to hold all public officials, including Mayor Byrne, accountable? Anybody to insist that there are standards of law and decency to govern the conduct of public officials, including hers?" If not,

Byrne's "policy of ruling by fear—of threatening the livelihood of families— . . . will not end. It will not be the exception—it will be the rule." Then he reminded the precinct workers that "to satisfy Mayor Byrne's ruthless desire for power," loyalty, the chief maxim of his father's political creed, had been sacrificed. "I know there is pressure on many of you, but isn't this the time to be truly loyal to . . . our city and our party? . . . Shouldn't we unite in the general election as we have always done, whether the candidate was my father, or Governor Walker, . . . or George McGovern—or Jane Byrne?"[91]

It was "a remarkable speech," as the *Chicago Tribune* characterized it. A Democrat named Daley addressed the Machine's foot soldiers and attacked the Democratic mayor. Accustomed only to responding on cue, most of the loyalists didn't know how to behave; so they sat in stunned silence. As usual, however, Alderman Vito Marzullo (25th Ward) wasn't speechless. "All is fair in war," he told a reporter. "And what do you think this is?"[92]

Marzullo was right; it was a war for power within the Machine, and Bernard Carey was to be its first casualty. He had to spend the final week of the campaign trying to distance himself from Byrne by defending Daley against her scattershot attacks. Carey claimed that the mayor's charges of racist scheming by Daley were "unfair, coming so close to the election," since there simply wasn't time to investigate them fully. "These are not my charges; I want to make that clear," he said. "[Daley] has enjoyed . . . fighting with the mayor," he claimed on election eve, because "that makes him appear to be a martyr or a victim." But by then Carey realized he was the victim. "I have stood outside the battle and got the fallout. It's like standing too close to Mt. St. Helens. Every time it erupts, I get covered with the ashes." He implored voters to decide between him and Daley on the basis of their relative qualifications and to disregard their feelings for Byrne. "If you are angry and outraged at Jane Byrne, don't make me the innocent victim of that battle."[93]

Carey was hardly an unoffending innocent, of course, but he did become a victim of the conflict between Byrne and Daley.[94] That battle captured the headlines, let Daley run as an underdog opposed by the leaders of the Machine, foreclosed discussion of the state's attorney's office, and created a context within which Carey's recitation of Daley's shortcomings appeared to be just another personal attack. By injecting herself into the campaign, Byrne let Daley make the election into a referendum on her popularity. She gave Daley what he needed—an issue to counter Carey's media endorsements, his scandal-free record, and his lack of significant political enemies. She also may have given him what he needed to mobilize black support. Daley won among blacks by a wider margin than among whites or Hispanics, and his edge was especially large in the Machine strongholds on the South and West Sides (see Table 12). Despite her charges of racism, blacks obviously did not regard Daley in the same way they had Hanrahan eight years earlier.[95]

By using the contest for state's attorney to gain power within the Machine, Byrne torpedoed Burke and Carey, while displaying her own lack of clout at the polls. She also made herself even more dependent on the anti-Daley faction among the committeemen. Without their backing, how could she prevent Daley from claiming his patrimony in 1983?

Jane Byrne and her husband—press secretary remained in the eye of the city's political storms over the next two years. She continued to act, change her mind, act again, explain that away, and then claim that none of it had ever happened, or that the media reported it inaccurately. But through it all, she made news, and her approval rating in the polls fluctuated widely and wildly, as the public responded to each imbroglio. She watched the poll reports, especially the early comparisons with the newly elected state's attorney, because she was convinced that "Daley and the entire Daley family have been running against me since the day I walked in the door."[96] And she prepared for Armageddon. In her four years as mayor, Byrne staged a series of splashy fund raisers that built her war chest to a reported $10 million, a sum which itself became an issue in the 1983 primary. She used those funds during her term to pay political advisers, including her husband; to dole out food and cash to black churches and community groups; and, finally, to finance her campaign for renomination, including an unprecedented and effective media blitz designed to present "New Jane" to the city's voters.

Byrne's political fund gave her clout, of a sort; but the clout that counted most in Chicago was the Machine's endorsement, especially for an incumbent whose popularity chart looked like a roller-coaster track. And grass-roots resentment lingered over from the 1980 primary fight; a cadre of Daley loyalists still remained among the committeemen, and Byrne especially suspected the loyalty of George Dunne, chairman of the Cook County Democratic Central Committee. Dunne had been as close (or closer) to the Daley family as any of the late mayor's longtime political associates, and he appeared to Byrne too eager to bestow his blessings on Richie after the 1980 primary. Byrne wanted her own allies in charge of the Central Committee, and they willingly took advantage of her insecurity to consolidate their power within the Machine.

By late March 1982, it was clear to reporters that Dunne's tenure was in jeopardy. On 22 March, Dunne charged that Byrne was "waging a campaign of patronage pressure and intimidation" to line up the committeemen to help replace him. As usual, Byrne denied the charge, while spending her time on the telephone and in closed-door meetings doing exactly what she was denying. Committeeman Matthew Bieszczat (26th Ward) reported that Byrne's patronage chief offered him jobs in return for his vote against Dunne. Even the mayor's political associates acknowledged that her fears of Daley prompted the move against Dunne. On 29 March, thirty-nine of the fifty city committeemen, including many who had committed their backing to Dunne previously, voted to replace him with Alderman Edward Vrdolyak. Chicago Park District Superintendent (and 47th Ward committeeman) Edmund Kelly, long a political associate of Vrdolyak and more recently of Byrne as well, became chairman of the party's executive committee, the group that played the key role in the slating process.[97]

Dumping Dunne was widely heralded as a move that increased Byrne's strength within the Machine. No doubt its timing came at Byrne's initiative; her use of patronage weaned support away from Dunne, and she eased the way for her own slating in the mayoral primary. But Dunne, who had neither dominated the Central Committee nor worked to obstruct Byrne's maneuvers, was replaced by Vrdolyak, who certainly did not see himself as a pliable figurehead, content merely to do the mayor's (or anyone else's) bidding. Both Vrdolyak and Byrne wanted to stop Daley, and Vrdolyak was more likely than Dunne to be willing and able to cajole or muscle doubtful committeemen into line. In that sense, but only in that sense, his replacement of Dunne represented a victory for Byrne.

Vrdolyak, however, was a hard-nosed political infighter who had shown earlier that he wasn't reluctant to slug it out for his share (and more) of the benefits, both political and tangible, that the Machine had to distribute.[98] Elected first as committeeman of the 10th Ward, with the cooperation of the incumbent alderman, Vrdolyak in 1971 challenged his partner and the Machine and was elected to the City Council, despite Tom Keane's campaign efforts on behalf of his opponent. In the City Council he became a leader of the "coffee club" rebels in 1972–1973, and in 1974, he unsuccessfully fought the Machine's candidate for county assessor. Not an Irishman and never an insider in Mayor Daley's court, Vrdolyak, if not the most ambitious, was certainly the most talented of the younger cadre of Machine committeemen. Outwardly amiable and disarmingly gracious, he was urbane, verbally facile, and more conscious of public relations than most of the ward barons. Yet his power ultimately derived from his leadership skills and his network of personal relations with those ward chieftains who, like him, had been kept on the periphery of power by Mayor Daley. Now in control of the Central Committee and aided by his associates and fellow outsiders, Edward Burke and Edmund Kelly, who presided over his own patronage preserve in the Chicago Park District, Vrdolyak was at the center of power.

With Vrdolyak, their leader and spokesman as party chairman, the parochial ward barons once again dominated the Machine. As mayor, Byrne still controlled the chief sources of jobs and lucrative contracts; but the ward politicians controlled the party, and she needed the Machine for her reelection bid more than it needed her. As a result, the private economic and political interests of the ward chieftains came to shape public policy in Byrne's Chicago.

Factional struggles within dominant parties sometimes open the way for previously underrepresented groups to gain leverage. When the factions are closely matched, one or both may seek to broaden its base of support by appealing beyond its core constituency. Excluded or underrepresented groups can then capitalize on this competition to gain a larger share of influence for themselves. However, the struggle between the factions of Chicago's Machine did not have that result for the city's black community. Both factions sought to control the Machine and to rule city politics, but without sharing power with blacks. Both were committed to maintaining white cultural dominance by subordinating the racial concerns and interests of black citizens to those of the party's white ethnic constituents. Regardless of which faction won the war, the black "plantations" and their people were its certain losers.

Leaders of the Machine's factions were simply unwilling to risk white ethnic support by representing black racial interests. That was a losing proposition electorally, given the low turnout among blacks and the high rates of mobilization among the city's white ethnic voters. Moreover, as long as black politicians relied more heavily on the Machine's backing than on the support of their communities, they could be controlled and counted on to sacrifice racial interests to the needs of the Machine. Under these conditions, blacks were treated as ciphers in the arithmetic of the power struggle. Black leaders were regarded as pawns to be manipulated, and black voters as subjects to be ruled, but neither was viewed by the white leadership as potentially coequal partners in the exercise of power.

But no conditions are forever unchangeable. By the late 1970s, blacks no longer passively accepted the Machine's rejection of their claims for fair and equal treatment. They were no longer content to be silent subjects of the regime, represented in its councils by persons indifferent or insensitive to the racial interests of the black community. Moreover, some of the leaders of the black community had learned the lessons of the recent primaries: the Machine was *not* invincible, and *black* voters could make the difference.

6. The Politics of Race
The Democratic Mayoral Primary, 1983

A vote for Daley is a vote for Washington. . . . It's a racial thing; don't kid yourself.
Edward Vrdolyak

■ Thousands of people streamed into Chicago's McCormick Inn on the evening of 22 February 1983. They filled one ballroom, then a second, and finally overflowed into the corridors. They burst into cheers and screams with every rumor of concession by the opposition candidates. "We want Harold. We want Harold," they chanted until many of them were hoarse. Typical of the Washington campaign, the gathering was part celebration and part religious revival. There was a cash bar dispensing drinks and a jazz band playing music, but the throng joined the Reverend Jesse Jackson in prayer and sang "We Shall Overcome," the anthem of their crusade. Even before the final results were in, the predominantly black crowd hugged, kissed, and congratulated each other. "We did it. We did it," they shouted. "I couldn't stay home," one young black woman told reporters. "This is history in the making."

She and the others had come there to share in Harold Washington's big night. But there was a larger reason for their joy. Washington's triumph was a symbol of their own political liberation. "Dr. Martin Luther King is surely smiling in heaven tonight," Jesse Jackson commented. "Fred Hampton and Mark Clark can sleep at night now. No more sharecropping precinct captains."[1]

The final tally showed what they had done. Harold Washington polled the support of 36.5 percent of the 1.21 million voters participating in the Democratic primary, and he won the party's mayoral nomination by a margin of 35,887 votes over his closest rival.

As both the revelers and the candidate knew, most of his votes came from black citizens. An extraordinary political contagion had swept through the black community and made itself felt in the high registration, turnout, and cohesive voting that had marked the November 1982 general election, even before Washington formally announced his candidacy for mayor. In turn, this political awakening shaped the 1983 revolution in Chicago's electoral politics.

"Come Alive October Five"

■ The most significant feature of Chicago's 1982 and 1983 electoral seasons was the political mobilization of its black community. After decades of control and manipulation by the city's Democratic Machine, Chicago's blacks awakened to their own racial interests and used the ballot box to advance them. By registering and voting in unprecedented numbers, blacks shook the standing order and permanently changed the shape of the city's politics. Both distant and local sources had aroused the political consciousness of Chicago's blacks. All over the country, blacks turned out at unusually high rates in November 1982, and they voted even more solidly Democratic than they had in the 1980 presidential election. Ronald Reagan, more than anyone else, was unwittingly responsible for this development.[2]

Blacks saw the Reagan Administration as indifferent, if not hostile, to their needs and aspirations. Its anti-inflation policies pushed unemployment among the black labor force to depression-era levels, while its budget cutbacks reduced employment opportunities for blacks in the public sector and cut social assistance to the poor. Reaganomics was "a rich man's economics," unfair and insensitive to the precarious economic situation of minorities. At the same time, the administration's stalling on the extension of the Voting Rights Act, its support for tax breaks to segregated private academies, and the Justice Department's intervention to oppose busing and affirmative action guidelines raised doubts concerning its commitment to basic civil rights. As early as spring of 1982, pollsters began detecting a marked racial difference in the assessment of Reagan's performance. "Black voters hate Ronald Reagan with a vengeance, and they will turn out," one Democratic pollster observed in late October. The blacks in Chicago were no exception, and their negative view of the Reagan Administration played a role in stimulating them to register and vote.[3]

In the United States, however, "all politics is local."[4] Organizing and mobilizing voters depends on grass-roots activity, and local developments often have greater impact than global events in shaping voters' evaluations of their political worlds. In Chicago, Jane Byrne gave blacks additional reasons for coming alive politically.

Some of Chicago's blacks may have linked Reagan with Byrne. While campaigning in 1980, Reagan phoned the mayor to assure her that when he was elected Chicago "will have a friend in the White House." For her part, Byrne, unlike the mayors of other northern cities, withheld criticism of Reagan's fiscal policies and publicly supported his "new federalism" initiatives. But most blacks didn't need to dig for links of this sort; the actions of the Byrne Administration gave them an even more powerful set of negative signals.[5]

If blacks thought Jane Byrne's election in 1979 marked the beginning of a new era of responsiveness to their needs and interests, she soon persuaded them otherwise. While her policy stances were often as mercurial and difficult to fathom as her revolving-door approach to personnel appointments, their effect was clear. She cast her lot with the anti-Daley Machine regulars, treated blacks as passive subjects of the regime, and courted the support of white ethnic voters by siding with them on integration issues. Whatever Byrne's mix of motives and calculations, blacks widely perceived her actions to be insensitive and even hostile. "Mayor Byrne has contributed to the development of a slave/master mentality even more than [Mayor] Daley," concluded Lu Palmer, head of Chicago Black United Communities. "Under Daley, you knew where you stood. The impression with Byrne is that she is working in the interests of black people when actually she is destroying our interests."[6]

Much of what occurred in the first two years of Byrne's administration aroused doubt and distrust among blacks because she seemed unconcerned with the effect of her actions on their well-being. The strikes by city employees had especially heavy impact on the black community. The CTA strike left blacks who depended on public transportation without a reliable and affordable means to travel to jobs or schools. Byrne's refusal to negotiate and her apparent effort to break the transit workers' unions, both of which were headed by blacks, prompted the Chicago chapter of the Coalition of Black Trade Unionists to criticize the mayor. In January 1980, thousands of black children with working parents and no adequate day-care facilities were deprived of adult supervision during the teachers' strike. The firemen's strike in February 1980 left minority areas, where living conditions were poorest, without protection; and the majority of deaths due to fires during the strike were in the black community.[7]

Byrne also displayed insensitivity to the interests of blacks on other policy questions. She accepted Governor Thompson's transit package, which called for a fare increase that hit poorer residents dependent on public transportation, and she supported an increase in the state sales tax to give the transit authority more money. When some Democrats in the state legislature, including State Senator Richard M. Daley, fought to provide relief for lower-income citizens

by eliminating the sales tax on food and medicine, Byrne successfully fought them. "Nobody cares if the sales tax goes up," one of her
$50,000-a-year aides remarked arrogantly.[8]

Byrne also disappointed blacks on issues that related to their racial interests. During the campaign, Byrne pledged to dismiss Police
Superintendent James O'Grady for politicizing the police force by
supporting Bilandic. Black leaders hoped for the appointment of a
black superintendent to help improve relations between their community and the police after years of mutual distrust and hostility.
They also expected a black superintendent to integrate the department and bring its hiring and promotion policies into compliance
with civil rights laws and court orders. Byrne lifted their hopes by
naming Deputy Superintendent Samuel W. Nolan, a black, as acting
police superintendent. Then, claiming that she wanted to bring in a
new superintendent from outside the department, Byrne eased Nolan
out of the picture and chose a white insider, Richard Brzeczek, as
superintendent.[9]

Byrne was also unwilling to relinquish white control of the Board
of Education. When Joseph Hannon resigned in November 1979,
Byrne rejected requests from black community groups, passed over
black Deputy Superintendent Manford Byrd, and appointed his subordinate, Angeline Caruso, a white woman, as acting superintendent. Many black leaders viewed Byrne's decision as "blatant racism." Then, in April 1980, as part of the package of measures that
had been worked out with the governor to ease the school system
past its financial crisis, Byrne reconstituted the entire Board of Education, making a show of appointing more minority members, including five blacks. When the new board decided to elect a black
president of its own choosing, the Reverend Kenneth Smith, she denounced its action as illegal and "immature" and refused for a time
to swear in the new members. Finally, in January 1981, the Board of
Education recommended a black woman from outside the Chicago
area, Ruth Love, for superintendent, again ignoring the pressures
from the black community for the appointment of Byrd. Byrne now
agreed to a black superintendent, since the 1980 bail-out package
had given control of the budget to a Chicago School Finance Authority, four of whose five members were whites. Black leaders did not
miss the significance of the change. "When they decided to allow a
black superintendent, they brought in a white dude to handle all the
money," Lu Palmer noticed. "The first black superintendent became
the first superintendent who is not handling the budget."[10]

Byrne's handling of the Nolan and Byrd cases implied that blacks
weren't good enough, or properly qualified, for positions of leadership over institutions that were critically important to the black
community. Her actions also indicated that she would not listen to

the recommendations of black community groups or their leaders. When blacks were appointed to important positions, they would be her blacks, or outsiders with no base of support in the city's black community. By using controlled blacks and continuing Mayor Daley's old divide-and-conquer policy, Byrne and the Machine hoped to maintain dominance over the "black plantations" and subordinate the racial interests of their populace to the needs of the city's ruling institution.

On integration issues, Byrne also came down on the side of the Machine's core white ethnic constituency. There were the customary zigs and zags in her approach, and some of her statements and actions confused and even infuriated the anti-integration groups. In the final analysis, however, she tilted in the direction of the white ethnics on questions of school and housing integration.

Mayor Byrne initially seemed more sensitive on integration issues than her predecessors. She was the first city official ever to admit that the school system had been deliberately segregated, and she suggested that things would be different under her administration. But then she rejected the plan by the Office of Civil Rights to use busing to remedy past abuses, and her strident defense of neighborhood schools echoed the sentiments of the white resistance groups. Byrne defended Superintendent Hannon's revised Access to Excellence scheme, which civil rights groups denounced as a sham and HEW rejected, and she showed insensitivity to the black community by appointing a white woman to succeed when Hannon resigned. She named five blacks to the Board of Education in the spring of 1980, used the new Board to negotiate a consent decree with the Justice Department to forestall another court order, and then attacked the Board's plan to comply with the decree. In the process she repudiated her earlier admission that segregation had been deliberate, publicly refused city funding for the Board's desegregation plan, and used the school system's need for new revenue to pressure the Board to change its plan.[11]

Of course even Hannon's pallid scheme and the 1980 consent decree drew fire from the white ethnic communities, and Byrne was the target of much of their criticism. The opposition grew more shrill in the early months of 1981, as the Board of Education worked on a desegregation plan to comply with the decree. Alderman Roman Pucinski, one of the more vocal defenders of the integrity of white neighborhoods and schools, called on Byrne and the Board of Education to repudiate the consent decree and to go back into court. "We don't feel we can do any worse with the Reagan Justice Department, we might do better," he said. While Byrne wasn't willing to go that far, she made clear how superficial her commitment to integration was. "Suppose we got moving on our cable TV program," she said at a press conference, "and suppose the channels from the Board of Education were giving classes to children all over Chicago. Wouldn't that be integration? That would be an integrated program."[12] No reporter bothered to remind her that Hannon had suggested such a scheme in 1977.

The cause of integrated public housing fared no better under Byrne. The mayor first unveiled a scattered-site housing program to comply with earlier court orders, a response which itself was a startling departure from the city's past practices. But Byrne stalled after that, and by late 1981, she repudiated her own scattered-site program. It was better, she said, to spend the money on improvements for existing units than to build new units in white neighborhoods. Blacks could only express their "outrage" at both her turnaround and her later expressions of sympathy and support for white groups that opposed CHA sites in their communities.[13]

Byrne's actions and her strident defenses of them created a generally negative impression among blacks. To repair her image, without jeopardizing her standing among the white ethnics, the mayor made a dramatic move. Prompted by an increase in gang violence at the Cabrini-Green housing project, a cluster of CHA high rises on the near North Side (42d Ward), Byrne announced on 21 March 1981 that she and her husband would move from their Gold Coast apartment and live in the project "for as long as it takes to clean it up." During the nearly three weeks of her highly publicized stay at Cabrini-Green, the number of police patrols and arrests in the area shot up. Even some of her black critics praised her for having "a lot of guts and courage" and took notice of the political benefits she stood to gain. Her action was merely symbolic, but it worked. Her popularity had dropped steadily since she took office, but a poll in April 1981 showed considerable recovery: 50 percent of the respondents approved Byrne's job performance, and nearly a third of those approving volunteered the move to Cabrini-Green as their reason. Some black leaders, however, remained unconvinced. "My reaction," Alderman Danny Davis (20th Ward) said, "is that the mayor has the perception that symbols with black folks can take the place of substance." Black community activists Lu Palmer, Dorothy Tillman, and Marion Stamps led protest demonstrations, charging that Byrne had invaded a law-abiding community and turned it into "a police state."[14]

Some of Byrne's actions and statements implied indifference and insensitivity to blacks; others seemed to be appeals for white ethnic support; and still others smacked of a determined hostility. Blacks saw four major actions by the Byrne Administration as nothing less than a frontal assault. Each aroused black leaders, stimulated their efforts to organize the opposition to Byrne within the black community, and led the way to the voting upheaval that occurred in February 1983.

The Ward Remap

■ When the Census Bureau released its 1980 population data, nineteen of Chicago's wards (under the 1971 boundaries) showed black majorities among their voting-age populations. This represented a gain of four black majority wards during the decade. Since wards are the jurisdictions electing both aldermen and committeemen, determining the location of the boundaries affected minority representation in both the city government and the Democrátic party. Byrne and the Machine regulars, aware of the importance of the redistricting question, designed a remap that diluted black and Hispanic voting power. As finally approved by the City Council, the new ward map restored white majorities to the 15th and 37th Wards, thus reducing the number of wards with a black majority to seventeen, and it split the Hispanic communities on the near Northwest and Southwest Sides among several wards each.

The Chicago Black United Communities, the Christian Action Ministry, and other neighborhood groups organized rallies to arouse public opinion. "Ward reapportionment! Will your ward be wiped out by the political machine and City Hall?" asked one CBUC flyer. They also fought the Byrne Administration in federal court. Several black and Hispanic plaintiffs filed separate suits against the mayor and the City Council, charging a violation of the Voting Rights Act. These actions were ultimately consolidated, and the U.S. Department of Justice joined the case in September 1982. The Council map remained in force through the general election of that year, but in late December the court found in favor of the plaintiffs and ordered a new ward map that restored the black majorities in the 15th and 37th Wards and created four Hispanic majority wards.[15]

Appointments to the Board of Education

■ In February 1981, when the Board of Education was working out its desegregation plan to comply with the 1980 consent decree, Byrne announced plans to replace two black members, whose terms expired on 30 April, with two white women. Her appointees, Betty Bonow from the Bogan area on the Southwest Side and Rose Mary Janus from the Northwest Side, had been vocal opponents of earlier desegregation efforts. The mayor claimed her move was made to "rotate" the terms of members of the Board of Education in keeping with her commitment to the Illinois legislature as part of the 1980 bail-out package. "I didn't write [the agreement]," she said, "but it's wise."[16]

Black legislators who had helped write the agreement indicated no knowledge of any rotation requirement, and the mayor was not replacing the Hispanic member whose term also expired on 30 April. It seemed more than coincidental that Byrne acted just a week after Alderman William Lipinski (23rd Ward), chairman of the City Council's Education Committee, vowed to fight to have the coming vacancies filled by white ethnics. To many blacks, Byrne appeared simply to be playing politics: the white ethnic groups were protesting the consent decree, so she changed the racial composition of the Board of Education to show her commitment to their racial interests. The move was an appeal to white ethnic voters, and it told blacks she did not regard them as an important factor in the city's politics.

The mayor miscalculated. Her appointment of "two racist white women," as one black activist described them, led to a firestorm of protest from the black neighborhoods.[17] Reaction was so strong that eleven of the sixteen black aldermen lined up in opposition, including several who routinely voted with the mayor. By providing community organizers with another symbol of her seemingly arrogant contempt for blacks, Byrne's actions focused grass-roots opposition and became another link in the chain of events leading to the electoral upheaval of 1983.

The Battle against Allan Streeter

■ Jane Byrne's attack on the black alderman from the 17th Ward classically illustrated her determination to keep control of the "plantation provinces." The battle developed from the controversy over the Bonow and Janus appointments.

Streeter, a longtime precinct captain and employee of the city health department, had been appointed by the mayor in January 1981 to fill the aldermanic vacancy caused by the resignation of the black incumbent, Tyrone McFolling. Black community organizations and independents objected to Byrne's choosing their representative for them and filed suit asking the federal court to order a special election. In the meantime, Streeter served in the City Council, was assigned a seat on its Education Committee, and dutifully followed the orders of his ward committeeman to vote for the Bonow and Janus appointments. He hadn't wanted to follow those orders, he later said, but "I did so anyway, against my conscience." As neighborhood groups denounced the appointments, pressure built on the black aldermen who were supporting them, and Streeter had second thoughts. He appealed to his committeeman, William Parker, pointing to "the resentment among the people in our ward"; but Parker repeated the original orders and reportedly told him "to hell with the people." Finally, Streeter rebelled. On 15 April he met with Byrne and informed her that he would vote against the nominations in the

full Council. Despite continuing pressure from his ward committeeman, Streeter stuck with his decision and voted against both appointments. "When race is involved, the machine does not ask for a
compromise," he explained. "The party wants us [the blacks] to sell
our souls and give up our self-respect for what the white bosses
want. I just couldn't take it."[18]

Streeter instantly became an outcast, even being evicted from the
regular Democratic ward office. When the federal court in January
1982 ruled that a special election had to be held for the remainder of
the aldermanic term, Byrne was handed an opportunity to discipline
Streeter and to show other blacks what would happen to them if
they strayed from the plantation. The court set 1 June 1982 as the
date for the special election, and Byrne and the Machine blacks mus-
tered their resources to defeat the rebellious Streeter. Although
Byrne claimed to be neutral in the contest, she injected herself into
it with charges that Streeter was under federal investigation for allegedly accepting bribes and kickbacks while an employee of the Chicago Department of Health. Her attempt to discredit Streeter back-
fired when the United States Attorney quickly dismissed Byrne's
claims, saying the charges were not worthy of prosecution. But the
effort focused public attention on the issue Streeter had used from
the outset—Jane Byrne.

In one of those strange twists that mark Chicago politics, Streeter's
display of independence made him a hero to the groups that originally opposed his appointment. With Byrne and the Machine using
all of the patronage muscle at their disposal, even sending in patronage workers from the 3rd, 9th, 15th, 16th, 21st, and 34th Wards,
the black neighborhood organizations and independents rallied to
Streeter's cause. He narrowly led the field in the 1 June election, and
he polled 55.6 percent of the vote in the bitterly contested runoff on
29 June against the candidate of the regular organization. "There's
no question but that Byrne was the issue," Streeter said after the returns were in. "People came out to register their protest. That was
the key."[19]

Appointments to the Chicago Housing Authority

■ Following a lengthy investigation and extended negotiation with
the city, the U.S. Department of Housing and Urban Development recommended the replacement of Charles Swibel, chairman of the CHA
and Byrne's chief fund raiser. Apparently to save Swibel's reputation, in July 1982 the mayor decided to make several new appointments. She nominated the executive director of the CHA, Andrew
Mooney, a white, to replace Swibel, and she named two white women
as replacements for two black members of the CHA. These appointments tipped the racial balance of the CHA from a black to a white

majority, while 84 percent of the Authority's tenants were black.

The mayor explained her action by claiming that the three new CHA members had the "management expertise" necessary to reform the troubled agency. Later, she contended that HUD had really wanted the city to dump all the CHA members and that her action therefore saved the seats of three blacks. She also claimed she was attempting to balance the CHA racially and to give blacks "full-time, day-in-and-day-out" operating control by naming a black to replace Mooney as executive director.[20]

None of her explanations were persuasive to black leaders. They saw the action as a "heavy insult" and another of Byrne's attempts to reassure white ethnics by guaranteeing their racial interests when the CHA selected future sites for public housing. Organizations within the black community again orchestrated the opposition and pressured the black aldermen. In a "raucous session" on 23 July, and after the administration majority engineered an early cutoff of debate, the City Council approved the appointments, with nine black aldermen dissenting on all of them. The Council debate left no doubt, and even Byrne's supporters acknowledged that the question had "clearly become a black and white issue."[21]

These actions aroused resentment within the black community. Virtually by fiat, Byrne and the Machine regulars in the Council had tried to dilute black voting power and representation, had reduced black influence over the schools and public housing, had chosen an alderman from a black ward, and then had tried to oust him after he voted in the interests of his constituents. Such actions encouraged a widespread belief among blacks that Mayor Byrne regarded them as subjects rather than citizens of their city.

Byrne maintained publicly that she was sensitive and committed to the interests of the city's blacks, even defending her appointments to the Board of Education and the CHA on those grounds. She also emphasized how many blacks she had appointed to city positions, and her appointees lauded that record even more frequently. But critics noticed her penchant for removing maverick black appointees in favor of whites or less independent minorities. They noticed, too, that her top black appointees lacked significant policy-making influence. "There is not one black person in the City of Chicago that controls any budgetary unit or agency," Renault Robinson observed. Were the mayor's black appointees, Alderman Danny Davis (29th Ward) asked, anything "more than figureheads? I don't find [Byrne's record] impressive when you understand that side of it."[22]

Another side of her record was more impressive, if only negatively. She used her political funds to distribute chickens, hams, and food baskets to low-income black families and to make cash donations to black churches. Ample publicity accompanied her largesse, and it all smacked of an older era, when political bosses used gifts to buy votes. Even Byrne had noticed in 1979 that the city's blacks were too sophisticated to be bought off in that way, but now it seemed she no longer believed what she had said earlier. "A lot of people consider giving these little Christmas trees to people in the housing projects an insult," Lu Palmer judged. "Giving them a two-pound ham, that's an insult. That's patronizing. . . . We consider that an insult—trying to buy off the black churches."[23]

Byrne's actions and patronizing insults to the black community sowed the seeds of the political revolution that came to fruition in 1983. Black civic leaders, ministers, community organizers, and political independents denounced and opposed each one of them. More important, they fought back, in the newspapers, in the courts, and in their organizations. As early as August 1981, Lu Palmer's Chicago Black United Communities held a citywide political conference to begin preparations for the 1983 city elections. "We Shall See in '83" served as the organization's slogan and its pointed reminder to Mayor Byrne. Over the next year, other conferences and meetings were held "to raise the level of awareness of black people about electoral politics" and to acquaint them with the basics of campaign and precinct work. By early 1982, black independents had organized a coalition as "a viable alternative to Chicago's plantation politics of the past. . . . We are rejecting machine tricks and their picks." The coalition demanded nothing less than political autonomy for the black community, and its leaders recognized that "only we can end plantation politics."[24]

Since at least the mid-1970s, a significant segment of the leadership of Chicago's black community had realized that blacks had to control their own fate. That they had to use their numbers to elect candidates responsible to their communities and not to the white leaders of the Machine. The larger problem was spreading that message through the black community and convincing the black populace that voting could make a difference. The statements and actions of Reagan and Byrne helped by bringing the battle lines into sharper focus, and the events of the spring and summer of 1982 channeled the discontent of the city's blacks into electoral politics.

Streeter's victory in the 17th Ward aldermanic election was a turning point of sorts, because it showed black citizens that they could out-organize and out-vote the Machine in a controlled ward and under conditions that usually worked to the advantage of endorsed candidates—a special election. Blacks had learned in 1979 that they could ally electorally with whites to defeat the Machine in a citywide race. In June 1982 blacks showed themselves that they could redeem their own community, despite the Machine's patronage muscle and precinct manpower. The event signalled the increased vulnerability of the Machine, while communicating to blacks a hopeful message concerning their prospects for success through collective action. The events of late July and August 1982 underscored that message, added impetus to the process of cognitive liberation, and gave rise to a larger movement aimed at rescuing the city from the dominance of its ruling institution.[25]

The breadth and intensity of sentiment within the black community was revealed by the boycott of Mayor Byrne's ChicagoFest, the centerpiece of her summer-long series of bread-and-circus festivals. The People's Coalition to Boycott ChicagoFest, an ad hoc grouping that drew together a wide range of existing community organizations, led the movement. The boycott reduced ChicagoFest's attendance and revenues, but its importance went beyond those indicators. The boycott tapped existing networks of associations within the black community, enlisted their support, and mobilized their participants in a common cause. It provided a rallying point that served "to sensitize, politicize, and mobilize black people toward eventual political empowerment." As "a coming together of black people," the boycott movement cut across standing divisions and leadership rivalries and demonstrated to blacks their potential for collective action. The ChicagoFest boycott was a vital step in the process of developing among the city's black populace an insurgent consciousness, a belief that blacks could alter their lot through their own actions.[26]

The enthusiasm generated by the boycott of ChicagoFest was quickly channeled into an expressly political movement—a voter-registration drive. The idea for a massive registration effort had originated before Byrne's CHA appointments and the boycott. In mid-June the leaders of People Organized for Welfare and Employment Rights (POWER), a coalition of sixteen community-based organizations, announced plans to conduct a campaign to register recipients of public aid. Even earlier, Operation PUSH had attempted to register students in high-school graduating classes, and a few businesses in the black community had encouraged registration by announcing sale days on which registered voters would be given discounts on purchases.[27] Of course, black organizations had staged voter-registration campaigns in earlier years, but the results had always been disappointing. So as late as June 1982, there was little reason to expect their current efforts to produce any different outcome.

The ChicagoFest boycott altered those expectations by showing black leaders what could be done if they cooperated with each other. It mobilized a wide range of community groups, gave them experience with collective action, and showed them how effective it could be. Involvement in the boycott gave black citizens a sense that they could act together effectively to assert their racial interests. By mobilizing community organizations and helping to change the outlook of the black populace, the boycott experience paved the way for the voter-registration movement to spread through the black community like a contagion.

In a sense, it was only a small step from the type of collective action involved in the boycott to the type that focused directly on acquiring greater political leverage; however, that step was neither inevitable nor automatic. It required decisions by community leaders to cooperate with each other and to develop tactics capable of stimulating the target population. The vital point is that these decisions were made by leaders of existing community groups, groups already mobilized by the boycott movement; and it was through their networks of person-to-person linkages—in the churches, the social action organizations, and the business community—that the political contagion spread. As a result, through the late summer and fall of 1982, Chicago's blacks came to see voting as "the advancement of the civil rights movement," and registering became as much "in vogue . . . as marching was in the 1960s."[28]

Black politicians played only a small role in the movement to register voters. The independents aided and abetted the drive, of course; but its dynamic force came from the grass roots, from black churches and from more than 200 community organizations, some of which were barely known beyond their own neighborhoods. The result was to bring the black, overwhelmingly poor population of Chicago, the segment least likely to participate in politics, into being as a new and major force in the city's political life.[29]

Since traditional registration efforts had not before been very successful among the black population, with its high proportions of low-income and unemployed persons, the leaders of the community organizations developed a new type of outreach program. POWER successfully battled the Chicago Board of Election Commissioners and the Illinois Public Aid and Labor Departments to conduct on-site registration at the city's public aid and unemployment compensation offices. The aim was to catch "the people at the very moment of their discontent" and encourage them to express that feeling through involvement in the electoral process. Chicago Black United Communities set up a People's Movement for Voter Registration to help coordinate the activities of other groups, such as Operation PUSH and the Chicago Urban League, and to enlist and train volunteers to work in the drive. The People's Movement also staged marches to escort interested persons to registration sites, and it pressured the Library Commission to publicize the fact that its local branches were empowered to register voters. On the welfare and unemployment lines, at the neighborhood branches of the public library, at churches, supermarkets, fast-food stores, the Cook County Hospital, and in the public housing projects, these groups conducted on-site registration.[30]

The black churches were also active in the effort. One well-known Catholic priest, Father George Clements, pastor of Holy Angels Church, condemned failure to register as a "sin." He told his congregation that "if you do not have a voter registration card, Holy Angels does not want your membership. . . . It should be obvious to everyone, black or white, that voter registration is bare minimum, a simple beginning, an opening gesture in the march toward freedom and liberation." The pastor of Mt. Pisgah Baptist Church announced that the church would no longer distribute free food to persons who could not present a registration card. And over 100 black ministers, meeting with the Reverend Jesse Jackson, pledged themselves to conduct registration drives at their churches. "Praise the Lord, and Register" became a common theme at services in the black neighborhoods.[31]

Black businessmen gave money for a three-week advertising campaign on the seven black-oriented radio stations, with over 500 jingles and commercials emphasizing the theme "Come Alive October Five." The same slogan appeared on thousands of posters and banners placed throughout the black community. Operation PUSH and the Chicago Urban League sponsored a "Voter Fever Family Registration Day" in Washington Park on 25 September, featuring a mixture of rock performances, gospel singing, and on-site registration. One of the performers, a six-year-old gospel singer, ended her rendition of "I'm Looking for a Miracle" by asking the audience to register. As one observer remarked, "We have been the coal that heated the pot. . . . Now it's time for us to get in that pot so that we can improve our social and economic plight in this city. It can be done through the ballot box."[32]

"It's amazing," Michael Lavelle, chairman of the Chicago Board of Election Commissioners, proclaimed, even before the final tally of new registrations. "This is the best outreach year ever. I give credit to the outstanding efforts of the community groups for this success." The leaders of the community groups believed that widespread antipathy toward Byrne among minorities and the poor fueled the registration effort. According to Slim Coleman (of POWER), "I think Mayor Byrne was very helpful, in a negative sort of way. I know a lot of people came out and registered just to get rid of her next year."[33]

The battle was only partially won with the close of general registration and the headlined announcement that "Black Registration Hits Record High." There was still the canvass by election judges to verify addresses, which in the past had purged thousands of names from the registration lists. To prevent the wholesale removal of the names of newly registered blacks, and to convert the registration fever into turnout fever on election day, the People's Movement remained active and vigilant. It monitored the activities of election judges as they canvassed the neighborhoods; it sent volunteers to contact people whose names were removed, urging them to register again; and it pressured the Board of Election Commissioners to permit those who were challenged to fill out affidavits in their own neighborhoods instead of going downtown to attest to their legal residence. To sustain enthusiasm, the black-oriented radio stations aired a new jingle—"Follow Through November Two." And on the Saturday before the November general election, the People's Movement sponsored a "Get Out the Vote Motorcade" in each of the city's predominantly black wards and distributed over 100,000 leaflets throughout the black community.[34]

Chicago's blacks came alive and followed through. In unprecedented numbers, they registered and voted in the 1982 general election. Table 13 allows us to assess their performance by comparing it with the registration and turnout rates of the city's major population groups since 1975.

Through 1979 the registration and turnout rates for whites were consistently higher than for blacks. Moreover, the difference between the turnout rates of the two groups was larger than the gap between their registration rates, indicating that even blacks who registered were less likely to vote than whites who registered. The pattern changed in the 1982 general election, when blacks registered and voted at higher rates than whites. A subsequent upturn in white registration reduced the size of the difference, but blacks still maintained a proportionate edge through the 1983 general election. White and black turnout rates were about the same in the 1983 primary, but in the general election black participation soared to an astounding 73 percent of the group's voting-age population, or 5.8 percentage points above the white rate. Finally, in all of these elections, Hispanic registration and turnout rates were consistently lower than the other groups, and they did not show any meaningful pattern of change over time.

The sharp increase in the black registration rate between 1979 and 1982 meant that a much larger number of blacks had become legally qualified voters. Between those years, the number of registered blacks showed a net gain of over 127,000, bringing the total number of black registrants to over 647,000 by November 1982. Between that time and the April 1983 general election, black registration showed another net gain of about 20,000. In contrast, between 1979 and 1982 white registration displayed a net gain of only 1,656; but the net increase between November and the April general election was just over 52,000.[35]

The voter-registration drive also changed the social profile of the

Table 13. Measures of Group Mobilization, 1975–1983: Registration and Turnout as Percentages of Voting-Age Population[1]

	Registration			Turnout		
	White	**Black**	**Hispanic**	**White**	**Black**	**Hispanic**
Primary 1975	81.1	70.9	34.5	48.5	34.1	24.9
Primary 1977	84.5	77.9	35.9	44.8	27.4	23.8
Primary 1979	77.4	69.4	31.5	48.9	34.5	18.3
General 1982	78.3	86.7	35.1	54.0	55.8	20.9
Primary 1983	82.2	87.2	36.1	64.6	64.2	23.9
General 1983	83.2	89.1	37.0	67.2	73.0	24.3

[1] The entries are citywide figures developed by weighting the estimates for each group within eight subareas of the city.

Table 14. Impact of the 1982 Registration Drive among Blacks: Percentages of Old and New Registrants by Age and Income[1]

	Old Registrants	New Registrants	Total Registrants
Age			
18–25	18.5	33.4	26.8
26–35	31.8	32.6	32.3
36–50	30.6	21.3	25.4
51–64	15.9	10.3	12.7
65+	3.2	2.4	2.7
Income			
Under $7,500	21.7	39.6	31.5
$7,500 to 14,999	18.1	19.1	18.6
$15,000 to 24,999	28.4	26.8	27.5
Over $25,000	31.8	14.6	22.4

The question: Did you register to vote during the past twelve months? (Old registrants are those who responded "no"; those who said "yes" are classified as new registrants.)

[1] Except for rounding error, the column percentages for each variable sum to 100 percent.

Source: WBBM-TV (CBS) Primary Exit Poll.

legally qualified electorate within the black community in some significant ways (Table 14). Voter-registration requirements have their greatest effect on poorly educated, low-income, and young voters. That was the case among Chicago's blacks: prior to 1982 the older and higher-income categories were overrepresented among the black registrants.[36] The voter-registration drive especially enrolled persons in the youngest and lowest-income groups, and thus significantly increased their relative shares of the legally eligible black electorate.

Unprecedented numbers of Chicago's blacks not only registered and participated in the 1982 general election, but they also voted cohesively against Republican candidates. That combination of high turnout and bloc voting upset the predictions of most pollsters and nearly upset Governor James Thompson's bid for reelection. Thompson ran reasonably well among the city's white voters, receiving the support of 23.4 percent of the white voting-age population to Adlai Stevenson's 30.6 percent. But among blacks he ran at a meager 3.5 percent, while 52.3 percent of the black voting-age population voted for Stevenson. Stevenson's margin over Thompson among black voters accounted for 75.7 percent of his 467,276-vote plurality in the city.

Stevenson's huge edge in Chicago led some observers to commend Vrdolyak and to speak of the revitalization of the Democratic Machine.[37] No analysis could have been further off the mark. It wasn't a "Vrdolyak Express" that ran over him, as Thompson claimed, but a black express fueled by a newly sharpened political consciousness and driven by community-based organizations.[38] To say the very least, that development would enormously complicate Jane Byrne's bid for reelection as mayor of Chicago.

Battle Plans

■ Electing a governor and congressmen was an entertaining diversion for Chicagoans, something to occupy their attention while they awaited the main bout. Once that preliminary skirmishing was over, they could "get down to the serious war—the election of a mayor."[39]

Two days after the November general election, State's Attorney Richard M. Daley announced his candidacy for the Democratic mayoral nomination. His declaration pushed the still unresolved gubernatorial race from the headlines and focused public attention on the contest for power in Chicago. Despite earlier promises not to run for mayor, Daley claimed "people" had urged him to enter the race. "Behind these appeals, I feel there is a deep concern—a concern about the performance and conduct of the present administration." Without mentioning Byrne by name, Daley lambasted her record. "People are worried about the future of Chicago because they have experienced the results of mismanagement. People are worried about the future of Chicago because they know the city has ineffective leadership." The increases in taxes and fees under the present administration, Daley added, "have cost the people of Chicago more every time they take a drink of water, make a phone call, buy a pair of shoes . . . or buy food and medicine." Since these burdens hit all residents, Daley promised a campaign that would appeal "to all the people of Chicago without regard to ethnicity." To underscore his point, he made his first campaign appearance at a rally held at a black church on the West Side, where he told his audience Chicago faced a "crisis in leadership."[40]

Six days later, on 10 November 1982, Congressman Harold Washington ended the suspense and announced that he would run for mayor of Chicago. For nearly a year, black community activists and independents had spoken of Washington as their preferred choice, although they had not tailored their efforts to his candidacy. But the congressman held back, saying he wanted first to see how the registration drive went. When that effort was obviously successful, he still hesitated, claiming on one occasion that there was not yet "a clearly compelling interest at the grassroots level" for a black candidate, and later saying that "other important factors" had to be settled before he could make the commitment. He was concerned, he said, with the availability of campaign funds, the likelihood of developing a strong organization, the possibility of other black candidates entering the race, and whether a black candidate would only help Byrne defeat Daley. Probably about a month prior to his announcement, when he finally became persuaded that a "sensible, skillful strategy" had been developed to enable a black candidate to win, Washington made his decision to run.[41]

Washington leveled two broad charges against the Byrne Administration. First he claimed that "Chicago was a city divided . . . where citizens are treated unequally and unfairly." Second, the "'city that works' doesn't work any more": its school system does not educate students, the crime problem continues to grow, "sewers are in disrepair, streets are marred with giant potholes, we have one of the highest infant mortality rates in the country and traffic is snarled permanently." To people out of work, without homes, and without food or hope, "the only answer the city government provides is fat consultant contracts for a few politically connected firms and jobs for a few patronage workers." The city suffers from these terrible problems, he concluded, "because [its] leadership . . . has perpetuated outdated politics and pie-in-the-sky financing."[42]

Mayor Byrne completed the field of major candidates on 22 November, when she formally announced her intention to seek reelection. The following day, the Democratic ward committeemen met in the Bismarck Hotel to engage in their slatemaking ritual, and Byrne humbly presented her candidacy before the committee, chiding Daley and Washington for refusing to appear. Then, on cue and according to script, committeeman after committeeman praised her record and her gutsy personality. The outcome was a foregone conclusion, but Chairman Vrdolyak's orchestra didn't play in perfect harmony. When 14th Ward Committeeman Edward Burke made the customary motion for a unanimous endorsement, George Dunne (42d Ward) stood up, looked squarely at the mayor, and demanded his vote be recorded as "No" on her endorsement. Twelve more committeemen joined Dunne, and the war for control over the Machine and the city was formally declared. "Chicago needs Jane Byrne," Vrdolyak warned, and "if anyone wants to take this organization on, they better pack a lunch because it will be an all day job."[43]

Each of the candidates began the campaign with a strategy for winning the contest. Their approaches reflected their separate judgments of what was possible politically, and these shaped their early campaign efforts and organizational arrangements. As later events and poll results altered their assessments, the candidates developed new tactics, switched campaign plans, and emphasized different themes, but they never really abandoned their original strategies.

Washington's plan involved solidifying his base in the black community, developing a coalition with Hispanics, and appealing for white support. His strategists publicly expressed the hope of winning up to 15 percent of the white vote, and Washington designed his campaign staff and steering committee with that goal in mind. Among his paid staff of thirty-one persons, there were thirteen whites; and his twenty-two-member "blue ribbon" steering committee, which was the core of his formal campaign organization, included six whites.

Washington's strategists expected little support from the white ethnics on the Northwest and Southwest Sides, although they did set up campaign offices in each of these areas. Washington also appeared at a forum sponsored by the Southwest Parish and Neighborhood Federation, where he discussed the "shared concerns" of blacks and whites for improved city services, education, and employment. "I wanted to show them that I didn't have horns," he quipped.[44] But he directed most of his campaigning among whites at the liberals in the Lake Shore wards and the University of Chicago community (Ward 5). There he tried to show that he was not a sectarian, racial candidate and that he supported the same social concerns as they did. He showcased his eighteen-year record in legislative politics, including his designation by *Chicago* magazine in 1977 as one of the state's ten best legislators. He scored the media for referring to him as "a black candidate," saying his record showed that "I have been more than fair and open [and] have never excluded any group . . . from becoming involved in the decision-making process." His campaign workers in the liberal areas, about 75 percent of whom were white, distributed literature emphasizing his positions on tenant rights, environmental issues, women's rights, and nuclear disarmament. He aired radio commercials on WBBM and WFMT, the favorite stations of the Lake Shore residents, and one of his television spots appealed to liberals by focusing on his positive qualifications for mayor.[45]

9. A scene from one of Washington's television spots emphasizing his experience and positions on issues. The voice-over urged viewers to "Elect the qualified candidate, Harold Washington."

Washington based his appeal to Hispanics on the experience of racial discrimination that they shared with blacks. He pointed to his support in Congress for bilingual education, pledged to work for the appointment of an Hispanic as district schools superintendent, and promised an affirmative action policy that would give Hispanics their appropriate share of city jobs. He included three Hispanics on his paid campaign staff, and two on his steering committee, made several dozen campaign stops in Hispanic areas, bought time for radio commercials on an Hispanic radio station (WOJO), and endorsed the aldermanic candidacies of two Hispanics who were challenging white incumbents (in the 22d and 25th Wards). Former New York Congressman Herman Badillo campaigned on Washington's behalf, and he was endorsed by the League of United Latin American Citizens and by several local Hispanic leaders, including Elena Martinez, who chaired Hispanics for Byrne in 1979.[46]

These and other efforts failed to spark much of a response among whites or Hispanics. Lingering friction between blacks and Hispanics over neighborhoods, jobs, appointments, and government funds blunted Washington's appeals, especially putting him at a disadvantage in competing with Byrne for Hispanic support. "A black-Hispanic coalition," as one Hispanic activist had said before the campaign, "is further down the road than any of us could have expected."[47] And whites were no more receptive to Washington's appeals. There was little payoff from his steering committee's attempts to raise funds from the white business establishment and to elicit endorsements from white liberals. In the end, only a handful of prominent whites publicly supported Washington, while most of the anti-Byrne liberals joined the Daley camp. The simple reality was that few whites, whether in the liberal establishment or the media, viewed Washington's candidacy as anything but a spoiler effort. Until quite late in the campaign, the white media evaluated Washington's effort in terms of its impact on Byrne's or Daley's chances of winning, giving little serious attention to the prospect of a Washington triumph.[48]

From the beginning, high turnout and cohesive voting among blacks was the central plank of Washington's strategy. Its shorthand expression was "80/80," or 80 percent support from an 80 percent turnout of black registrants. But the original plan called for Washington to concentrate on appeals to the entire city, while his Task Force for Black Political Empowerment, an ad hoc grouping that evolved from the ChicagoFest boycott and the registration drive, ran the campaign in the black community. That tactic was modified somewhat as Washington's lack of success in attracting white and Hispanic support became clear. During January, for example, about 35 percent of Washington's campaign stops were in white and Hispanic communities, but he scaled back those efforts in February and spent about 75 percent of his time in black neighborhoods. "This campaign started in the 'hood, and it will end in the 'hood," Washington claimed near the end of the campaign. The effort was also financed and staffed largely by blacks. Nearly all of the $1.1 million campaign fund was raised among black businessmen, and blacks made up a plurality among his paid campaign staff, a majority on his steering committee, and nearly 80 percent of his 6,000 volunteers.[49]

Given the heart of his electoral strategy, it was crucial for Washington to persuade blacks that he was a serious candidate and to present himself as a symbol of black pride and progress. He had to convert anti-Byrne sentiment among blacks into support for his candidacy, rather than Daley's, and to counter the long-standing belief that the Machine had a lock on a sizable share of the black vote. To do that, Washington attacked Byrne's racial policies, ridiculed the "hocus-pocus" character of her earlier stay at Cabrini-Green, and criticized the black politicians supporting the mayor. But Washington's appeal to blacks did not rely exclusively, or even primarily, on anti-Byrne sentiment. He appealed to racial pride and self-respect and aimed at convincing blacks to identify voting for him with community values, to see it as a means of political liberation, and one that could succeed. "We have given the white candidates our vote for years and years and years," he told a black audience a few days after entering the race. "Now it's our turn, it's our turn, it's our turn." There was no reason to be hesitant or doubtful: "Every group, when it reaches a certain population percentage, automatically takes over. They don't apologize . . . they just move in and take over."[50] His rhetoric may have frightened white ethnics and puzzled the white media, but it was intended to remind blacks of their long peonage to the Machine, the enforced subordination of their racial interests, and to evoke feelings of pride and confidence in his campaign for their political autonomy.

To show that he was a serious candidate, Washington unveiled a series of endorsements from blacks prominent in local, state, and national affairs. In addition to support from three black state legislators, the city's independent black aldermen, as well as endorsements by every black community newspaper and the Chicago Defender, a nearly steady stream of black politicians came to Chicago to campaign for Washington, including members of the Black Congressional Caucus and the Conference of Black Mayors. The endorsements and campaign activities were news and produced invaluable publicity for the campaign, especially since a chronic shortage of funds prevented Washington from matching Byrne's or Daley's media advertising.

Of the three candidates, Daley faced the toughest task in developing a strategy to mobilize a plurality in the divided city. He may have presumed originally that he could translate black dissatisfaction with Byrne into support for his candidacy, as he had in both the primary and general elections in 1980, but that possibility began to evaporate on the day Washington entered the contest. From that point on, with Washington appealing to black pride and Byrne relying on Machine loyalists in the black wards, Daley was left without a viable basis on which to compete for the votes of blacks.

Daley was endorsed by two black officeholders, but Washington's candidacy drew away his potential allies among the black independents and kept his black supporters on the defensive throughout the campaign. An early effort to show support for Daley among black ministers fizzled when reporters discovered that most of the 150 were storefront preachers with small (if any) congregations. The Daley campaign opened nine offices to service the nineteen black majority wards, while there was a separate office in each of the predominantly white and Hispanic wards; and there were a few blacks among Daley's top campaign staff. But even the whites and blacks on his central campaign staff ran "separate but equal operations" and were never fully integrated into a single effort. The same type of racial separation marked his grass-roots efforts. "He's got his white precinct workers on the west side of Western Avenue and his black workers on the east side, and the two shall never meet," quipped one black resident of the Chatham area.[51] Perhaps better than anything else, Daley's organizational arrangements symbolized both his dilemma and the degree to which an aroused black consciousness had changed the terms and conditions of coalition building since Byrne's election in 1979.

Daley was never able to develop a positive strategy to compete with Washington in tapping the widespread anti-Byrne feelings that existed among blacks. Daley's appeal to blacks focused on crime control, unemployment, and his record of hiring blacks in the state's attorney's office. "No other major city has the percentage of minority staff attorneys" that Chicago does, he often told his black audiences. But he avoided discussing issues that touched on the racial concerns of blacks—integrated schools, open housing, and police brutality. He never explicitly acknowledged past discrimination against blacks in Chicago but spoke instead in general terms of his aversion to prejudice, blaming Byrne's policies for any existing racial strife and condemning her allegedly race-baiting campaign tactics. He was especially sensitive to charges that his own neighborhood, Bridgeport, resisted open housing and had a reputation for racism. "I'm sick and tired of these vicious and unworthy attacks," he responded to a questioner during the second debate among the candidates. "There are many good people in my neighborhood, and I'll defend them. And there are a few bad people, and I'll prosecute them." On a radio talk show the next day, attempting to repair the damage, he responded to another question about Bridgeport's reputation for violence against blacks by saying that "no candidate represents the worst in society."[52]

Daley's dilemma lay in the fact that he needed votes from blacks, but his base of support was among the white ethnics on the Southwest Side, and on integration issues they were as sensitive as blacks. If he could appeal directly to the racial interests of blacks, or even recognize past acts of racial discrimination and violence against them, he might win more votes in the black community, although that was no sure bet with Washington in the contest. But the tactic would be dangerous, because it could anger the white ethnic voters whose support was vital to his candidacy. So all Daley could do was to engage in an elaborate "juggling act," hoping to keep "it all glued together until after the election." Appearing before white audiences, he avoided direct references to race, even substituting code words like "low-income residents," and he avoided attacking Washington. To black audiences, Daley spoke of the economic and social policies that concerned minorities, but he ignored or downplayed matters that involved their racial interests.[53]

The balancing act proved difficult, and at times Daley appeared evasive, awkward, and without a clear sense of how to respond as campaign developments highlighted the race question. But he had a consistent approach, similar to the one his father used prior to the late 1960s. By stressing his support for programs that appealed to the welfare interests of blacks and emphasizing his efforts to unite the city, Daley tried to minimize the importance of the racial interests of blacks, because he knew he couldn't win if they became the focal point of the contest.

Daley was on surer and safer ground with his strategy for garnering support from white voters. In the liberal areas, where distrust of the Daley name was strong, he presented himself as an independent. He attacked Byrne's misuse of patronage, her enormous campaign fund, and her deceptive television advertising. "The mayor's word is no good," he said at one rally. She "doesn't know what's true and what's false, and after four years, it's very difficult to teach these basic elements." He stressed his own record of professionalism in staffing the state's attorney's office, promised reform of political fund raising, and proudly pointed to a series of endorsements by prominent independents and liberals, including Adlai Stevenson and Walter Mondale.[54]

But it was in the ethnic communities, especially on the Southwest Side, that Daley was truly at home. He knew and understood those neighborhoods and could relate his general themes to their local concerns. There he was at ease, able to depart from his prepared speeches and arouse his audience with scathing attacks on the Byrne Administration. In the white ethnic communities, it was "a fight amongst clans," one observer remarked. "It's the shanty Irish versus the lace-curtain Irish." Daley pitched his appeal to the hardworking, taxpaying homeowners, blistering Byrne for her fiscal mismanagement, her tax increases, and her lack of leadership. He also countered the mayor's appeal by matching her support for the effort by the Southwest Parish and Neighborhood Federation to get the CHA to sell two apartment buildings earmarked for public housing. And he told white audiences in Marquette Park and on the Northwest Side that he supported the right of residents to veto public housing projects in their neighborhoods. Finally, beginning in early February, he did what Byrne couldn't do: he invoked his father's name and the memory of an earlier and better Chicago, "the city that worked."[55]

More so than her two rivals, Mayor Byrne's strategy from the outset was based on being able to win significant shares of the vote among whites, blacks, and Hispanics. Her campaign slogan, "Mayor Byrne for *All* Chicago," expressed that strategy symbolically, and her campaign organization reflected it concretely. She located six of her ten main campaign offices in black and Hispanic neighborhoods and targeted one of her special committees to blacks, another to Hispanics, and the third to women. Her campaign staff was racially in-

10. Richard M. Daley campaigning on the near Northwest Side, 21 February 1983. (*Chicago Tribune.*)

tegrated, with twenty blacks and five Hispanics among its fifty-four paid members; and about a third of her 6,000 volunteers worked in the black neighborhoods.[56] "The black vote is probably the most important targeted vote that we need," William Griffin, Byrne's campaign manager, admitted. Conceding that Washington would get a majority among blacks, Griffin calculated that "whoever wins [the primary] has to come in second" with that vote. Byrne's strategy was to cut into Washington's plurality and to try to win as much as 25 percent of the black vote for herself.[57]

Byrne moved early to recover her sagging popularity with black voters. In October 1982, she appeared on a WBMX call-in show to face the criticism directly. She acknowledged "extreme slippage" in her standing among blacks and attributed it to a "lack of communication from my office." She denied that any of her actions were intended to show disrespect toward blacks. "When I hear that, it hurts a lot. It's not true." She then defended her record, emphasizing that more blacks had been appointed to key positions during her term than in any previous administration.[58]

After entering the race, Byrne backed her claims with action. She reestablished a black majority on the CHA by replacing Angeline Caruso with Earl L. Neal, a prominent black attorney; she filled a vacancy on the Board of Education with a black businessman, Leon

11. A frame from one of Daley's television spots highlighting his family and his connection to an earlier and better Chicago. His mother, Eleanor "Sis" Daley, told viewers: "I'm very proud of him. And I'm sure his father if he were alive would be proud of him, too. . . . He'll be a professional mayor of the city of Chicago."

Jackson; she named another black, Bennett Stewart, to her cabinet as interim director of the Inter-Governmental Affairs Office; and she engineered the appointment of still another black, Harry Reddrick, as the CTA's manager of transportation. The mayor continued to make donations from her campaign funds to black churches, and she met with leaders of the local advisory councils of the CHA to announce plans for distributing more than 40,000 hams to residents of the public housing projects. She was concerned, she said, "that each CHA family have a Christmas dinner." In January she doubled garbage pickups and transferred $10 million from community development funds to set up a temporary jobs program for 3,800 unemployed Chicagoans.[59]

Byrne campaigned aggressively in black neighborhoods, especially in the black churches. Sometimes she appeared in tandem with an elected black official and even more often with one of her black appointees, who extolled her for naming blacks to positions in the city government. She boasted about that record, called for a crackdown on street gangs, reminded audiences of her stay at Cabrini-Green,

12. Mayor Jane Byrne speaking to the congregation of the St. Paul Missionary Baptist Church, 6954 South Union Avenue, on Sunday, 9 January 1983. "I . . . recruited [black] department heads and deputies in this government that weren't included before . . . so they would represent you and you can relate to them," she said. (*Chicago Tribune.*)

and bragged about her temporary jobs program and the hams she had given away. Like Daley, she spoke largely to the economic concerns of blacks; but unlike him, Byrne was at ease before such audiences and made efforts to show that she understood the black experience. At a black church on the West Side in late January, Byrne defended her use of political funds to buy food for the poor, claiming that she had learned what it was like to suffer when she was a widow with a young baby to rear on government pensions. "I know what it's like at the end of the month when that little blue-and-green card [the government check] isn't there," she said. "I know what it's like. So I know how people suffer." [60]

In searching for votes among blacks, Byrne used her endorsement by Senator Edward Kennedy, who sent a letter urging blacks to vote for her. She also depended on the backing of a number of black ministers, one of whom introduced her to his West Side flock as "the greatest mayor that ever lived." She knew of the traditional friction between blacks on the West Side and those on the South Side, and she expected that to reduce enthusiasm among West Siders for a black candidate from the South Side. But she depended most on support from prominent black officials, especially the nine black committee-men who voted to slate her, and on the Machine's presumed ability to deliver votes in several black wards.[61]

To mobilize Hispanic support, Byrne relied on their traditional commitment to Machine candidates, appealed to their ethnic pride, and exploited the standing tensions between them and the black community. She produced literature targeted at Hispanic voters; and Raul Villalobos, president of the Chicago Board of Education, and Dr. Hugo Muriel, the city health commissioner, her top Hispanic ap-pointees, often appeared with her at rallies. Their presence vividly showed her audiences how she had "opened the doors of city govern-ment" to Hispanics. Her supporters also fanned racial fears to un-dercut Washington's appeal. The mayor's assistant press secretary for Spanish communications told a Spanish-language television au-dience that past administrations had favored blacks over other mi-norities in hiring. "We can go to the Department of Human Services, and we will see how dark that department is," he said. "Can you imagine how it would be with a mayor with a face of that color?"[62]

But it was for the white vote that Byrne fought most vigorously, and her competitor there was Daley. If the state's attorney's name evoked memories of an earlier and better Chicago, then Byrne coun-terattacked on several fronts. In speeches and TV spots, she pre-sented herself as a heroine who inherited a huge budget deficit, had guts enough to cut expenses and raise taxes, and saved the city from financial disaster. "No one would know better than I what fiscal defi-cits were like, and no one would know better than I that it must never happen to Chicago again." The claim implied that Bilandic, and even Mayor Daley before him, by playing tricks with the city's finances, had created the crisis she had so resolutely resolved. Sec-ond, she raised the specter of the 11th Ward's being restored to domi-nance over the Machine and the city through a Daley victory. She had opened up the government to all groups, she told a rally of pre-cinct captains, and "I fail to believe that this group, these neighbor-hoods, would want one neighborhood only to run Chicago."[63]

To counter Daley's appeal to white liberals, the mayor produced her own endorsements from prominent independent politicians, in-cluding former Alderman William Singer. She was also endorsed by the Chicago Federation of Labor, the Chicago Gay and Lesbian Democrats, and the Chicago chapter of the National Organization of Women. The endorsement by NOW was controversial, since a number of feminists were active in the Washington campaign; and a 1982 study by the American Federation of State, County, and Municipal Employees had criticized the city government for sex discrimina-tion. Nevertheless, it fit in with the mayor's larger gender strategy—

to portray herself as a competent administrator who was being picked on because of her sex. She needed their support, she told audiences of women, because "with two versus me, it's about equal to the uphill battle last time."[64]

Campaigning in the white ethnic communities, Byrne pointed to her accomplishments, their benefits to the neighborhood, and her earlier opposition to locating CHA sites in areas where the homeowners disapproved. She appealed to the neighborhood pride of the Northwest Siders, while telling Southwest Siders not to "let anybody tell you that I don't love the Southwest Side, because I do." Police Superintendent Richard Brzeczek's television spot endorsing Byrne, and his speeches at rallies of policemen, probably bolstered her law-and-order image among white ethnic voters. And her own claims that she would "not let race become a campaign issue" could only have reminded whites that it was a factor.[65]

While Byrne traveled the campaign's high road, some of her workers on the streets, especially the Machine's precinct captains, took a different path. As early as the final week of January, some tried to scare whites by exaggerating the number of blacks who had registered on the final day and by portraying Byrne as the "white hope" candidate, the best bet to stop Washington. "'Man the barricades,' white Americans, the blacks are going to take over Chicago. Only St. Jane of Arc can save us.' That's the message," one columnist reported. Publicly, the Byrne campaign denied these early reports, but her campaign manager gave them credence by saying that "when we hear about it, I call and . . . tell them to stop that."[66]

The mayor's targeted appeals to particular groups were parts of a broader effort to enhance her popularity. It was no secret that her frequent shifts in policy and personnel, as well as her abrasive manner and confrontational approach, had weakened her standing with the city's voters. Byrne's popularity dropped from one public opinion poll to the next over the first two years of her administration, rebounded in the wake of her move to Cabrini-Green, and then resumed its slide through the autumn of 1981. The *Chicago Tribune*'s polls in January and July of 1982 recorded majorities saying that Byrne was not "honest and trustworthy," and both showed Daley ahead in a hypothetical matchup for mayor. The *Chicago Sun-Times* reported in September that a plurality of the city's voters disapproved of Byrne's job performance, and its October poll registered a 10-point lead for Daley, with the state's attorney running ahead of the mayor in almost every political and demographic category.[67] So, to improve her public image and catch up in the polls, Byrne hired David Sawyer as a media consultant and campaign strategist in July 1982. His task was to analyze the causes of her lagging support and to develop a strategy to turn the situation around.

13. "Old Jane" as she appeared on 24 June 1982, announcing plans to promote Chicago as the site of the 1984 Democratic Convention. (*Chicago Tribune.*)

14. "New Jane" as she appeared on 22 November 1982, announcing her candidacy for mayor. (*Chicago Tribune.*)

"The Sawyerization of Jane Byrne" was a phenomenal success. The mayor as a candidate became "New Jane," as local commentators dubbed her. She dressed more conservatively, exchanging "her circus costumes for a businesslike look out of the old Peck & Peck windows"; she spoke more deliberately, avoiding wisecracks and her usual biting sarcasm; and she shied away from the confrontational politics that had been her earlier hallmark. "The harsh, petulant, mercurial Old Jane was replaced by a softer, friendlier chief executive."[68]

There was more to "New Jane" than a change in demeanor. Sawyer's television spots took what the public saw as her weaknesses and tried to make them into strong points. The commercials didn't try to change the public's judgments of Byrne's characteristics; they attempted to put them into a new context and thus change people's overall evaluations of her performance as mayor. What the public saw as a revolving door of high-level personnel appointments, Sawyer presented as an honest trial-and-error search for the best possible administrative team to run the city. "I think we've got a good team. It takes a while to put a good team together," Byrne remarked softly at the end of one spot. Her combative and abrasive manner be-

15. An example of Byrne's television spots in which she tried to create a new and more favorable view of her reputation for conflict and combat. As she speaks to an interviewer of the tough problems she's had to face as mayor, the voice-over tells viewers: "She was twenty-four; her husband died, and she had to put her life back together. Today she still draws on that same determination, that same toughness. She's feisty, with a mother's protective instincts. . . . She's one of a kind, Jane Byrne."

came the type of no-nonsense toughness needed to run a city like Chicago. "I'm feisty. And I'm combative," she told viewers. "But this is a very tough city and you have to be feisty." And "New Jane" was contrite, willing to admit mistakes, rather than blame others or deny they happened. "I've made some mistakes, some big ones," a somber Byrne acknowledged on one commercial. "But I've learned." [69]

Reporters first noticed "New Jane" after she returned from her summer vacation, and most Chicagoans got their initial view before the November elections in a series of commercials plugging the Democratic ticket. Then in December, Byrne caught the opposition completely off guard. While Daley and Washington were nearly out of public view, preoccupied with assembling their campaign staffs and raising funds, Byrne's commercials saturated the airwaves. Her effort to reeducate voters worked: by early January, "New Jane" had pulled well ahead in the polls, a position she held until the final week of the campaign.

The notion that they had created a "New Jane" rankled both Byrne and Sawyer. "My hair and my clothes aren't different," the mayor said. "I haven't changed anything." To Sawyer the new image was the "Real Jane." It simply deemphasized certain things, while emphasizing others, and was intended to "change—and control—the context in which the campaign would be waged [so] we would have a greater opportunity to explain the positive aspects of her plans and create an environment where the public would listen to her." [70]

In addition to fashioning a new image, Byrne took other precautions to avert a public relations disaster during the campaign. She kept husband Jay away from the media, sending him to work in an out-of-the-way office in Charlie Swibel's Marina City, and she packed Swibel himself off to Florida to enjoy the sun. With these sources of embarrassment under wraps, her opponents on the defensive, and Sawyer running her media effort, cool, calm, and collected Jane seemed to be in command and headed for reelection.

The Process of Winning

■ January's bright expectations turned to dark forebodings a few days before the election. Suddenly, it all came apart, and on the night of 22 February gloom enveloped the Byrne camp. Why did it happen? With the Machine, the money, the volunteers, the media campaign, how could it have ended in defeat? In part the mayor was a victim of campaign developments she could not control and of a strategy based on the faulty assumption that Daley was the major threat. In even larger measure, however, she was done in by a mobilized and assertive black community and by a campaign that turned into a crusade for political liberation.

The patterns of voting behavior that marked the election cast light on how the events of the campaign helped shape its outcome. Table 15 shows how each of the city's major voting groups divided its support. [71]

Whites split the bulk of their vote between Byrne and Daley, giving very little support to Washington. Hispanics gave most of their vote to Byrne, as they had to every endorsed candidate since 1975. But since the mayor also ran better than Daley among blacks, only 77.9 percent of Byrne's total vote came from whites, compared with 90.3 percent of the ballots for Daley. Most critically, however, blacks delivered the preponderance of their vote to Washington. Their citywide turnout was trivially below the rate for whites, and it missed the target of 80 percent of the registered blacks by just over 6 percentage points. But blacks voted even more cohesively than community leaders had hoped: 84.7 percent of the blacks who came to the polls cast ballots for Washington. [72] As a result, and because he received relatively little support from whites and Hispanics, 92.1 percent of Washington's citywide total came from black citizens.

Table 15. The Democratic Mayoral Primary, 1983: Regression Estimates of Group Voting Behavior [1]

	Washington	Byrne	Daley	Nonvote
Citywide [2]				
Blacks	54.3	7.9	1.9	35.7
Whites	2.6	30.4	31.4	35.3
Hispanics	2.8	12.6	8.3	76.0
Blacks				
Dawson wards	54.1	8.2	2.5	35.1
Other South Side	57.8	7.3	1.4	33.3
West Side	46.3	8.9	1.5	43.1
Whites				
Northwest Side	0.8	33.2	29.1	36.8
South Side	0.5	28.3	45.7	25.4
Lake Shore	5.8	30.6	25.5	37.9
Ward 5	24.3	17.3	24.3	33.9
Hispanics				
Puerto Rican [3]	3.8	31.2	15.1	49.6
Mexican [4]	2.1	10.4	7.6	78.6
Total citywide	20.2	18.5	16.4	44.4

[1] Entries are percentages of voting-age population, and rows sum to 100 percent, except for rounding error.

[2] Developed by weighting the estimate of each group's voting behavior within eight subareas of the city.

[3] Estimates of Hispanic behavior in predominantly Puerto Rican Wards 26 and 31.

[4] Estimates of Hispanic behavior in predominantly Mexican Wards 22 and 25.

The solidarity of black support for Washington was truly impressive. Both the WMAQ-TV (NBC) and the WBBM-TV (CBS) primary exit polls showed relatively little difference in the level of Washington's support from one category of black respondents to another. In the NBC polls, for example, Washington registered at least 80 percent support among all but three categories of blacks, and each of those was relatively small. Blacks who identified themselves as Republicans gave him 60 percent of their votes; "very conservative" blacks gave him 78.7 percent support; and blacks sixty-five years of age and older voted 70.4 percent for Washington.[73] Table 16 presents the results from the WBBM-TV (CBS) exit poll for income and age categories, which show two meaningful patterns. First, Washington's support among blacks increased as income increased, with middle- and upper-income respondents giving him 6 to 7 points more support than those in the bottom category. Byrne's support among blacks moved in the opposite direction; she polled her largest percentage at the bottom of the income scale. Second, support for Washington dropped off among older blacks, and Byrne was the chief

Table 16. Patterns of Black Voting by Income and Age: The Democratic Mayoral Primary, 1983[1]

	Washington	Byrne	Daley	(N)
Income				
Under $7,500	80.5	16.2	3.3	(666)
$7,500 to $14,999	83.8	13.7	2.6	(388)
$15,000 to $24,999	86.2	12.0	1.7	(581)
Over $25,000	87.3	9.9	2.7	(473)
Age				
18–25	86.4	11.4	2.2	(597)
26–35	85.4	13.3	1.3	(714)
36–50	84.9	12.2	2.9	(581)
51–64	75.5	19.1	5.4	(298)
65+	69.1	16.2	14.7	(68)

[1] Entries are percentages. Each row sums to 100 percent, except for rounding error.
Source: WBBM-TV (CBS) Primary Exit Poll.

beneficiary of that decline, except among the oldest group, where Daley's percentage nearly tripled from the preceding category.

These patterns suggest some lingering traces of Machine influence among blacks. This probably accounts for Byrne's relatively better showing among low-income, older blacks, and for the sudden spurt in Daley's percentage among the oldest group. The age patterns also confirm how important the registration drive was: it nearly doubled the proportion of registrants among the eighteen-to-twenty-five-year-old group, the category giving Washington his highest level of support. In fact, 55.8 percent of the blacks who reported voting for Washington also said they had registered within the past year.

While these patterns of difference within the black group are mildly revealing, what is much more impressive is how little variation occurred. To notice that the smallest-sized age category gave Washington his lowest level of support at 69.1 percent simply emphasizes how cohesively blacks voted in the primary. No subgroup of black respondents reported giving Washington less than 60 percent of its vote, and most gave him 80 percent or more.

In stark contrast, the white vote divided almost evenly between Byrne and Daley, with no significant subcategory of white respondents giving either candidate as much as 60 percent of its vote. For example, Byrne had a 3-point edge among Republicans and a 2-point lead among Jewish voters, but those were among her largest margins, and Daley offset them by running about 1 point ahead among Democrats and Catholics, both of which were larger groups. The largest difference was the gender gap: Byrne ran 3.5 points ahead of Daley among women and 3.3 points behind among men, for a total gap of 6.8 percentage points.[74] The mayor's appeal to women worked but was offset in the final tally since slightly more men participated.

It's no surprise that the white vote failed to show sharp differences across these types of categories. It was evenly split to begin with, and its division primarily followed geographic lines (Map 2). As the estimates in Table 15 indicate, Byrne had a 5.1-point margin over Daley among white voters in the Lake Shore wards, and she won by 4.1 points among the white ethnics on the city's Northwest Side, carrying all but two wards (the 32d and 45th) in the northern part of the city. But her only victories in its southern half came in three Machine bastions—the 10th, 14th, and 25th Wards. The mayor's losing percentage among the South Side's white ethnics was only a shade under Daley's losing level on the Northwest Side, but Daley's support in his home base was much larger than Byrne's in her core area of strength. Because of the very high turnout of his white supporters on the South Side, Daley swamped Byrne there by 17.4 percentage points, offsetting her edge among whites elsewhere (except in Ward 5). As a result, Daley eked out a 1-point lead among white voters citywide.[75]

Washington carried twenty wards, all on the South and West Sides, and all but one with black majorities. The exception was the 1st Ward, where blacks were a plurality of the voting-age population and combined with Hispanics to give him a narrow 166-vote edge. Washington's margins among blacks were decisive in every area of the city (see Table 15), although Byrne was correct in suspecting that he would be weaker among black voters on the West Side. Less than a majority of the black voting-age population there voted for him, and his support was 7.8 points lower than it was in the Dawson wards on the South Side. However, most of that difference was due to lower turnout among blacks on the West Side, and there Byrne still trailed Washington by 37.4 percentage points. By a small margin, Washington ran best among the blacks in the "Other South Side" wards, several of which were middle-class communities, and their voters turned out at a slightly higher rate than those in the Dawson wards. But both differences were small, especially considering the generally larger disparities in income and education between the two groups of voters.

Finally, Byrne outpolled both of her rivals among Hispanics citywide and in the wards with the largest concentrations of Puerto Ricans and Mexicans. But Hispanics are the smallest of the three major components of the city's voting-age population, and only 12.6 percent cast ballots for her. The most revealing fact is that 76 percent of the city's voting-age Hispanics didn't participate at all.[76]

What should be apparent by this point is that the 1983 Democratic primary was *not* a three-way race. It involved two separate two-way

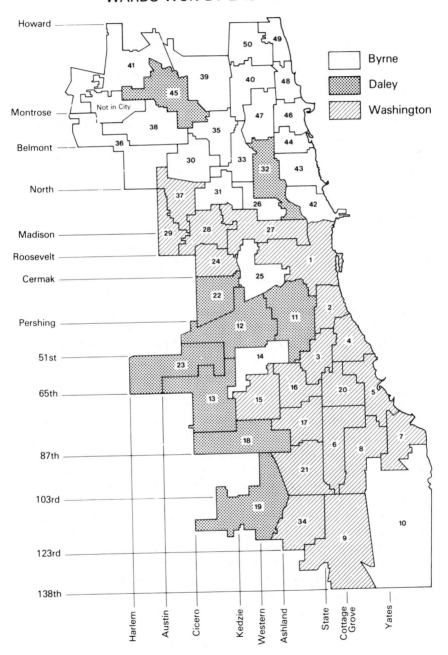

MAP 2
THE DEMOCRATIC PRIMARY, 1983:
WARDS WON BY EACH CANDIDATE

Byrne
Daley
Washington

Howard
Montrose
Belmont
North
Madison
Roosevelt
Cermak
Pershing
51st
65th
87th
103rd
123rd
138th

Harlem
Austin
Cicero
Kedzie
Western
Ashland
State
Cottage Grove
Yates

Not in City

races. The first was fought in the white community between Byrne and Daley, and it proved to be an extremely close contest. The second and decisive battle, as it turned out, was in the black community between Byrne and Washington, and that proved to be no contest. The city's white ethnic voters split their support between the white contenders, as they had in 1977 and 1979; but, unlike those earlier contests, black voters enthusiastically and cohesively supported a black candidate. Their high turnout and bloc voting made the difference and determined the outcome.

The close division of the white vote and the solidarity of the black vote were the keys to the result, and neither was assured at the outset of the campaign. In a mid-October poll, Daley was the preferred choice of both white and black voters, and among every other demographic grouping as well (Table 17).[77] By the second week of January, following her media blitz, Byrne pulled into a 10-point lead among white voters, widened that to 25 points during the next week, then saw the gap close, open, and finally close again during the last days of the campaign. Rebounding from his low point among whites at the end of the third week of January, Daley gained strength over the next two weeks, remained pretty stable after that, and attracted new white supporters in the final days. Among blacks, Daley's October lead evaporated by mid-January, as both Byrne and Washington made gains of about equal size. After that, Daley was not a factor in the battle for the black vote. Washington's support from blacks moved upward after early January, reaching 60 percent about a week before the primary, then surging forward during that week. Byrne's share of the black support fell after early January and, even before the final week, hovered precariously close to the minimum she needed from blacks to win the election.[78]

Despite the fact that almost every poll from December onward showed Daley running last, Mayor Byrne and her campaign strategists were slow to recognize Washington as the major threat. Even when her strength among blacks dropped in the wake of the first debate, there was no alarm, because it was offset by a larger increase in support among white voters. When Daley began to bounce back among whites in early February, there may have been somewhat more concern; but the mayor still led overall, and her private polls showed her citywide support holding steady at about 38 percent. Besides, myths die hard, especially when they involve the Machine and an Irish blood feud. As late as a week before the election, Vrdolyak claimed Daley was in second place (10 points behind), and he predicted Byrne would win 30 percent of the black vote. Then Byrne's private polls taken on 17 February showed her support dropping to 36 percent, the first significant change in about six weeks. It fell to 34 percent in the poll taken on 18 February with Washington's sup-

Table 17. Trends in Racial Support: Poll Reports, October 1982 through February 1983[1]

Interview Dates	Washington	Byrne	Daley	Undecided
Whites				
9–13 October[2]	4	33	47	16
10–11 January[3]	5	49	39	6
19–22 January[2]	6	55	30	9
11–16 February[2]	5	46	39	10
18 February[4]	4	43	39	14
19–20 February[3]	9	47	37	7
22 February[5]	6	47	46	—
Blacks				
9–13 October[2]	27	20	33	20
10–11 January[3]	41	35	13	11
19–22 January[2]	49	29	11	11
11–16 February[2]	59	21	6	14
18 February[4]	61	25	4	11
19–20 February[3]	61	23	6	10
22 February[5]	84	12	4	—

[1] Entries are percentages, and each row sums to 100 percent, except for rounding error.

[2] Conducted by the Gallup Organization.

[3] Conducted by Market Shares, Inc.

[4] Conducted by Richard Day Research, Inc.

[5] WMAQ-TV (NBC) Primary Exit Poll.

port moving to 30 percent and Daley dropping deeper into third place at 25 percent. "We're not even worried about Daley anymore," Sawyer said for publication. "It's Washington we're concerned about."[79] By then Vrdolyak was concerned, too, and the publicity generated by his appeal to the precinct workers on Saturday, 19 February, provided a final stimulus to the black crusade.

The final days of the campaign only witnessed the culmination of trends that began earlier. Compared with the January results, the interviews conducted between 11 and 16 February showed the white vote splitting more evenly between Byrne and Daley, while the black vote was solidifying for Washington. If that type of movement continued, Washington would win the primary. Moreover, the movement that occurred in the polls from October through early February was itself evidence of how volatile public opinion was, and how it was responding to campaign events.

Several developments helped crystallize public opinion. Byrne's media blitz in December was the first of these. By dominating the airwaves, Byrne's commercials framed the context for evaluating her candidacy, put her opponents on the defensive, and pushed her ahead in the polls. The four debates among the candidates, between 18 and 31 January, had a similar effect for Washington. Coming after the faltering start of his campaign, the debates gave him valuable exposure when he needed it, when many blacks still had to be convinced he was a serious challenger.[80]

Despite his years in legislative politics, Washington wasn't as well known throughout the city as his opponents. With less money than Byrne or Daley, he wasn't able to air television commercials early to frame the context for the public's perception of his candidacy. What Chicagoans did learn of Washington during the early days of the campaign was not positive. The day after Washington announced his candidacy, one television commentator discussed his past conviction and jail sentence for failing to file income tax returns, and Washington later addressed the matter in a speech to the Chicago Rotary Club. Then, on Christmas Day, Washington made a campaign visit to the inmates of the Cook County Jail, and a local television station used the occasion to show his old mug shot on its nightly news. These reminders of his past errors were bad enough, but the reports on his current campaign made matters worse. The campaign seemed to be in a shambles, lacking coherence and centralized direction, and Washington himself seemed unable to seize control and project himself as a forceful and decisive leader.[81]

The debates gave Washington the opportunity to prove himself, and he made the most of it. He dominated much of the action, displayed his knowledge of city government, showed his considerable oratorical skills, and finally provided voters with a framework for assessing his candidacy. He attacked Byrne, sketched his own remedies for the city's ills, and largely ignored Daley. "I'm running for the office of Mayor of the City of Chicago because Jane Byrne is destroying our city," he began his opening statement in the first debate. "Chicago can no longer afford Jane Byrne, because what is at stake is the very life blood of Chicago—jobs, jobs, jobs." The second debate focused on crime and public safety, and Washington again went on the attack, referring to Chicago as "the organized crime capital of the world" and calling for the ouster of Police Superintendent Brzeczek, "the top cop who's become a political prop." Washington again assailed Byrne's record on jobs in the third debate, accusing her of fostering downtown development at the expense of the neighborhoods. Her media image "as a competent administrator and effective leader is a fraud," he claimed. "The real Jane Byrne has created an atmosphere in Chicago that is totally inhospitable to business."[82]

Through the first three exchanges, Washington, like Daley, presented himself as an anti-Byrne candidate. He forcefully, sometimes stridently, attacked the mayor, distinguishing his candidacy from hers on jobs, fiscal management, and the need to end cronyism and patronage in city government. His references to Daley were usually indirect and general, because he was competing against Byrne for votes among blacks. Finally, in the last debate, on 31 January, at Roberto Clemente High School, Washington framed the context for blacks to evaluate his candidacy. "There are some who believe that I should avoid the race issue," he said in his opening statement. "But I will not avoid it because it permeates our entire city and has devastating implications. . . . I'm running to end Jane Byrne's four-year effort to further institutionalize racial discrimination in this great city."[83]

Simply "standing toe-to-toe" with his opponents gave his candidacy "an air of legitimacy" that its fumbling start and lack of advertising had denied it to that point.[84] The 5 million viewers who watched the debates, and especially blacks, saw a dynamic and knowledgeable candidate, who upstaged his rivals and took control of the situation. Washington showed himself to be a viable candidate, a real contender, not just a spoiler helping one of his white opponents by siphoning support from the other. And Washington identified his candidacy with the racial interests of the black community, not just with its economic and social concerns. He attacked discrimination directly and specifically, reminding blacks of their own experiences, appealing to their self-respect, and offering them his own candidacy as a means of saying "never again."

Washington's performance in the fourth debate came three days after a highly publicized racial gaffe by Byrne, which may have heightened its impact. Speaking to students at DePaul University, Byrne was again itemizing her record of minority appointments. She listed their names, cited their credentials, and mentioned that the persons happened to be black. When she got to Commissioner of Human Services Lenora Cartwright, the mayor said "she happens to be black, but she's good." Again, when she came to Elmer Beard, Jr., the CHA's executive director, she noted that he "also happens to be black but [he] also happens to be good."[85] The audience gasped audibly at both these references; the mayor seemed to be saying that these appointees were good despite being black, implying that it was unusual for blacks to be qualified. Such comments simply reinforced the view, held by many blacks, that Byrne was insensitive and contemptuous of them.

Whatever the effect of Byrne's comments, blacks were clearly impressed with Washington's performance in the debates. Workers for Market Facts, Inc., who were interviewing in the neighborhoods between 17 and 23 January, caught some of the early reactions. "The debates show he's the better man. He's qualified," one black resident of the West Side told an interviewer. While another said he supported Washington because of "the attitude he could foster for blacks. . . .

The young kids need that image, someone they can look up to." Washington was becoming a symbol of black pride, and the analysts of the survey admitted that their poll couldn't measure the impact of that development.[86] Other polls (see Table 17) did detect a spurt in Washington's support among blacks between early January and early February, which suggests the effect of the debates. Moreover, on election day, 57.4 percent of the blacks voting for Washington said the debates helped them make their decision.[87]

Washington gained most from the debates, but he was not their only beneficiary. Despite verbal assaults from two sides, "New Jane" kept her cool demeanor, appearing low-key and professional and showing none of the traits of "Old Jane." Daley also scored with his attacks on Byrne's media advisor and her campaign funds. Most important for Daley, his performance showed he could hold his own and undermined claims that he lacked the intellectual equipment to run the city.

While the debates were vital to Washington, so was the development that kept Daley's candidacy alive. Mid-January was the low point in the Daley campaign: published polls showed him trailing and losing ground, and his campaign staff worried about the effect on the morale of his precinct volunteers and voters. Then, on 23 January, the *Chicago Tribune* editorially announced that Byrne's "roller-coaster administration" and Washington's "polarizing campaign" left it "no alternative but to endorse Daley." Byrne had proven adept only at raising "obscene" amounts of campaign funds and using the power of the mayor's office to reward cronies and punish enemies. Daley, the editorial concluded, "offers hope, and that makes him unique among the candidates." Ten days later, on 3 February, the *Chicago Sun-Times* gave a more enthusiastic endorsement to the state's attorney. Its full-page editorial blasted Byrne for selling "the city to buy reelection," and it praised Daley for keeping "his [past] campaign promises—a rare and wonderful thing in a politician. . . . He has a reputation for reliability and integrity."

By endorsing Daley, the city's two major newspapers implied that he was still a viable candidate, with a decent chance of winning. The Daley staff quickly jumped on the suggestion and spread the message by distributing a million reprints and quoting the endorsements in television commercials. The stepped-up newspaper attack on Byrne's record aided their effort, and so did the endorsement by the Firefighters Union on 9 February. And to counter negative reports from published polls, the Daley staff began circulating stories that their own straw polls showed him in the lead and picking up momentum.[88] With this activity and vigorous stump campaigning, especially on the Southwest Side, Daley's white support turned upward. As that occurred, and Washington's black support continued to

Editorial Why we picked Daley

Daley's the best hope

16. A scene from one of Daley's television spots in which he used endorsements by newspapers in an effort to revive his candidacy. In this commercial, the voice-over tells viewers, "Both newspapers agree that only Richard Daley has a program for Chicago that will work."

grow, the race tightened. "Of course it's getting closer," Byrne's campaign manager admitted. "We're getting our brains beaten in by the papers everyday, so it stands to reason that the thing is going to tighten up."[89]

If Byrne's strategists hadn't been preoccupied by the contest with Daley for the white vote, they might have noticed yet another development in the campaign, one which changed the odds in the Byrne-Washington battle for black support. But they seem to have missed the way the Washington campaign was being transformed into a crusade.

The Washington campaign all along had something of the appearance of a social movement, but the massive rally on 6 February at the Pavilion of the University of Illinois at Chicago revealed its crusading character. A capacity crowd of 12,000, the largest of the primary campaign, braved an all-day snowfall to consecrate themselves to the cause. They waved Washington placards, chanted, sang, and filled the arena with applause. The throng escorted Washington to the podium with "thunderous applause and foot stomping," and it roared approval when he denounced Byrne as a "flunky of Ronald

Reagan." They cheered, too, as Washington unleashed his strongest attack yet on Daley; and when he repeated his pledge to fire the police superintendent, the audience shouted back "Fire Brzeczek. Fire Brzeczek."[90]

The rally was more a religious revival than a typical political gathering. Those attending were already converted, but coming together strengthened their commitment, raised their expectations, and stimulated them to greater activity. The rally showed the city "that we are serious," one Washington supporter concluded; and showing that to blacks ignited an enthusiasm that swept through the black community. "The mood is there; the commitment is there," Washington sensed by the end of that week. And later he explained: "The critical point was slightly after the debates when everything came together in one, cohesive whole. . . . I was certain we had it won the day after the rally [at the Pavilion]."[91]

The final development that crystallized public opinion came during the last week of the campaign, when "the race thing" burst into the open, and Byrne's "All Chicago" strategy fell apart. Not many white voters originally chose between Byrne and Daley because one was more likely to prevent a black candidate from winning the primary. Most of them probably dismissed the likelihood of high and cohesive turnout for Washington among blacks and underestimated his strength. As the campaign wore on, Washington's black support solidified, Byrne's strength softened among blacks and marginal groups of whites, and Daley still ran last. However, as the state's attorney's white support began to bounce back from its January low point, Byrne's strategy was in some danger.

It was at that point that Byrne began attacking Daley. She had generally avoided direct criticisms of her opponents, probably fearing that attacks would simply remind voters of Old Jane. In the fourth debate, under Daley's heavy assault on her campaign fund, she responded by criticizing his own fund-raising activities, and possibly she mentioned the theme at some later campaign stops. But it was during the second week of February that she picked up the theme, used it more often, and added that the budget for the state's attorney's office had gone up sharply under his administration. The Byrne campaign also began airing a television commercial claiming that Daley had raised millions of dollars in campaign funds from persons doing business with City Hall or with the state's attorney's office. Byrne's moves were an attempt to slow Daley's gains and to shore up her own support among white voters.[92]

Even before the mayor launched her attack, some precinct captains were circulating news that Byrne's polls showed Daley to be out of the running. In a Byrne-Washington contest, they argued as early as mid-January, a vote for Daley would only help elect a black mayor. From the second week of February onward, the tempo of this type of activity increased. Leaflets began appearing in white neighborhoods claiming that Washington as mayor would break up the Northwest and Southwest Side communities. "Vote No. 10 [Byrne's ballot line] and at least you will secure your neighborhood," the Concerned Citizens of the Neighborhood urged. In some places precinct workers distributed photographs of Jesse Jackson as "hysteria bait," arguing that he would be the real mayor if Washington was elected. Then a week before the primary, a letter signed by former Republican Governor Richard Ogilvie was circulated widely in white areas on the Northwest Side. Ogilvie, who had endorsed Byrne in January, now claimed that the contest had narrowed to a choice between her and Washington. As other stories surfaced, it seemed that the Machine's printing presses and mimeograph machines were working overtime "cranking out scare letters and brochures" for circulation on the white Northwest and Southwest Sides. The appeals were clearly intended to arouse the anxieties of white voters, reminding them that their continued cultural dominance was at stake, in the hope of stampeding them away from Daley toward Byrne.[93]

Some voters didn't need overt appeals. From reading the newspapers, or listening to the comments of local television reporters, white voters knew the gap was narrowing and that Washington, not Daley, was in second place. "My precinct captains aren't bringing up the race thing; they don't have to say a thing," Alderman Thomas Cullerton (38th Ward) observed. "The people bring it up themselves. They read about the polls and they have an impact." Other committeemen went beyond tacit silence. In Roman Pucinski's 41st Ward, precinct captains distributed Ogilvie's letter and hammered the theme repeatedly during the final week of the campaign.[94]

Byrne, Griffin, Sawyer, and probably Vrdolyak, knew what was happening in the days prior to 19 February. They knew from Byrne's private polls that the mayor had dropped 4 points between Wednesday and Friday (16 to 18 February), that Washington was gaining, and that the mayor's lead was down to an insecure 3.9 percentage points. They may also have known that Washington had a higher proportion of firmly committed supporters than either Byrne or Daley. And, of course, they had earlier heard, and denied, the reports that precinct workers were playing up "the race thing."[95]

This was the context for Vrdolyak's now-famous speech to white precinct workers at a rally on the Northwest Side the Saturday before the primary. "A vote for Daley is a vote for Washington," he told them. "It's a two-person race. It would be the worst day in the history of Chicago if your candidate . . . was not elected. It's a racial thing. Don't kid yourself. I'm calling on you to save your city, to save your precinct. We're fighting to keep the city the way it is."[96]

17. Edward Vrdolyak addressing an early meeting of precinct captains. "Who are these people . . . that make these endorsements from various media places?" he asked them. "Have they ever been to your neighborhood? Have they ever gone to a wake there? Have they ever gone to a christening or a wedding? Have they ever helped somebody who needed help on your block? That's what this organization is all about."

Since he was simply repeating a theme that had been making the rounds in the precincts for some time and which some columnists and reporters had already described, Vrdolyak may have been unprepared for the firestorm that developed when the press and television reported his comments. He may have thought it just wasn't news. But there was a difference. When Vrdolyak voiced the argument, he phrased his appeal baldly and bluntly, without any of the usual code words. Moreover, he was a close advisor to Byrne and chairman of the Democratic Central Committee of Cook County, not merely a precinct captain or simply another alderman, so his comment made the front pages and became the lead story on news broadcasts. From that point until election day, charges and countercharges concerning Vrdolyak's appeal and Byrne's racial tactics preoccupied the candidates and the media.[97]

Daley's reaction contributed to the focus on race, while underscoring the dilemma that plagued him throughout. Daley assailed Vrdolyak for "the fear, the hysteria he's using. . . . It isn't good for the

city." On Sunday and again on Monday, he denounced Byrne for trying to frighten his white supporters by injecting race into the campaign. "It is an insult to anyone's intelligence and it is a desperate
political strategy. It is a disgrace." The contest is now and always has
been a three-way race, he claimed. And the Daley campaign underscored the claim by releasing the results of a straw poll taken on Saturday, showing the state's attorney with a slight lead. "Every indicator we have except the telephone polls show[s] we are winning," his
campaign manager concluded.[98]

While Daley could counter the mayor's efforts to panic whites, he
was not able to use the weekend's developments to fashion an effective appeal for black support. He condemned Vrdolyak for encouraging fear among whites, but he declined opportunities to go beyond
that to a specific charge of racism and a call for Vrdolyak's removal
as party chairman. When Daley appeared on a popular WGN radio
show and was pressed on that and other matters touching on the
racial interests of blacks, he simply repeated his familiar campaign
stances. He would not single out any government or political officials to be fired; he favored open housing in general but wanted
neighborhoods to have more say in the location of public housing
projects, and he claimed that incidents of racial violence in his home
area of Bridgeport were simply "individual criminal acts that can
happen anywhere in the city."[99] To the end of the campaign, Daley's
sensitivity to his white ethnic base, especially on the Southwest
Side, simply prevented him from developing any strategy to tap the
racial concerns of blacks and their anti-Byrne feelings and translate
these into voting support. The absence of such an appeal had effectively defined Daley out of the competition for the black vote from
the beginning.

Only Byrne was a contender in both of the simultaneous contests
that made up the primary, and the late focus on race exposed the
two-sided character of her campaign strategy. On the one hand,
the Byrne campaign followed Vrdolyak's advice to fight hard out in
the precincts over the weekend. The precinct captains are "busting
their tails, really doing a number" for the mayor, Vrdolyak boasted,
and he was right. On election day nearly two thirds of the white voters
reported having been contacted by a precinct captain, and Byrne
drew 53 percent of her white support from among these voters.[100]
There is also evidence that Vrdolyak and other Byrne supporters set
up an elaborate phone bank to warn whites of a possible Washington
victory. Thousands of white voters received phone calls over the
weekend urging them not to waste their vote on Daley but to support
Byrne as the best "white hope" of defeating Washington. In Vrdolyak's own 10th Ward, the precinct captains were telling voters to
"stop the nigger" on behalf of Byrne. "They are making it a black-

18. Mayor Byrne, on the Saturday before the primary election, campaigning at the Cabrini-Green building in which she had stayed for several weeks in 1981.

and-white issue," complained one Democratic committeeman who supported Byrne. "It's deplorable. They are trying to get all the whites to vote for Byrne." [101]

At the same time, the events of the final weekend put Byrne on the defensive and threatened her effort to cut Washington's support among blacks. To control the damage, the mayor campaigned in the black community and tried to separate herself from Vrdolyak's remark. "Nobody speaks for the mayor. We've made no statements nor will we with racial overtones," she said. "I don't think any candidate, including Mr. Washington, should make it [race] an issue." Later she told another black audience that she was "annoyed with anybody who made race an issue," including Vrdolyak and Washington. "I have campaigned for all Chicago," she added. She went door to door in the housing projects, traveled into the heart of Washington's congressional district, and visited black churches to preach what she described as her message of "love" and "caring." No mayor could get everything done in less than four years, but she had cared enough to begin, she told a black audience on the South Side, "and it's much more than was ever done before." [102]

The late concentration on race caused Washington none of the tactical problems that it created for his opponents. Since early Febru-

19. A confident Washington greeting supporters while campaigning in the Loop, 21 February 1983. (*Chicago Tribune.*)

ary, he had worked to solidify his "black base," as he referred to it, and the public attention surrounding Vrdolyak's statement aided the effort. Campaigning on Sunday and Monday at L stations, black churches, and rallies, Washington spoke of Vrdolyak's "scurrilous racist statement" and demanded Byrne "publicly denounce" the chairman or pull out of the primary. He branded the chairman's remark as "a desperate appeal to racism," an eleventh-hour effort to frighten and intimidate voters. Then he used the statement to reassure his supporters and to encourage his workers. "This hysteria, this pointed racism on the part of Mr. Vrdolyak, is a result of the fact that they can count. They can see. They can hear. We're going to win this campaign." [103]

Throughout these final days, Washington was a picture of total confidence. Attacking Byrne and linking her with Vrdolyak, Washington now personified black pride and self-respect. "We Shall Overcome," sang the throng at the final campaign gathering, a candlelight spiritual service at the South Side headquarters of Operation PUSH. "We've run the course," Washington told them. "We met the enemy on the battlefield. We fought him on his own terms. We pushed him, whipped him to his natural knees." [104]

High turnout and bloc voting by Chicago's blacks delivered the mayoral nomination to Harold Washington, as Byrne and Daley fought to a virtual draw among the city's white voters. To be sure, Washington received some support from whites and Hispanics, but their ballots together came to about 3,200 votes less than his margin of victory.[105] Without the performance of his "black base," the newspaper columns and television commentaries after the election would have extolled the Machine's performance, instead of trying to explain how Washington snatched victory from its grasp.

How did he do it? Why did blacks rally around his candidacy? Why didn't whites stampede to Byrne? These questions simply point to a larger one: Was Washington's victory a fluke, an outcome made possible by anti-Byrne sentiment combined with an unexpected campaign incident? Or did it represent a politically focused racial awakening among black citizens?

The immediate postmortems pointed to the chancy character of the result. When Daley's strength among white ethnic voters proved lower than their projections, his aides attributed it to Vrdolyak's racial remark. Referring to the politics of "the lost weekend," they claimed that efforts to portray the contest as a two-person, white-vs.-black race "killed us on the Southwest and Northwest Sides."[106] The evidence in Table 18 casts strong doubt on that explanation. If the late focus on race panicked white voters and drove them into Byrne's camp, she should have outpolled Daley among whites who made their decisions in the final days of the campaign. In fact, the opposite was the case—Daley ran 11.7 points ahead of the mayor among the late-deciding whites, and they made up nearly one fifth of all the white voters supporting him. Indeed, Daley outpolled Byrne among all whites who decided *during* the campaign, with the mayor's only edge coming among those who knew their decision all along.

Moreover, there is no evidence that a large number of whites chose between Byrne and Daley in order to stop Washington. Given an opportunity by the WBBM-TV (CBS) exit poll to mark one or more reasons for their voting decision, only 8.6 percent of the responses by whites indicated that voting *against* another candidate was a factor, and more Daley voters checked that reason than Byrne supporters (by 7.4 percentage points). Some respondents may be reluctant to admit supporting one candidate to stop another, especially when it makes their decision appear to be racially motivated. But voters aren't very likely even to consider the possibility unless they believe the undesirable candidate has a chance to win, and interviews conducted over the final weekend showed that only 19 percent of the whites thought Washington had a good chance of winning. Despite the events of the campaign, the published poll results, and the efforts by Byrne's workers to convince them, most white voters simply didn't believe that a black candidate could win the primary.[107] Most

Table 18. Vote by Race by Time of Decision [1]

	Whites			Blacks		
	All Along	Few Weeks	Few Days	All Along	Few Weeks	Few Days
Washington	5.2	14.9	18.4	81.5	93.7	84.1
Byrne	59.5	40.5	34.8	16.2	4.6	12.3
Daley	35.2	44.3	46.5	2.3	1.7	3.6
(N)	(1037)	(370)	(256)	(906)	(302)	(138)

The question: How long ago did you decide who to vote for?

[1] Entries are percentages, and each column sums to 100 percent, except for rounding error and scattering for other candidates.

Source: WBBM-TV (CBS) Primary Exit Poll.

had been nurtured on the myth of the Machine's invincibility, and many probably also believed that without white leadership blacks were incapable of organizing a successful political effort. As a result, most whites never came to see Washington's candidacy as a realistic threat, and thus they felt free to choose between the rival white candidates, the contending white factions of the Machine, without fear of jeopardizing their racial interests.

David Sawyer, Byrne's chief campaign strategist, offered another explanation. From the November elections until the day before the primary, he claimed Byrne was in control of the campaign; then the roof fell in after Vrdolyak's comment. "So *suddenly*," Sawyer said. "We had that race in our pocket and then, like *that*, she was gone." The late publicity concerning the race question turned victory into defeat. "The thing we feared most was the race issue. That's why we couldn't attack Washington—she was already seen as unfair to blacks, and whites, simply perceiving her as unfair would switch their support to Daley." That's why the "'alleged' comment [by Vrdolyak] was a disaster," he concluded. "As soon as the press picked it up we lost control of the campaign. And there was nothing we could do to get it back." [108]

Sawyer at least recognized that most of the late-deciding whites opted for Daley, although it's hard to imagine their doing so because they suddenly remembered Byrne was unfair to blacks. Although Sawyer didn't say so explicitly, he also implied that Vrdolyak's statement contributed to Byrne's defeat by eroding her support among blacks. However, the blacks who decided in the final days gave the mayor considerably more support than those who made their choices a few weeks earlier (see Table 18).

Both the postmortem by Daley's aides and the one by Sawyer exaggerated the impact of Vrdolyak's remark. The swing to Washington among blacks was in progress before Vrdolyak appealed to the precinct workers, and it was sparked by a new and assertive sense of racial pride among Chicago's blacks, a politically focused racial consciousness. Washington's aides often spoke during the final weeks of the "almost religious fervor his campaign has engendered in the black community, where his blue-and-white button has become a symbol of racial pride." There was "a groundswell of support among all levels of blacks . . . for Washington," one columnist observed, and it has been developing "over the last two weeks." And Washington's pollster noticed "very clear movement within the last couple of weeks, and it was accelerated movement."[109]

Byrne's private polls detected this developing groundswell among blacks by Thursday, 17 February, well before Vrdolyak's remark and the massive publicity surrounding it. It was to arrest that movement that the mayor adjusted her campaign schedule for 19 February and added stops in the black community. "We're concentrating where we have slippage," she admitted to reporters, and her aides explained that Washington had made a point-a-day gain among blacks over the past week. Byrne's heavy campaigning among blacks on Saturday probably slowed Washington's momentum, and the poll taken for the mayor on Sunday showed her making a 4-point gain. But that was a temporary deviation from the longer trend: when they saw the results of the Monday survey, her pollster, Richard Dressner, admitted later, "we felt we were dead."[110]

From the boycott of ChicagoFest, through the registration drive, to the early stages of the Washington campaign, negative attitudes toward Byrne were probably the key factors motivating most blacks. Even at the end, of course, most blacks disapproved of Byrne, and those who did voted heavily for Washington (Table 19). We expect that pattern, just as we expect voters who approve any incumbent's job performance to give heavy support to that candidate. Although white voters approving of Byrne did that, blacks who approved her overall performance gave the mayor only 55.1 percent of their votes. And she received only 50 percent support from the small proportion of blacks who judged her to be sensitive to the needs of minorities.[111] Moreover, blacks who approved of Byrne but made their choices during the campaign gave majorities to Washington (Table 20).

The overall pattern is impressive. First, there are no signs that the last few days of the campaign witnessed any unusual surge of black voters toward Washington. Second, even blacks approving of the job Byrne had done as mayor gave her a considerably smaller share of their votes than whites who approved. Third, the blacks who approved of Byrne but made their decisions during the campaign gave her less support than the corresponding categories of approving whites, and less even than the approving blacks who made their choices at the outset. However, those who made up their minds a few

Table 19. Vote by Race by Byrne's Approval Rating [1]

	Whites			Blacks		
	Approve	Dis-approve	No Opinion	Approve	Dis-approve	No Opinion
Washington	3.1	16.5	10.4	44.1	96.7	90.7
Byrne	91.2	4.9	28.2	55.1	0.4	6.9
Daley	5.7	78.3	60.7	0.3	2.9	2.5
(N)	(864)	(649)	(163)	(290)	(753)	(321)

The question: Do you approve or disapprove of the job Jane Byrne has done as Mayor of Chicago?

[1] Entries are percentages, and each column sums to 100 percent, except for rounding error and scattering for other candidates.

Source: WBBM-TV (CBS) Primary Exit Poll.

Table 20. Vote by Race by Time of Decision for Respondents Approving Byrne's Performance as Mayor [1]

	Whites			Blacks		
	All Along	Few Weeks	Few Days	All Along	Few Weeks	Few Days
Washington	0.8	5.0	15.2	33.3	72.9	64.3
Byrne	96.8	84.3	66.3	66.1	27.1	35.7
Daley	2.4	10.7	18.5	0.5	0.0	0.0
(N)	(595)	(159)	(92)	(186)	(48)	(42)

The questions are those used for Tables 18 and 19.

[1] Entries are percentages, and each column sums to 100 percent, except for rounding error and scattering for other candidates.

Source: WBBM-TV (CBS) Primary Exit Poll.

weeks prior to the election gave Washington more support than the late deciders.

It seems plausible that the debates helped to change Washington's campaign into a crusade, and as that occurred, blacks developed a positive and potent motive for voting—pride in their candidate, their community, and themselves. Despite the fact that on the eve of the election most blacks (57 percent) still thought Byrne would win and only a minority (49 percent) thought Washington had a good chance, they turned out in large numbers and voted cohesively for their candidate.[112] Developing this sense of solidarity, of racial pride, and channeling it into electoral politics was the accomplishment of the primary campaign and the major reason for Washington's victory.

7. Race War Chicago Style
The Election of a Mayor, 1983

Epton for Mayor—before It's Too Late! *Campaign slogan*

■ The feast of St. Patrick is always a grand day in Chicago. Whether the sun shines brightly or the day is wet and cold, a spirit of exuberant celebration fills the air. City workers dump dye into the Chicago River, turning its waters green. The Irish societies and bands, the neighborhood groups and organizations march in a gala parade, the highlight of the city's formal festivities. And in the neighborhood bars and taverns, Irish and would-be Irish celebrate into the wee hours of the morning.

St. Patrick's Day in Chicago is as much a time for the trooping of political colors as for the wearing of the green. The city's politicians, incumbents as well as office seekers, make appearances at the neighborhood festivities, and none would think of missing the downtown parade. Brandishing shillelaghs, sporting leprechaun hats, or simply wearing green ribbons, the pols strut along the line of march, waving to the crowds, basking in the limelight, and identifying themselves with the city's best-known ethnic group. Seeing the politicians may be as big an attraction to the crowd as hearing the drum and bugle corps, and many grizzled veterans of City Hall still regard the reaction of the onlookers as a better barometer of a politician's popularity than the latest poll results.

Typically, the Democrats use the St. Patrick's day parade to showcase the candidate who is heading their ticket at the next election. But 1983 was an exceptional year. The Democratic nominee for mayor of Chicago, Harold Washington, a black from the South Side, was denied a place of honor in the front rank and marched beside

George Dunne, the ousted chairman of the party. Onlookers stirred as the Washington-Dunne group came toward their locations. Some strained to catch a glimpse of the Democratic candidate; there was a smattering of applause, a few shouts of recognition, but none of the enthusiastic outpouring that normally greets the party's standard-bearer for mayor.

The cool, passive reception given Washington by the St. Patrick's Day crowd contrasted sharply with the welcome his Republican opponent received four days earlier at the annual South Side Irish Parade. Bernard Epton, a wealthy Jewish Republican from the lakefront, was an unlikely hero to working-class Catholic Democrats. But thousands of onlookers yelled and cheered wildly as Epton, resplendent in his green sweater, walked along Western Avenue. He marched through the heart of Daley Country, smiling, waving acknowledgment, and enjoying the warmth of his reception. "It looks like he just won the war or something," his press secretary commented to reporters. "Do you think they're getting [him] confused with the Pope?"[1]

At one point along the route, a woman in the front row of onlookers shouted his name. As Epton turned in her direction, she yanked open her jacket to reveal a bright green T-shirt emblazoned with the slogan, "Vote Right, Vote White." Epton didn't react visibly, and it's likely he didn't even see the lettering on the T-shirt. But its message came to dominate the election.[2]

The contest for mayor brought Chicago's long-standing and sharp racial divisions into political focus. The prospect of a black mayor stirred deep feelings of pride in some neighborhoods, while it aroused equally strong fears in others. "Black people were energized," the Reverend Jesse Jackson said. "White people were traumatized."[3] As a result, Chicago's general election for mayor in 1983 was not a battle between two parties, or even simply between two candidates; it was a political war between two races.

Washington vs. the Regulars

■ The overflow crowd at the McCormick Inn had been celebrating since the polls closed. They sensed victory, and their expectations rose with every news release. They cheered reports of heavy turnout in the black wards and the sullen comments of the West Side blacks who were tied to Byrne. "I'm afraid the mayor is not going to do as well as expected in the 24th Ward," lamented Cardis Collins, the only black member of Congress to endorse Byrne. "There is a groundswell for Washington."[4]

At 11:40 P.M., a somber Richard M. Daley appeared before his tearful supporters at the Hyatt Regency Chicago. Knowing now that he was denied his patrimony, he called for "all neighborhoods and all people" to support the next mayor. Then, shortly before midnight, reports circulated that Mayor Byrne's chief field organizer projected a narrow victory for Washington. A few minutes later, Byrne herself descended from the penthouse suite at the Ambassador West to address her supporters. Still hoarse from the cold that bothered her during the last week of the campaign, she told her workers to "calm down" but keep their spirits up. "The election is too close to call." She was going home to bed, she said, advising them to follow her example. They'd all know the outcome by tomorrow morning. The television reporters were stunned; they had expected Byrne to concede, and so had Harold Washington: "Lord," he grumbled, still fearing the Machine's vote-counting tricks, "those barracudas are going to steal us blind."[5]

His advisors were sure of the victory, but Washington cautiously decided to wait for still more returns, telling his staff to bring in other speakers to keep the throng in the ballrooms livened up. Chief among these speakers was the Reverend Jesse Jackson. "Today we had a retirement program," he told the cheering crowd. "We retired Daley, the relic of the past. We retired Jane Byrne, the curse of the present, and we elected Harold Washington, the hope of the future." Referring to the primary as "a stepping stone to higher ground," Jackson reminded them that the general election for mayor, "the Super Bowl" of politics, was still ahead. "We want the Super Bowl! We want the Super Bowl! We want it all! We want it here! We want it now!" Television commentators wondered aloud whether Jackson's rhetoric might only galvanize the fears of apprehensive whites, but its immediate effect was on the crowd of listeners at the McCormick Inn. They cheered and cheered and then broke into the now familiar rhythmic chant, "We want Harold. We want Harold." At about 2 A.M., they got him. With Jesse Jackson standing beside him, Washington quieted the crowd and announced that he "proudly and humbly" accepted the Democratic nomination for mayor of Chicago. "To those who have opposed us, we open our arms and offer you to join in our movement."[6]

Washington spoke that night not just to his black supporters but to all Chicagoans, and both his text and his tone were conciliatory and inviting. Since 53.7 percent of the city's registered voters were white, to win the general election Washington knew he had to reach beyond his black base. There was no immediate reason to doubt the outcome of that effort.

On election night, after it became clear that Byrne had lost, several Democratic committeemen told reporters they were uncertain about backing Washington. "I'll go back to my organization and discuss it with them," one remarked. But Vrdolyak assured that there would be "no obstructionism. . . . The Democratic party will give its full support to the Democratic candidate." When Mayor Byrne read her statement to the media on Wednesday morning, she congratulated Washington on his victory and pledged her support for his candidacy in the general election. It was the city's tradition to elect the Democratic nominee as mayor, and "that's the proper way," she added. "The people have spoken. And now we must continue to work for Chicago and for one Chicago." Even Vito Marzullo, the longtime boss of the 25th Ward, said he could back Washington: "I've never had any problems in all my political life with anyone," he told reporters at City Hall. Asked if he was waiting for Washington to request his support, Marzullo responded, "He don't have to do anything. He's the Mayor of Chicago."[7]

Like Marzullo, Washington and his campaign staff viewed his election as a foregone conclusion. Democratic mayoral nominees had won every general election in Chicago since 1931, and most of them by wide margins, so Washington had good reason to be confident. He could expect the leaders of the party, however reluctantly, to accept the results of the primary and work for his election in April. After all, hadn't they done as much on Jane Byrne's behalf four years earlier, despite her continuing attacks on the evil cabal? As the party's nominee, in a city where Republicans were nearly an endangered species, Washington would attract new support from among white and Hispanic Democrats, and he could count on virtually all the black vote against a Republican. "He might not win as big as some other Democrats have, but he should win," Don Rose calculated a few days after the primary.[8]

In those euphoric days immediately following the primary, Washington behaved like the mayor-elect. He announced the appointment of Edwin Berry, former executive director of the Chicago Urban League, to put together a transition team, one of whose tasks was to be a talent search for people to appoint to executive positions. He deflected Brzeczek's charge that the police department would "be a circus" under Washington by calmly saying that the police superintendent was "hysterical" and "out of control." He met with leaders of the city's business community, indicated his general backing for projects such as the improvements at O'Hare International Airport, the North Loop Development, and the 1992 Chicago World's Fair, and assured the executives of a healthy business climate under his administration. He spoke to the businessmen and other groups of programs and plans that would permit "all Chicago to move forward."[9]

While Washington was delivering his message of unity and conciliation, strange things were going on in the precincts. Democratic voters were rallying to the cause of a Republican candidate. Volunteers turned up by the dozens at Epton campaign offices. So many came, in so short a period, that his small staff had difficulty even

20. Republican mayoral candidate Bernard Epton acknowledging cheers from the throng that greeted him outside Wrigley Field before the Cubs' scheduled home opener on 5 April 1983. (*Chicago Tribune.*)

keeping track of them. Bridgeport residents, many saying they'd be voting Republican for the first time in their lives, overflowed the Epton office near their neighborhood. On the Northwest Side, groups came under banners announcing themselves as "Democrats for Epton." Some sported buttons with slogans such as "Polish for Epton-ski" and "Italians for Epton-ini." The outpouring was so great that the Epton campaign eventually operated thirty volunteer offices, ten times the number originally planned.[10] This same enthusiasm marked Epton's early campaign stops. Wherever he appeared, the Polish, Italian, Lithuanian, Greek, or Irish audiences received him warmly, chanting "Ber-nie, Ber-nie." It was a spontaneous and enthusiastic outpouring from the grass roots, a groundswell unlike anything "I've seen . . . in 30 years in politics," his deputy campaign manager observed.[11]

As ordinary Democrats flocked to Epton's banner, the leaders of the party remained cool toward their own nominee. On the night of the primary election, only two of the ward committeemen who had worked for Byrne or Daley called for support of Washington, and they were both blacks. As one of them said, party officials should not refuse to accept the verdict of the people; "it could cause unbelievable social fragmentation and political schism that would cause total distrust on the part of minorities."[12] At that point, most of the white committeemen were probably still stunned by Washington's nomination and, like Marzullo, also took the election of any Democratic nominee for granted. Perhaps, too, some assumed that Washington would come around, as Byrne had four years earlier. Hadn't he begun his career as a precinct worker for the Machine? Wouldn't his inside knowledge lead him to respect its power and court its support? Surely Washington knew better than Byrne did in 1979 how the city's ruling institution operated, and he did not yield to the wishful thinking so common among Chicago's independents by writing a premature obituary for the Machine. He knew it was still alive, although seriously wounded, and that its precinct activities remained important. But he had experienced the Machine as a black, witnessed its neglect of black interests, and chafed under its domination. That experience had encouraged his maverick behavior as an elected official and now cemented his resolve to push forward with reforms ending the Machine's control over the government of the city and the lives of its people.

Washington publicly said he expected the party organization to endorse and work for his election. "I am the nominee. I expect the support of the Democratic committeemen," he told reporters two days after the primary. He would talk with the committeemen, but "there will be no deals made relative to that accommodation," he added. There will be "no erosion" of his campaign promises, including the one to end patronage by removing the Democratic party organization from its control of city government and city workers. Later, after receiving the endorsement of the Independent Voters of Illinois—Independent Precinct Organization (IVI-IPO), Washington pledged to issue an executive order and seek changes in city or state laws to dismantle the patronage system. "It's got to end. . . . It's costly. It's wasteful. It's a shutout mechanism that keeps people out of government rather than bringing them in." [13]

Washington's assault on patronage was a threat to the self-interest of the committeemen, just as Byrne's attack on the evil cabal had been four years earlier. They wondered whether their families, their friends, and members of their political organizations would keep access to city jobs and promotions under a Washington Administration. They wondered, too, whether they would still be able to funnel millions of dollars to politically connected firms, and to influence building inspections and police transfers. "Harold says he doesn't want to wreck the organization and in the same breath he says he doesn't want the committeemen to have any influence in city government," one disturbed ward leader complained. "It doesn't make any sense." [14]

The first break in the facade of party unity came on the last day of February when Alderman Aloysius Majerczyk (12th Ward) announced his support for Epton. His constituents, he explained, "are giving me a message of racial pride. . . . They're afraid of scattered-site housing. They're concerned about the stability of our neighborhood. . . . We're against open housing in my ward and we always have been." Five days later, Lou Reda, Byrne's deputy commissioner of consumer services and a former assistant to her patronage chief, addressed a meeting of Democrats for Epton in a predominantly white ethnic neighborhood on the Northwest Side. "While Daley and Byrne were out there fighting, the troops didn't know there was a little—I don't want to use the word—guy in the woodpile," Reda told the cheering crowd. "We don't want Chicago run from 63d and Halsted." Other party officials and officeholders kept silent for the time, although some were meeting privately and working out of public view. "The question isn't Epton or Washington; everyone's for Epton," one insider observed. "The question is whether it would help or hurt Epton for them [the white committeemen] to come out openly and say so."[15]

In the meantime, Washington acted on two fronts to prevent public defections. In late February he traveled to the state capital to confer with the city's legislative leaders. There he secured the endorsement of House Speaker Michael Madigan (13th Ward committeeman), who publicly advised him to meet with the committeemen and request their support. On 8 March he spoke briefly with Vrdolyak, by telephone, and told reporters he had received the chairman's "personal assurances" of support in the general election. It was certain, Washington continued, that the regular Democrats would "lick their wounds and get back into the fray" on his behalf. At the same time, Washington and his campaign staff publicly stressed the obligation of the committeemen to support the nominee and the consequences of failing to perform their duty. "We expect 100 percent support from every Democratic ward committeeman," Washington said on 13 March. "If they play games with this election . . . then I submit that the county ticket of the Democrats is going down to inglorious defeat in 1984." And Alderman Danny Davis (29th Ward) warned that anyone who wants to run for citywide office "can just about forget about black support" unless they've endorsed Washington.[16]

But neither tactic worked. Concerned about their future prerogatives, power, and income, and aware of the developing groundswell for Epton among their white constituents, most committeemen pondered their options. "There are alternatives," warned Alderman Edward Burke (14th Ward). Some observed that Washington hadn't yet made "any formal request" for support, and others complained that he was making no effort to appeal to voters beyond the black community. Still others, admitting that they couldn't sell Washington in their wards, were reluctant to speak publicly because they didn't want to be assailed as racists. Besides, "this is going to be a populist election," Roman Pucinski (41st Ward) concluded. "The voters are going to make their own minds up. . . . I don't think it's very important what the [precinct] captains do, what the committeemen do, what the editorial writers do."[17]

It was apparent by early March that the party organization was not going to give Washington the type of unified support he had expected. While black committeemen and some of the whites representing black majority wards, such as Edward Quigley (27th Ward) and Frank Damato (37th Ward) endorsed Washington, most of the others remained quiet, planning either to sit out the election or to do the unthinkable and publicly endorse Epton.[18] The prospect of a Democratic party openly divided and formally indifferent, if not hostile, to the election of its own nominee was a novel condition for Chicagoans to witness.

Then, on the day before St. Patrick's Day, Jane Byrne announced she would give the committeemen another alternative. She had "looked carefully" at the candidacies of Epton and Washington and had concluded "that neither of them represents the best interests of the city." Consequently, she had decided to wage "the uphill battle" and seek reelection as a write-in candidate. She conceded that some party leaders had advised her against the effort, and she admitted that it was a great risk to her own political future. But she was "willing to take that risk" because the future of this "fragile city" depended upon the election of a strong and able mayor.[19]

Observers marveled at Byrne's audacity. Write-in campaigns are always difficult to win, and especially under Illinois and Chicago laws. The election codes required voters at the polls to write in the name of the office, the name of the candidate, and draw a box beside the candidate's name and mark an "X" inside it. The laws also prevented the use of preprinted stickers. Byrne's lawyers were prepared to challenge these technical provisions of the election codes; but they had only an outside chance of success, since the lower courts had upheld them in earlier cases, and these decisions had not been reversed by the state supreme court. Moreover, the uncertainty and delay involved in the court challenges would complicate matters by making it impractical to launch the intensive television campaign necessary to educate voters about how to mark the ballot.

The mayor's decision to reenter the campaign revived memories of Old Jane, mercurial, vindictive, and unfair to blacks. Only two weeks earlier, after returning from a vacation in Palm Springs, Byrne had scoffed at the idea of a write-in campaign and repeated her earlier endorsement of Washington. Her latest change of mind, an angry Washington told a hastily called press conference, is "representative of how she ran City Hall." He characterized her move as an act of "political desperation" that will be "destructive" of the Democratic party. "She does not realize that she is finished. She'd rather destroy the City of Chicago and her own party." Most people like fairness, he continued. "They like to know that when you strike out, you're out and you don't come back and ask for three more strikes."[20] Privately, however, some of Washington's strategists expressed no dismay at Byrne's decision. The aura of unfairness that her candidacy evoked might actually increase Washington's appeal among liberal voters in the Lake Shore wards. And, her entry enhanced his chances by splitting the votes of white Chicagoans who resisted the idea of a black mayor.

Epton was certainly aware of the potential impact of Byrne's decision on his chances. "I certainly would assume her candidacy hurts me," he said, explaining that they both would be appealing to the same voters. Nevertheless, if Byrne hoped her announcement would drive him from the race, he publicly informed her that she was badly mistaken. He was determined and bitingly struck back at her, playing to the feeling that her action was unfair. "Three weeks ago the voters wrote Jane Byrne off, and now she wants us to write her in."[21]

Byrne's decision to wage a write-in campaign also complicated matters for the party regulars. If her long-shot legal challenges were successful, and the court simplified the procedures, she might attract enough votes to win. Otherwise, she might simply split the white vote and give Washington an easy route to the mayor's office. The anti-Washington leaders of the party preferred no uncertainty, and so they worked to push Byrne out of the race.

Moments after Byrne's announcement, Vrdolyak issued a public statement separating himself from her effort. "I am not, nor will I be, participating in any write-in campaign." Some of the mayor's other primary supporters followed their chairman's lead in shunning Byrne's renewed candidacy. Later in the day, Park District Superintendent Edmund Kelly (47th Ward) and Alderman Vito Marzullo (25th Ward) announced their endorsements of Epton. Other committeemen from the white ethnic wards who were planning to aid Epton held off while they tried to figure out the effect of Byrne's move. "I've been talking to a lot of guys, and no one knows what the hell to do any more," one North Side committeeman said. "Everything's at a standstill for the moment."[22]

But Byrne was being pressured to withdraw. National party officials denounced her betrayal of Washington and renewed their commitment to him. David Sawyer, her media expert, under pressure from national Democratic leaders, withdrew from the campaign, saying it would be "virtually impossible" for her to win. Key figures from her primary staff, including her campaign manager and press secretary, refused to join the write-in effort, and Senator Edward

Kennedy, a former ally, criticized her publicly when he came to Chicago to campaign for Washington. Private polls showed little support for the write-in bid, and she was soundly booed when appearing before a group of senior citizens on the Southwest Side, where she expected strong support for her candidacy. Finally, one week into her new campaign, Byrne again stunned Chicagoans by abruptly ending her write-in candidacy.[23] When Washington heard the news, he tacitly admitted that Byrne's withdrawal was no boost to his campaign. "It's back to the drawing board," he said. "We've just got to work a bit harder." Making a campaign stop on the Northwest Side, Epton praised the mayor's latest decision and told his cheering supporters, "Now we have a contest."[24]

With Byrne finally out of the picture, Epton's momentum resumed. The flow of volunteers and campaign contributions picked up again and so did the movement of the committeemen. Matthew Bieszczat (26th Ward) and Theodore Swinarski (12th Ward) joined Kelly and Marzullo in the Epton camp on 24 March, and William Banks (36th Ward) and Anthony Laurino (39th Ward) followed the next day. Then John Geocaris (40th Ward) and finally Roman Pucinski (41st Ward) publicly endorsed the Republican candidate for mayor. The defectors claimed that their actions reflected the sentiments of the people of their wards. Referring to a survey of 7,000 voters in his ward, Banks conceded that resistance to a black mayor contributed to their overwhelming sentiment. Geocaris spoke of a survey done by his precinct captains that showed "a real groundswell for Epton." Washington's support for an income tax increase and his past personal income tax problems were among the reasons, Geocaris explained. But just as other Northwest Side and Southwest Side Democratic committeemen had acknowledged earlier, Geocaris admitted that race was a major factor in his community's preference for Epton. "I've been in this business a long time, and I know people vote along racial and ethnic lines."[25]

No one could mistake the Democratic party's lack of unity. When Vrdolyak called a meeting of the Central Committee for 24 March to endorse Washington, ten committeemen, mostly from the Northwest and Southwest Sides, stayed home, and twelve others sent representatives in their places. It was only by sparing them the embarrassment of a roll call that Vrdolyak engineered the endorsement without open conflict.

In the end, no more than six white committeemen publicly supported Washington, while eight openly opposed him; and most of the others quietly aided Epton's cause. Democratic precinct workers on the Northwest and Southwest Sides were "all out for Epton," according to one whose committeeman was nominally for Washington. The Democratic nominee received no major financial support from any of the Democratic organizations in white wards, while money flowed to Epton from close friends, business associates, and law partners of several Democratic committeemen. There were also rumors that Vrdolyak, who kept in touch with the Epton camp throughout the campaign, channeled Democratic party money into Epton's organizations and tacitly encouraged efforts to get out the vote for him in white ethnic areas. Many of the Democratic precinct captains in Vrdolyak's own 10th Ward urged voters to support the Republican mayoral candidate.[26]

Why did so many Democratic committeemen prefer Epton? In part, of course, because he was white; they were all aware of, and some probably shared, the dominant anti-black sentiments of their constituents. More important, the election of Epton posed no danger to their control. The committeemen knew that whatever Epton planned or proposed was irrelevant: there was no way he could muster majority support in the City Council. With no Republicans and only a handful of independents in the Council, Epton could not count on enough votes to support any of his initiatives or even to block the proposals of the Council's traditional leaders. As mayor, Epton could cut ribbons, dedicate playgrounds, and hold press conferences, but he could not exercise executive power. The ward barons, led by Vrdolyak and Burke, would run the city. Washington, on the other hand, posed a serious threat to the power of the committeemen. He pledged to undercut their control over the city; he had a strong base of popular support in the black community; and he could count on a solid bloc of votes in the Council. He might not have a majority there, but even a healthy minority combined with the mayor's veto was enough to force compromise and accommodation. That sort of restraint on the committeemen's power to run the city was not a prospect the ward barons found appealing.

Desertion by the leaders of the party wrecked Washington's initial plan to run as the nominee of a united and dominant party and forced him to rely on national Democratic figures to establish the legitimacy of his claim to the votes of Democratic partisans. House Speaker Thomas O'Neill urged local Democratic leaders to aid Washington, and he offered his own support. Senators John Glenn, Gary Hart, and Edward Kennedy campaigned for Washington in Chicago, along with a delegation of twelve Democratic party leaders from southern states, led by Bert Lance, the Georgia state Democratic party chairman. Former Vice President Mondale, who had supported Daley in the primary, came to Chicago to make amends; and Representative Claude Pepper, the congressional champion of the elderly, spoke to groups of senior citizens on Washington's behalf. Lane Kirkland, president of the AFL-CIO, and Douglas Fraser, president of the

United Auto Workers, addressed a Washington rally and lauded the candidate's strong pro-labor record.

None of these efforts could really overcome the outright opposition or tepid support of the local leaders of the party. While the defecting committeemen, and those who worked silently against Washington, probably followed rather than shaped the opinion of their constituents, their actions were important because they gave a public signal to rank-and-file Democrats. If officials and officeholders could abandon their party's nominee, then it seemed legitimate and proper for ordinary voters to defect. As that message spread among white voters, Chicago's mayoral election became a close and hard-fought contest, one in which party loyalties proved no match for racial identifications.

Washington vs. Epton

■ At the opening of the campaign, Washington and his staff assumed that he could coast to a relatively comfortable victory as the Democratic nominee in strongly Democratic Chicago. By striking a conciliatory and statesman-like posture immediately after the primary, Washington hoped to attract support from the party's organized constituencies and to quell open criticism by the committeemen. Behaving like the mayor-elect and treating the outcome of the general election as a foregone conclusion might also undermine the opposition's morale. However, Washington seriously underestimated the willingness of the Democratic committeemen to work for his defeat, the determination of his opponents, and the readiness of his own campaign organization to fight a tough battle in which party loyalties counted for little.

Washington's organization in the primary never developed the centralized direction that Byrne's and Daley's had attained. Coordination and planning improved from a bad start in December; but even after the victory was in hand, his campaign manager admitted that "the race was not won by the management of the campaign." Since Washington's advisers didn't anticipate a bruising and close general election campaign, they spent no effort right after the primary to repair the organization's weaknesses. Some of the inexperienced and overconfident staff spent as much energy jockeying for position as preparing to win the general election; and the campaign organization never developed the tight discipline, the clear line of command, necessary for close and timely coordination of its activities. The scheduling foul-ups, conflicting agendas, and slow and uncoordinated decision making that resulted made the entire effort seem confused and inept. At the very time when Washington's fitness and competence to manage the city came into question, the apparent mismanagement of his campaign reinforced people's doubts.[27]

Washington also failed to use the spotlight the media gave him after the primary to define a context for whites to evaluate his candidacy. He adopted a conciliatory tone and made some gestures to deemphasize the city's racial divisions. For example, the week after the primary, Washington went to Cicero, a stronghold of anti-black feeling, and joined its mayor in a pledge to stop a factory closing. But this was a single event, easily lost sight of in the welter of staff problems and party conflicts, and not part of a concerted campaign effort to surmount racial differences by focusing on shared economic concerns. By not using this type of initiative to give a reassuring image to his candidacy, Washington forfeited his chance to dictate the campaign's issue agenda and shape voters' perceptions of him. When Epton later took advantage of that opening to make Washington himself the central issue of the campaign, the Democratic nominee suddenly found himself on the defensive.

Although not many Chicagoans noticed at the time, the Republicans also held a primary to select a mayoral candidate on 22 February. Their campaign was low-key, to say the least: it was virtually ignored by the media and attracted fewer than 15,000 voters. Bernard Epton was the slated and only candidate, and no one doubted his election-day claim that "after I voted this morning, I was satisfied I was the nominee."[28]

Epton was a native Chicagoan, spending most of his life in South Shore and Hyde Park, and he had been active in politics since first becoming a Republican precinct captain when he was seventeen years old. He was elected to the Illinois House of Representatives in 1968 from the 24th Legislative District on the South Side. Centering on Hyde Park and the University of Chicago community (Ward 5), his district was racially mixed and strongly Democratic. But the state's system of multiple-member districts guaranteed representation to the minority party, and Epton served for fourteen years as the district's Republican representative. When a statewide referendum in 1980 reduced the size of the house and created single-member districts, Epton's career in the legislature was at an end. He gave up his post as the Republican committeeman from the 5th Ward, moved to the Gold Coast, and entered the mayoral race "only after a genuine, certifiable draft" by the GOP when they could find no other suitable candidates.[29]

Neither his long involvement in party politics nor his seven successful campaigns for the state legislature adequately prepared Epton for the rough-and-tumble game of running for mayor in Chicago. Educationally, economically, and in the attitudes of its voters, the Hyde Park district was a world apart from the city's ethnic enclaves, and Epton's success there depended more on the system that guaranteed minority representation than on his skills as a coalition builder. Moreover, he did not have a serious primary challenge or a difficult general election until 1978; and even then, with ample campaign funds and the support of the IVI-IPO, he easily led the minority field, although most of the district's voters cast Democratic ballots. Finally, contests for state legislative seats, especially under the multiple-member system, received comparatively light attention from the media; and Epton's record and personality were not exposed to the constant glare of publicity they received during the mayoral election.

As a legislator, Epton was known for his sardonic wit, his quick temper, and his intelligence; and he once remarked facetiously that he had the highest IQ in the legislature. As a successful insurance lawyer, Epton knew the insurance industry and became the General Assembly's recognized expert in that area. His critics claimed that he simply did the industry's bidding. They singled out his opposition to mandatory auto insurance and his bill eliminating the requirement that insurance firms explain cancellations to policyholders. But he fought against the industry for his plan to create a fund to protect policyholders when insurance companies went bankrupt, and he chaired the Insurance Laws Study Commission, whose report criticized the influence of insurance lobbyists in the legislature.[30]

While Epton twice served in the Republican leadership and regularly supported Republican Governor James Thompson, he still maintained a reputation as an independent, voting conservatively on fiscal issues and often siding with the Democrats on social questions. He opposed banning the use of Medicaid funds for abortions and voted for the Equal Rights Amendment, but he also supported the Republican leadership by voting against changing the rules to reduce the majority needed for passage of a constitutional amendment. He regularly supported the good-government and election-reform issues favored by the IVI-IPO, and he received its backing in his campaigns throughout the 1970s. He also had a strong record on racial questions, although his fiscal conservatism sometimes led him to oppose measures bearing on the economic interests of blacks; for example, in 1979, he voted against a bill to exempt food and prescription drugs from the state's sales tax. However, his image as a supporter of black rights was solid enough that the *Chicago Defender*, two days after the primary, praised his "long history of support for causes affecting the black and poor" during his years in the General Assembly. If Byrne or Daley had won the Democratic nomination, it isn't hard to imagine Epton's using his legislative record to pull together a voting coalition of blacks and white liberals.[31]

The general outline of Epton's strategy for the mayoral race was in place before the outcome of the Democratic primary was known. As any Republican running for office in Chicago, he had to play down his party label. "You don't win office in a city full of Democrats by stressing the fact that you're a Republican," one Epton strategist said. "You won't be hearing the word Republican too much during this campaign." Second, since the Democratic primary was hotly contested, Epton had planned to pick up the pieces by appealing to those who had supported the losing candidates. His brother, Saul Epton, a retired Cook County Circuit judge, explained, "From the start, Bernard felt that there would be two losers and great unhappiness as a result."[32]

Before Washington won the Democratic primary, few observers gave Epton's strategy much chance of success. Neither did many of Chicago's Republicans, who were so accustomed to losing that they regarded it nearly as a natural event. Only thirty-seven of the fifty ward committeemen even bothered to attend the Central Committee's slating session, since most of them probably assumed, as Epton's brother had, that either Byrne or Daley would be the Democratic nominee and that party loyalty would be very hard to overcome. Even the leaders of the state party, while encouraging Epton to make the race, were reluctant to associate themselves publicly with his candidacy. At a fund-raising dinner for Senator Charles Percy in late January, the slated Republican candidate for mayor of Chicago was not even introduced or seated at the speakers' table. Then, almost overnight, when the Democratic voters narrowly nominated Harold Washington, "the Epton pumpkin [turned] into a sleek campaign coach."[33]

Anyone familiar with Chicago's history of race relations knew why the odds against Epton suddenly shifted. They knew, too, why the Republican party establishment moved so quickly to bolster his campaign effort. James Fletcher, who had managed Governor Thompson's first campaign, came aboard to direct the general election race, replacing the candidate's daughter, Dale Epton, who had run the primary campaign. Spurred by Fletcher, Republican businessmen opened their checkbooks to finance the campaign. And John Deardourff, of Bailey & Deardourff, the Washington, D.C., political consulting firm that Thompson had used in each of his three races, signed on as Epton's media consultant and chief strategist.[34]

Epton launched his campaign even before these arrangements were completed. On Wednesday, 23 February, he told businessmen meeting for a breakfast in the Union League Club that "I really intend to be the Mayor of Chicago." He was optimistic despite the tradition of Republican defeat because "the majority of people who voted in the primary backed a loser. I will appeal to the disenchanted Democrats." At the Union League Club and in a later appearance that day on a WLS-TV (ABC) talk show, Epton disavowed any intention of making race an issue in the campaign. "I do resent anyone who would vote for me because I'm white," he said. "This is one city that should not be divided." On the same day, Epton told the *Chicago Defender* that he would "repudiate any efforts by white racist Democrats" to support him "to save Chicago from the blacks. . . . I have no desire to win a vote, because an opponent is black and I am white," he continued. "A bigot is a bigot, and I want no part of it."[35]

Frequently during the campaign, both candidates complained that the media kept bringing up race, each implying that somehow the black-and-white difference would disappear if reporters ignored it. In fact, neither Epton, nor Washington, nor the media, nor anyone else had to *make* race an issue in the election. Racial feelings were long-standing facts of Chicago's political life, and a biracial contest for the mayor's office inevitably had to evoke and focus them. This had routinely occurred whenever a black candidate and a white candidate ran against each other, even for aldermanic seats (Table 21). In the twenty-two biracial contests for alderman between 1975 and 1981, blacks tilted marginally toward black candidates, while whites decisively preferred white candidates. Only 3.9 percent of the white voting-age population cast ballots for any of the black candidates, and even most of that low figure was due to the behavior of the white voters in the Hyde Park–University of Chicago area (Ward 5).[36] There was no reason to expect the city's white voters to be any more likely to support a black candidate for mayor.

Regardless of what Epton said or did during the campaign, he was white, and that by itself was reason enough for many white Chicagoans to prefer him over Washington. The white ward committeemen and precinct captains knew that and said as much. "Voters on the Southwest Side are more worked up than ever before," Alderman Edward Burke (14th Ward) testified. "You're talking about people who feel threatened, and they're going to vote." Another ward leader observed that whites "on the Southwest Side have been pushed out of their neighborhoods 2 or 3 times by blacks. This is a chance to get even." On the Northwest Side, a Democratic precinct captain working for Epton saw it as "more than an election. We're fighting for everything we have this time." Alderman Anthony Laurino (39th Ward) bluntly summarized the attitude of his constituents: "The people in my area just don't want a black mayor—it's as simple as that."[37]

Moreover, the political movement in the black community and Epton's Republican label meant that he had little hope of winning many votes from blacks, despite his earlier legislative support for civil rights issues. His only realistic chance was to appeal to those who had supported Byrne and Daley in the primary, and these were over-

Table 21. Racial Patterns in Aldermanic Elections, 1975–1981: Regression Estimates of Group Voting Behavior[1]

	Candidates			
	White	**Black**	**Hispanic**	**Nonvoting**
All Contests[2]				
Blacks	8.3	12.6	0.3	78.0
Whites	45.2	3.9	0.7	49.3
Hispanics	11.2	0.1	7.3	81.2
Contests in Ward 5[3]				
Blacks	7.8	13.1	—	78.9
Whites	34.5	13.4	—	51.9

[1] Entries are percentages of voting-age population, and each row sums to 100 percent, except for rounding error.

[2] Includes twenty-two biracial contests: twelve in 1975, seven in 1979, two special elections in 1977, and one special election in 1981.

[3] Includes three biracial contests: the preliminary and runoff in 1975 and the election in 1979.

whelmingly white voters. Thus, while Epton expressly disavowed racial appeals and racist support, the only electoral strategy open to him involved mobilizing white voters, which gave his campaign the aura of a white movement from the outset.

In developing their plans to attract voting support, Epton's strategists didn't have the problem that Washington's opponents faced in the primary. Both Byrne and Daley had hoped to win a reasonable share of black support, so they avoided direct criticisms of Washington, fearing that attacks would increase his popularity among blacks and undercut their own attempts to attract black voters. As a result, Washington emerged from the primary battle virtually unscathed by his white opponents and unprepared to deal with direct attacks on his candidacy from the opposition. Since Epton's strategists never counted on winning many votes in the black community, this was exactly the tactic they pursued.[38]

The opening forays of the Epton campaign gave little hint of what was to come. During his first appearances, Epton touched on a number of issues, especially addressing the city's financial problems. Taxes will be an important issue in the campaign, he said, promising that the city would have to "live within the budget" under his administration, even if that meant cutting some city services. Before groups of businessmen, at neighborhood rallies, and on talk shows, Epton repeated that theme, sometimes adding that Washington "isn't a very fiscally wise individual." Epton held back from endorsing the 1992 World's Fair, saying his support would depend on how much tax money would be needed. He claimed $10 million could easily be cut from the city's payroll. "If I have to lay off people, I'll do so," he vowed, indicating also that he opposed paying the prevailing wage scale for city construction workers.[39]

Apart from a few general references, Epton apparently did not attack Washington directly during the first week or so of the campaign. The day after the primary he referred to the Democratic nominee as "articulate and intelligent," adding that "he's going to be a tough opponent. He's done a fine job in Washington [D.C.] and I hope he'll continue to do a fine job [there]." Epton told an interviewer later that Washington had been "a very articulate spokesman for lost causes" when they served together in the state legislature. These positive references to Washington's personal capabilities were not surprising; other Republicans shared that assessment. In October 1982, J. Robert Barr, chairman of the Cook County Republican party, hinted to reporters that the Republicans could endorse Washington if he entered the mayoral race. Barr then described the congressman as "one of the finest, most outstanding political leaders of this city, black or white," and he added that Washington "could well provide the city with the fresh, new ideas that could get [it] out of the mess it's in."[40] Needless to say, both Barr and Epton changed their public evaluations of Washington as the campaign progressed.

From the outset, the flood of volunteers, the enthusiasm at the rallies, and the results of the polls pointed to a single conclusion—white voters were moving to Epton. By mid-March, before Epton's media campaign began, Washington already trailed by 14 percentage points among white voters, although more than a third were still undecided (Table 22). Thereafter, his white support changed very slightly, while Epton's strength snowballed as undecided whites moved into his camp. The mid-March poll also showed Washington holding on to his black base from the primary, with Epton running at about 1 percent and only 13 percent undecided. But Epton didn't target his campaign at the small number of blacks who remained undecided; he aimed it at the 80 percent of the undecided voters who were white.[41]

During the first week of March, while Washington was still cancelling campaign appearances to "meet with staff and field people to put his campaign strategy in place," Epton went on the attack. He accused Washington of ignoring his responsibilities in Congress and of offering unworkable and costly programs for Chicago, especially criticizing a scheme Washington suggested during the primary for creating 11,000 jobs. "If my distinguished opponent wants to get rough, I'm perfectly willing to get rough," Epton told a cheering crowd of supporters on the Northwest Side. "I used to think that Harold was an amiable fellow and an intelligent one. I guess I was wrong on both counts."[42]

Table 22. Trends in Racial Support: Poll Reports, March and April 1983[1]

Interview Dates	Washington	Epton	Undecided
Whites			
15 March[2]	25	39	37
22 March[3]	18	41	41[6]
24 March[3]	27	55	17
26–30 March[4]	20	64	16
29 March[2]	18	58	25
5 April[3]	20	61	18
10 April[2]	20	66	14
12 April[5]	19	81	—
12 April[3]	23	77	—
Blacks			
15 March[2]	86	1	13
22 March[3]	86	0	13[6]
24 March[3]	90	1	8
26–30 March[4]	92	1	7
29 March[2]	92	3	5
5 April[3]	95	0	4
10 April[2]	93	2	5
12 April[5]	98	1	—
12 April[3]	99	1	—

[1] Entries are percentages, and each row sums to 100 percent, except for rounding error.

[2] Conducted by Richard Day Research, Inc.

[3] Conducted by Market Shares, Inc., and the 12 April results are from the WBBM-TV (CBS) exit poll.

[4] Conducted by the Gallup Organization.

[5] WMAQ-TV (NBC) exit poll.

[6] Includes support for Mayor Byrne: 23 percent of whites and 5 percent of blacks.

By the next week, Epton and his campaign planners had mapped their strategy. Their private polls showed two holes in public opinion. Most voters didn't know very much about Epton; he "is really an unknown quantity," Deardourff told reporters. Second, most voters were unaware of Washington's record. "Our polling is very clear that there is not a perception that this guy [Washington] has a history of failure to meet his basic obligations." To fill these gaps, Deardourff outlined a two-phase media campaign. The first phase involved "putting flesh on the bones" by emphasizing biographical information about Epton and his positions on issues such as crime, jobs, and city finances. In the second phase, "there was to be some effort to characterize the past record of Washington," especially his past legal problems.[43]

As Deardourff described it to reporters, the campaign strategy sounded conventional enough. Usually, a virtually unknown candidate like Epton uses the early stages of the campaign to build name recognition and a positive image of himself. That gives voters a context for evaluating his candidacy and reasons for supporting him. Then, as his recognition and approval ratings inch upward, he works at turning public discontent into voting support by attributing to his opponent negative characteristics which contrast with his own positive traits. In practice, however, Epton reversed this conventional sequence and attacked his opponent before presenting a picture of his own strong points. In his speeches, and later in his media spots, Epton concentrated on creating a context in which the public could assess Washington, and he emphasized positive advertising to build his own image only in the week before the election. By taking this tack, Epton made Washington the issue in the campaign and encouraged Chicagoans to vote against the Democratic nominee.[44]

Epton's attack on Washington began in earnest during the second week of March, dominated the only debate between the candidates on 21 March, and became the centerpiece of the media campaign that began the following day. Reporters noticed the shift on 10 March, and Epton's strategists told them it marked "a tough new phase" of his campaign for mayor. Asked about Washington's past legal problems during a radio interview on that day, Epton said it was "extremely unfortunate" that a man who is a lawyer "is heading a mayoral ticket with that type of record." There was "absolutely no excuse" for Washington's legal problems, Epton added. "The people must decide if he has the capacity and integrity to run this city." But the news media, Epton again claimed, were ignoring Washington's past record out of a fear of being called racist. Depicting himself as a victim of "reverse racism," Epton noted that due to intimidation, several blacks had declined to serve on his transition team and that he had been forced to cancel a meeting at a home for elderly persons in a black neighborhood because he feared reprisals against the residents there. "I'm not suggesting Harold is doing this," he observed. "But you only have to go to Operation PUSH on a Saturday morning to see who is bringing up the issue of racism."[45]

During their televised debate, Epton pounded the "integrity issue." The voters have a right to ask each of us certain fundamental questions: "Will he obey the law? Will he do what he promises? Will he tell the truth?" Brandishing a three-inch-thick looseleaf binder that he claimed documented Washington's past legal problems, Epton continued, "The only way I know what a person will do in the future is to look at what he's done in the past." Then he detailed Washington's past record—the jail term in 1972 for failing to file income tax returns, the suspension of his law license in 1970 for not doing work for which clients had paid, the failure by Washington to disclose that five lawsuits were pending against him when he petitioned to regain his law license in 1975. This "disquieting" past, Epton suggested, should be the overriding consideration when voters make their choice for mayor.[46]

Washington seemed to reel under what he characterized as a "scurrilous" attack. "What happened in 1972 has been explained over and over and over again to the people of this city," he replied. "We did wrong. We were punished for it. Since that time we have had an exemplary record. We have outlived that issue." But Epton pressed his advantage at every opportunity, often using his caustic wit to underscore his opponent's vulnerability. When Washington promised to promote affirmative action at City Hall, Epton quipped: "I'm glad the congressman is going to follow the law. It would be refreshing."[47]

To capitalize on his debate performance and to reinforce the anti-Washington theme of his campaign, Epton launched his television advertising the following day. The media campaign depicted Washington as a tax fraud, a shady lawyer, and an ex-convict. Some of the television spots included a pitch aimed at countering the guilt Democrats might feel about voting for a Republican. One commercial, for example, quoted President Kennedy saying "sometimes party loyalty asks too much. Surely this is such a time."

Both Epton and Deardourff vigorously denied charges that the attack on Washington's character pandered to white racism. They had decided to zero in on Washington's personal history, Deardourff explained, because "more important than where a candidate stands on any issue is the question of his or her basic fitness to serve in public life." Particular issues rise and then fade away, and many future issues can't even be anticipated during a campaign; but character is permanent, can be judged from the individual's past record, and serves as a guide to future conduct. But Deardourff admitted that Epton's voters were fearful of Washington, adding that he didn't know "how much of that attitude comes from their perception of Harold Washington as an individual and how much comes from him as a black. I'd like to think it comes from him as an individual."[48]

Washington and his advisers had a different interpretation. They portrayed the attack on Washington's integrity as a smoke screen to give whites a convenient reason for opposing him without having to admit bigotry. "We feel it's a below-the-surface thing," one strategist said. "It's more than taxes; they're using the race issue. We are quite concerned about it."[49]

They became more concerned as new accusations about Washington hit the front pages and the air waves almost daily. There were stories of unpaid water bills, electric bills, and real estate tax bills, and he was revealed to be involved with the ownership of a slum building in the black community whose tenants were evicted by the city because the buildings were unsafe. From these disclosures, Washington appeared to be a slumlord and a deadbeat who failed to pay his bills; these added up to a "pattern of disregard for the law," Epton charged. Washington's claims that some of the bills were for earlier campaign offices, and staff people should have paid them, led to more publicity and seemed like a feeble effort to dodge responsibility. On top of the tax conviction and suspension from law practice, "the drip, drip, drip of all the other goofey disclosures" fanned the flames of the integrity issue and magnified its effect.[50] Each new revelation lent credibility to Epton's attack on his opponent's character, and Washington's attempts to respond to the charges only increased the media coverage and diverted attention from his own issues and themes.

These disclosures and the way Epton linked them to the character issue contributed to intense scorn of Washington, especially among white ethnics, and reinforced negative stereotypes of blacks as irresponsible and incapable. "That's just the way blacks are around here," one elderly white woman remarked. "They never obey the rules, even the traffic laws."[51]

At times, Epton's caustic wit and penchant for sarcasm encouraged ridicule of his opponent. On one occasion, when informed that Washington had gone to the East Coast for a fund-raising effort, Epton cracked that he should also "bring back some brains." On other occasions, his references seemed condescending and patronizing. Epton's repeated claim that Washington "is not the best qualified candidate the black community can produce" belittled the collective judgment of the black community, and his constant reference to Washington as "Harold" struck some as an attempt to give "the impression of being the superior person talking down to his inferior." But, as Mike Royko observed, it could have been worse: "He hasn't called him 'boy' yet." Finally, Epton unfavorably compared Washington's role in the black community to his own past benevolence. "I've done more for the black community in one year than Harold has in a lifetime," he said two days before the election. "I gave more in charity than most people earn."[52] Like Byrne's comments about her hams and Christmas trees, Epton's remark suggested that black enthusiasm for Washington was a display of ingratitude to him and other whites, a violation of the implicit bargain by which blacks gave political support in return for white largess. Blacks regarded such implications as insults, as contempt for their sense of citizenship and their right to control their own fate.

Epton's negative advertising and sardonic comments didn't create fear and resentment among white ethnic voters. Those sentiments existed long before Epton began his campaign. His strategy tapped those attitudes, served as a rallying point for them, gave them a re-

21. Epton supporters shouting at Mondale and Washington outside St. Pascal's Church, Palm Sunday, 27 March 1983.

spectable political outlet, and generated an enthusiasm akin to the fervor for Washington in the black community.

Buoyed by the warmth of the crowds, and spurred by their rhythmic chants of "Ber-nie, Ber-nie, Ber-nie," Epton often seemed to tell his listeners what they wanted to hear. Whether he offered another cut at Washington's character or a pledge of his commitment to neighborhood pride, they viewed him as one of their own. Republican or not, since he was Chicago's "Last White Hope," lifelong Democrats, white and mostly working class, jammed his rallies, cheered his remarks, and sang his praises. "Your record, Bernie, shows you're tough / And as for us, we've been pushed enough / For Chicago—Epton!" The lyrics were light and vague enough, but their message was in the familiar tune. As most of those who heard it probably knew, it was "Bye, Bye, Blackbird."[53]

Widespread scorn of Washington, open expressions of racial bias, and Epton's caustic comments helped create the campaign's mean and ugly tone. Two incidents, both publicized by the national media, illustrated the tenor of the battle.

On Palm Sunday, 27 March, a crowd of shouting, placard-waving supporters of Epton taunted and jeered Washington and former Vice President Mondale as they tried to attend religious services at St. Pascal's Roman Catholic Church on the city's Northwest Side. The

22. Mondale and Washington leaving St. Pascal's Church through a throng of placard-waving and jeering Epton supporters. (*Chicago Tribune.*)

words "NIGGER DIE" were freshly spray-painted on one of the doors of the church, and the visitors had to walk a gauntlet of angry demonstrators shouting "Go home," "Tax cheater," "Carpetbagger," and "Epton, Epton, Epton." "The big thing is fear," Father Francis Ciezadlo, St. Pascal's pastor, explained later. "People have either heard of neighborhoods changing or have lived in neighborhoods that changed. . . . They can say it's Harold Washington's tax problems or his criminal record, but it's really a black-white thing. We cannot deny that there is prejudice." One of his parishioners put it more succinctly: "There's hate here." For his part, when informed of the incident, Epton expressed regret. "You should be able to go to church and worship without being bothered. If they were supporters of mine, I apologize."[54]

On the following day, the octogenarian hero of the elderly, Congressman Claude Pepper of Florida, campaigned for Washington before audiences of senior citizens. Before one group in a Northwest Side restaurant, just the mention of Washington's name evoked a round of boos. "This is America," Pepper exploded. "It isn't the color of a man's skin. . . . It's character and the spirit they possess that determine excellence. I wouldn't be here if I didn't believe Harold Washington would be a good mayor for every man, woman, and child in the city."[55]

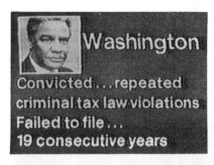
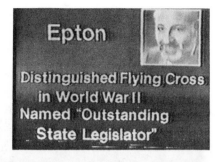

23. Scenes from a television spot in which Epton's controversial slogan was used to underscore the stark contrast between Washington's and Epton's records.

The attack on his character made Washington the central issue of the campaign. "We've given people a reason to vote against Washington" by concentrating on his past misdeeds, one Republican strategist surmised.[56] To convert this anti-Washington sentiment into a vote for the Republican candidate, Epton's television spots ended with what became the most controversial line of the campaign, the slogan "Epton for Mayor—Before It's Too Late!"

Epton insisted the slogan had no racial implications. He claimed it was developed even before the Democratic primary, when he assumed Byrne would be his opponent in the general election. Regardless of the identity of the opposing candidate, he argued that the slogan was intended to have "only one meaning: Chicago was in a deep financial crisis. . . . All I was saying was, 'You'd better let Epton handle it before bankruptcy hits us.' . . . It never occurred to me that it could mean anything else."[57]

The possibility of a veiled meaning did occur to others. One nationally syndicated columnist characterized it as "a lightly coated message to whites to resist the election of the city's first black mayor."[58] The *Chicago Tribune* denounced the slogan as "disgraceful evidence of either insensitivity or outright exploitation"; it is "a blatant appeal to the worst of Chicago." Epton's incessant disavowals of race in the campaign make him sound like "a man who doth protest too much," the editorial writers continued; he "is . . . running a campaign founded on [race baiting]."[59] Even Epton's daughter Dale, who worked as an aide in the campaign, initially had some doubt. When she saw the slogan before it was aired, she asked Deardourff, "What the hell does that mean?" He told her that it referred to the city falling into financial ruin, and she explained later, "I just thought it was my own paranoia that made me read anything else in it."[60]

Whatever message Epton and Deardourff intended to convey with the slogan is less important than the character of the line itself. Because it didn't refer to anything specific, listeners and viewers could read into it whatever message they chose. Some may have seen it as a reminder of Epton's qualifications to tackle the city's financial woes; but others could just as easily have read it as an appeal to racial feeling, a warning that only a vote for Epton could prevent a black from becoming mayor. Since race had become so dominant a factor in the campaign that pollsters said "it confounds traditional demographic analysis," it's hard to imagine that the slogan's economic implication was anywhere near as important as its racial effect.[61] And since those who planned the Epton campaign were not rank amateurs, it's also hard to imagine that they were not aware of how the slogan would be perceived and of its value in attracting white support.

While Epton aired his television and radio commercials and stumped the white neighborhoods, especially on the Northwest and Southwest Sides, another type of campaign raged in the precincts. That campaign involved the distribution of racist literature and open racial appeals to "stop the nigger." Handbills were circulated depicting a police insignia that read "Chicongo Po-lease." On the insignia in the center were a pair of lips, a watermelon slice, a can of beer, and a slab of ribs; and the written commentary on the side deprecatingly linked these to black heritage and traditions. Another piece of racist propaganda, displayed in some of the police stations in white areas, posed a series of questions emphasizing the danger that with a black mayor, Chicago would become another Gary, In-

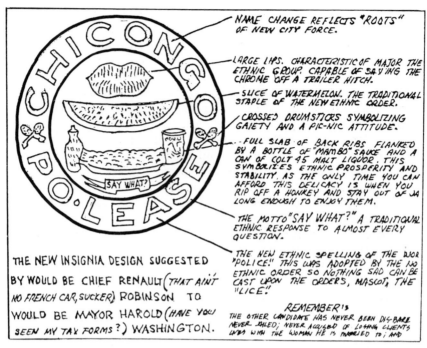

24. One of the handbills using racial stereotypes to fuel opposition to the candidacy of a black for mayor. Such handbills were widely distributed in white precincts.

diana. "No matter what anyone tells you, this election has come down to *race*," it warned. Readers were urged to "make the difference" by voting for Epton and to "make copies" of the handbill "and get the word around." [62]

Many of the Democratic precinct captains and other volunteers for Epton were actively involved in these racist activities, although neither Epton nor his campaign managers approved or directed their efforts. "The campaign was out of control," Dale Epton explained after the election. "It was mass hysteria. At the beginning we said we didn't want anyone to vote for us because we were white, but then we gave up saying it because it just didn't matter, nobody listened to us. Epton offices all over the city were printing their own literature, spending their own money. . . . We tried to ignore it because we couldn't do anything about it. Nobody could." [63]

Epton himself was appalled by the character of these appeals. "But I had 9,000 volunteers," he said later. "I couldn't be responsible for every one of them." Whenever racial literature or remarks were drawn to his attention during the campaign, Epton invariably con-

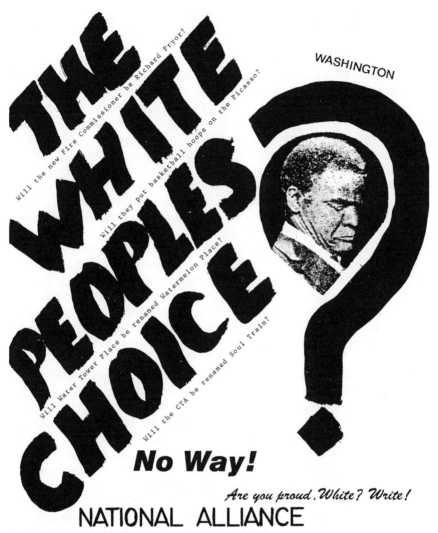

25. Another handbill: "The White People's Choice?"

demned them, and he just as regularly rebuked his questioners for injecting race into the campaign. "It's you people in the press that keep bringing up race. You do it," he said on several occasions, as if blaming the messenger for the bad news.[64]

Epton's outbursts, several of which were recorded by television cameras and shown to nightly news audiences, made him appear testy, ill-tempered, and unable to control his emotions. These appearances became a campaign liability when a local television reporter put them into a larger context by raising questions about his past mental health. Medical records, apparently stolen from Michael Reese Hospital, showed that he underwent psychiatric evaluations there in 1975 and again in 1978. The release of the records infuriated Epton, who explained that any depression he experienced at the time was due solely to the inability of his doctors to pinpoint the cause of severe abdominal pains he was experiencing (later diagnosed as ulcers). He rejected Deardourff's advice to hold a press conference, refused to release his complete medical record, and tried to end the discussion by saying, "I'm perfectly healthy."[65] The matter generated considerable attention, not simply because the media reported it, but because Epton's earlier outbursts and seeming lack of emotional discipline made questions concerning his psychological stability appear plausible. In that sense, Epton was more harmful to his cause than the media he criticized.

The racist literature made no converts for Epton. Whites likely to be impressed by it needed no convincing, while those who found it repugnant may have been influenced to vote against him. Its larger significance lay in its relatively wide and open distribution and the publicity it produced. This sort of open racism and Epton's campaign attacks worked to solidify Washington's support among blacks and to boost their turnout to a rate surpassing even their showing in the primary.

Washington's campaign needed whatever boost it could find. From the beginning, it was disorganized, unfocused, and unsure about how to develop a winning strategy. Washington's strategy problem in the general election was similar to that faced by Byrne and Daley in the primary. His black base was not large enough by itself to win the election, so he needed to appeal beyond the black community for white and Hispanic support.[66] But there was a vital difference between Washington's calculations and those his primary opponents had to factor into their solutions to similar situations. Most of Washington's black support was firm to begin with, and the character of Epton's campaign removed even the remote possibility of a split in the black vote. Thus, since Washington's position with his core support group was more secure than Byrne's or Daley's had been with theirs, he was freer to appeal for votes from other groups without risking losses among blacks. Until the final week of the campaign, however, Washington failed to make the most of his tactical options.

The various parts of Washington's organization weren't tightly coordinated, and often it seemed that no one was in charge. Responses to new developments were slow, incomplete, and sometimes contradictory. The candidate frequently was scheduled to appear in more than one place at the same time, and the last-minute corrections only added to the appearance of chaos. The turmoil that surrounded his campaign simply reinforced doubts among some voters concerning Washington's ability to manage the city in an orderly and efficient way. "How's he going to run the city if he can't run his own campaign?" one precinct captain wondered aloud.[67]

Some of the rough edges came from the nature of the organization. "I think it's still a combination of . . . a movement and a campaign," Al Raby, his campaign manager, observed in late March. There was also a struggle for control within the organization, with Raby himself getting pushed aside only eight days before the election and members of Washington's congressional staff assuming more influence. Finally, there was a battle over strategy, pitting the staff with movement connections against the more electorally experienced and pragmatic members of the organization. Most of the white staff and some of the older, more conservative blacks pushed Washington to campaign hard for white support. On the other hand, those who had been involved in the ChicagoFest boycott and the registration drive advised against moves to allay the concerns of whites for fear of dampening the enthusiasm of blacks. The political consciousness of many of the movement people had been shaped during battles over integration issues, and they were skeptical of the effectiveness of appeals to white voters. Their judgments were as limited by memories of past racial conflicts as were those of the white ethnics who flocked to Epton's banner.[68]

With these types of differences simmering just beneath the surface, Washington's campaign limped along, moving now in one direction and then in another, but never appearing to be a disciplined and focused effort. By fumbling the early opportunity to frame his candidacy and define the campaign's issue agenda, Washington defaulted that initiative to Epton. And, once the attack on his character began, Washington found himself on the defensive, responding to one charge after another and increasing the publicity each received as he did so. It was poor planning to have made no effort to anticipate the charges and therefore clear up the unpaid bills before the campaign began. It was even worse planning to allow the accusations to come out one by one, without acting to defuse their effect. But his staff often couldn't respond to questions about the charges, or they gave incomplete explanations that later had to be withdrawn or clarified. As a result, each incident lingered in the headlines and newscasts for several days, which only increased its impact. And Washington himself, probably due to a combination of pride and stubbornness, refused to address the issue fully. He admitted his past mistakes and said he regretted them, but he never offered what even sympathetic observers regarded as a reasonable explanation. Saying "I forgot" didn't seem to be a persuasive explanation for not filing income tax returns, especially since his birthday was also 15 April. And his glib dismissal of unpaid utility bills as trivial incidents failed to take into account how this struck people who routinely paid all their bills, often scrimping and saving to do so.[69]

The inept handling of the integrity issue concerned Washington's advisers, who correctly saw how it had pushed him onto the defensive. But they should have been equally concerned when Washington went on the attack. Replying to Epton's complaint that he was a victim of "reverse racism" because the media wouldn't publicize his opponent's personal history, Washington accused the Republican candidate of "playing with fire." Epton "doesn't know what he is doing. You cannot play with people's emotions in the form and manner he so insidiously tries to do and slink away and say, 'It's not my fault.'" When he repeated the argument later before a group of ministers, Washington added that if his supporters "get the feeling that this campaign is going to turn into a race war, then it might turn bitter, evil, angry." In that case, he warned, the campaign could get out of hand, and "some innocent person . . . may wind up dead."[70] Statements of that sort simply fanned the fears of those whites who were determined to prevent the election of a black mayor, while raising doubts about Washington's commitment and capacity to unify the racially polarized city, even among whites without racial motives. Whatever their intended effect, by frightening white voters, Washington's references to the possibility of racial violence reinforced Epton's strategy and appeal.

Hindered by a disorganized campaign apparatus and kept on the defensive by Epton's attacks, Washington seemed to be converting victory into defeat. "We haven't run a very smart campaign since the primary," an adviser acknowledged in one of the few understatements of the campaign. The polls told the story (see Table 22): after Byrne's withdrawal, the white undecided voters began moving decisively to Epton. Washington's citywide lead, which was as large as 28 percentage points in mid-March, was being eroded almost daily, and by the end of the month his advisers were jittery. If the movement continued, Chicago would elect its first Republican mayor since 1927. "We don't expect to make great gains between now and the election," one of Washington's strategists said glumly after examining the prospects. "What we want to do is hang onto what we have against this onslaught from Epton."[71]

Hanging on for Victory

■ On 12 April 1983, the 122d anniversary of the firing on Fort Sumter, South Carolina, which began the war to maintain slavery, black Chicagoans ended their political enslavement to the city's ruling institution. In the closest mayoral election since 1919, Harold

Washington barely hung on, defeating Bernard Epton by the razor-edged margin of 46,250 votes—out of 1.29 million ballots cast.[72]

When they recorded their votes in the race for mayor, most citizens selected between Washington and Epton on the basis of their skin colors, not because of party or policy differences. More than any other factor, race dominated voting choices.[73] No matter which voting data we examine, or how we explore them, the degree of racial polarization is striking.

"Except for the accidents," as Deardourff had predicted, Washington got all of the black vote (Table 23). Black turnout was lower on the West Side than elsewhere, but even there two thirds of the black voting-age population cast ballots for Washington. No demographic subgroup of blacks gave Washington less than 95 percent of its vote, while black professionals, voters over sixty-five years of age, and the top income group supported him almost unanimously. Blacks not only voted cohesively, they were highly mobilized: their citywide turnout rate (73 percent) was 5.8 percentage points higher than white participation.[74]

Among Hispanics, Washington outpolled Epton by just under 3 to 1, although the group's turnout remained low. The vote division was closest among Mexicans, but among the Puerto Ricans, whose turnout was higher, Washington beat his Republican opponent by just under 4 to 1.[75] Within both of these major subgroups of Hispanics, support for Washington dropped at the higher income levels. Puerto Ricans with incomes under $10,000 voted 91.9 percent for Washington; those in the top income category voted 77.6 percent for him. Mexicans in the two bottom income categories preferred Washington by 78.8 percent; the next two categories gave him about 60 percent of their votes, and the top income category only 55.6 percent. Shared economic status and party identification played the important roles in shaping the black-brown voting alliance in April 1983.[76]

Finally, whites voted strongly for Epton, although they behaved less cohesively than blacks. Citywide, about 58.8 percent of the white voting-age population turned out for Epton, and 8.3 percent supported Washington. Expressed in the more familiar way, that means Washington was the choice of 12.3 percent of the whites who voted, while 87.6 percent favored Epton.[77]

In the Lake Shore wards, Washington's white support was twice the size of his citywide level, and it was five times larger in Ward 5, where he outpolled Epton among whites by about 2 to 1. On the Northwest and South Sides, however, the white ethnics were cohesively mobilized for Epton. Their turnout for him was considerably higher than that of whites in other areas of the city, while their support for Washington was only about half the size of his citywide pro-

Table 23. The General Election for Mayor, 1983: Regression Estimates of Group Voting Behavior [1]

	Washington	Epton	Nonvote
Citywide [2]			
Blacks	72.7	0.2	26.9
Whites	8.3	58.8	32.7
Hispanics	18.0	6.2	75.6
Blacks			
Dawson wards	74.1	0.1	24.9
Other South Side	76.0	0.0	23.9
West Side	66.9	0.0	33.0
Whites			
Northwest Side	5.0	63.0	31.9
South Side	3.2	72.0	24.6
Lake Shore	17.3	48.9	33.6
Ward 5	42.3	25.3	32.3
Hispanics			
Puerto Rican [3]	35.6	9.4	51.5
Mexican [4]	10.8	9.2	78.3
Total citywide	31.9	29.6	38.4

[1] Entries are percentages of voting-age population, and rows sum to 100 percent, except for rounding error and scattering for a minor candidate.

[2] Developed by weighting the estimate of each group's voting behavior within eight subareas of the city.

[3] Estimates of Hispanic behavior in predominantly Puerto Rican Wards 26 and 31.

[4] Estimates of Hispanic behavior in predominantly Mexican Wards 22 and 25.

portion of the white voting-age population.[78] However, since the precinct-level census data used for the estimates in Table 23 don't allow us to distinguish among whites according to ethnic ancestry, they may overstate white ethnic opposition to Washington. Fortunately, the WMAQ-TV (NBC) exit poll asked respondents their ethnic and religious identities. Table 24 uses that information to provide a more complete picture of white ethnic voting behavior.

Looked at individually or collectively, the four ethnic groups shown in this table gave scant support to Washington. Their total vote for him (18.3 percent) even fell slightly below this exit poll's estimate of his overall white support (19.6 percent). The strongest opposition within each group came among its Catholic, blue-collar component, the segment that is most commonly thought of as the core of the white ethnic community. Indeed, Washington's support among whites generally was weakest at the bottom ends of the income and occupation scales and increased, although still only marginally, at the higher ranges.[79]

Table 24. Vote by Ethnicity, Religion, and Occupation[1]

	Italian	German	Polish	Irish	Total
All Religions					
Epton	90.4	78.0	82.7	79.3	81.6
Washington	9.6	22.0	17.3	20.7	18.3
Catholics: White-collar and Professional					
Epton	84.8	77.5	80.7	73.1	78.7
Washington	15.2	22.5	19.3	26.9	21.3
Catholics: Blue-collar Occupations					
Epton	100.0	87.1	89.8	81.1	89.8
Washington	0.0	12.9	10.2	18.9	10.2

[1] Analysis confined to white respondents; entries are percentages, and for each category, the columns sum to 100 percent, except for rounding error.

Source: WMAQ-TV (NBC) exit poll.

Even at the higher income and education levels, Catholics, the city's largest and most Democratic subgroup of whites, lagged behind Protestants and Jews in supporting the Democratic candidate for mayor. On the whole, Catholics were more resistant to the idea of a black mayor and more likely to vote against Washington than other white Chicagoans.[80] While very few voters, white or black, admitted that race was the deciding factor in their choice for mayor, more white Catholics (22.2 percent) than non-Catholics (16.3 percent) said so. And the Catholics who singled out race voted 97.4 percent for Epton, while other whites who said race was the most important factor preferred him by only 70.5 percent. Finally, more non-Catholics (48.2 percent) than Catholics (41.8 percent) felt strongly about their choice, but the Catholics who did voted 88.8 percent for Epton, while other whites with similar feelings gave him 69.7 percent. Thus, while racial attitudes influenced the voting choices of some portion of every subgroup of whites in the city, they seem to have been especially widespread among Catholics, the religious group to which most residents of the Northwest and Southwest Sides belonged.

Some election postmortems claimed a much larger number of white ethnic voters supported Washington than was the case. By looking only at the ward totals, one study counted over 49,000 votes from the white ethnic strongholds for Washington, and another claimed he received 80,000 votes from the white ethnic neighborhoods.[81] Both claims are far off the mark and for the same reason: each incorrectly assumed that all of the votes for Washington from predominantly white wards on the Northwest and Southwest Sides were cast by whites. In fact, of Washington's total vote in those two

Table 25. Support for Democratic Candidates at the General Election, 1983: Regression Estimates of Group Voting Behavior[1]

	Mayor[2]	City Clerk	City Treasurer[2]
Citywide[3]			
Blacks	72.7	65.6	69.7
Whites	8.3	47.0	40.0
Hispanics	18.0	20.2	18.0
Whites			
Northwest Side	5.0	51.2	40.0
South Side	3.2	55.6	40.5
Lake Shore	17.3	34.2	35.1
Ward 5	42.3	40.4	41.1
Hispanics			
Puerto Rican[4]	35.6	38.2	37.9
Mexican[5]	10.8	16.4	16.0
Total citywide	31.9	48.1	45.2

[1]Entries are the percentages of each group's voting-age population supporting the Democratic candidate for each citywide office.

[2]Black Democratic candidates.

[3]Developed by weighting the estimate of each group's voting behavior within eight subareas of the city.

[4]Estimates of Hispanic behavior in predominantly Puerto Rican Wards 26 and 31.

[5]Estimates of Hispanic behavior in predominantly Mexican Wards 22 and 25.

areas, only 36.4 percent came from white voters, while 53.5 percent of it came from blacks and 10 percent from Hispanics. Using the gross ward totals seriously underestimates the willingness of whites in these ethnic areas to vote against their party's black nominee for mayor.

The information in Table 25 gives another insight into the selectiveness underlying the voting choices of white Chicagoans. In the Lake Shore wards, about half the whites voting for the Democratic candidates for city clerk and city treasurer apparently crossed over and voted for the Republican nominee for mayor. But the crossover percentages were much higher among whites living on the Northwest and South Sides, and there white voters were also less willing than elsewhere to vote for the black Democratic nominee for city treasurer.

It isn't hard to pin down the geographic location of Washington's white voting support. Applied to the size of the white voting-age population, the citywide regression estimates (see Table 23) indicate that he received about 78,518 votes from whites throughout the city, which accounted for 11.7 percent of his total vote. The estimates for Ward 5 and the Lake Shore wards show that a total of 42,649 whites in those areas chose him over Epton, and that figure represents over half (54.3 percent) of all his white voters. On the Northwest Side, 15,013 whites voted for Washington, and so did 8,879 whites on the South Side, for a total of 23,892 white voters in these two areas of ethnic concentration. In other words, less than a third (30.4 percent) of Washington's white votes came from the two areas that held three fifths (60.2 percent) of the city's white voting-age population. In fact, Washington received nearly twice as many votes from Hispanics (43,286), despite their low turnout and the fact that there are less than half as many voting-age Hispanics in the city as there are white voters living on the Northwest and South Sides.

The geography of Washington's white support suggests its social composition, and the data in Table 26 allow us to examine that more closely. There are two columns of percentages in the table. The unadjusted percentage simply indicates the proportion of each category that voted for Washington. The adjusted percentage can be thought of as a "corrected" score that takes into account the effect of all the other factors itemized. For example, Jews voted 30.6 percent for Washington, higher than Protestants or Catholics. But since liberals also gave more support to Washington than conservatives or moderates, the unadjusted rate of Jewish voting could be due to the fact that there are more liberals among Jews than among the other major religious groups. To adjust or correct for that possibility, we want to know how the religious groups would have voted if they were all composed of the same proportions of ideological and party identifiers and had the same age, income, education, and sex ratios. By correcting for these compositional differences, we can see how the variables influenced each other and isolate those with the largest independent effect.[82]

Only education and ideology (in that order of strength) operated independently to boost support for Washington. Whites who held a liberal ideology gave him over a third of their votes, and those who had attended graduate school gave him nearly half. The slight tilt among Independents toward Washington, and the larger one among Jews, have to be explained on compositional grounds, while the gender gap increased when corrected for the effect of the other variables. Finally, Democratic party identification (even when adjusted) didn't add much to the likelihood of preferring Washington, and on election day, an astounding 79.3 percent of the city's white Democrats voted for the Republican candidate.[83]

In the city as a whole, whites who had voted for Daley in the primary were about 5 percentage points more likely to vote for Epton (85 percent) than those who had supported Byrne (80.1 percent). However, on the Southwest Side, the opposite pattern occurred (by 2.2 percentage points), because 3.5 percent of Daley's primary vot-

Table 26. Support for Washington among White Voters: General Election, April 1983

	Unadjusted Percentage	Adjusted Percentage [1]	(N)
Sex			
Male	21.4	22.8	(546)
Female	19.0	17.5	(519)
Religion			
Protestant	25.0	24.7	(275)
Catholic	16.2	18.0	(679)
Jew	30.6	19.1	(88)
None	43.4	37.3	(23)
Party			
Republican	9.9	11.8	(151)
Independent	24.2	21.0	(384)
Democrat	20.3	22.1	(530)
Ideology			
Liberal	39.0	35.3	(356)
Moderate	12.3	14.3	(431)
Conservative	8.6	10.1	(278)
Education			
Not HS graduate	9.6	9.1	(114)
HS graduate	11.7	12.3	(298)
Some college	11.5	13.6	(303)
College graduate	25.7	25.0	(171)
Graduate school	50.8	47.3	(179)

[1] Each variable controlled for the effects of all the other variables and for age and income.

Source: WMAQ-TV (NBC) exit poll.

ers didn't participate in the general election. On the Northwest Side and in the Lake Shore wards, virtually all of Daley's supporters voted for Epton; nearly 7 percent of Byrne's primary supporters on the Northwest Side voted for Washington and another 6 percent didn't vote at all. Washington did better in recruiting from Byrne's coalition in the Lake Shore wards, where over a quarter (27.2 percent) of her primary voters went to him, while 17.6 percent didn't make a choice for mayor. In the Puerto Rican areas (Wards 26 and 31), two thirds of Byrne's voters, but none of Daley's, cast ballots for Washington; but in the Mexican areas (Wards 22 and 25) Byrne and Daley voters were about equally likely to favor Epton, with the Republican candidate attracting three quarters of their supporters. Washington did comparatively better among "new" voters, whites and Hispanics who had not voted in the February primary. Among this newly mobilized group, about 23 percent of the whites and 60 percent of the Hispanics chose Washington over his Republican rival.[84]

Despite these variations in the voting behavior of the city's whites, we need to bear in mind that Washington's overall support among white Chicagoans was quite low—only 19.6 percent according to the exit poll used to construct Table 26. Of course, since the election was very close, even that level of support was vital to the outcome. Indeed, the sum of the votes cast for Washington by whites and Hispanics was 2.6 times the size of his 46,250-vote margin over Epton. The significance of white and Hispanic support grows when we realize that the result would have been changed if only about 24,000 Washington voters had switched to Epton. When the outcome can be reversed with the swing of so small a number of voters, virtually any group can claim to have made the decisive difference.

But claims of that sort miss the central reality of the 1983 mayoral election—without extraordinarily high turnout and cohesive support among the city's blacks, the smaller-sized components of Washington's vote would have been irrelevant to the result. No one would ask which group made the difference in electing Washington if he hadn't won, and without the performance of his "black base" Chicago would now have a Republican mayor. Since over eight tenths (81.8 percent) of the votes cast for Washington in the general election came from blacks, their behavior was the one truly indispensable element in his victory.[85]

Washington won the primary by solidifying his black support, a trend that began in earnest with the debates and continued through 22 February. As the mid-March polls showed (see Table 22), that black base carried over intact into the general election campaign. Epton's attacks and negative advertising simply increased Washington's popularity among blacks as the previously undecided voters moved into his column, and by election day his black support approached unanimity. Epton's campaign strategy, as well as a sense that the election was close, also stimulated blacks to participate. Alderman Danny Davis (29th Ward) predicted a "record-breaking, phenomenal turnout" for the West Side, an area which traditionally recorded the lowest turnout in the city. "There is a resolve on the West Side of Chicago, and in the black community as a whole, that is hardcore. No one has to tell people to do it or ask people to do it. They're going to do it on their own." The story was the same on the South Side, where blacks were so galvanized that several ward committeemen confidently predicted a 90 percent turnout rate.[86]

Their predictions proved mildly optimistic, of course, and Washington's staff didn't fail to work on election day to encourage blacks to vote. Cars with loud speakers mounted on them toured the black areas and campaign workers boomed the message: "Wake up, everybody. Vote for Chicago. You've got the power to make history today." Whether they heard that last-minute message or not, blacks woke up, turned out, and voted cohesively for Harold Washington. Their behavior was not a tribute to the activity of precinct captains or campaign volunteers. Only slightly more than a third (36.2 percent) of the blacks reported being contacted by a precinct captain, and only 27.9 percent said that anyone else had contacted them. Whether contacted or not, blacks gave Washington 99 percent of their vote. Their behavior was a sign of a political enthusiasm that swept through the black community, producing strong feelings of support for Washington among an incredible 84.3 percent of the black voters on election day.[87]

Another type of sentiment had swept through the city's white neighborhoods. Epton's attacks and negative advertising crystallized anti-Washington feelings among previously undecided whites, prompting their movement into his column and narrowing the projected citywide outcome. Table 27 shows that most of this movement occurred among whites on the Northwest and Southwest Sides, areas where Washington's support was initially weak and where it didn't change much through the election.[88] Before the end of March, there was also some softening of Washington's strength among Hispanic voters, although Epton gained only about half of those who drifted away from his opponent. The integrity issue had its most critical impact, however, among the mostly white voters in the Lake Shore wards. There Epton scored a 30-percentage-point gain between 15 March and 10 April, while the number of undecided voters fell by 16 percentage points and Washington's support by 14. It was this loss of support along the Lake Shore that especially jeopardized Washington's election, and a private tracking on 7 April showed him losing the mayoral race to Epton.[89]

As Washington's campaign managers looked at the poll results in early April, they knew their candidate could become the first Democratic nominee to lose a mayoral contest since 1927. The 10 to 12 percent still undecided were mostly whites; and in other biracial contests, whites who decided late in the campaign voted almost unanimously for the white candidate. Moreover, Epton's blunt attacks on his character and the "drip, drip, drip" effect of the disclosures had kept Washington on the defensive, obscured his own campaign themes, and eroded his support even among whites who otherwise were willing to vote for a black candidate. As one potential Washington backer, a well-educated career woman from a Lake Shore ward, put it:

> I'm getting disgusted. My God, I don't want to vote with the bigots. But everyday it's something new. He doesn't pay this bill, he didn't pay that bill. I work hard and I pay all my bills. I'm getting fed up. I'm not sure I'll vote. Epton and his people are disgusting. I just may skip it.

Table 27. Trends in Support by Areas of the City: Poll Reports, 15 March through 12 April 1983 [1]

Interview Dates [2]	Washington	Epton	Undecided
Whites: Northwest Side			
15 March	21	38	41
29 March	18	60	23
10 April	19	69	12
12 April	16	84	—
Whites: Southwest Side			
15 March	21	46	33
29 March	28	50	22
10 April	21	60	19
12 April	23	77	—
All Respondents: Lake Shore			
15 March	50	22	28
29 March	42	41	17
10 April	36	52	12
12 April	44	56	—
Hispanics: Citywide			
15 March	57	19	24
29 March	51	22	27
10 April	67	26	7
12 April	67	33	—

[1] Entries are percentages, and each row sums to 100 percent, except for rounding error.

[2] Polls conducted by Richard Day Research, Inc., and the 12 April results are from the WLS-TV (ABC) Exit Poll.

A white business executive from the Belmont-Sheridan area, who had voted for Washington in the primary, admitted that he was "just disgusted. . . . I can't vote for Epton, but I don't think I can vote for Washington either. The tax thing was bad enough. But it just goes on and on, and there are never any real explanations." Among many liberal and moderate whites, "there's a fear that Washington represents turmoil," one political analyst concluded. Bungling by Washington's campaign organization reinforced that fear. "He doesn't show up for this, he doesn't show up for that. I get the feeling that everything is completely disorganized," observed a young professional in the New Town area. Some veteran politicians suggested another reason why white voters in the Lake Shore wards were swayed by Epton's attacks and Washington's fumbling campaign efforts. As one Democratic leader in the area put it, "There are people who don't like to admit that they are uncomfortable about a black mayor who have been given a legitimate reason to turn their backs on Washington." [90]

Because Washington stopped this hemorrhaging of his support in the Lake Shore wards, he was able to hang on to win the general election. Washington switched his tactics in the final days of the campaign: he went on the attack against Epton and vigorously competed for votes on the Lake Shore battlefield. It's not clear how much of this new initiative was planned all along, how much was simply good luck, and how much resulted from the increased influence of his congressional staff within the campaign organization. The timing of the switch, coupled with the character of the staff struggle—a conflict between the movement activists and the electoral veterans—suggests that resolving the internal tension was critical to developing a coherent strategy. In any case, the new initiative worked. Among late-deciding whites generally, and especially among the types who populated the Lake Shore wards, Washington received a larger share of support than he had among those who made their decisions between one and four weeks prior to election day (Table 28). As a result, between 10 and 12 April, Washington picked up enough new support along the Lake Shore to hang on for his narrow victory. If late-deciding whites had divided in the same proportions as those who made their choices during the preceding four weeks, Washington's overall strength among whites responding to the WMAQ-TV (NBC) exit poll would have dropped to about 16 percent, and Epton would have polled the support of 50.2 percent of all its respondents.[91]

The final days witnessed a fittingly odd end to what had become, even by Chicago's none-too-lofty standards, "the meanest, dirtiest and most contentious general election . . . in decades." Epton, who earlier claimed "the more I talk the more I seem to alienate people," took his words to heart. He maintained a low profile over the last week, making relatively few campaign stops, softening his references to Washington, and relying mostly on a new series of television commercials that emphasized his positive attributes. In sharp contrast, Washington stumped vigorously, toughened his rhetoric, attacked Epton on the integrity issue, and aired his own television spots that played to the disquiet that many liberal and moderate whites felt over the racist nature of much of the opposition to him. Both camps agreed that the vote in the Lake Shore wards "is as fluid as the vote in the other areas is fixed," and the contrast in tactics reflected their judgments of how best to win the battle in that pivotal area.[92]

Washington increased his campaign stops in the Lake Shore wards and emphasized four themes designed to attract support from their normally liberal and independent electorate. First, he confronted the integrity issue and tried to contain its damage and to raise doubts about Epton's character. As he had on other occasions, Washington

Table 28. Vote by Time of Decision: Percentage for Washington[1]

	Last 3 Days	1 to 2 Weeks	2 to 4 Weeks	Over 4 Weeks
Whites	27.8	17.5	14.6	20.0
Blacks	88.8	92.8	97.5	97.4
Hispanics	44.1	50.0	61.9	65.5
White Respondents Only				
Liberal	38.6	33.3	35.9	45.7
Moderate	26.9	11.5	9.6	8.6
Conservative	17.2	9.1	2.9	9.1
Democrat	26.5	15.3	14.8	21.4
Independent	33.3	30.0	16.4	22.8
Republican	28.5	10.0	3.5	10.0
Not HS graduate	18.5	6.1	13.8	14.1
HS graduate	26.9	11.0	10.8	6.8
Some college	16.0	18.5	8.1	12.9
College graduate	35.3	29.6	13.6	29.0
Graduate school	42.9	37.9	45.2	59.1
Protestant	28.9	18.4	18.9	28.2
Catholic	22.5	15.8	10.3	14.5
Jew	47.6	25.0	26.1	36.7

[1] The percentage for Epton is the reciprocal of each entry.

Source: WMAQ-TV (NBC) exit poll.

acknowledged his responsibility for past mistakes, while arguing that Epton had blown them out of proportion. "You would think I had committed homicide and should go to the guillotine or a life sentence," he told one rally of liberals at the Belmont Hotel on North Sheridan Road. "I don't reduce them to peccadilos, but they were not much more." One of the new radio advertisements that Washington's staff targeted to the lakefront audience repeated that theme. The announcer likened his conviction for failure to file income tax returns to a parking ticket, adding that "Bernie Epton's lack of decency would have him pay for his mistake for the rest of his life."[93]

Washington also went on the offensive against Epton's integrity. A study released on 2 April by the Illinois Public Action Council alleged that Epton's law firm earned over $1.3 million in fees from the insurance industry while Epton served as the General Assembly's unofficial expert on insurance legislation. The executive director of the council, Robert Creamer, claimed that Epton's actions, while not illegal, were worse than those in Washington's troubled past. "Epton was so enmeshed in conflict of interest so pervasive that, in effect, he sold his seat in the House to the state's insurance industry." Epton had denied the general charge earlier, but the release of a study

26. Mayoral candidate Harold Washington jubilantly greeting a crowd of supporters from the Lake Shore precincts at the Belmont Hotel, Saturday, 9 April 1983. (*Chicago Tribune.*)

based on the records of the Illinois Department of Insurance gave Washington new ammunition. "Since Mr. Epton has claimed he's 'Mr. Integrity,' it's incumbent upon him to respond to that alleged conflict," Washington told a rally in New Town. In other speeches, he referred frequently to Epton's law firm growing rich on insurance business while he supported the industry's positions as a state legislator. "And he would dare to try to sully my character?" Washington asked sarcastically. "Mr. Epton cure yourself. Come clean, Bernie, before it's too late."[94]

To complete his characterization of Epton, Washington hit his legislative voting record, his affluence, and his ability to lead the city. The Washington campaign ran a full-page advertisement in the *Chicago Reader*, which circulated heavily on the lakefront, comparing the voting records of the two candidates on selected social and consumer issues. The comparison portrayed Epton as a conservative, out of touch with the liberal and moderate lakefront voters. And Washington attacked his opponent's vow to be a one-term mayor, saying it showed Epton "thinks the City of Chicago is a toy to be played with by some rich man like himself." Washington also repeatedly jabbed at Epton's ability to manage the city government: "He's not a serious candidate. . . . He would be a puppet . . . for the next four years," he told one group of voters.[95]

The second theme that Washington emphasized in the final days was that his campaign for mayor was a battle against the Democratic Machine. "The battle cry of this campaign never was and never will be race," he said. "The battle cry is reform." In speech after speech, on the lakefront and in black neighborhoods, Washington pounded that theme over the final weekend. Speaking to black audiences, he linked his anti-Machine message with opposition to Mayor Byrne. "There is a direct connection between this outgoing mayor and Epton," he told a South Side rally. "Bernie Epton will be there to deliver for her." But in the Lake Shore wards, where Byrne had run well in the primary and was still popular, Washington refrained from criticizing the mayor. There he concentrated on the "greed merchants," the Machine Democrats who were working against him because they saw Epton's election as their best bet to keep control over the city. "Greed is involved in this campaign, profit is involved in this campaign—and they're using race to cover it up," he told one cheering lakefront crowd. In this version of the theme, Washington and his supporters cast the contest as a struggle within the Democratic party between reformers and regulars. "I think people should realize that this isn't really a battle between Washington and Epton; it's a battle between Washington and Eddie Vrdolyak," said Democratic state Representative Ellis Levin. "Epton would be just a figurehead if elected."[96]

Third, Washington courted Hispanic voters, including those who made up 11.2 percent of the voting-age population of the Lake Shore wards. To a luncheon gathering of Hispanic youths on the near North Side, he uncharacteristically spoke about his personal background, telling them of the importance of his father as a role model and identifying his experience with their struggle for education and opportunity. To other gatherings, he promised again to forge the black-brown coalition, "not a negative but a positive coalition, designed to help . . . make [this city] fairer for everyone within it." And over the last four days, the Washington campaign aired specially produced commercials on all local Spanish-language radio and television stations and ran ads in the city's Spanish newspapers.[97]

Finally, about a week before the election, the Washington campaign began running television spots that attacked the race question directly. Bill Zimmerman, Washington's media consultant, felt that since "the Epton campaign had polarized the city around race, . . . we had to talk about race to [white] liberals." One of the ads interspersed shots of an integrated group of children pledging allegiance to the flag with scenes of angry demonstrators. Then, on the Saturday before the election, the staff unveiled what it dubbed the "ashamed

27. Frames from a commercial interspersing shots of the St. Pascal's incident with pictures of youngsters quietly reciting the pledge of allegiance to the flag. In the final week of the campaign, Washington's television spots used such visual images to tap the guilt feelings of undecided white liberals.

commercial," the most striking and most controversial ad of its media effort. The television spot featured a series of still photos of a Ku Klux Klan rally, the Kennedy and King assassinations, and the Kent State shootings, interspersed with scenes of Epton's supporters jeering at Washington and Mondale in front of St. Pascal's Church on Palm Sunday. As the scenes flashed across the screen, the announcer said, "There are moments in our history of which we are thoroughly and profoundly ashamed. One of those moments may be happening

28. A scene from a commercial that presented idyllic images of Chicago's diversity, while the voice-over told viewers: "Here in Chicago, we're people of a thousand different backgrounds and beliefs. But we can be united, too, by our belief in a better Chicago, and by our faith in the miracle called democracy. On April 12th, . . . we'll send a message to the entire nation. . . . Chicago can rise above corruption and strained race relations. We're going to vote with our hearts, not with our fears. . . . On April 12th, we're going to vote for Harold Washington, because this is Chicago and, here in Chicago, we know what makes America strong."

in Chicago right now." Then the voice concluded by urging citizens to cast a "vote they can be proud of."[98]

The commercials were aimed at two audiences. They played to the consciences of white liberals and moderates, those who had developed doubts about Washington but who wanted to separate themselves from the blatant racism displayed by some of Epton's supporters. The theme was also targeted to blacks, to remind them of what was at stake and to reinforce their intention to vote.

Five days before the election, Washington's appeal to the guilt feelings of whites took on a new dimension. A week or so earlier, an anonymous leaflet surfaced that claimed the *Chicago Tribune* was suppressing a story that Washington had once been arrested on a charge of child molestation. The leaflet claimed that the event had been expunged from police records, but the arresting officer and the family of the young man involved were willing to confirm it. Rumors of such a past event had been circulating for several weeks in some of the white precincts, and when the leaflet appeared, reporters for the *Tribune* and other media outlets investigated the claims. They found, and law enforcement authorities confirmed, that the claim of a past arrest on a morals charge was completely unfounded. A reporter for WLS-TV (ABC) traced the leaflet to Epton volunteers working out of a 26th Ward front organization originally set up for Jane Byrne by one of Vrdolyak's close aides. After some internal debate, the *Tribune* decided to run a story about the leaflet, making clear that no evidence existed confirming its allegations.[99] That decision eventually aided Washington, because it cleared the air of a troubling rumor and showed the depths to which the attacks on his character had sunk.

On Thursday, 7 April—the same day on which he opened himself to more criticism by missing a scheduled appearance on a popular WGN talk show, and the same day on which Caddell's tracking showed him running behind Epton—Washington decided to deal openly with the leaflet and the rumors of a past morals charge. Speaking that night at Mundelein College, on the North Side, Washington noted that he had become something of a "folk hero" among black children and denounced the leaflet's description of him as a child molester. The assault "on my basic, fundamental character . . . is not going to be tolerated." Addressing his remarks to Epton, he went on: "Do you want this job so badly? . . . Are you so singularly minded that you would try to destroy character? If that is the kind of man you are, and if these are the kinds of dogs of racism and scurrilism that you are going to unleash, I say to you, Mr. Epton, I will fight you day and night." After naming the news media, Epton, and Deardourff as the sources of the charges, Washington recited a list of other recent disclosures of unpaid bills and claimed he was being attacked because he was black. "Lies. Lies. Lies," he exclaimed. "Anything goes. Old Harold can take it. After all, he's black. That's what it's all about. He's black. The press will print it and then they'll ask questions after they print it."[100]

By that stage of the campaign, Washington's staff felt the barrage of personal attacks against him had begun to backfire. "A lot of whites have been turned off by the attacks," one of his planners told reporters. By openly discussing the leaflet, Washington tapped the unease those whites felt at putting themselves into the same camp with those who would stoop to any level to defeat a black candidate for mayor. It was a sound tactic to expose the nature of the grass-roots campaign being waged against him and to use the leaflet's reprehensible and bogus claim, which Epton had called "vile" and had immediately repudiated, to undercut the effect of the earlier attacks on his integrity. It was also a relatively low-risk tactic: persons likely to believe such anonymous and undocumented claims were also likely to have decided much earlier to vote against Washington, while he might gain sympathy and support among whites who had come to doubt his competence and integrity but saw this sort of attack as going too far.[101]

While Washington went on the offensive during the final week, with a hard-hitting attack on several fronts, Epton took the opposite approach. His switch in tactics was a calculated part of Deardourff's larger strategy. Having raised doubts about Washington's character and fitness throughout the campaign, Deardourff used the closing days to give undecided voters positive reasons to support Epton by emphasizing his background and proposals. The switch also guarded against a backlash to the earlier negative approach.[102]

Campaigning in the last week, Epton avoided confrontation and sarcasm and projected an image of serenity, often acting as though he had already won the election. He generally made no direct mention of Washington, except for a few references at rallies to "voters like you who file your taxes and pay your bills." On 8 April, appearing on the WGN show that Washington had missed the preceding day, Epton was calm and restrained, again withholding direct criticism of Washington. Throughout the last days, Epton emphasized his familiar themes—no new taxes, a strong police force, and neighborhood pride. "I want you to know that nothing will be done in this city without the consent of the neighborhoods involved," he told the residents of Marquette Park on the Southwest Side, who for years had opposed scattered-site public housing in their community.[103]

The tone of Epton's television and radio commercials also changed. Beginning on 6 April, the "before it's too late" slogan disappeared from his ads, and the new spots were lighter and more positive than the earlier ones. Most featured straightforward shots of Epton extolling his record as a businessman, lawyer, and legislator, and one talked of Epton's integrity, without mentioning Washington. Most were aimed at voters in the Lake Shore wards, according to Deardourff, and they highlighted "his votes in the Legislature on the Equal Rights Amendment, consumer protection, and anti-red-lining as well as the support he's gotten from the Independent Voters of Illinois and the AFL-CIO." In his final radio address, aired on Monday evening, Epton again listed his opponent's financial problems, saying they summed to "a long and disturbing pattern of behavior," but he also pledged to "bridge the gap" between the city's racial and religious groups and asked voters not to make their choice based on race or religion.[104]

The Epton campaign projected a reserved, positive, but confident image during the final week. Instead of campaigning relentlessly, as Washington did, Epton made fewer appearances than he had in earlier weeks. There was neither the frenetic last-minute drive that the media had expected, nor the shrill, negative tone that had been the campaign's earlier hallmark. Some political reporters were puzzled by these unconventional tactics, but they fit well with what Epton's staff judged to be the best way to win the election.

Except to provide a final boost to turnout, Epton didn't need to campaign on the Northwest and Southwest Sides. His support there was solid; Washington couldn't really compete for those votes, and the Machine's precinct captains were lined up and working for Epton. He had no reason to doubt that the voters there who were still undecided would opt overwhelmingly for him. "We don't need a pitch," one of his workers on the Northwest Side remarked. So Epton could cut back his campaign stops in these areas, shorten them, and confine himself to comments that weren't controversial. "I look around, and all I can say is I love you and God bless," he said as he was mobbed by one group of cheering supporters on the Northwest Side.[105]

Epton's campaign managers knew that the more unpredictable group of undecided voters was in the Lake Shore wards. They knew, too, that the best way to attract those voters was to quiet the shrill rhetoric and identify Epton with their positions on issues, while putting some distance between him and the blatantly racist appeals of some of his supporters. The new commercials and Epton's calm and restrained demeanor were designed to present him as an experienced, stable, and moderate person, capable of running the city competently without the turmoil that Washington's election threatened.

Still, the Epton camp was worried about a possible sympathy effect on the race question among liberal and moderate whites. On the Sunday before the election, a group of clergy from the North and Northwest Sides held a press conference to endorse Washington and decry the "racist character" of the election. Blaming Epton for exploiting racial fears, their spokesman said bluntly that "this election is . . . a choice between justice and racism." It was to prevent such sentiments from spreading among undecided whites that Epton struck a clearly conciliatory tone over the final week. "We have had a bitter, divisive campaign, but it's not too important now to place the blame on me or my opponent," he told one North Side group. "Bitterness and hatred" are the price we pay for freedom. "Unfortunately, sometimes it is the freedom to hate. But the fact remains . . . we are going to live together." On 10 April, appearing on ABC-TV's "This Week with David Brinkley," Epton played down the race issue, saying that "the main issue is not my race or my religion or his [Washington's], but integrity, honesty, and open government." And he repeated his earlier denials that his campaign or his slogan intended to capitalize on racial feelings. He made comments on race, he told reporters, only in response to persistent questions from the media, and their "erroneous and false" reports, "magnified out of all proportion," were giving Chicago "a bad rap."[106]

At last, on election day, Chicagoans had their opportunity to speak. The contest drew a record turnout to the polls, as 61.7 percent of the city's voting-age population, or 74.3 percent of its registered voters, cast ballots for mayor. The outpouring in the black community caught even some of Washington's advisers by surprise. In some precincts, the lines of people extended halfway down the block when the polls opened at 6 A.M., and by mid-afternoon several of the black precincts on the South Side reported that all the registered voters had cast their ballots. "People have, I guess, been dreaming of this day for a long time," Alderman Eugene Sawyer (6th Ward) said, accounting for the turnout. "It's hard to explain how important this is to people in my community." The same fervor marked the white ethnic neighborhoods, especially those on the Southwest Side, where resistance to a black mayor was evident from the outset. "I'm surprised it's so high," Congressman William Lipinski said, commenting on the turnout in his 23rd Ward. "But they just kept coming, and it was 'Epton, Epton, Epton.'"[107]

Despite their generally higher education and income levels, whites along the Lake Shore didn't match the turnout of blacks or white ethnics. The Democratic candidates for city clerk and city treasurer handily carried all six wards along the lakefront, while Washington lost them all, running best in the 42d and 46th wards.[108] While his strategists had hoped for a better showing, the votes Washington did attract from Lake Shore whites, added to his black and Hispanic support, were enough to push him over the top. Both Caddell, Washington's pollster, and his counterpart in the Epton camp, Robert Teeter, agreed that a crucial share of the lakefront's undecided voters swung into Washington's column over the final three days. "History was working against us," Caddell said, referring to other biracial contests for mayor, where the undecided white vote went to the white candidate. "In many ways this was a miracle."[109]

By making Epton and his campaign strategy the issue in the final week, Washington stopped and then reversed the erosion of his support among key categories of white voters. While only a minority of the whites who decided in the final three days opted for Washington, those who did accounted for over a fifth (21.6 percent) of all his white voters. But they were generally unenthusiastic about their choice, with 87 percent saying they had reservations or that Washington was the least objectionable candidate. Most of them may have echoed the view of one Hyde Park liberal who said on election eve, "Washington is almost the last person I would vote for as mayor, but Epton *is* the last."[110]

29. The polling place at 54 West Cermak Road on the near South Side. The heavy turn-out by blacks typically produced long lines such as this one. (*Chicago Tribune.*)

The 1983 mayoral election was not a traditional Chicago election. "It used to be that . . . many people would have chosen sides according to party, and the campaign would be over," Caddell observed shortly before election day. "This time, people also have chosen sides, but the controlling fulcrum here is race not party."[111]

Many Chicagoans, including some reporters and politicians, proved unwilling to admit the implication of Caddell's remark. Surely it wasn't true, one columnist suggested, that all of Epton's voters were white racists and all of Washington's black racists. Other reporters noted Washington's 19 percent among white voters, compared it with other biracial contests for mayor and concluded that it was higher than most other black candidates had received in their initial elections. And one columnist especially scored the national media for looking only at Washington's race, while ignoring his legal and financial problems, as the basis for opposition to him. "Race is an easy issue" to pick up on, she wrote, "and so Chicago has been portrayed as an intolerant city. . . . Or so *they* say."[112]

Despite their defensive tone, there is some credibility in these claims. Whites in other cities have been reluctant to support black candidates for executive offices; and some of Chicago's white voters were genuinely disturbed by the apparent chaos surrounding Washington's campaign effort and by his past legal and financial problems. Indeed, a national poll released the day before the election showed that nearly three of five people (including 41 percent of the blacks) thought Washington's past troubles—and not his race—would be responsible if he lost the mayoral election.[113] But most of these respondents had no exposure to politics Chicago style, hadn't experienced its history of bitter and often violent racial conflicts, and didn't know the code words and symbols its politicians used to tap racial feelings.

Washington's personal history was an appropriate matter for any opponent to raise, but the reaction to it seemed out of proportion to the character of his misdeeds. True, he had been convicted for failing to file income tax returns, but the charge was a misdemeanor and the federal audit discovered that he owed the government a total of $508.05. The Chicago Bar Association had suspended his law license for not performing services for which clients had paid, but the fees involved amounted to less than $300. In these instances, and those of the unpaid bills, there was evidence of carelessness and inattention to his personal finances, but there was never a hint of fraud or misuse of public office. Perhaps in some other locales, offenses of this type might merit the rank of major scandals, but they should have been barely noticed by Chicago's standards. In its indifference to or tolerance of the misdeeds of its public servants, Chicago has never been the nation's second city. "Open deals, openly arrived at," that's the Chicago style, the *Tribune* editorialized, referring to campaign contributions given to Byrne by contractors doing business with the city. "It is a Chicago tradition that other cities must marvel at."[114]

Neither the city's voters nor its Democratic politicians seemed much upset earlier when Edward Barrett, Earl Bush, Paul Wigoda, and Thomas Keane were convicted on far more serious felony charges. Indeed, the voters of the 31st Ward elected Keane's wife to stand in for him on the City Council while he served time in the federal penitentiary. And there were no righteous outcries from his Republican colleagues when William Scott, the incumbent attorney general of Illinois, was convicted of income tax fraud in March 1980. Instead, they joined with several prominent Chicago Democrats to fete him at a $100-a-head "Appreciation Night"; and Governor Thompson, who had prosecuted the wayward Democrats, called him "the best attorney general in the history of the State of Illinois," overlooking the fact that Scott's defense involved claiming he had accepted secret, but nontaxable, gifts of cash from several persons with whom his office dealt officially.[115] Finally, while Washington's earlier failure to pay $508 in income taxes was becoming a *cause célèbre*, the fact that Alderman Edward Vrdolyak ended a four-year dispute with the Internal Revenue Service in early March by agreeing to pay the government $118,000 in back income taxes, penalties, and interest passed almost unnoticed.[116]

In a city with a long history of misdeeds and shady deals by public officials, and one where voters displayed a high tolerance for public corruption, the news about Washington should not have been a bombshell. Moreover, the poll data (in Tables 22 and 27) show that Washington's white support, especially on the Northwest and Southwest Sides, was low even in mid-March, before Epton's media blitz and at a time when Deardourff claimed their polls indicated little public awareness of the Democratic nominee's troubled past. Unlike 1979, white Democrats didn't move immediately to the winner of their party's primary; they remained doubtful and undecided, although most (68 percent) thought Washington would win the general election.[117] Their choice was between two unpleasant possibilities: voting for a *black* Democrat or voting for a white *Republican*. Epton's negative advertising and slashing attack on Washington's character reinforced racial stereotypes, confirmed doubts about a black as mayor, and provided many white Democrats with an ostensibly respectable reason to vote their racial feelings.

Of course on election day, relatively few whites (19.8 percent) admitted that race was the most important factor guiding their choice, although 93.2 percent of those who did voted for Epton. More white voters (47.4 percent) agreed with the claim that Chicago was not ready to have a black mayor, and they cast 98.2 percent of their ballots for Epton, making up over three fifths (61.1 percent) of all his white voters.[118]

Racial identifications operated in two distinct ways to determine the outcome of the election. They shaped popular assessments of the candidates and issues, with most whites coming to see Epton as the more experienced leader and better able to deal with the police force, the neighborhoods, and the city's business community. Second, even independently of this impact, race still had a sizable direct effect on voting choices. Thus, whites who saw no difference between the candidates on issues relating to the police, neighborhoods, and business community still gave 85 percent or more of their vote to Epton. The Republican candidate appears to have been the choice of these citizens because he "had all that [they] demanded: white skin and a pulse beat."[119]

Black Chicagoans faced no dilemma in making their voting choices. Party identification reinforced racial pride, and blacks who had supported Byrne or Daley in the primary quickly moved into Washington's column, leaving only a small share of the black vote undecided. Epton's failure to campaign extensively for black support and his bruising attack on his opponent drove the undecided blacks to Washington by election day.[120]

"It was black for black and white for white," and Chicago had become "a city divided against itself," the *Tribune* lamented editorially two days before the election. But its judgment was needlessly morose. On election day, a majority of Hispanics and a small proportion of whites joined with blacks to support a black candidate for mayor. By doing so, they ended the Democratic Machine's uncontested control over the city, its public institutions, and its people, and opened the way to a new era in Chicago politics and government.

8. Beyond Chicago and April 1983

Chicago is one city. We must work as one people for our common good and our common goals. . . . I want to reach out my hand in friendship and fellowship to every living soul in this city.

The healing that we see . . . is economic and social and more. And it includes justice and love, not just for ourselves as individuals alone, but for all, all, all in this city. *Mayor-elect Harold Washington*

■ The mostly black crowd that gathered in Donnelley Hall at 23rd and Martin Luther King Drive on the South Side was in a joyous mood. The Sunshine Festival Band played rock music, and souvenir salesmen peddled T-shirts and beanies. The people danced and clapped, laughed and wept, and they cheered the early reports that Harold Washington was piling up a huge lead in the black wards. At 7:01 P.M., WLS-TV (ABC) called him the winner, with an estimated 55 percent of the vote. The WBBM-TV (CBS) and WMAQ-TV (NBC) exit polls also showed Washington ahead, but those stations hedged their bets and held back their predictions.

When the returns from the white wards poured in, WLS-TV scaled back its estimate to 52 percent, and the other networks still claimed the result was too close to call. At about 11 P.M., Bernard Epton appeared before his crowd of mostly white supporters in the Grand Ballroom of the Palmer House. He told them that he was then running only about 5,000 votes behind, but "I think most of the outstanding wards are our wards." The crowd cheered. "Keep smiling, keep praying, and keep waiting. I'll be back down just as soon as we get those figures," he assured them. But Epton made no second appearance that night. He left the hotel about an hour later, after his analysts confirmed that his bid had fallen short. On the way out he told reporters that he wished Washington luck in managing the city, especially in coping with its financial problems. "Maybe he'll learn to pay his bills promptly and his taxes," he added. A few steps later, apparently referring to his almost complete lack of votes from blacks, he said, "I certainly will save a lot of money in the future on charitable causes." One of his key supporters called it a "graceless" exit, one last note of bitterness ending a divisive and racially polarizing campaign.[1]

While Epton was leaving the Palmer House, the crowd at Donnelley Hall awaited the arrival of the mayor-elect. At about 1:30 A.M., Harold Washington made his way through the throng and responded to their chants of "Harold, Harold, Harold." "You want Harold?" he asked. "Well here is Harold." Under a banner proclaiming "Washington for All Chicago," the mayor-elect spoke of the meaning of his triumph. "Out of the crucible of this city's most trying election, . . . blacks, whites, Hispanics, Jews, gentiles, Protestants and Catholics of all stripes have joined hands to form a new Democratic coalition and to begin in this place a new Democratic movement." We have been victorious, he continued, "but I am mindful that there were many other friends and neighbors who were not a part of our campaign." But now "each of us must . . . rededicate [our] efforts to heal the divisions that have plagued us. . . . Together we will overcome our problems[.]"[2]

Later that day, Washington met with several of his former campaign foes for a symbolic "ecumenical prayer unity luncheon" at the Conrad Hilton Hotel. Saul Epton represented his brother, who was then on route to Florida, and delivered "a clear-cut good will message" from the losing candidate to the mayor-elect. Mayor Byrne and State's Attorney Daley attended the luncheon, as did eighteen of the city's religious leaders, including Joseph Cardinal Bernardin, the Roman Catholic archbishop. Speaking later to reporters, Washington said "we are now in the process of building a new city, a multi-ethnic city," and he pledged "to reach out to every area of the city."[3]

The mayoral contest opened old wounds and brought unresolved tensions and fears into public view. In a city with a long and bitter history of racial conflict, the campaign inflamed group relations and complicated the task of reconciliation. With no reservoir of mutual trust to draw on, whites and blacks were not likely to heed Washington's call to "reach out and open our arms" to each other. Too many Chicagoans silently shared the cynical outlook of Mike Royko's mythical friend Wally. "You open your arms to somebody in this town and they'll either yell for the cops or hit you in the mouth because you've left yourself wide open."[4]

The electoral war between the races changed the shape of Chicago's politics, but its importance reached beyond the city. What happened among Chicago's blacks was both part of and made its own contribution to a larger national movement, which has enormous significance for the future course of race relations and for the operation of the political system.

Beyond April 1983

■ On Friday, 29 April 1983, in ceremonies at Navy Pier, Harold Washington became Chicago's forty-second mayor and its first black chief executive. Addressing his inaugural remarks to the invited guests and to the citywide television audience, Mayor Washington called for a new approach to the government of the city, while offering a stunning indictment of the outgoing administration. "My transition team advises me that the city government is . . . in far worse financial condition than we thought," the mayor said, calling attention to a gap as large as $150 million in the current budget. To remedy financial problems he described as "enormous and complicated," Washington promised cuts in executive salaries, a hiring freeze, and the release of "the several hundred new city employees who were added because of political considerations" in the closing days of the Byrne Administration.[5]

The 4,000 invited guests, many of whom were Washington campaign workers, applauded his promise to heal the "racial fears and divisiveness [that] have hurt us in the past." And they cheered thunderously when he pledged to remain true to the reform spirit of his campaign, vowing a more open government and greater citizen involvement. "My election was made possible by thousands of people who demanded that the burdens of unfairness and inequity be lifted so that the city can be saved," he told them. "One of the ideas that held us together said that neighborhood involvement has to take the place of the Machine."

To the newly sworn members of the City Council, including its Machine stalwarts, the mayor issued both a challenge and an appeal. "Today, I am calling on all of you . . . to respond to a great challenge: Business as usual will not be accepted. . . . Help me institute reform and bring about a renewal of this city while we still have time."

Washington's tough words probably didn't surprise the party regulars, although several claimed publicly that the tone of his speech discouraged harmonious relations. "He came off like Attila the Hun," Alderman Thomas Cullerton (38th Ward) remarked. "That's not going to help him win the aldermen over."[6] But as Cullerton knew, the battle for control over the city was already raging behind the scenes, and nothing Washington said during his inauguration could have changed many minds or altered the balance of forces.

On 2 May, when the City Council met for the first time under

30. Alderman Edward Vrdolyak (10th Ward) calling for quiet in the City Council chambers after taking control following Mayor Washington's hasty adjournment of the session on 2 May 1983. (*Chicago Tribune.*)

the new mayor, the Democratic regulars, led by Alderman Edward Vrdolyak (10th Ward), formed a solid voting bloc of twenty-nine members. Knowing that he didn't have the votes to prevent the adoption of resolutions that created new committees, distributed their chairmanships, and adopted new rules shackling the mayor, Washington hastily adjourned the meeting, ignoring verbal demands for a roll call on the motion. As the mayor and his twenty-one allies walked out of the Council chamber, Vrdolyak seized the gavel and the Council majority adopted its resolutions. The "Council wars" had formally begun, with Vrdolyak and Alderman Edward Burke (14th Ward), his chief ally and the newly designated chairman of the powerful Finance Committee, in control of the Council.[7]

The battle had begun before the Council's initial session. "That's when I knew how it was going to be," Vrdolyak said, referring to Washington's demand on 19 April that Vrdolyak yield the chairmanship of the Building and Zoning Committee. "That's when I knew it would be war. . . . I'm not the kind of guy you can tell 'Go sit in the corner'—and I just go sit there. I never was. That's not how I got where I got. . . . Nobody can blow me off like that." He wasn't going to be a passive bystander while Washington and his allies were "trying to take my manhood away." They "read me all wrong. I'm a fighter. I don't go down easy."[8]

According to Vrdolyak, his decision to resist came on the occasion of a highly publicized unity meeting between the mayor-elect and the aldermen on 19 April. The breakfast at the Bismarck Hotel was intended as a peace-making session. Washington spoke briefly, telling the aldermen he would "not overly interfere with the council" and would cooperate and communicate with them. "I look forward to four years of hard work, but there will be controversy." The mayor-elect then made the rounds of all the tables, chatting at length with several aldermen who had opposed him in the general election. After the breakfast, in a private meeting with Alderman Wilson Frost (34th Ward) and Vrdolyak, Washington told the alderman and committeeman from the 10th Ward and the chairman of the Democratic Central Committee of Cook County that he should relinquish his post as the Council's president pro tem and take a committee chairmanship other than Building and Zoning. Vrdolyak agreed to give up the honorific position but objected to losing his control over the powerful (and profitable) committee. "You're attacking my manhood," he told Washington.[9]

Needless to say, Vrdolyak's version of the details serves his own purpose. It presents him as willing and ready to cooperate with the new mayor, while depicting Washington as ungratefully rebuffing Vrdolyak's gracious offer and pushing him out of the leadership. In this version, the responsibility for conflict falls heavily on the mayor, with Vrdolyak and his allies appearing as the aggrieved parties. "None of this would have happened if Harold had come to us the way Byrne did," Alderman Burke said.[10]

But Washington was not another Jane Byrne, willing to yield control over the city to the parochial ward barons. Vrdolyak, Burke, and the other party regulars knew that from the outset, and because they did, they worked for Epton's cause, some openly and others covertly. Vrdolyak himself played all ends against the middle, verbally backing Washington, secretly aiding Epton, and all the while organizing his own bloc among the aldermen. When Washington won the general election, Vrdolyak stepped up his organizing efforts, cleverly exploiting the racial fears of white aldermen, playing to their desire for the prestige and patronage of committee chairmanships, and taking advantage of conflicting signals and indecisive counterefforts by Washington's camp. Acting as both coach and cheerleader, Vrdolyak "created a sense among these guys [i.e., his allies] that they could win," one insider observed. He called frequent meetings, kept in touch with everyone, set up a "buddy system" to keep tabs on the freshman aldermen, and even sent flowers to the wives of the twenty-nine on Mother's Day. And the Vrdolyak group did its homework thoroughly: they checked the statutes and precedents with lawyers and were ready for any eventuality.[11]

Washington wasn't unaware of Vrdolyak's early efforts to organize his own majority on the Council. Cook County Board President George Dunne and others warned him of the behind-the-scenes maneuvering, and the unity breakfast on 19 April was a response to those warnings. In his meeting with Vrdolyak after the breakfast, Washington told him directly, "You supported Epton, bullshitted me, and you've been organizing from day one. Let's get it out front."[12] But Washington's attempt to slow the opposition's momentum was limited by his own commitment to reform, which prevented him from outbidding Vrdolyak for support, and the continuing fear of a black mayor among most white Chicagoans, which made even those white aldermen who were uncomfortable with Vrdolyak reluctant to join Washington's bloc of supporters on the Council.

Earlier and better organizing by Washington and his followers might have recruited more support on the Council. But no amount of maneuvering, no matter how skillful, could have prevented the battle, since it is simply another episode in the ongoing war for control over the city. At one level, that war involves competition between racial groups for dominance over the city's culture-transmitting institutions; at another level, it represents a contest for power, prestige, and profits between Machine and anti-Machine politicians. And in the real world of Chicago politics, these two separate threads of conflict have been closely interwoven.

While the "Council wars" are a direct continuation of the primary and general election skirmishes, their roots lie in the demographic changes the city has experienced since the 1940s, and the ways in which its political leaders responded to them. The growth and residential expansion of the black population raised integration issues and strained the bonds that tied blacks and lower-income whites to Chicago's Democratic Machine. With the civil unrest of the 1960s and the rise of a more assertive black leadership, Machine politicians came to view blacks as an undependable part of their electoral coalition and become increasingly dependent on the white ethnic neighborhoods for voting support. The Machine's responsiveness to its white constituency forestalled the type of white backlash that occurred in other northern cities, while further alienating and demobilizing black voters. But it also made the Machine vulnerable to continuing "white flight," which threatened its electoral base. Thus, pursuing policies designed to stop or slow white out-migration became linked with preserving the Machine's electoral control and its status as the city's ruling institution. This reciprocal relationship between the Machine and the white ethnic areas is the context that gives meaning to the politics of the city's culture-transmitting agencies over the past twenty years. Appointments to the police and fire departments, to the Board of Education, and to the Chicago Housing Authority have been focal points of the ongoing competition between whites and blacks for cultural dominance. Because it defended their racial interests, white voters supported the Machine and developed a high tolerance for fiscal mismanagement and outright corruption.

The relationship worked as long as the white ethnics turned out at high rates and supported the Machine's slated candidate, or when the opposing groups turned out at low rates or split their votes among competing anti-Machine candidates. Although in different ways, the formula worked in 1975 and again in 1977; it faltered in 1979, and it finally collapsed in the 1983 primary election. Then most whites simply underestimated the seriousness of Washington's challenge and split their support between the white candidates, both with Machine links and identifications. A mobilized and cohesive black community took advantage of the split and delivered the nomination to its own candidate. The result gave a new twist to the guiding adage of politics Chicago style: blacks not only got mad, they also got even.

Writing the Machine's obituary has been a routine post-election exercise for some time, but it always seems to rise again to fight another battle and discredit the news of its death. Fighting battles, however, is not the same as winning them, and since Mayor Daley's day, the regular Democratic organization has barely limped along, losing every major Democratic primary contest since 1979.[13] Thus, for some years, there has been more myth than reality to the notion of the Machine's invincibility, and there are solid reasons to suppose that its decade-long decline is not going to be reversed.

After Washington won the primary, white voters took his candidacy seriously. Faced with the prospect of a black Democrat as mayor, most of the city's white Democrats, and especially those in the ethnic neighborhoods on the Northwest and Southwest Sides, chose the "lesser evil" and voted for a Republican. Despite this breakdown of party loyalty, and despite the absence of a significant third candidate to siphon off some share of the anti-black vote, Washington won the general election, although narrowly. He won primarily because black turnout was unprecedentedly high and cohesive. Of course, Epton's defeat can be "explained away" on the grounds that he was a Republican, a weak campaigner, and so forth. The search for disingenuous explanations will no doubt continue, because it springs from an implicit disbelief that blacks could have conceived, organized, and carried out Chicago's electoral revolution. In the final analysis, however, that is the simple reality, which cannot be wished away or explained away, and to which white politicians and voters must accommodate.

Add one more ingredient to that reality: Washington's support among Hispanics, a group not yet fully mobilized politically. A black-brown coalition even now makes up a bare majority (51.5 percent) of the city's voting-age population, and it will have even greater potential in the future. Population projections point to stabilization in the size of the black population, a further slight decline in the number of whites, and a near doubling of the size of the Hispanic component.[14] Chicago's minority groups are well on their way to becoming the numerically dominant part of the city's electorate. Moreover, as the outcome of the April election showed, the Machine's formula for electoral success no longer works. High turnout and solid support among white ethnic voters no longer assures a citywide victory. The tactic of patching a variety of ethnic fragments into a majority coalition can no longer offset mobilized and cohesive support among blacks and Hispanics, whose numbers now give them the political "clout" they previously lacked.

Still, many white Chicagoans cling to the myth of the Machine, hoping somehow that it will rescue them again in four years. And regular party leaders, taking advantage of racial anxieties to secure their electoral base and assure their continued power, prestige, and access to profits, encourage that popular belief in the Machine's unique ability to restore white control over the city. The "Council wars" reflect this complex mix of conflicting racial outlooks, powerful egos, and driving personal ambitions. They involve both a struggle for power between leadership blocs and a clash of vital constituency interests.

By organizing a majority bloc, Vrdolyak and Burke tried to win what they had already lost in the primary and general elections—executive control over the city.[15] Their creed remains what it always had been—politics, patronage, and profits as usual. And their aim is to continue Machine politics, with no effective limits on the power of the parochial ward barons to channel city business to favored companies and contractors.

But the alignment on the Council also reflects the racial polarization that exists in the city. With four exceptions, the "Vrdolyak 29" represent heavily white wards, whose populations are sensitive to integration issues and gave Washington relatively little support in the general election (Table 29). The members of the "Washington 21," again with four exceptions, represent areas of strong black concentration and voting support for Washington.[16] This obvious racial division at the leadership level encourages voters of both races to view the contest as a continuation of the struggle for cultural domi-

Table 29. Racial and Political Base of City Council Blocs

	Vrdolyak 29	Washington 21
Voting-age Population		
% White	68.8	21.9
% Black	10.8	71.7
% Hispanic	16.9	3.9
Support in Mayoral Election		
% Washington	25.9	86.1
% Epton	73.7	13.6

nance. Through their actions and statements, the leaders on both sides reinforce that perception, because it strengthens the resolve of their electorates and keeps the pressure on their aldermanic supporters. Alderman Vrdolyak, for example, spread the word through the publishers of community newspapers on the Northwest and Southwest Sides that the mayor intended to encourage "white flight" by abolishing the residency requirement for public employees and concentrating public housing in white areas. For similar reasons, Washington and his supporters haven't hesitated to portray the struggle as a "war" with distinct racial overtones.[17]

On a number of specific issues of public policy, such as tax support for the city's schools, funds for the Chicago Transit Authority, and the distribution of resources by the police and fire departments and the Chicago Park District, the tangible interests of the white and black communities diverge. And there is a clear and long-standing racial conflict over the siting of future public housing projects. Indeed, despite Washington's post-election effort to soothe fears by assuring that "no neighborhood is going to be inundated by public housing," his refusal to obstruct the Chicago Housing Authority's scattered-site program is a prime source of the distrust that persists among the city's white ethnics. In a fund-raising letter distributed in November 1983, the Southwest Parish and Neighborhood Federation claimed that "Mayor Washington is running City Hall with a vengeance. Either we build a more powerful organization with which to confront this administration or we decide it's not worth it and leave the city."[18]

Although it would be a difficult task, some of the tensions might be resolved if they could be addressed concretely rather than symbolically. But as long as both sides see specific disagreements within the larger context of a struggle for cultural dominance, their competing demands will remain indivisible and uncompromisable. Because they emphasize and strengthen that symbolic view of the racial competition, the "Council wars" complicate the task of assuaging the legitimate concerns that exist on both sides of the city's racial divide.

31. The Reverend Jesse Jackson being interviewed by WBBM-TV's news team during its election-night report. "There was an unfounded fear," Jackson told the television audience. "The idea that blacks once they take power will engage in retributive justice is just not so. There will be a process of healing. . . . And now we've got a chance to really show just how gracious black people can be with power."

The struggle also encourages white voters to hunker down and await redemption by the city's Democratic Machine—their Great White Hope. By prompting whites to see black political empowerment as a transitory phase, a period to be lived through until the Machine restores white dominance, it discourages accommodation. Under that condition, whites will continue to see flight or resistance as their only viable options. Only when white voters recognize the city's changed demographic and political realities are they likely to realize that Machine politicians are jeopardizing their long-term interests by exploiting their current anxieties. That realization will not occur, however, until the actions of the Washington Administration persuade them that "it's our turn" does not have to mean "we want it all."

Beyond Chicago

■ What happened in Chicago in April 1983 was not an isolated event. In other places, blacks have also awakened to the strength of their numbers, and in the future they are likely to do so in still more locales, especially where there are reasonably sized concentrations of black voters. Biracial contests elsewhere may not involve the open and strident racial appeals that characterized Chicago's mayoral contest. But we should not mistake tone for substance; each biracial contest will bring latent tensions and hostilities to the surface and strain intergroup relations.

Philadelphia's Democratic primary is a good example. That contest pitted a black candidate, W. Wilson Goode, the city's managing director, against its former mayor, Frank Rizzo. During the campaign and after the primary election on 17 May, Philadelphians congratulated themselves, while accepting the plaudits of the national media, because their contest was free of the open anger that marked Chicago's.[19] While the tone of Philadelphia's campaign surely was less heated than Chicago's, the difference stopped there: the voting results were quite similar in both cities. In a very high turnout election, Goode scored a relatively narrow win, although most observers (and pollsters) had originally predicted a landslide. Like Washington, he forged his victory in the black community, polling 98 percent of a high turnout among black voters. But despite having none of the personal liabilities that troubled Washington's candidacy, Goode received only 24 percent from Philadelphia's white voters, which was only slightly higher than the level the exit polls gave to Washington in Chicago's general election. Moreover, Philadelphia's white ethnics, especially its blue-collar Catholics, voted about as heavily against Goode as their Chicago counterparts did against Washington (Table 30).[20]

It's not surprising that Philadelphia's election results show about as much racial polarization as Chicago's.[21] Beneath the self-congratulatory hoopla, there were clear signs of its development. Goode complained throughout that "the Rizzo camp was running an 'underground campaign' that included racist slanders and personal rumors such as one accusing him of wife-beating." And Rizzo repeatedly dismissed the preelection poll results and professed a nearly mystical faith in what he called the "hidden vote," those whites who would not admit to pollsters their unwillingness to support a black candidate. The erosion of Goode's support among white voters during the final two weeks of the campaign suggests that Rizzo was on target; he simply overestimated the size of his "hidden vote" and underestimated black turnout.[22]

More so than the Washington-Epton contest, the Goode-Rizzo battle illustrates the problem black candidates confront. When even exceptionally qualified blacks run for highly visible public offices, they are less likely to win support from voters who are not their own ethnic compatriots than are candidates from most other groups. Thus, without a large-sized black voting constituency, black candi-

Table 30. White Ethnic Voting for Black Mayoral Candidates: Chicago and Philadelphia, 1983[1]

	Italian	German	Polish	Irish	Total
Catholics: White-collar and Professional					
Chicago	15.2	22.5	19.3	26.9	21.3
Philadelphia	14.0	38.2	31.8	22.0	22.3
Catholics: Blue-collar Occupations					
Chicago	0.0	12.9	10.2	18.9	10.2
Philadelphia	12.2	18.2	5.9	10.5	11.9

[1] Entries are the percentages for Washington in the 12 April general election and for Goode in the 17 May primary election.

Source: NBC exit polls.

dates normally have little chance of election. However, a black base heightens white fears and increases the likelihood of racially polarized voting patterns, because whites apparently presume that black officeholders will respond vigorously to black interests and ignore white concerns. In fact, where some white support is required for election, black candidates and officeholders have generally avoided postures and actions that antagonize the white component of the electorate. They have been sensitive to the requirements of building a biracial coalition, even at the expense of criticism from more militant blacks. The problem lies in communicating this record and its message of political accommodation to white voters. And the problem is magnified when entrenched white politicians seek to avoid displacement by polarizing white voters through coded (or overt) appeals to their standing suspicions and anxieties.[23]

The developments in Chicago and Philadelphia in the spring of 1983 were parts of the larger national movement that produced extraordinarily high turnout and partisan cohesiveness among blacks in November 1982. In nine states, black turnout actually exceeded the white participation rate; and the white edge nationally was only 6.9 percentage points, the smallest difference since the U.S. Census Bureau began reporting the data in 1964.[24] These turnout gains reflected the success of voter registration drives in black communities throughout the country. Between 1980 and 1982, reported registration among blacks in the United States showed a net gain of 573,000, compared with a net increase of only 93,000 among white voters and 107,000 among Hispanics.[25]

Blacks not only turned out to vote at higher rates than usual, they voted overwhelmingly for Democrats. They gave over two thirds of their vote to Democratic candidates in twelve of the twenty gubernatorial races and seventeen of the twenty-three senatorial contests surveyed by the CBS—New York Times exit poll. And cohesive black support made the difference in several key races, including the gubernatorial contests in New York and Texas and the Senate race in New Jersey.[26]

This surge in black turnout was propelled by their evaluation of the Reagan Administration. While white voters may have been ambivalent toward Reagan's policies, concerned about unemployment but willing to give the Reagan formula more time, blacks had made up their minds. On election day, whites narrowly approved Reagan's overall performance (by 50 percent to 47.3 percent), while blacks registered clear disapproval (by 87 percent to 6.3 percent); and blacks expressed even stronger dissatisfaction with Reagan's economic performance (by 89.4 percent to 5.8 percent).[27]

The off-year voter mobilization drives channelled this discontent among blacks into the political process, inaugurating a much-delayed second phase of the civil rights movement. The first phase began in the South during the 1955–1960 period, with the mobilization of the indigenous institutions of the black community, especially the campus- and church-based organizations. As the initial wave of insurgency attracted external resources, organizations formally dedicated to the movement (e.g., SCLC, SNCC, CORE) grew in size and prominence, and over the 1961–1965 period they assumed leadership. The transformation was relatively quick and successful, since these formal movement organizations incorporated the existing institutions and resources of the southern black community into their programs, and support for the movement was broadly based in the early 1960s. Its strength was further increased by the fact that its insurgent campaign was sharply focused. Between 1955 and 1965, three quarters of the actions initiated by the movement occurred in the seventeen southern and border states, and 65.2 percent of them had racial integration as their goal. Thus, through the mid-1960s, the civil rights movement rallied a broad base of support around an issue consensus focusing on exclusionary racial practices in the South.[28]

As the movement shifted its focus from the South to the North, and broadened the range of its issue concerns, this consensus rapidly dissolved. External support declined and internal conflict over goals increased and fragmented the movement. The urban riots of the mid-1960s, which completed the process of transferring racial conflict from the South to the cities of the North, mobilized a powerful political opposition in the form of a "white backlash," which made itself felt in the 1966 off-year elections. The growing importance of racial issues in northern elections polarized the Democrats' traditional urban coalition, as white ethnics abandoned the party in droves. As a result, the political strategists of both parties reestimated the value of mobilizing black voters at the cost of antagonizing large numbers of whites. Under conditions of strong racial polarization, the black vote ceased to be a political asset.[29]

The George Wallace phenomenon contributed immensely to this devaluation of the black vote. In 1968 the two major parties polled roughly equal shares of the popular vote, with Richard Nixon running slightly ahead and winning the presidency, but Wallace garnered an additional 14 percent of the total vote. Thereafter, the electoral strategies of both major parties gave priority to the perceived political interests of the Wallace voters, thus further diminishing the political influence of blacks.

In the face of these developments, a sense of pessimism and impotence regarding prospects for racial change spread among blacks. Their responses on national surveys provide unmistakable evidence of the trend in black public opinion. Beginning around 1970, blacks became more pessimistic about their future prospects and less confident of their capacity to improve conditions. For example, the proportion of blacks who said that they "usually get to carry things out the way" they planned in their personal lives dropped by half between 1964 and 1970. At the same time, the proportion of black respondents who said things were improving for them declined. Through the mid-1960s, nearly 60 percent felt that the position of blacks had improved "a lot" in the past few years, but the percentage was only about half as large in 1976. The judgment that their collective status was no longer improving led more blacks to express a sense of impatience with the pace of change on civil rights questions. Through 1968 only about a quarter of them indicated that the pace was "too slow"; in 1970 the proportion jumped to 39.6 percent, and it has remained in the mid-30s since then.[30]

As white opposition mobilized politically and impressed itself on the strategists of the major parties, an increasing proportion of blacks began to express pessimism about their future status and disillusionment with the pace of change through the political process. In turn, these developments led blacks to become increasingly negative and distrustful of government. By 1970, for the first time since 1958, more blacks (by 25 percentage points) gave cynical responses than trustful ones when queried about their confidence in government, and the gap grew thereafter to a peak of 55 percentage points by 1974. Much more so than whites, blacks also became dubious about whether they could have an impact on the political process. Among whites the difference between those who doubted their capacity to influence politics and those who felt they had impact has never been larger than 23 percentage points (in 1978), but since 1970 it has never been smaller than 37 percentage points among blacks. Finally, while most whites believe that government and public officials pay attention to popular opinion, from 1970 on, the blacks who doubted the government's responsiveness have been a larger group than those who believed in it.[31]

It was this context of pessimism, impotence, distrust of government, and lack of confidence in the responsiveness of political institutions to their interests that shaped black political participation in the late 1960s and 1970s. Of course, in the South, voting rights legislation and mobilization campaigns boosted black turnout over its pre-1960 levels, but the rate never moved much above the 59.2 percent recorded in 1968, and by 1980, black turnout was only 58 percent. Among the black electorate in the North, the decline was steeper, from a high of 75.3 percent in 1964 to only 53.2 percent in 1980.[32]

The disillusionment and fatalism that prompted northern blacks to withdraw from electoral politics also nurtured separatist inclinations. Some blacks rejected a political process that had frustrated their aspirations and denounced cooperation with whites, whose mobilization had constricted their opportunities for political gains. A few also rejected racial integration as a goal and preached instead a doctrine of black exclusiveness. Because it seemed to be only the other side of the same coin, black power became as odious a phrase to whites, including many supporters of the civil rights movement, as Jim Crow had been only a decade or so before.[33]

The developments of 1982 and 1983 provide unambiguous evidence that blacks have refocused their attention on electoral politics and have once again displayed their faith in the ballot box. Using the sole resource indisputably available to them—their sheer numbers—blacks have chosen to pursue their legitimate group goals and demands for group benefits through the traditional political process.[34]

This rising political awareness will surely bring blacks into conflict with other groups assertively defending their own prerogatives, and the ensuing struggles may become overheated at times. But like similar contests in the past, these battles for political leverage will also necessarily involve compromising group interests to build a majority coalition. That insures that no combatant will score an unconditional victory, but it also guarantees that none will suffer an unconditional defeat. Whatever the short-term pain, operating through the political process increases the likelihood of eventually reconciling conflicting demands and reducing group tensions.

Notes

Notes to Chapter 1

1. Eugene Kennedy, *Himself! The Life and Times of Mayor Richard J. Daley* (New York: Viking Press, 1978), pp. 212–13. See Mike Royko, *Boss: Richard J. Daley of Chicago* (New York: E. P. Dutton, 1971), pp. 5–7, for the driving route from Bridgeport to City Hall; and see *The Report of the National Advisory Commission on Civil Disorders* (Washington, D.C.: Government Printing Office, 1968), pp. 32 and 35–108, for information on the 1967 riots.

2. Bill Gleason, *Daley of Chicago: The Man, the Mayor, and the Limits of Conventional Politics* (New York: Simon and Schuster, 1970), pp. 36–48.

3. These quotations are from Royko, *Boss*, pp. 149–50, 161, and 151. Also see Kennedy, *Himself*, pp. 207–8; and Gleason, *Daley of Chicago*, pp. 46–47. Len O'Connor, *Clout: Mayor Daley and His City* (Chicago: Henry Regnery, 1975), pp. 192–93, incorrectly dates this Lawndale riot as occurring in mid-summer 1967. There had been a two-day riot in Lawndale on 12 and 13 August 1965.

4. Quoted in Gleason, *Daley of Chicago*, pp. 51–52.

5. The Sullivan quotation and the information in the following paragraph are from Gleason, *Daley of Chicago*, pp. 53–55, 62–63.

6. Kennedy, *Himself*, pp. 215–17; Gleason, *Daley of Chicago*, pp. 59–60, 52, and 70.

7. Daley made these comments to Corporation Counsel Raymond Simon prior to his 15 April 1968 press conference; quoted in Kennedy, *Himself*, p. 219.

8. The quotations are from a partial transcript of Daley's remarks; see Gleason, *Daley of Chicago*, pp. 73–76; Kennedy, *Himself*, pp. 219–32.

9. The text of Daley's statement to the City Council is in Gleason, *Daley of Chicago*, pp. 78–79; the other quotation is on p. 75.

10. Charles W. Roll and Albert H. Cantril, *Polls: Their Use and Misuse in Politics* (New York: Basic Books, 1972), pp. 39–64; Larry J. Sabato, *The Rise of Political Consultants: New Ways of Winning Elections* (New York: Basic Books, 1981), pp. 68–110. For an overview of the historical development of polling, see Richard Jensen, "Democracy by the Numbers," *Public Opinion* 3 (February/March 1980): 53–59.

11. Thomas E. Patterson, *The Mass Media Election: How Americans Choose Their President* (New York: Praeger, 1980), pp. 21–30.

12. Kurt Lang and Gladys Engel Lang, "The Impact of Polls on Public Opinion," *The Annals of the American Academy of Political and Social Science* 472 (March 1984): 129–42.

13. On the technical standards, see Roll and Cantril, *Polls*, pp. 65–116; and Graham Kalton, *Introduction to Survey Sampling* (Beverly Hills, Calif.: Sage Publications, 1983). For a recent discussion of the major sources of bias and an evaluation of the accuracy of polls in general, see Burns W. Roper, "Are Polls Accurate?" *The Annals of the American Academy of Political and Social Science* 472 (March 1984): 24–34.

14. Or, the undecideds may have opted overwhelmingly for the candidate with only 8 percent in the preelection poll. There is a simple way to make better comparisons between preelection polls and voting results: drop the percentage assigned to the undecided category in the preelection poll; sum the remaining percentages; and then divide each of the candidate's percentages by that sum. In effect, this assumes that the undecideds will divide in the same proportions as those who have reached a decision.

15. On the accuracy of exit polls, see Mark R. Levy, "The Methodology and Performance of Election Day Polls," *Public Opinion Quarterly* 47 (Spring 1983): 54–67.

Notes to Chapter 2

1. This information is from Milton Rakove, *Don't Make No Waves—Don't Back No Losers* (Bloomington: Indiana University Press, 1975), pp. 21–27; the quotations are on pp. 23–24.

2. David Ward, *Cities and Immigrants: A Geography of Change in Nineteenth-Century America* (New York: Oxford University Press, 1971); and Stanley Lieberson, *Ethnic Patterns in American Cities* (New York: Free Press, 1963).

3. The series reported in Table 1 has been developed from data in the appropriate volumes of the federal decennial census, 1870 through 1970. However, the censuses of 1870, 1880, and 1940 did not report the number of native-born persons of foreign-born parents. The data series conveniently reported in *The People of Chicago* (Chicago: Department of Planning and Development, 1976) is not entirely compatible with the one reported here. Its native-stock category includes whites and blacks, and the native-born of foreign-born parents are counted in *both* the native-born and foreign-stock categories.

4. This series has been developed from the same sources as Table 1. For each group the data include those born in the country and their children born in the United States.

5. On differences within the Polish group, see Edward R. Kantowicz, *Polish-American Politics in Chicago, 1888—1940* (Chicago: University of Chicago Press, 1975), pp. 33—37; and for the Jews, see Edward Mazur, "Jewish Chicago: From Diversity to Community," in *The Ethnic Frontier*, ed. Melvin G. Holli and Peter d'A. Jones (Grand Rapids, Mich.: William B. Eerdmans, 1977), pp. 279—83.

6. These data are reported in U.S. Bureau of the Census, *Religious Bodies: Censuses of 1906, 1916, 1926, and 1936* (Washington, D.C.: Government Printing Office, 1906, 1919, 1929—1930, and 1941).

7. For an explanation of the statistical technique, see Stanley Lieberson, "Measuring Population Diversity," *American Sociological Review* 34 (December 1969): 850—62.

8. John L. Sullivan, "Political Correlates of Social, Economic, and Religious Diversity in the American States," *Journal of Politics* 35 (February 1973): 70—84; the diversity indexes are in Table 3, p. 73.

9. Richard Jensen, *The Winning of the Midwest: Social and Political Conflict, 1888—96* (Chicago: University of Chicago Press, 1971); Paul Kleppner, *The Cross of Culture: A Social Analysis of Midwestern Politics, 1850—1900* (New York: Free Press, 1970); and Paul Kleppner, *The Third Electoral System, 1853—1892: Parties, Voters, and Political Cultures* (Chapel Hill, N.C.: University of North Carolina Press, 1979).

10. Martin Shefter, "The Electoral Foundations of the Political Machine: New York City, 1884—1897," in *The History of Electoral Behavior*, ed. Joel H. Silbey, Allan G. Bogue, and William H. Flanigan (Princeton, N.J.: Princeton University Press, 1978), pp. 263—98; the quotation is on pp. 297—98.

11. Shefter, "Electoral Foundations," p. 266. For insightful comments by a reformer, see Jane Addams, *Democracy and Social Ethics* (New York: Macmillan, 1902), pp. 224—28; and see Joan S. Miller, "The Politics of Municipal Reform in Chicago during the Progressive Era: The Municipal Voters' League as a Test Case, 1896—1920" (M.A. thesis, Roosevelt University, 1966), for a useful analysis of the reform movement in Chicago.

12. Peter W. Colby and Paul Michael Green, "The Consolidation of Clout: The Vote Power of Chicago Democrats from Cermak to Bilandic," in *Illinois Elections*, ed. Caroline A. Gherardini et al., 2d ed. (Springfield, Ill.: Sangamon State University, 1982), p. 31.

13. For similar conditions and their impact on party organizations in another city, see Paul Kleppner, "From Party to Faction: The Dissolution of Boston's Majority Party, 1876—1908," in *The Evolution of Urban Politics: Boston, 1750—1980*, ed. Ronald P. Formisano and Constance Burns (Westport, Conn.: Greenwood Press, 1984), pp. 111—32.

14. For some indication of the effect of the ward system on political representation, see Diane Marie Pinderhughes, "Interpretations of Racial and Ethnic Participation in American Politics: The Cases of Black, Italian and Polish Communities in Chicago, 1910—1940" (Ph.D. dissertation, University of Chicago, 1977), pp. 163—265.

15. Claudius O. Johnson, *Carter Henry Harrison I: Political Leader* (Chicago: University of Chicago Press, 1928), pp. 188—99 and 202.

16. Carter H. Harrison II, *Stormy Years* (Indianapolis: Bobbs-Merrill, 1935), pp. 118—19.

17. The data on the partisan composition of the city council are from the *Chicago Daily News Almanac and Year-Book for 1932* (Chicago: Chicago Daily News, 1931), p. 696.

18. These summary indicators have been developed from data reported by Colby and Green, "Consolidation of Clout," pp. 32, 34.

19. On Cermak, see Alex Gottfried, *Boss Cermak of Chicago: A Study of Political Leadership* (Seattle: University of Washington Press, 1932); and for Cermak's coalition-building efforts, see John M. Allswang, *A House for All Peoples: Ethnic Politics in Chicago, 1890–1936* (Lexington: University of Kentucky Press, 1971), esp. pp. 152–56.

20. Allswang, *House for All Peoples*, pp. 118–19; the quotation is on p. 120.

21. On Cermak's party-building efforts, see Harold F. Gosnell, *Machine Politics Chicago Model* (Chicago: University of Chicago Press, 1937), pp. 13–14; and Len O'Connor, *Clout: Mayor Daley and His City* (Chicago: Henry Regnery, 1975), pp. 38–39.

22. The quotations are from Eugene Kennedy, *Himself! The Life and Times of Mayor Richard J. Daley* (New York: Viking Press, 1978), pp. 51–52. In December 1922, the party slated William Dever, an Irish Catholic and a reform candidate, for the 1923 mayoral race.

23. O'Connor, *Clout*, p. 55; Kennedy, *Himself*, pp. 58–59.

24. O'Connor, *Clout*, pp. 54–55. Sorting out the personalities, alliances, and maneuvering involved in factional strife is always difficult. There are useful comments at various points in O'Connor; in Kennedy, *Himself*; and in Mike Royko, *Boss: Richard J. Daley of Chicago* (New York: E. P. Dutton, 1971). The discussion here is based on information culled from these sources.

25. Bill Gleason, *Daley of Chicago: The Man, the Mayor, and the Limits of Conventional Politics* (New York: Simon and Schuster, 1970), pp. 178, 180.

26. The Arvey quotation is in Royko, *Boss*, p. 55; see Kennedy, *Himself*, p. 97, for the Bauler quotation, and p. 90 for the attitude of other Democratic regulars. On the latter, also see Gleason, *Daley of Chicago*, p. 143.

27. The best description of the mechanics of the Daley Machine is in Rakove, *Don't Make No Waves*, esp. pp. 90–162.

28. Since 1900, except for Harrison, Cermak, and Harold Washington, all Democratic candidates for mayor have been Catholics.

29. Strong anti-Semitism among the Poles was another obstacle; see Kantowicz, *Polish-American Politics*, pp. 117–19.

30. Harold F. Gosnell, *Negro Politicians: The Rise of Negro Politics in Chicago* (Chicago: University of Chicago Press, 1935), pp. 13–63; Allan H. Spear, *Black Chicago: The Making of a Negro Ghetto, 1890–1920* (Chicago: University of Chicago Press, 1967), pp. 111–26, 181–200; and see Ira Katznelson, *Black Men, White Cities*, Phoenix ed. (Chicago: University of Chicago Press, 1976), pp. 86–103, for an analytic overview.

31. Allswang, *House for All Peoples*, pp. 146–48, 153. On the white reaction to the growth of the black population, see Spear, *Black Chicago*, pp. 201–22; and William M. Tuttle, Jr., *Race Riot: Chicago in the Red Summer of 1919* (New York: Atheneum, 1970).

32. Allswang, *House for All Peoples*, pp. 155, 161–62; also see O'Connor, *Clout*, p. 38, for Cermak's approach to Dawson.

33. The information is from Pinderhughes, "Interpretations of Racial and Ethnic Participation," pp. 234—40.

34. On the nature of the process, see the comments by Cecil Partee in Milton Rakove, *We Don't Want Nobody Nobody Sent: An Oral History of the Daley Years* (Bloomington: Indiana University Press, 1979), pp. 156—57. Also see the discussion by James Q. Wilson, *Negro Politics: The Search for Leadership* (Glencoe, Ill.: Free Press, 1960), pp. 48—76.

Notes to Chapter 3

1. St. Clair Drake and Horace R. Cayton, *Black Metropolis: A Study of Negro Life in a Northern City*, rev. ed., 2 vols. (New York: Harper & Row, 1962), 1:61.

2. The data reported in Table 3 are from the appropriate volumes of the federal decennial census. If Hispanics who classified themselves as white in 1980 are added to the number of whites reported in the table, the white share of the city's population increases to 49.5 percent.

3. Pierre de Vise, *Chicago's Widening Color Gap* (Chicago: Interuniversity Research Committee, 1967), p. 17. If white Hispanics are added to the number of whites reported in Table 3, the net loss between 1940 and 1980 is reduced to 1.6 million.

4. Map 1 uses the 1983 ward boundaries. While the precise boundaries shifted several times over the forty-year period, the location and general shape of each ward remained basically unaltered. For the other information in the paragraph, see Drake and Cayton, *Black Metropolis*, "Appendix: Black Metropolis 1961," 1:liii; Allan H. Spear, *Black Chicago: The Making of a Negro Ghetto, 1890—1920* (Chicago: University of Chicago Press, 1967), p. 223; and Brian J. L. Berry, *The Open Housing Question: Race and Housing in Chicago, 1966—1976* (Cambridge, Mass.: Ballinger Publishing Company, 1979), pp. 5—6, 500—501.

5. The quotations are from two real estate dealers in the Austin area; see Berry, *Open Housing Question*, pp. 258—59. On the paths of black expansion, see de Vise, *Chicago's Widening Color Gap*, p. 42.

6. For examples of these different reactions, see the case studies in Berry, *Open Housing Question*; and for a detailed study, see John Hall Fish, *Black Power/White Control: The Struggle of the Woodlawn Organization in Chicago* (Princeton, N.J.: Princeton University Press, 1973).

7. Drake and Cayton, *Black Metropolis*, "Appendix: Black Metropolis 1961," 1:lii—liii; Martin Meyerson and Edward C. Banfield, *Politics, Planning, and the Public Interest: The Case of Public Housing in Chicago* (Glencoe, Ill.: Free Press, 1955), p. 103. On the paranoia over racial change that some communities experienced, see the discussion of Garfield Ridge in Berry, *Open Housing Question*, pp. 227—28.

8. Spear, *Black Chicago*, pp. 12—16. For more complete time-series data, see Stanley Lieberson, *Ethnic Patterns in American Cities* (New York: Free Press, 1963), p. 122; Karl E. Taeuber and Alma F. Taeuber, *Negroes in Cities: Residential Segregation and Neighborhood Change* (Chicago: Aldine Publishing Company, 1965), p. 54; and Annemette Sørensen, Karl E. Taeuber,

and Leslie J. Hollingsworth, Jr., "Indexes of Racial Residential Segregation for 109 Cities in the United States, 1940 to 1970," *Sociological Focus* 8 (April 1975): 125–42.

9. Quoted in Spear, *Black Chicago*, p. 22; see pp. 21–23 for the full discussion of these events.

10. Drake and Cayton, *Black Metropolis*, 1:175–77; Spear, *Black Chicago*, pp. 129–46, is the best discussion of the 1915–1920 migration.

11. William M. Tuttle, Jr., *Race Riot: Chicago in the Red Summer of 1919* (New York: Atheneum, 1970), provides the most complete account. Also see Drake and Cayton, *Black Metropolis*, 1:65–76; and Spear, *Black Chicago*, pp. 214–16.

12. Spear, *Black Chicago*, pp. 217–28; the quotation is on p. 221; Drake and Cayton, *Black Metropolis*, 1:77–97.

13. Spear, *Black Chicago*, pp. 219–21; the quotations are on p. 220. Also see Chicago Commission on Race Relations, *The Negro in Chicago: A Study of Race Relations and a Race Riot* (Chicago: University of Chicago Press, 1922), pp. 212–24.

14. Drake and Cayton, *Black Metropolis*, 1:182–87. In 1949, the U.S. Supreme Court held the use of racially restrictive covenants to be unconstitutional; see Shelley v. Kramer, 334 U.S. 1 (1948).

15. Both quotations are in Spear, *Black Chicago*, p. 217.

16. After the riot, white Chicagoans increasingly thought of blacks as a "problem"; see Drake and Cayton, *Black Metropolis*, 1:69–72.

17. Drake and Cayton, *Black Metropolis*, 1:91–97; the quotation is on p. 96.

18. Spear, *Black Chicago*, p. 224.

19. Quoted in Meyerson and Banfield, *Politics, Planning, and the Public Interest*, p. 32. I have relied on this study for the background and chronology of the early phase of the public housing issue.

20. Kennelly is quoted in Meyerson and Banfield, *Politics, Planning, and the Public Interest*, p. 62; see pp. 29–30 for details concerning the city's housing shortage.

21. Meyerson and Banfield, *Politics, Planning, and the Public Interest*, pp. 34–35.

22. *Chicago Tribune*, 6 December 1946; Meyerson and Banfield, *Politics, Planning, and the Public Interest*, pp. 125–31; Bill Gleason, *Daley of Chicago: The Man, the Mayor, and the Limits of Conventional Politics* (New York: Simon and Schuster, 1970), pp. 92–93.

23. Meyerson and Banfield, *Politics, Planning, and the Public Interest*, pp. 105–7.

24. The executive secretary of the Southwest Neighborhood Council, quoted in Meyerson and Banfield, *Politics, Planning, and the Public Interest*, p. 110; and see pp. 182–87 for discussion of the City Council's hearings on the package of sites.

25. *Chicago Defender*, 17 December 1949; Meyerson and Banfield, *Politics, Planning, and the Public Interest*, pp. 100–105, 196–99, 218–21.

26. Memorandum Opinion of Judge Richard Austin, Gautreaux v. Chicago Housing Authority, 296 F. Supp. 910, 911 (1969).

27. Gleason, *Daley of Chicago*, pp. 97–102; the quotation is on p. 101.

28. Austin's opinion cites an affidavit from the Executive Director of the CHA admitting pre-clearance by aldermen; Gautreaux v. Chicago Housing Authority, 296 F. Supp. 910, 911 (1969).

29. Gautreaux v. Chicago Housing Authority, 296 F. Supp. 907 (1969), and see 265 F. Supp. 582 (1967) for Austin's critical ruling on the defendants' motion to dismiss on the grounds that the suit was an improper class action.

30. Gautreaux v. Chicago Housing Authority, 304 F. Supp. 736 (1969); also 741 for the quotation and orders to the Chicago City Council. In addition, the judgment called for immediate integration of three of the four projects that were almost exclusively white, stipulated that future buildings could be no more than three stories high and contain no more than 120 units, and provided a detailed tenant selection and assignment plan.

31. Gautreaux v. Chicago Housing Authority, 296 F. Supp. 909 (1969).

32. See the decision of the Court of Appeals, 7th Circuit, Gautreaux v. Chicago Housing Authority, 436 F. 2d 306 (1970), and 308–10 for a detailed review of the informal conferences. For the list of sites, see Chicago Today, 6 March 1971, and Chicago Daily News, 6 and 7 March 1971.

33. The quotations are in Chicago Tribune, 8–10 March 1971. Vrdolyak (10th Ward) was first elected to the City Council in the February 1971 aldermanic election.

34. Chicago Today, 9 March 1971; Chicago Daily News, 10 March 1971. Daley later outlined his four-point housing plan in a speech to the City Club of Chicago; see Chicago Tribune, 23 March 1971.

35. Chicago Sun-Times, 15 March 1971; Chicago Defender, 8 March 1971.

36. Gautreaux v. Romney, 332 F. Supp. 366 (1971); Austin's comment about Daley is at 370. For Austin's ruling that the CHA could bypass the City Council on site selection, see Gautreaux v. Chicago Housing Authority, 342 F. Supp. 827 (1972). The Court of Appeals, 7th Circuit, upheld that ruling in Gautreaux v. City of Chicago et al., 480 F. 2d 210 (1973).

37. Chicago Tribune, 11 December 1977, 26 April and 4 May 1978.

38. Chicago Tribune, 25 April and 7 June 1980. Judge Crowley's order in April 1979 called for an additional 900 units of housing for the elderly, but the family units were the ones at the center of the controversy.

39. Chicago Tribune, 25 October 1981. An editorial in the Chicago Sun-Times, 29 October 1981, pointed out that Byrne's action violated the CHA's April 1979 agreement with Judge Crowley and HUD. For criticism of Byrne's move by blacks, see Chicago Defender, 16 December 1981 and 13 January 1982.

40. Southtown Economist, 18 April and 17 December 1982; Chicago Tribune, 23 December 1982 and 17 April 1983; Chicago Sun-Times, 19 June and 19 September 1983; and Chicago Reader, 4 February 1983.

41. Chicago Daily News, 2 July 1969; for the April 1983 court appearance, see the Southtown Economist, 28 February and 20 May 1983.

42. The goal of blacks was stated by Henry McGee, a black member of the Board of Education, in the Chicago Defender, 22 March 1978. For the Board of Education's goal and the quotation from its 1967 plan, see Paul E. Peterson, School Politics Chicago Style (Chicago: University of Chicago Press, 1976), pp. 173–76; the quotation is on p. 174. Also see Mary J. Herrick, The

Chicago Schools: A Social and Political History (Beverly Hills, Calif.: Sage Publications, 1971), pp. 303–92, for a review of the early developments.

43. Gleason, *Daley of Chicago*, p. 37, indicates that in 1963, 81 percent of the city's elementary schools had enrollments that were either all white or all black, and the percentage rose to 82 by 1965. The other details are from a useful chronological summary in *Southtown Economist*, 12 April 1982.

44. Albert Raby quoted in Gleason, *Daley of Chicago*, p. 38. Also see Mike Royko, *Boss: Richard J. Daley of Chicago* (New York: E. P. Dutton, 1971), pp. 138–42; and Len O'Connor, *Clout: Mayor Daley and His City* (Chicago: Henry Regnery, 1975), pp. 189–90. Willis actually retired in the summer of 1966, after James Redmond was chosen as his successor.

45. O'Connor, *Clout*, pp. 181–82; Peterson, *School Politics*, p. 31. Robert Havinghurst conducted the second study, and it was submitted in November 1964. Philip Hauser headed the panel of experts that issued the first report; for his later reflections on the questions of school and housing integration, see *Chicago Sun-Times*, 11 September 1983.

46. Peterson, *School Politics*, pp. 153–55; the Pucinski quotation is on p. 154, and the quotations from Daley are on pp. 160–61.

47. Peterson, *School Politics*, pp. 155–58; the quotation is on p. 157. A week later, the Board approved a voluntary busing plan for Austin.

48. *Chicago Sun-Times*, 6 June 1978; Peterson, *School Politics*, p. 144. The data in Table 4 are the Board of Education's statistics reported in: *Chicago Tribune*, 28 August 1977, 5 April 1981, and 13 February 1982; and *Chicago Sun-Times*, 7 January 1983.

49. *Chicago Sun-Times*, 13 January 1977; *Chicago Tribune*, 25 January 1977. Also see *Chicago Tribune*, 13 January 1977, for earlier opposition by mothers from the Bogan community. Mrs. Betty Bonow, who would be appointed to the Board of Education by Mayor Byrne in 1981, was one of the leaders of the opposition to this and later suggestions for integration.

50. The quotations are in *Chicago Defender*, 11 June 1977; also see *Southtown Economist*, 10 August 1977; and *Southwest News Herald*, 9 June 1977.

51. *Southtown Economist*, 10 and 14 August 1977; *Chicago Tribune*, 9 August 1977.

52. *Chicago Tribune*, 10 August 1977; *Southwest News Herald*, 25 August 1977; *Chicago Daily News*, 17 August 1977. Jeff Lyon, the author of the *Tribune* story, concluded: "You encounter things like this and it makes you hope the integration plan doesn't go through. Why inflict these people on blacks?"

53. *Southwest News Herald*, 9 June and 25 August 1977; *Chicago Sun-Times*, 11 June and 11 August 1977.

54. *Chicago Sun-Times*, 24 August and 2 September 1977; *Chicago Daily News*, 24 August and 15 October 1977; *Chicago Defender*, 8, 19, 13, and 17 September 1977.

55. *Chicago Tribune*, 8 November and 20 December 1977; *Chicago Daily News*, 10 November 1977; and *Chicago Sun-Times*, 25 October, 17 November, and 8, 13, and 20 December 1977. For a detailed summary of Welling's plan, see *Chicago Daily News*, 17 November 1977.

56. Hannon is quoted in *Chicago Tribune*, 21 March 1978. A *Southtown*

Economist editorial, 29 March 1978, praised Hannon for accepting the views of the neighborhood groups.

57. *Chicago Tribune,* 7 April 1978.

58. *Southtown Economist,* 16 June and 7 September 1978; *Southwest News Herald,* 14 and 28 September 1978; *Chicago Tribune,* 16 and 17 September 1978.

59. *Chicago Metro,* 9 September 1978. For the other details, see *Southtown Economist,* 7 September 1978; *Chicago Tribune,* 7 September 1978; and *Chicago Sun-Times,* 26 September 1978.

60. *Chicago Sun-Times,* 11 April 1979; *Chicago Tribune,* 12 April and 31 August 1979. Civil rights groups in Chicago praised the federal intervention; see *Chicago Sun-Times,* 12 April 1979.

61. For Byrne's admission, see *Chicago Tribune,* 28 August 1979, and *Southtown Economist,* 29 August 1979; her attack on the OCR plan is in *Chicago Tribune,* 1 September 1979.

62. For Lipinski's views, see *Chicago Tribune,* 7 September 1979, and *Southwest News Herald,* 6 September 1979, which also contains the statement by Pucinski. For criticism of the OCR plan by Mrs. Betty Bonow, see *Southtown Economist,* 23 September 1979.

63. The quotations are in *Chicago Tribune,* 20 February 1981, and *Chicago Sun-Times,* 25 March 1981. For the other details, see *Chicago Tribune,* 21 February, 28 March, and 4 April 1981; *Chicago Sun-Times,* 24 March 1981.

64. For the quotations, see the *Southwest News Herald,* 9 April 1981; *Chicago Sun-Times,* 4 April 1981; and *Chicago Tribune,* 7 April 1981. For other reactions by groups on the Southwest Side, see *Chicago Tribune,* 7 April 1981.

65. The Byrne statement is in *Chicago Sun-Times,* 7 April 1981. Also see *Chicago Tribune,* 8, 9, and 15 April 1981.

66. *Chicago Sun-Times,* 13 February and 6 April 1982.

67. *Chicago Sun-Times,* 7 January and 3 November 1983. Civil rights groups criticized Shadur's ruling; see *Chicago Sun-Times,* 8 and 16 January 1983; *Chicago Tribune,* 14 January and 10 February 1983; *Chicago Defender,* 10 January 1983. The Board of Education is now suing the state and federal governments to force them to help pay for the city's voluntary desegregation plan; and the NAACP is appealing an earlier ruling by Shadur that prevented it and two Hispanic groups from intervening in the case.

68. Quoted in Meyerson and Banfield, *Politics, Planning, and the Public Interest,* p. 185.

Notes to Chapter 4

1. Eugene Kennedy, *Himself! The Life and Times of Mayor Richard J. Daley* (New York: Viking Press, 1978), p. 131; see also p. 123 for the *Chicago Sun-Times* poll that was published on St. Patrick's Day. Daley's description of himself came in a speech during the primary campaign; see Bill Gleason, *Daley of Chicago: The Man, the Mayor, and the Limits of Conventional Politics* (New York: Simon and Schuster, 1970), p. 199.

2. The data are from reports in the decennial federal census, 1940 through

1980. Precise comparisons of the white voting-age population are not possible, since prior to 1980 the census did not report Hispanic voting-age population separately. In 1980, 49.6 percent of Chicago's Hispanics reported themselves as white, 1.9 percent as black, and the remainder as "other races." If we allocate the 1980 Hispanic voting-age population according to these figures, the total number of whites goes to 1,071,568 (or 54.7 percent of the total), and the number of blacks to 763,462 (or 39.0 percent of the total). The larger number for whites is the better one to use for comparisons with earlier years.

3. Len O'Connor, *Clout: Mayor Daley and His City* (Chicago: Henry Regnery, 1975); the quotation is on p. 103.

4. Gleason, *Daley of Chicago*, pp. 196–97; the quotation is on p. 196.

5. O'Connor, *Clout*, p. 114; the election returns used throughout are from City of Chicago, Board of Election Commissioners, *Statement of the Results of the Canvass of the Election Returns*. The Dawson sub-machine included wards 2, 3, 4, 6, and 20; the West Side wards were 1, 24, 27, 28, 29, and 31. The boundaries of these and other wards changed slightly after 1955, and I took these changes into account by using precinct data to reconstruct the original wards. I followed the same procedures for the other categories of wards. The Lake Shore wards are 42, 43, 44, 46, 48, and 49. The Northwest Side ethnic wards are 30, 35, 36, 38, 39, 41, and 45; and the South Side white ethnic wards are 10, 11, 12, 13, 14, 18, 19, and 23.

6. It is more common to examine election results expressed as percentages of the vote cast; therefore, it is useful to notice the relationship between that measure and the mobilization indicator used here. In the 1955 primary, 753,340 votes were cast, and Daley polled 369,362, or 49.0 percent of the total. There were over 2.27 million adults of voting age in Chicago in 1955, and only about 33.0 percent actually voted in the Democratic primary. So, Daley's 369,362 votes meant that he had the support of 16.2 percent of the voting-age population. One can arrive at the 16.2 percent figure by dividing the number of votes cast for Daley by the size of the voting-age population, or by multiplying his proportionate share of the vote cast by the citywide turnout percentage (i.e., .490 × .330 = .1617). The difference between Daley's citywide mobilization percentage and the total citywide turnout gives the percentage of the voting-age population that cast votes against him. Finally, if we subtract the total citywide turnout percentage from 100, the remainder is the proportion of the voting-age population that did not vote.

7. Only Hearst's *Chicago American* supported Daley; the *Chicago Sun-Times*, *Chicago Daily News*, and *Chicago Tribune* endorsed Merriam. See Gleason, *Daley of Chicago*, pp. 201–6; and O'Connor, *Clout*, pp. 115–21.

8. In 1943, Edward J. Kelly polled 54.5 percent and beat George B. McKibben, the Republican nominee, by 114,020 votes. Daley's citywide plurality was 126,667 votes. For the data on the pre-1955 elections, see Peter W. Colby and Paul Michael Green, "The Consolidation of Clout: The Vote Power of Chicago Democrats from Cermak to Bilandic," in *Illinois Elections*, ed. Caroline A. Gherardini et al., 2d ed. (Springfield, Ill.: Sangamon State University, 1982), p. 32.

9. In 1960, blacks were a majority of the population in two of the six West Side wards, the 24th and 29th, but in the latter they were less than 60 percent of the population. By 1970, these two wards, and the 27th and 28th, were over 80 percent black.

10. O'Connor, *Clout*, pp. 163–76; Gleason, *Daley of Chicago*, pp. 222–26, 248–50.

11. Of the South Side white ethnic areas, Daley carried only the 11th and 14th Wards. See O'Connor, *Clout*, pp. 175–77; Joseph Zikmund II, "Mayoral Voting and Ethnic Politics in the Daley-Bilandic-Byrne Era," in *After Daley: Chicago Politics in Transition*, ed. Samuel K. Gove and Louis H. Masotti (Urbana: University of Illinois Press, 1982), pp. 37–40. For claims that Daley lost the white vote to Adamowski, see Joe Mathewson, *Up Against Daley* (LaSalle, Ill.: Open Court Publishing, 1974), pp. 63–64; Gleason, *Daley of Chicago*, p. 339.

12. Also see the discussion and electoral maps in Zikmund, "Mayoral Voting and Ethnic Politics," pp. 30–51.

13. Also see Kathleen A. Kemp and Robert L. Lineberry, "The Last of the Great Urban Machines and the Last of the Great Urban Mayors? Chicago Politics, 1955–77," in *After Daley*, ed. Gove and Masotti, Table 4, p. 17. Especially compare the correlations between candidate support and the percent black for the *contested* elections between 1955 and 1967.

14. For the general formulation, see Robert K. Merton, *Social Theory and Social Structure* (Glencoe, Ill.: Free Press, 1957), pp. 71–82; and for Chicago, see Milton Rakove, *Don't Make No Waves—Don't Back No Losers* (Bloomington: Indiana University Press, 1975), pp. 106–31; and Thomas M. Guterbock, *Machine Politics in Transition: Party and Community in Chicago* (Chicago: University of Chicago Press, 1980).

15. James Q. Wilson, *Negro Politics: The Search for Leadership* (Glencoe, Ill.: Free Press, 1960), pp. 47, 71–76.

16. Wilson, *Negro Politics*, pp. 50, 81; interview with Cecil Partee, in Milton L. Rakove, *We Don't Want Nobody Nobody Sent: An Oral History of the Daley Years* (Bloomington: Indiana University Press, 1979), p. 156; and Joel Weisman and Ralph Whitehead, "Untangling Black Politics," *Chicagoan* 1 (July 1974): 74.

17. Quoted in Weisman and Whitehead, "Untangling Black Politics," p. 75.

18. Rakove, *Don't Make No Waves*, pp. 258–60. For the different styles of leadership and types of leaders in Chicago's black community, see Wilson, *Negro Politics*, pp. 214–80.

19. For evidence that the relationship did not bring blacks rewards commensurate with their electoral loyalty, see Michael B. Preston, "Black Politics in the Post-Daley Era," in *After Daley*, ed. Gove and Masotti, pp. 92–93; and Harold M. Baron, "Black Powerlessness in Chicago," *Transaction* 6 (November 1968): 28–31.

20. See the interviews with James Taylor and Madison Brown, in Rakove, *We Don't Want Nobody Nobody Sent*, pp. 165, 188; Rakove, *Don't Make No Waves*, pp. 260–61; and Paula P. Wilson, "Black Aldermen Search for Power in Post-Daley Era," *Chicago Reporter* 7 (January 1978): 1–7.

21. The quotation is in Kennedy, *Himself*, p. 209; see pp. 192–211 for the

larger discussion of King's marches in Chicago. Also see John M. Allswang, *Bosses, Machines, and Urban Voters: An American Symbiosis* (Port Washington, N.Y.: Kennikat Press, 1977), pp. 137–41.

22. On the distinction between racial and welfare objectives, see Wilson, *Negro Politics*, pp. 278 and 185–99. On the developing restlessness of blacks, see Gleason, *Daley of Chicago*, pp. 68–69. One of the black independents elected to the state senate in 1966 was Richard H. Newhouse, who challenged Daley for the mayoral nomination in 1975.

23. Mathewson, *Up Against Daley*, pp. 121–33; Weisman and Whitehead, "Untangling Black Politics," p. 75.

24. For identification of the Dawson wards and the white ethnic wards, see n. 5, above. For 1963 and 1967, the West Side wards: wards 24 and 29; for 1971, wards 24, 27, 28 and 29; for 1975, wards 24, 27, 28, 29, and 37. The Other South Side black wards: for 1963 and 1967, wards 5 and 17; for 1971, wards 5, 8, 16, 17, 21, and 34; for 1975, wards 5, 7, 8, 9, 15, 16, 17, 21, and 34. The results are not changed materially if for 1975 we use only the wards that had a majority black voting-age population in the 1970 census. That change reduces the number of black wards to fifteen for 1975, and Daley's mobilization rate is 16.5 percent.

25. In the white ethnic areas, Daley beat his combined opposition by better than 2 to 1 in 1975.

26. Mike Royko, *Boss: Richard J. Daley of Chicago* (New York: E. P. Dutton, 1971), pp. 205–9; O'Connor, *Clout*, pp. 219–20.

27. Bill Granger, "Men and Machine: Part Two," *Chicago Guide* (December 1975): 137–38; Rakove, *Don't Make No Waves*, p. 230. The conspiracy charges against Hanrahan were dismissed in 1977; see *Chicago Tribune*, 16 April 1977.

28. Mathewson, *Up Against Daley*, pp. 233–34; the quotation is from Moore's campaign literature, and the emphasis is in the original.

29. The quotation is from Ralph Whitehead, Jr., and Joel Weisman, "Is LaSalle Street Grooming the Black Mayor?" *Chicagoan* 1 (August 1974): 80; and see Mike Royko, "Boss: The Legacy and the Loss," *Chicagoan* 1 (October 1973): 56–57, for the impact of the Hanrahan race on the Machine. While Hanrahan carried Chicago, Carey offset that in the suburbs and won the election. The general election for state's attorney coincided with a presidential contest, so the mobilization levels were generally higher than in the primary or in earlier general elections for mayor.

30. Don Rose, quoted in Mathewson, *Up Against Daley*, pp. 249–50.

31. Appearances to the contrary, after the operation, Daley quietly left his office every afternoon for a two-hour nap. See Len O'Connor, *Requiem: The Decline and Demise of Mayor Daley and His Era* (Chicago: Contemporary Books, 1977), pp. 36–37. See pp. 31–32 for information on the operation and on the inoperable blockage of Daley's right carotid artery.

32. *Chicago Tribune*, 8, 9, and 12 December 1972, 1 March, and 11 April 1973; and Bill Granger, "Men and Machine: Part Three," *Chicago Guide* (March 1974): 102–3.

33. O'Connor, *Clout*, p. 240; and Mathewson, *Up Against Daley*, pp. 240–41. For Conlisk's resignation, see *Chicago Tribune*, 11 October 1973.

34. From an unidentified Chicago reporter, quoted in O'Connor, *Clout*, p. 252.

35. For the Bush case, see *Chicago Tribune*, 3 and 4 August 1973, 22 February, and 12 October 1974, and 5 September 1975. For the Wigoda case, see *Chicago Tribune*, 13 and 14 March, 6 and 11 April, 9 May, 11 October, and 3 December 1974, and 2 December 1975. For Keane, see *Chicago Tribune*, 31 March, 1, 3, 4, 10, and 25 April, 5 May, and 16 June 1973, 3 May, 12 September, and 10 October 1974. On Danaher, see Mathewson, *Up Against Daley*, pp. 261—62.

36. *Chicago Tribune*, 10 October 1974. For the comments by Daley and Marzullo, see O'Connor, *Clout*, pp. 251—53. Danaher died on 15 December 1974, before going to trial on these charges.

37. For the Singer comment, see O'Connor, *Clout*, p. 252. The poll was sponsored by the *Chicago Sun-Times* and WBBM-TV; see Mathewson, *Up Against Daley*, p. 263.

38. *Chicago Tribune*, 19 February 1975.

39. *Chicago Tribune*, 9 February 1973; also see the editorial on 10 February 1973.

40. *Chicago Tribune*, 15 February 1973. At a later press conference, Daley still refused to provide an explanation; *Chicago Tribune*, 28 February 1973. For a view of the family networks among the city's Irish politicians, see Royko, *Boss*, pp. 72—74.

41. Mathewson, *Up Against Daley*, p. 231; O'Connor, *Clout*, p. 241.

42. *Chicago Tribune*, 26 February 1975. Daley had no major news media support in his 1975 primary contest.

43. Precinct-level voting returns were obtained in machine-readable form from the Chicago Board of Election Commissioners. The block-level census data are from the 1980 census and were provided by the Census Data Laboratory, Social Science Research Institute, Northern Illinois University, which also did the programming to aggregate the block data to the precinct level. The 1980 census data were used, rather than an interpolation between 1970 and 1980, because the 1970 census did not report the Hispanic voting-age population separately at the block level.

44. The match required comparing precinct maps with maps of the census blocks. Whenever a census block was split between two (or more) precincts, a proportionate allocation was made by checking the voter registration lists and determining how many voters lived at each street address in the census block. Since some precinct boundaries changed between elections, the match was done separately for each election.

The calculation of the regression estimates follows these steps. First, for each precinct, express the number of votes cast for each candidate and the number of voting-age persons of each racial group as a percentage of the total voting-age population in the precinct. Second, regress a particular candidate's percentage of the voting-age population on the proportion that a particular racial group (for example, blacks) made up the voting-age population. From that equation we can derive a statistically unbiased estimate of the proportion of the voting-age members of the group who cast ballots for that candidate. The estimate equals the sum of the regression constant and the regression coefficient. The procedure is then repeated to develop estimates of the voting support of the other racial groups for that candidate. Third, in the same way, calculate the estimates for the other candidates and for the percentage of nonvoters. For the mathematics underlying the technique, see Leo A. Goodman, "Ecological Regression and the Behavior of Individuals," *American Sociological Review* 18 (December 1953): 663—64; and Leo A. Goodman, "Some Alternatives to Ecological Correlation," *American Journal of Sociology* 64 (May 1959): 610—25.

45. To develop citywide estimates, I divided Chicago's precincts into eight geographic areas and calculated separate estimates for each. Then I weighted the estimate for each group by each area's proportional share of that group's voting-age population in the city and used these weight factors to calculate the estimates of the group's behavior in the city as a whole.

46. There was another entrant in the 1959 primary: Lar Daly, who campaigned in an Uncle Sam costume and ran for a variety of offices in the late 1950s and 1960s. His candidacy was treated humorously by the local media, and in the 1959 primary he polled 42,965 votes.

47. See Chapter 3 for Daley's role in the struggles for integrated schools and public housing.

48. Alderman Anna Langford (16th Ward), quoted in *Chicago Defender*, 11 March 1971; the Daley comment is from *Chicago Today*, 9 March 1971. Governor Richard Ogilvie attributed the defeat of the Republican mayoral candidate to Daley's strong stand against Austin's desegregation order; see *Chicago Daily News*, 7 April 1971. Also see Bill Granger, "Men and Machine: Part One," *Chicago Guide* (November 1973): 108.

49. *Chicago Sun-Times*, 31 December 1975 and 11 January 1976; *Chicago Tribune*, 9 January 1976; *Hyde Park Herald*, 18 February 1976; and Ron Dorfman, "Daley's Bluff," *Chicago* 25 (April 1976): 123—29, 222—23. For the Marshall quotation, see *Chicago Sun-Times*, 6 January 1976; Daley's reaction is in *Chicago Daily News*, 6 January 1976, and *Chicago Tribune*, 7 January 1976.

50. Mathewson, *Up Against Daley*, pp. 187—89.

51. The quotations, respectively, are in Mathewson, *Up Against Daley*, p. 189, and *Chicago Tribune*, 11 May 1972.

52. *Chicago Tribune*, 10 May 1972, for the quotation, and 11, 12, 15, 16, 20, and 21 May 1972, for the other details. Also see Mathewson, *Up Against Daley*, pp. 190—91. Several of the black representatives backed off under pressure from the Machine; and Tyrone Kenner, one of the two black aldermen originally supporting the charges of police brutality, was the Machine's candidate in 1976 to defeat Metcalfe for the post of committeeman from the 3rd Ward. Metcalfe won by the slim margin of eleven votes.

53. Alderman Anna Langford (16th Ward), quoted in Mathewson, *Up Against Daley*, p. 192.

54. The quotation is in Whitehead and Weisman, "Is LaSalle Street Grooming the Black Mayor?" p. 80 (emphasis in the original). In the 16 March 1976 primary, Erwin A. France, formerly head of Chicago's Model Cities Program, was endorsed by the Machine to oppose Metcalfe. For discussion of the significance of Metcalfe's primary victory, see *Chicago Tribune*, 21 and 24 March and 12 April 1976.

55. Thomas N. Todd, member of Metcalfe's executive campaign committee, quoted in *Chicago Tribune*, 21 March 1976.

56. The quotation is in *Chicago Tribune*, 24 February 1975; also see *Chicago Tribune*, 22 September and 11 December 1974.

57. *Chicago Defender*, 20 February 1975; *Chicago Tribune*, 24 January 1975.

58. *Chicago Tribune*, 23 February 1975; see 26 and 31 January 1975 for his earlier statements.

59. *Chicago Tribune*, 26 January 1975.

60. *Chicago Tribune*, 13 February 1975; and see 21 January 1975 for other support for Singer from independent blacks.

61. *Chicago Tribune*, 24 February 1975. Even the fact that Newhouse had a white wife produced criticism from some blacks; *Chicago Tribune*, 22 September 1974.

62. *Chicago Tribune*, 5 February 1975.

63. For example, Daley did not permit a citywide registration drive after 1964; see Joel Weisman and Ralph Whitehead, "The Day Cook County Lost the Pennant," *Chicagoan* 2 (October 1974): 68.

Notes to Chapter 5

1. See Len O'Connor, *Requiem: The Decline and Demise of Mayor Daley and His Era* (Chicago: Contemporary Books, 1977), pp. 1–20, for the details concerning Daley's death and funeral. Despite the attempts to revive him, Daley had suffered cardiac arrest and probably died instantly.

2. Bill Gleason, *Daley of Chicago: The Man, the Mayor, and the Limits of Conventional Politics* (New York: Simon and Schuster, 1970), p. 253.

3. The reference to Daley is from Haynes Johnson's column in the *Washington Post*, quoted in O'Connor, *Requiem*, p. 193; see pp. 185–95 for the details of the public visitation and funeral.

4. Len O'Connor, *Clout: Mayor Daley and His City* (Chicago: Henry Regnery, 1975), p. 124.

5. O'Connor, *Clout*, p. 129, quoting Alderman Joseph Burke (14th Ward), father of the current alderman from that ward, Edward Burke; and see Mike Royko, *Boss: Richard J. Daley of Chicago* (New York: E. P. Dutton, 1971), pp. 17–21, for another description of the mayor's attention to the details of patronage and benefits. The *Chicago Tribune*, 25 February 1955, reported Daley's post-primary statement, and, shortly after the April general election, he repeated his public commitment to resign the party chairmanship.

6. Milton L. Rakove, *Don't Make No Waves—Don't Back No Losers* (Bloomington: Indiana University Press, 1975), p. 106, uses the feudal analogy, and pp. 107–31 provide a good description of how the ward organizations worked. However, Rakove underestimates the degree of control that Daley came to exercise within the party organization.

7. O'Connor, *Clout*, p. 124, for the quotation; see pp. 122–24 for the early concern of the committeemen about Daley's outside connection with the city's labor unions.

8. On the importance of this gatekeeping function, see Kathleen A. Kemp and Robert L. Lineberry, "The Last of the Great Urban Machines and the Last

of the Great Urban Mayors? Chicago Politics, 1955–77," in *After Daley: Chicago Politics in Transition*, ed. Samuel K. Gove and Louis H. Masotti (Urbana: University of Illinois Press, 1982), pp. 7–8.

9. Vernon Jarrett, "City Hall Displays More Than Racism," *Chicago Tribune*, 20 October 1978. Frost had announced that he would meet with reporters in the mayor's fifth-floor conference room; but when they arrived the doors were locked, and a stand bearing a book for mourners' signatures stood in the doorway; see *Chicago Tribune*, 24 December 1976, for the details.

10. These arrangements were reported in *Chicago Tribune*, 24 and 27 December 1976; see the issue of 29 December 1976 for the council's action.

11. *Chicago Tribune*, 24 and 26 December 1976; Kemp and Lineberry, "Last of the Great Urban Machines," pp. 19–20. George Dunne, president of the Cook County Board of Commissioners and a longtime associate of the late mayor, was chosen as chairman of the Democratic Central Committee of Cook County.

12. *Chicago Tribune*, 24 January 1977.

13. *Chicago Tribune*, 22, 24, and 29 January 1977.

14. Quoted in Paula P. Wilson, "Black Aldermen Search for New Power in Post-Daley Era," *Chicago Reporter* 7 (January 1978): 7. And see Michael B. Preston, "Black Politics in the Post-Daley Era," in *After Daley*, ed. Gove and Masotti, p. 106, for the "total disrespect" shown to Frost.

15. For the Bilandic quotation, see *Chicago Sun-Times*, 27 January 1977. For the other details and reactions, see *Chicago Tribune*, 2, 3, 6, 7, 8, 13, and 23 February 1977; *Chicago Daily News*, 12 January 1977; and *Chicago Defender*, 1 and 7 February 1977.

16. For a thorough airing of that suspicion, see Vernon Jarrett, "Ralph Metcalfe Takes His Stand," *Chicago Tribune*, 23 January 1977. For the other details, see *Chicago Tribune*, 3, 9, 20, 22, and 26 January 1977.

17. *Chicago Tribune*, 29 January, 19 and 20 February 1977.

18. The other was the Independent Precinct Organization, which endorsed no candidate in the Democratic primary. Washington is quoted in *Chicago Tribune*, 20 February 1977; and for the other details, see *Chicago Tribune*, 21, 25, and 28 February, 2, 17, and 18 March 1977. It is interesting to notice that the details of Washington's conviction on charges of not filing income tax returns for four years, the prosecutor's claim that he had not filed for as many as nineteen years, and the suspension of his license by the Chicago Bar Association were detailed in the papers during the campaign and aired by the IVI prior to its endorsement.

19. Reid is quoted in *Chicago Tribune*, 28 February 1977; the issue of 27 March 1977 reported Jackson's endorsement. For other details, see *Chicago Tribune*, 29 January and 22 February 1977; Wilson, "Black Aldermen," p. 3. The columns by Vernon Jarrett, *Chicago Tribune*, 9, 23, and 25 March 1977, also provide valuable insights.

20. Lu Palmer, a black journalist and community organizer, quoted in Wilson, "Black Aldermen," p. 3. Also see the discussion by Preston, "Black Politics in the Post-Daley Era," pp. 101–5.

21. Both quoted phrases are from Vernon Jarrett, "The Politics of Fear Enter the Race," *Chicago Tribune*, 23 March 1977; also see his columns of 4 and 25 March 1977.

22. *Chicago Tribune*, 19 April 1977; see the issues of 30 March, 1, 6, and 17 April 1977 for the other details. The anti-patronage stance taken by Pucinski and Washington probably reflected their sense of the impact of the 1972 Shakman consent decree that prohibited the discharge of city employees for political reasons, and which later was extended to the hiring of city workers. For the details, see Robert J. McClory, "Shakman: The Man and His Battle against Patronage," *Illinois Issues* 9 (September 1983): 7–12.

23. The poll data are reported in *Chicago Tribune*, 13 March 1977. Washington polled just under 6 percent, ranking fourth behind Hanrahan, and only 23 percent of his supporters thought he could win. Bilandic had a solid lead among all the city's white ethnic groups, and he also was favored by six of ten black respondents.

24. It is important to notice that Table 10 reports estimates of the behavior of *voters* and not of geographic areas (i.e., wards). The figures derive from regression equations that used precinct voting and census data. While the number of precincts varied slightly from one election to another, in 1977, there were 279 precincts in the old Dawson wards; 536 in the other South Side black wards; and 238 on the West Side. The Northwest Side had 526 precincts, and there were 549 in the South Side white areas. The city-wide estimates are weighted sums of the separate estimates of white, black, and Hispanic behavior in each of eight subareas of the city.

25. The election-day poll was conducted by NBC; see *Chicago Tribune*, 21 April 1977, and see the issue of 17 April 1977 for other indications of strenuous efforts by the precinct captains.

26. Turnout can be calculated from Table 10 simply by subtracting the nonvoting proportion of each group from 100 percent. For discussion of the voting preferences among blacks, see Preston, "Black Politics in the Post-Daley Era," pp. 94–97; and *Chicago Tribune*, 20 April 1977, which also reports Washington's inaccurate claim that "we won a plurality in the black community."

27. The difference was smaller than the estimated number of votes that white ethnics cast for Hanrahan. The *Chicago Tribune*, 20 April 1977, incorrectly equated the appeal of Pucinski with Adamowski; and see Joseph Zikmund II, "Mayoral Voting and Ethnic Politics in the Daley-Bilandic-Byrne Era," in *After Daley*, ed. Gove and Masotti, pp. 43–46, for the regional concentration of Pucinski's support.

28. Alderman Casimir Laskowski (35th Ward), quoted in *Chicago Tribune*, 13 March 1978. The balance tilted in 1982 when Vrdolyak became chairman of the Democratic Central Committee of Cook County.

29. Quoted in *Chicago Tribune*, 13 March 1978; also see the issue of 14 March 1978.

30. *Chicago Defender*, 17 September and 14 June 1977, respectively, for the quotations. Also see *Chicago Daily News*, 17 August 1977; *Chicago Sun-Times*, 18, 21, 23 August, 2 and 21 September 1977; and *Chicago Tribune*, 21 August, 14, 16, 21, 23, and 28 September 1977. And for a more complete discussion, see Chapter 3.

31. *Chicago Sun-Times*, 11 June 1977; *Chicago Tribune*, 24 March, 15 April, and 8 June 1978. In the City Council, four black aldermen and three white independents voted against the reappointment of the two white women, and

one black and one white independent opposed the reappointment of the black male; see *Journal of the Proceedings of the City Council of the City of Chicago for the Council Year 1978* (Chicago: John C. Marcin, City Clerk, 1979), pp. 7787–88, 8082.

32. The Washington quotation is in *Chicago Tribune*, 10 November 1978; and the characterization of Stewart is by Vernon Jarrett, "City Hall Displays More Than Racism," *Chicago Tribune*, 20 October 1978; also see his column of 10 November 1978. The Machine made no effort to punish Pucinski for his campaign against Bilandic, since that might run the risk of antagonizing his voters; and Washington, unlike Pucinski, had refused to support Bilandic in the general election. See Washington's description of Bilandic as a "third-rate boss Daley," in *Chicago Tribune*, 1 June 1977.

33. Only 6.6 percent of the mortgages financed home purchases in the black and Hispanic communities; the majority (53.4 percent) went for condominium purchases along the lakefront on the near North Side, and the second-largest share (44.8 percent) went for homes in the white communities on the Northwest and Southwest Sides. See *Chicago Tribune*, 31 December 1978.

34. Peter W. Colby and Paul Michael Green, "The Consolidation of Clout: The Vote Power of Chicago Democrats from Cermak to Bilandic," in *Illinois Elections*, ed. Caroline A. Gherardini et al., 2d ed. (Springfield, Ill.: Sangamon State University, 1982), p. 40. This article containing their prediction was first published in February 1979 and was probably written a month or two prior to its appearance.

35. For the description of Marzullo and the quotation, see Kathleen Whalen FitzGerald, *Brass: Jane Byrne and the Pursuit of Power* (Chicago: Contemporary Books, 1981), p. 203. The maxim was also one of Mayor Daley's favorites; see Eugene Kennedy, *Himself! The Life and Times of Mayor Richard J. Daley* (New York: E. P. Dutton, 1971), p. 54.

36. On her background, see Bill Granger and Lori Granger, *Fighting Jane: Mayor Jane Byrne and the Chicago Machine* (New York: Dial Press, 1980), pp. 61–83; and FitzGerald, *Brass*, pp. 134–60.

37. FitzGerald, *Brass*, p. 178; see p. 137 for Daley's mispronunciation of Byrne's name.

38. The Depres quotation is in FitzGerald, *Brass*, p. 161; see Granger and Granger, *Fighting Jane*, pp. 136–38, for the attitude of the regulars toward her, and pp. 139–41, for Daley's pleasure with her attempts to include more women in party affairs.

39. Granger and Granger, *Fighting Jane*, pp. 95–101.

40. The quotation is in Granger and Granger, *Fighting Jane*, p. 87.

41. FitzGerald, *Brass*, p. 181; also see Granger and Granger, *Fighting Jane*, pp. 160–61.

42. Granger and Granger, *Fighting Jane*, pp. 165–71; FitzGerald, *Brass*, p. 182. Public Vehicle Commissioner James Y. Carter was eventually indicted, convicted, and jailed on federal bribery charges.

43. Granger and Granger, *Fighting Jane*, pp. 176–77. Burke quietly shelved his earlier lawsuit.

44. See the report in *Chicago Tribune*, 16 November 1977; and Granger

and Granger, *Fighting Jane*, pp. 182–84, for a partial transcript of Bilandic's television interview.

45. The text of the memo is in *Chicago Tribune*, 17 November 1977; see the issue of 22 November 1977, for the report of Bilandic's news conference and Byrne's response. The connection between Byrne and the *Chicago Daily News* was through Jay McMullen, who had been the paper's City Hall reporter between 1949 and 1976, when he was reassigned to its real estate section. Byrne and McMullen had been dating and were married on 17 March 1978. On McMullen's career and his outlook, see Granger and Granger, *Fighting Jane*, pp. 143–49, 189.

46. *Chicago Tribune*, 25 April 1978.

47. FitzGerald, *Brass*, pp. 193–94; Granger and Granger, *Fighting Jane*, pp. 189, 202; *Chicago Tribune*, 30 March 1978.

48. For an excellent analysis, see Jeff Lyon, "Will Byrne Tell All, or Is She All Mouth?" *Chicago Tribune*, 25 April 1978.

49. See the columns by Mike Royko and Basil Talbott, Jr., in *Chicago Sun-Times*, 21, 25, and 28 February 1979.

50. The quotation is in Granger and Granger, *Fighting Jane*, p. 210. For the other details, see *Chicago Tribune*, 27 November, 2, 3, 8 December 1978, and 2, 3, 14, 15, 16, and 17 January 1979.

51. *Chicago Tribune*, 16 January 1979, quoting a CTA transportation director.

52. *Chicago Tribune*, 14 January 1979; Granger and Granger, *Fighting Jane*, p. 211.

53. On the snow command, see Mike Royko, "A Chip Off the Old Payroll," *Chicago Sun-Times*, 14 February 1979. On the Sain contract, see *Chicago Tribune*, 1 February 1979; *Chicago Sun-Times*, 22 February 1979; and Granger and Granger, *Fighting Jane*, p. 211.

54. *Chicago Tribune*, 30 January, 1 and 3 February 1979; and Vernon Jarrett, "Why the Trains Passed Us By," *Chicago Tribune*, 2 February 1979.

55. The Byrne quotation is in *Chicago Sun-Times*, 27 February 1979; and the text of Daley's testimonial is in FitzGerald, *Brass*, p. 200.

56. Jeff Lyon, "Will Byrne Tell All," *Chicago Tribune*, 25 April 1978.

57. *Chicago Sun-Times* and *Chicago Tribune*, 15 February 1979.

58. Both quotations are in *Chicago Sun-Times*, 21 February 1979; the first is by Alderman Wilson Frost. For similar predictions by Machine loyalists, see *Chicago Sun-Times*, 22 and 24 February 1979. The *Chicago Sun-Times* endorsed Bilandic on 18 February 1979, the *Chicago Tribune* on 18 February 1979, and WBBM-TV, reported in *Chicago Sun-Times*, 27 February 1979.

59. The WBBM-TV poll was conducted by Mid-America Research and the WLS-TV poll by Richard Day Research, Inc. All three sets of poll results are reported and discussed in *Chicago Sun-Times*, 21 February 1979. For the media's belief in the Machine's invincibility, see *Chicago Tribune*, 23 February 1979, and Mike Royko, "If Chicago Got Byrned," *Chicago Sun-Times*, 25 February 1979. By the weekend prior to the election, another WLS-TV poll gave Byrne a three-point lead, while the final WBBM-TV poll showed her with a two-point margin; *Chicago Sun-Times*, 26 and 27 February 1979.

60. *Chicago Sun-Times*, 22, 23, and 25 February 1979.

61. Granger and Granger, *Fighting Jane*, pp. 1–5; the quotation is on p. 4.

62. Mike Royko quoted in Granger and Granger, *Fighting Jane*, p. 21. For additional evidence of the Machine's waning control, see William J. Grimshaw, "The Daley Legacy: A Declining Politics of Party, Race, and Public Unions," in *After Daley*, ed. Gove and Masotti, pp. 71–79.

63. In the 1983 WMAQ-TV (NBC) Primary Exit Poll, respondents were asked for whom they had voted in 1979. Analysis of that recall indicates that among whites, Byrne ran best among self-professed liberals and political independents. She was also stronger among blacks who had at least attended college than among those with only high school educations or less. Moreover, there was considerably less variation in Byrne's support among subgroups of blacks than among the corresponding categories of whites, and her overall level of support among blacks was 14 percentage points higher than among whites. For the data and its analysis, see Paul Kleppner, "Chicago Elects a Black Mayor: An Historical Analysis of the 1983 Election" (Chicago: American Jewish Committee, 1983), pp. 45–49. The data from the WMAQ-TV (NBC) poll were obtained from the Roper Center for Public Opinion Research.

64. *Chicago Sun-Times*, 21 February 1979; and see *Chicago Tribune*, 2 March 1979, for comments by Harold Washington and Cecil Partee concerning the impact of the closings on black voters.

65. Since all of the regression estimates use voting-age population, they will understate the actual participation rates among Hispanics. Except for Puerto Ricans, some of the voting-age Hispanics are ineligible to vote because they are not citizens. The amount of understatement cannot be measured precisely, but when the 1979 estimates were calculated separately within Mexican and Puerto Rican areas, the turnout rate for Hispanics in the latter areas was only about 5 percentage points higher than for Hispanics in predominantly Mexican areas. However, the difference was much greater in 1983. On these matters and others, see Luis M. Salces and Peter W. Colby, "Mañana Will Be Better: Spanish-American Politics in Chicago," in *Illinois Elections*, ed. Gherardini et al., pp. 43–45; and Joanne Belenchia, "Latinos and Chicago Politics," in *After Daley*, ed. Gove and Masotti, pp. 118–45.

66. Granger and Granger, *Fighting Jane*, pp. 218–19; and see *Chicago Sun-Times*, 24 and 28 February 1979, for examples of her denunciations of Vrdolyak and Burke.

67. Alderman Roman Pucinski predicted as much on the night of the primary. His statement and Burke's are both in *Chicago Sun-Times*, 28 February 1979; also see Granger and Granger, *Fighting Jane*, p. 222, for a similar comment by George Dunne.

68. For the Rose quotation, see *Chicago Tribune*, 24 April 1983. Rose had managed Byrne's campaign in 1979.

69. The argument here and in the following paragraphs relies on Milton L. Rakove, "Jane Byrne and the New Chicago Politics," in *After Daley*, ed. Gove and Masotti, pp. 230–35; also see Rakove, *Don't Make No Waves*, pp. 85–88, 213–32.

70. FitzGerald, *Brass*, p. 203; Rakove, *Don't Make No Waves*, pp. 43–44.

71. Granger and Granger, *Fighting Jane*, pp. 223–25.

72. For the quotations and details, see *Chicago Tribune*, 17–21 December 1979.

73. *Chicago Tribune*, 8 February 1980, and for the earlier details, see the issues of 17 December 1979; 31 January, 2, 3, and 4 February 1980.

74. *Chicago Tribune*, 15 and 19 February 1980; Granger and Granger, *Fighting Jane*, p. 226.

75. The public opinion poll was conducted by Market Facts, Inc., and was reported in *Chicago Tribune*, 17 February 1980. For the other developments, see *Chicago Tribune*, 21, 22 February, 1 and 9 March 1980.

76. *Chicago Tribune*, 15 December 1979; Granger and Granger, *Fighting Jane*, p. 227.

77. For the quotations, see *Chicago Tribune*, 25 and 28 January 1980; and for the settlement and other developments, see *Chicago Tribune*, 24, 26, 27 January, 1, 3, 4, 10, and 11 February 1980.

78. Alderman Martin Oberman, quoted in Granger and Granger, *Fighting Jane*, pp. 229–30. Alderman Edward Vrdolyak summed up the charge against Mayor Daley: "The 'city that works' was for 20 years the city that juggled its books," *Chicago Tribune*, 29 January 1980.

79. Rakove, "Jane Byrne and the New Chicago Politics," pp. 233–34. Obviously, Vrdolyak and Burke didn't want another mayor with the power that Daley accumulated, but it isn't likely that they saw Byrne in that light.

80. Rakove, "Jane Byrne and the New Chicago Politics," pp. 234–35.

81. Peter W. Colby and Paul Michael Green, "The Irish Game: Watch Byrne Watch Daley Watching Byrne," in *Illinois Elections*, ed. Gherardini et al., pp. 46–47; *Chicago Tribune*, 20 November 1979.

82. *Chicago Sun-Times*, 30 November 1979; *Chicago Tribune*, 24 November 1979.

83. *Chicago Tribune*, 16 and 17 March 1980; Colby and Green, "Irish Game," p. 47.

84. *Chicago Sun-Times*, 19 March 1980.

85. *Chicago Sun-Times*, 19 March 1980; the first quotation is from William Daley, Richard M. Daley's brother and campaign manager.

86. *Chicago Sun-Times*, 21 March 1980.

87. *Chicago Tribune*, 18 and 19 September 1980; *Chicago Sun-Times*, 18 September 1980.

88. *Chicago Tribune*, 12 October 1980; see *Chicago Sun-Times*, 30 October 1980, for William Daley's assessment of the number of committeemen supporting his brother.

89. *Chicago Sun-Times* and *Chicago Tribune*, 10 and 11 October 1980.

90. *Chicago Sun-Times* and *Chicago Tribune*, 23 October 1980. Byrne also charged that a similar discrimination scheme kept minorities out of the 19th Ward, Assessor Hynes's bailiwick. While Byrne attacked Daley, she did not expressly endorse Carey, although Harold Washington did.

91. *Chicago Sun-Times*, 29 October 1980.

92. *Chicago Tribune*, 29 October 1980; the Marzullo quotation is in *Chicago Sun-Times*, 29 October 1980.

93. *Chicago Tribune*, 29 October and 3 November 1980.

94. Carey's record as state's attorney was ridiculed in a series of columns

by Mike Royko, who was a longtime critic of the Daley family; see *Chicago Sun-Times*, 15, 28, 30, 31 October, and 2 November 1980.

95. Compare the data for blacks in Tables 8 and 12. The data in Table 8 are ward-level totals and are not as precise as the regression estimates in Table 12. However, since the black wards in Chicago are quite homogeneous racially, the difference in Carey's support in the two contests can't be explained away on those grounds.

96. Quoted in *Chicago Tribune*, 26 July 1982. For poll reports of Byrne's approval rating, see *Chicago Tribune*, 10 January and 8 February 1980; 18 January, 9 and 10 April, 26 and 28 July, 30 August 1981; 18 July, 28 September, and 22 October 1982.

97. *Chicago Tribune*, 23 March 1982; for the other details, see the issues of 24–28 and 30 March 1982. *Chicago Defender*, 29 March 1982, reported that fifteen of the sixteen black committeemen were lined up with Vrdolyak.

98. See the comments by Vrdolyak, in Milton L. Rakove, *We Don't Want Nobody Nobody Sent: An Oral History of the Daley Years* (Bloomington: Indiana University Press, 1979), pp. 133–38; and Bill Granger, "Men and Machine," *Chicago Guide* (March 1974): 102.

Notes to Chapter 6

1. The description and quotations are in *Chicago Sun-Times*, 23 February 1983. Hampton and Clark were the Black Panther leaders killed in Hanrahan's raid in December 1969.

2. For more discussion of this, see Chapter 8; also see Thomas E. Cavanagh, "The Reagan Referendum: The Black Vote in the 1982 Election" (paper presented at the annual meeting of the Midwest Political Science Association, Chicago, April 1983).

3. Peter Hart made both quoted remarks; see *Chicago Sun-Times*, 28 October 1982. For discussion of Reagan in local black sources, see *Chicago Defender* editorials, 30 September, 7 and 11 October 1982; and see the attack on Reagan's economic policies by the Reverend Jesse Jackson, in *Chicago Defender*, 12 October 1982. In the WMAQ-TV (NBC) exit poll of 22 February 1983, only 5.6 percent of the blacks rated Reagan's performance as excellent or good, while 73.9 percent gave him a poor score. The corresponding figures for Chicago's whites were 31.2 and 37.1 percent, respectively. The NBC exit poll data were obtained from the Roper Center for Public Opinion Research.

4. The quotation is from Speaker of the House Thomas P. O'Neill. See Jack Beatty, "The Life of the Party," *New Republic* (24 January 1983): 16–20; the quotation is on p. 17.

5. Reagan is quoted in *Chicago Sun-Times*, 27 October 1980. For criticism by blacks of Byrne's support for Reagan, see *Chicago Defender*, 30 March and 16 September 1982.

6. Quoted in Ronni Scheier and Laura Washington, "Byrne's Record on Race: Little Fire behind the Rhetoric," *Chicago Reporter* 11 (September 1982): 2.

7. Michael B. Preston, "Black Politics in the Post-Daley Era," in *After Daley: Chicago Politics in Transition*, ed. Samuel K. Gove and Louis H. Ma-

sotti (Urbana: University of Illinois Press, 1982), p. 110; *Chicago Tribune*, 20 December 1979.

8. Quoted in Bill Granger and Lori Granger, *Fighting Jane: Mayor Jane Byrne and the Chicago Machine* (New York: Dial Press, 1980), p. 228.

9. Preston, "Black Politics in the Post-Daley Era," pp. 109–10; and *Chicago Tribune*, 19 April 1979 and 12 January 1980. Under Brzeczek and Byrne, there was no substantial progress toward resolving the discrimination suit against the city; see Federal Judge Prentice Marshall's observations in *Chicago Sun-Times*, 16 May 1981.

10. Respectively, the quotations are from Reverend Jesse Jackson, in *Chicago Tribune*, 14 December 1979; Jane Byrne in Granger and Granger, *Fighting Jane*, pp. 227–28; and Lu Palmer in Paul McGrath, "The Washington Strategy," *Reader* (Chicago) (26 November 1982): 29. Also see Casey Banas, "Why the School Board Bypassed Byrd—Again," *Chicago Tribune*, 8 January 1981.

11. For the details of the consent decree, the Board of Education's integration plan, and Byrne's maneuvers, see Chapter 3.

12. *Chicago Sun-Times*, 17 April 1981; the Pucinski quotation is in *Chicago Sun-Times*, 6 April 1981.

13. *Chicago Defender*, 16 December 1981; see Chapter 3 for the details.

14. The poll is reported in *Chicago Tribune*, 10 April 1981; see the issues of 22, 23 March and 14 April 1981, for the quotations.

15. *Chicago Defender*, 27 October 1981, reports some of the community action. The Justice Department sided with the plantiffs; see the statement by U.S. Attorney Dan K. Webb, *Chicago Defender*, 16 September 1982. The case was Ketchum and the United States *v.* Byrne et al., heard by Judge Thomas R. McMillan in the Northern Illinois District. McMillan found a violation of the Voting Rights Act but said that it was the unintended consequence of the City Council's attempt to draw the ward lines to protect incumbents. Under the new map approved by McMillan, the black majorities in the 15th and 37th Wards were smaller than they had been under the 1971 lines, and Hispanics had only bare majorities of the total population in three of the four wards in which they were given majority status. Several of the original plaintiffs rejected McMillan's solution and appealed that portion of his decision; see *Chicago Defender*, 22, 28, 30 December 1982, and 1 January 1983. In May 1984, the United States Court of Appeals for the Seventh Circuit upheld this appeal and remanded the case to the district court for reconsideration. In doing so, the Court of Appeals provided these guidelines: establishing an effective black majority in at least nineteen wards and creating four wards with an effective Hispanic majority. And it defined an "effective majority" as being 65 percent of the total population or 60 percent of the voting-age population. Despite the objections of Mayor Washington and the city's corporation counsel, the majority bloc on the City Council has instructed its lawyer to appeal the decision to the U.S. Supreme Court.

16. For Byrne's original explanation, see *Chicago Tribune*, 12 February 1981, which also reports reactions by black and white ethnic leaders. Byrne later claimed the appointments were made to balance the appointment of a black superintendent; see her comments, in Ed McManus, "Jane Byrne Interview," *Illinois Issues* 9 (February 1983): 14.

17. Lu Palmer, quoted in McGrath, "Washington Strategy," p. 29. For the City Council vote, see Ben Joravsky, "City Council Records Show Byrne Support," *Chicago Reporter* 11 (December 1982): 5.

18. The quotations are from columns by Vernon Jarrett, *Chicago Tribune*, 1 May 1981 and 28 May 1982.

19. Streeter was quoted in *Chicago Tribune*, 30 June 1982; for other information on the campaign, see the issues of 31 May and 27 June 1982, and the column by Vernon Jarrett, 4 June 1982.

20. Paul M. Green, "Washington's Victory: Divide and Conquer," *Illinois Issues* 9 (April 1983): 15–16; and McManus, "Jane Byrne Interview," p. 14.

21. The quotations are from Lu Palmer, in McGrath, "Washington Strategy," p. 29; and Alderman John Madrzyk (13th Ward), in *Chicago Tribune*, 24 July 1982, which also described the Council meeting. For the votes of the black aldermen, see Joravsky, "City Council Records Show Byrne Support," p. 5.

22. For a thorough evaluation of Byrne's record on minority appointments, see Scheier and Washington, "Byrne's Record on Race," pp. 1–5; both quotations are on p. 5.

23. Quoted in McGrath, "Washington's Strategy," p. 29.

24. *Chicago Defender*, 15 August 1981 and 6 March 1982.

25. On the importance of the subjective meanings that people attach to situations, see Murray Edelman, *Politics as Symbolic Action* (New York: Academic Press, 1971), p. 133; and for the concept of cognitive liberation and its vital role in generating social movements, see Doug McAdam, *Political Process and the Development of Black Insurgency* (Chicago: University of Chicago Press, 1982), pp. 48–51.

26. The quotations are from Lu Palmer, in McGrath, "Washington's Strategy," p. 24. Also see the *New York Times* (15 March 1983) and the Reverend Morris H. Tyne's "Analysis of Fest Boycott" (*Chicago Defender*, 16 and 18 October 1982) for a critique of the boycott. On the cognitions necessary for the development of insurgent social movements, see Frances Fox Piven and Richard A. Cloward, *Poor People's Movements* (New York: Vintage Books, 1979), pp. 3–4; and McAdam, *Political Process*, pp. 49–50.

27. *Chicago Sun-Times*, 29 April 1982; *All Chicago City News*, 25 January and 11 June 1982. The co-chairpersons of POWER were Walter "Slim" Coleman, Heart of Uptown Coalition, and Nancy Jefferson, Midwest Community Council.

28. Respectively, the quotations are from a retired black postal employee working in the registration drive, in *Chicago Sun-Times*, 27 September 1982; and Vernon Jarrett, "A Way to Achieve Respect," *Chicago Tribune*, 12 September 1982.

29. *Chicago Journal*, 22 December 1982; and *Chicago Tribune*, 12 September 1982.

30. Dorothy Tillman, quoted in *Chicago Tribune*, 12 September 1982. For the other details, see *Chicago Sun-Times*, 6 and 17 August 1982; *Chicago Tribune*, 9 and 24 August 1982; *Chicago Defender*, 1, 8, 21, 22, 25 September, and 4 October 1982.

31. *Chicago Sun-Times*, 18 and 29 August 1982; *Chicago Tribune*, 27 and

31 August 1982; *Chicago Defender*, 21 and 29 September 1982; *New York Times*, 20 September 1982.

32. County Commissioner John Stroger, quoted in *Chicago Defender*, 28 September 1982. Also see *Chicago Sun-Times*, 7 October 1982; *Chicago Defender*, 1, 23, 29 September and 4, 5 October 1982; *New York Times*, 15 March 1983. The final day for registration prior to the November general election was 5 October 1982.

33. The quotations are in *Chicago Sun-Times*, 27 September 1982, and *Chicago Tribune*, 7 October 1982; also see their issues of 3 and 11 October 1982 for other statements supporting Coleman's judgment.

34. *Chicago Defender*, 7 October 1982, carried the headline; see the issues of 11 and 30 October 1982, for the activities of the People's Movement. Black leaders claimed that in 1980 nearly 107,000 of the 140,000 new registrants were purged from the voting rolls as the result of challenges by the Chicago Board of Election Commissioners, and in 1982, the Board challenged 116,143 new registrants; see *Chicago Defender*, 13 October and 9 November 1982.

35. These numbers derive from applying the regression estimates of group registration to the known size of each group's voting-age population. All of the estimates refer to *net* changes and not to the total number that had to be added to compensate for names dropped because of death, change of residence, and so forth. For discussion of the increased number of black registrants, see *Chicago Defender*, 7 and 28 October 1982; see the issues of 11 and 18 December 1982 and 1 January 1983, for the post-November registration efforts and their targets. In the period after the November 1982 general election, the Board of Election Commissioners issued reports at least implying that recent black registrants continued to outnumber recent white registrants. Whether those were based on miscalculations, or were efforts to stimulate white registration, is problematic. In any case, they were in error.

36. I am assuming the profile of the Total Registrants in Table 14 is a good representation of the distribution of these categories among the total black population. Overall, 55.5 percent of the black respondents in the WBBM-TV (CBS) Primary Exit Poll reported having registered during the past twelve months, and the total number of black respondents was 2,341. The WBBM-TV (CBS) poll was conducted by Market Shares Corporation, and I am grateful to Nick Panagakis, president of Market Shares, and Greg Caputo, news director of WBBM-TV, for making the primary and general election exit polls available for secondary analysis.

37. For example, Basil Talbott, Jr., "Machine Back in Gear," *Chicago Sun-Times*, 4 November 1982; the same issue quotes Seymour Sudman, University of Illinois Survey Research Laboratory. Also see *Chicago Tribune* editorial, 8 November 1982; and Ed McManus, "'Punch 10' Power: The Machine Rolls On," *Illinois Issues* 8 (December 1982): 39.

38. Thompson publicly attributed the margin of his defeat in Chicago to Vrdolyak; see David Axelrod, "Revived Machine Facing Tough Tests," *Chicago Tribune*, 7 November 1982. For explanations of the outcome by blacks, see the comments by Harold Washington, quoted in Axelrod, "Revived Machine," *Chicago Tribune*, 7 November 1982; the comments by Reverend Jesse

Jackson, in *Chicago Defender*, 6 November 1982; and that paper's editorial of 4 November 1982.

39. Mike Royko, *Chicago Sun-Times*, 3 November 1982, quoted in Green, "Washington's Victory," p. 17.

40. *Chicago Sun-Times* and *Chicago Tribune*, 5 November 1982; *Chicago Defender*, 6 November 1982.

41. For Washington's professions of reluctance, see *Chicago Sun-Times*, 7 October 1982; and the columns by Vernon Jarrett, in *Chicago Tribune*, 1, 8, and 15 October 1982. For some of the activities by community leaders that prompted Washington's decision, see *Chicago Defender*, 30 October and 9 November 1982; and McGrath, "Washington's Strategy," p. 30.

42. *Chicago Defender*, 11 November 1982; Green, "Washington's Victory," p. 17.

43. Vrdolyak quoted in Green, "Washington's Victory," p. 17. Three minor candidates were entered in the Democratic primary, but together they received only 5,068 votes, or 0.4 percent, of the total number of ballots cast.

44. Harold Washington quoted in Laura Washington, "80% Solution," *Chicago Reporter* 12 (March 1983): 6; also see *Chicago Tribune*, 25 January 1983. The March 1983 issue of the *Chicago Reporter* contains three unusually perceptive and detailed articles on "Race in the Race: The Candidates and Their Strategies." Much of the factual information in the discussion that follows comes from these pieces.

45. Washington characterized his legislative record in a question-and-answer session with Alfredo S. Lanier and Andrew Patner, in *Chicago* 32 (February 1983): 102. The other details are from Washington, "80% Solution," p. 6; *Chicago Tribune*, 13 February 1983; and *Chicago Defender*, 14 December 1982.

46. *Chicago Tribune*, 30 January and 19 February 1983; Washington, "80% Solution," p. 6.

47. Juan Andrade, Director, Midwest Voter Registration Education Project, quoted in *Chicago Tribune*, 12 November 1982. For evidence of the tension between blacks and Hispanics, see *Chicago Defender*, 25 October and 6 December 1982; and James Martinez and Jorge Caruso, "Black, Latin Interests May Differ in Elections," *Chicago Sun-Times*, 21 February 1983.

48. Washington, "80% Solution," p. 6; David Axelrod, "Washington Mounting a Campaign of Confusion," *Chicago Tribune*, 16 January 1983; James Ylisela, Jr., "Washington Forced Press to Grapple with Race in Campaign," *Chicago Reporter* 12 (March 1983): 7–8; and McGrath, "Washington's Strategy," p. 22.

49. On the sources of Washington's campaign funds, see the comments by Edwin C. Berry, who chaired the steering committee, quoted in Richard Reeves, "A Tale of Two Chicagos, One White, One Black," *Chicago Sun-Times*, 29 April 1983. For the other details and the quotation from Washington, see Laura Washington, "80% Solution," pp. 5–6; McGrath, "Washington's Strategy," p. 17; and Basil Talbott, Jr., "Whites Fail Washington," *Chicago Sun-Times*, 6 February 1983. Robert Starks, Center for Inner City Studies, Northeastern Illinois University, chaired the Task Force, and I gratefully acknowledge his willingness to discuss its origins and operations with me.

For other information on the Task Force, see Lillian Williams, "Washington Campaigning on Two Fronts," *Chicago Sun-Times*, 27 March 1983.

50. Washington's remarks are quoted in Laura Washington, "80% Solution," pp. 5–6; and Barbara Brotman, "Washington Makes Plea for Support from Blacks," *Chicago Tribune*, 15 November 1982. And also see Leanita McClain, "The Racial Truth of Politics," *Chicago Tribune*, 29 November 1982. The other details are reported in *Chicago Sun-Times*, 2 February 1983; and *Chicago Tribune*, 31 January, 2, 6, 9, 10, and 18 February 1983.

51. For the quotations and details, see Ben Joravsky, "Western Avenue," *Chicago Reporter* 12 (March 1983): 3–4. For Daley's black support and reactions to it, see *Chicago Tribune*, 21 February 1983; and *Chicago Defender*, 18 and 22 November 1982.

52. Joravsky, "Western Avenue," pp. 4–5; *Chicago Tribune*, 24 and 25 January 1983.

53. See Joravsky, "Western Avenue," p. 4, for the quotations.

54. Green, "Washington's Victory," p. 18; *Chicago Tribune*, 28 January, 3, 5, 8, 10, 14, 16, and 19 February 1983.

55. The quotations are in *Chicago Tribune*, 4 and 6 February 1983.

56. Willie Cole, "Save Our City," *Chicago Reporter* 12 (March 1983): 2.

57. *Chicago Tribune*, 13 February 1984; see Cole, "Save Our City," p. 2, for the statements by Griffin, which make clear that at the outset Byrne did not regard Washington as having a serious chance to win the primary.

58. Byrne quoted in *Chicago Defender*, 25 October 1982. The Black Public Opinion Poll, reported in *Chicago Defender*, 16 November 1982, indicated that only 17 percent of the blacks (but 38 percent of the whites) rated Byrne's performance as good or excellent, and 28 percent of the blacks (but only 17 percent of the whites) gave her a poor rating. A Gallup poll, conducted for WMAQ-TV (NBC), showed that whites were evenly divided over their approval of Byrne's job performance, while blacks tilted 45 to 35 percent for disapproval; *Chicago Sun-Times*, 22 October 1982.

59. *Chicago Defender*, 2, 11, 13, and 27 December 1982; *Chicago Sun-Times*, 24 and 25 December 1982; *Chicago Tribune*, 24 December 1982 and 13 February 1983; Cole, "Save Our City," p. 2; Green, "Washington's Victory," p. 18. The garbage pickups and jobs program were not confined to blacks.

60. *Chicago Tribune*, 31 January 1983; and also see Cole, "Save Our City," pp. 2–3. Byrne had frequently used the general theme before late January, but this was the first time she linked it with a defense of her political funds. When Byrne was widowed, she never had to depend exclusively on her government pension.

61. *Chicago Tribune*, 25 and 31 January; and 5 and 13 February 1983. For evidence of the continuing tension between West Side and South Side blacks, and for Byrne's support among the former, see *Chicago Defender*, 4 September, 5 October, and 22 November 1982. Byrne may also have attempted to pressure School Superintendent Ruth Love into endorsing her; see Vernon Jarrett, "What Supt. Ruth Love Isn't Saying," *Chicago Tribune*, 11 February 1983.

62. Respectively, the quotations are from Dr. Muriel and Fernando Prieto, in *Chicago Tribune*, 7 and 20 February 1983. Also see Cole, "Save Our City," p. 3.

63. Bob Wiedrich, "Ingrates Trample on Daley Legacy," *Chicago Tribune*, 16 February 1983; McManus, "Jane Byrne Interview," p. 14. Also see *Chicago Tribune*, 19 and 28 January, and 6 February 1983.

64. Byrne quoted in *Chicago Tribune*, 22 February 1983, and also see the issues of 19–21 January, 2 and 11–13 February 1983; Green, "Washington's Victory," p. 18.

65. *Chicago Tribune*, 21, 26, and 30 January 1983.

66. The quotations are from Vernon Jarrett, "Byrne Campaign Scaring Whites," *Chicago Tribune*, 30 January 1983 (emphasis in original); and William Griffin, in Cole, "Save Our City," p. 3. There is no intention here even to imply that Byrne or her campaign manager designed a two-track approach. That was wholly unlikely, since at the outset they simply didn't see Washington as a serious threat.

67. *Chicago Tribune*, 17 January and 18 July 1982; *Chicago Sun-Times*, 28 September and 22 October 1982. The July and October polls also showed Washington attracting more votes from Daley than from Byrne, especially among blacks. For responses by Byrne and Vrdolyak, see Harry Golden, Jr., "Byrne Insists Polls Don't Worry Her," *Chicago Sun-Times*, 23 October 1982.

68. Basil Talbott, Jr., "Daley Advisers Divided," *Chicago Sun-Times*, 24 October 1982.

69. *Chicago Tribune*, 13 February 1983; Green, "Washington's Victory," p. 17; and Alfredo S. Lanier and Andrew Patner, "Jane Byrne Interview," *Chicago* 32 (February 1983): 95–96.

70. See *Chicago Tribune*, 13 February 1983, for Byrne's claim; and Rick Soll, "Sawyer Still Stunned by Byrne Loss," *Chicago Sun-Times*, 3 April 1983, for Sawyer's explanation.

71. The Lake Shore wards are 42, 43, 44, 46, 48, and 49; together they have 352 precincts. Wards 26 and 31 have 94 precincts, and there are 65 precincts in Wards 22 and 25. Ward 5, the University of Chicago–Hyde Park area, has 60 precincts. The wards contained in the other subareas are the same as those identified in nn. 5 and 24, Chapter 4, for 1975. In the 1983 elections, the Northwest Side wards had 469 precincts, and the South Side white ethnic wards had 541. The old Dawson wards on the South Side held 319 precincts; the other South Side black wards had 444 precincts, and the West Side black wards had 260 precincts. The citywide estimates for each group are not based only on the subareas of their concentration but derive from estimates of their behavior in all areas of the city.

72. See Table 13 for voter registration and turnout figures. Voter turnout shown in that table and nonvoting in Table 15 are expressed as percentages of the voting-age population. To express turnout as a percentage of the registered voters, divide the turnout figure by the estimate that is given for the percentage of the group's voting-age population that was registered. Similarly, to translate the figures in any row of Table 15 into the customary measure, i.e., the percentage of the vote cast, add the percentages for the three candidates and divide the figure for each candidate by that sum.

73. The number of black respondents in the WMAQ-TV (NBC) Primary Exit Poll is 1,010. Eighty-four percent reported a vote for Washington, 12 percent for Byrne, and 4 percent for Daley. The data were obtained from the Roper Center for Public Opinion Research, University of Connecticut.

74. The figures come from an analysis of the WMAQ-TV (NBC) Primary Exit Poll data. I used multiple classification analysis, confined to white respondents reporting a vote for Byrne or Daley, and took into account the simultaneous effects of sex, religion, party identification, ideology, education, income, and age. The differences reported in the text are net of the effects of the other variables, and only the sex difference is statistically significant (at .01). For the category-by-category results of an earlier version of this analysis, see Paul Kleppner, "Chicago Elects a Black Mayor: An Historical Analysis of the 1983 Election" (Chicago: American Jewish Committee, 1983), Table 3.5, p. 86.

75. Following the raw results of the exit polls, most commentators have assigned Byrne an edge among white voters. But the difference reported by the polls was usually smaller than the sampling error for the poll; e.g., the gap in the WMAQ-TV (NBC) poll is 1 percentage point, with a sampling error of 3 percentage points. It is also not certain that analysts of the exit polls have been able to take into account the differences in white turnout between the two major areas of white ethnic concentration. However, I should also notice that the difference reflected in the regression estimates is also within the range of standard error. All of this simply confirms the key point—the division of the white vote was very close. Joravsky, "Western Avenue," pp. 3–4, also gives Daley an edge over Byrne among white voters.

76. The Midwest Voter Registration Education Project, *Special Report: Chicago Mayoral Election* (Columbus, Ohio: MVREP, March 1983), estimates that 66,000 Hispanics voted, which would put the turnout rate at 27.6 percent of the voting-age population. That figure comes from examining homogeneous precincts, while the regression estimates place the number of Hispanic voters at 57,097 citywide, for a turnout rate of 23.9 percent. The exit poll conducted by MVREP also shows that Byrne ran ahead among Puerto Ricans, Mexicans, and other Hispanics, and the WBBM-TV (CBS) and WMAQ-TV (NBC) exit polls also give her a margin among Hispanic voters.

77. The full report on the 9–13 October survey is in *Chicago Sun-Times*, 22 October 1982; and the issue of 19 February 1983 conveniently compares the January and February Gallup polls. Reports on the January and February polls conducted by Market Shares Corporation were generously made available by the company's president, Nick Panagakis. The February poll conducted by Richard Day Research, Inc., is reported in Richard Day, Jeff Andreasen, and Kurt Becker, "Polling in the 1983 Chicago Mayoral Election," in *The Making of the Mayor: Chicago 1983*, ed. Melvin G. Holli and Paul M. Green (Grand Rapids: William B. Eerdmans, 1984), pp. 90–91.

78. Byrne's strategists estimated that she needed about 20 percent of the black vote. Since these polls had a sampling error of plus or minus 3 to 4 percentage points, she was either just at or just under that level from about 11–16 February.

79. For Vrdolyak's claim that Daley was running second, see *Chicago Tribune*, 16 February 1983; the issue for 20 February 1983 has the Sawyer quotation. Two days before Vrdolyak's claim, Byrne warned her supporters against overconfidence; *Chicago Tribune*, 14 February 1983. The daily results of the Dressner-Sykes polls done for the Byrne campaign during the

period 16–21 February were published in Rick Soll, "Sawyer Still Stunned by Byrne Loss," *Chicago Sun-Times*, 3 April 1968.

80. See *Chicago Defender*, 1 and 21 December 1982, editorials, for some expressions of doubt.

81. For good enumerations of the low points in the Washington campaign, see *Chicago Tribune*, 13 and 18 February 1983. Washington replaced his first campaign manager, Renault Robinson, with Al Raby. Some of the appearance of disorganization came from the involvement of a large number of black organizations and leaders who often acted on their own. It was a kind of "creative chaos," according to Raby, quoted in Laura Washington, "80% Solution" (p. 5).

82. *Chicago Sun-Times*, 21 January 1983, published a full transcript of the first debate; for reports on the second and third, see *Chicago Tribune*, 24 and 28 January 1983.

83. *Chicago Tribune*, 1 February 1983. For a good discussion of Washington's general approach to the race question in the campaign, see Ylisela, "Washington Forced Press to Grapple with Race," pp. 7–8.

84. David Axelrod, "Three Winners Emerge from Mayor Debates," *Chicago Tribune*, 2 February 1983. Green, "Washington's Victory," p. 18, offers a similar judgment.

85. *Chicago Tribune*, 29 January 1983. For Byrne's sensitivity to the general charges, see Lanier and Patner, "Jane Byrne Interview," p. 96.

86. The quotations are in *Chicago Tribune*, 1 February 1983; the other articles in the series appeared on 30 and 31 January, and 2, 3, 4, and 6 February 1983. The interviewing was concluded before the final debate and still showed Byrne running slightly over 30 percent among blacks on the South and West Sides.

87. WMAQ-TV (NBC) Primary Exit Poll. Blacks who said the debate helped voted 84.4 percent for Washington, while those who said the debates weren't helpful gave him 69.8 percent of their votes. Overall, 52.7 percent of the blacks, but only 34.7 percent of the whites, said the debates were helpful.

88. *Chicago Tribune*, 10, 11, and 20 February 1983; Green, "Washington's Victory," p. 18; and Doris A. Graber, "Media Magic: Shaping the Public's View of Chicago's Next Mayor" (paper presented at the annual convention of the Midwest Political Science Association, Chicago, April 1983), see especially Table 7, which presents a week-by-week content analysis of the major print media.

89. William Griffin, quoted in *Chicago Tribune*, 13 February 1983, and David Sawyer is also quoted to the same effect. But Byrne's strategists noted that she still held a 12-point lead over Washington and a 13-point lead over Daley.

90. *Chicago Tribune*, 7 February 1983.

91. For the quotations, see *Chicago Tribune*, 7, 14, and 19 February 1983. And see Vernon Jarrett, "Blacks Show Faith in the Ballot Box," *Chicago Tribune*, 9 February 1983, for the significance of the rally.

92. Reporters observed that Byrne was switching tactics by going on the attack against Daley; see David Axelrod, "As Election Gets Closer So Does Race for Mayor," *Chicago Tribune*, 13 February 1983.

93. The quoted phrases are from Vernon Jarrett, "Evidence of Pre-Election

Racism," *Chicago Tribune*, 18 February 1983; and Bill Granger, "How to Get Rich, Not Burned, by Election," *Chicago Tribune*, 22 February 1983. For other details, see David Axelrod, "Offensive Use of Polls Is Offensive," *Chicago Tribune*, 20 February 1983, and the reports in the issues of 16 and 19 February 1983; Charles Nicodemus, "Dirty Tricks Jolt Campaigners," *Chicago Sun-Times*, 20 February 1983; and *Chicago Defender*, 22 February 1983.

94. The Cullerton quotation is in David Axelrod, "Candidates Pulling No Punches in Last Round," *Chicago Tribune*, 21 February 1983. For activities in Pucinski's ward, see Basil Talbott, Jr., "Charges Fly as Campaign Winds Down," *Chicago Sun-Times*, 21 February 1983. And also see Jon Margolis, "Northwest Side's Voters 'Like It Like It Is,'" *Chicago Tribune*, 30 January 1983, for indications of latent racism.

95. The data from Byrne's polls are in Soll, "Sawyer Still Stunned." Other polls also caught the movement away from Byrne during the last week; see *Chicago Sun-Times*, 24 February 1983. The January and February polls by Market Shares Corporation used a ten-vote-distribution technique to distinguish "firm" from "soft" support. Between the interviews on 10–11 January and 19–20 February, Byrne's firm support among whites increased by 3 percentage points, to 31 percent; Daley's dropped by 1 percentage point, to 25 percent; and Washington's increased among blacks by 18 percentage points, to 42 percent. The statement in the text does not suggest that the Market Shares data were made available to the Byrne staff; I presume, however, that at least some of the polls done for Byrne by Dressner-Sykes did tap this dimension.

96. *Chicago Sun-Times* and *Chicago Tribune*, 21 February 1983. Vrdolyak later denied making the statement, but there were several reporters present at the rally who confirmed it.

97. In addition to heavy reportorial coverage, columnists, television commentators, and editorial writers hit the tactics. For examples, see Mike Royko, "Racist Finale: An Odorous Byrne Ploy," and Roger Simon, "Dull Politics? Not in Chicago," both in *Chicago Sun-Times*, 22 February 1983; and "The Campaign of Distortion," *Chicago Tribune* editorial, 22 February 1983.

98. *Chicago Sun-Times*, 22 February 1983; *Chicago Tribune*, 21 and 22 February 1983.

99. *Chicago Sun-Times*, 22 February 1983.

100. Vrdolyak quoted in *Chicago Tribune*, 21 February 1983; the data on contacting are from the WBBM-TV (CBS) Primary Exit Poll. Only 40.7 percent of Daley's white supporters reported that they had been contacted by a precinct captain.

101. Alderman Ralph H. Axelrod (46th Ward), quoted in *Chicago Sun-Times*, 21 February 1983; Green, "Washington's Victory," p. 19, reports the information on the weekend phone calls; and David Moberg, "The Man Who Wants to Break the Mold," *Chicago* 32 (October 1983): 172, describes the activity in Vrdolyak's ward.

102. *Chicago Tribune*, 21 February 1983. And also see *Chicago Defender*, 23 February 1983; and Sarah Snyder, "Byrne Looks for Salvation on S[outh] Side," *Chicago Sun-Times*, 21 February 1983.

103. Basil Talbott, Jr., "Charges Fly as Campaign Winds Down," *Chicago*

Sun-Times, 21 February 1983; Lillian Williams, "Washington Rips Byrne Tactics," *Chicago Tribune*, 22 February 1983; also see the issues of 20 and 21 February 1983 for reports of Washington's other campaign appearances.

104. Lillian Williams, "Washington: 'We've Run the Course,'" *Chicago Tribune*, 22 February 1983.

105. The regression estimates (Table 15) indicate that Washington received about 26,297 votes from whites and 6,362 from Hispanics, for a total of 32,659. Brian J. Kelly and Basil Talbott, Jr., "Washington Key: Lakefront Votes," *Chicago Sun-Times*, 24 February 1983, overestimate white support for Washington in these wards. The regression estimates for the six Lake Shore wards indicate that Washington polled 11,814 votes from whites. No other area gave him so large a number of white votes, although his proportionate strength among whites was greater in Ward 5. Only 3,829 whites on the Northwest and Southwest Sides voted for Washington.

106. Unidentified Daley aide, quoted in *Chicago Sun-Times*, 23 February 1983. Also see Green, "Washington's Victory," pp. 18–19.

107. The figure is from a poll conducted by Market Shares Corporation and is reported in Nick Panagakis, "Why Jane Byrne Lost Round One," *Chicago* 32 (April 1983): 180; the interviewing was done on 19–20 February 1983. Respondents were asked to assess the chances of all three candidates. Among whites, 73 percent said Byrne could win, and 40 percent said Daley could win. An earlier Gallup poll showed that 52 percent thought public opinion polls in Chicago were usually inaccurate in gauging the results of the election; see *Chicago Sun-Times*, 20 February 1983.

108. Quoted in Soll, "Sawyer Still Stunned."

109. Respectively, the quotations are from David Axelrod, "The Countdown," *Chicago Tribune*, 20 February 1983; Vernon Jarrett, "Whites May Surprise Washington," *Chicago Tribune*, 20 February 1983; and *Chicago Sun-Times*, 24 February 1983, quoting Paul Maslin, an associate of Patrick Caddell, whose firm did Washington's polling.

110. Byrne quoted in *Chicago Tribune*, 20 February 1983; and Dressner quoted in *Chicago Sun-Times*, 24 February 1983; the issue of 3 April 1983 published Byrne's poll results for the final week.

111. WMAQ-TV (NBC) Primary Exit Poll. Only 16.4 percent of the black respondents agreed that Byrne was sensitive to minorities. For the WBBM-TV (CBS) data, the correlation between Byrne approval and the vote is .78 for whites and .32 for blacks. The correlation measure is Kendall's tau-c, and the vote has been dichotomized between Byrne and all others.

112. The data are from the 19–20 February 1983 poll conducted by Market Shares Corporation. A path model of the relationships, using the WMAQ-TV (NBC) Primary Exit Poll, shows the importance of race. The model used race, education, ideology, and indices of candidate and issue assessments to explain vote choices. Together these variables explain 58.5 percent of variance of the vote, and race is by far the dominant predictor. Controlled for the impact of all the other variables, the path coefficient measuring its direct effect on the vote is .682. For the model and analysis, see Paul Kleppner and Stephen C. Baker, "Electoral Revolution Chicago Style: The Democratic Primary 1983" (paper presented at the annual meeting of the Midwest Political Science Association, Chicago, April 1984).

Notes to Chapter 7

1. Rick Murray quoted in *Chicago Tribune*, 15 March 1983.

2. The incident is described by Douglas Franz, "A One-Issue Mayoral Race," *Chicago Tribune*, 27 March 1983.

3. Quoted in Clarence Page, "Harold Washington's Biggest Challenge," *Chicago* 32 (April 1983): 175.

4. Basil Talbott, Jr., "Washington Forces Claim Close Victory," *Chicago Sun-Times*, 23 February 1983.

5. Page, "Harold Washington's Biggest Challenge," p. 175; also see *Chicago Defender*, 23 February 1983, for Washington's concern about vote fraud.

6. Jackson is quoted at length by Anne Keegan, "Washington Should Take Tip from Byrne and Hide Jesse Jackson," *Chicago Tribune*, 26 February 1983; Washington's statement is in *Chicago Sun-Times*, 24 February 1983.

7. *Chicago Sun-Times*, 24 and 25 February 1983; *Chicago Defender*, 24 February 1983.

8. *Chicago Tribune*, 27 February 1983.

9. *Chicago Tribune*, 25–27 February and 4 March 1983; Paul M. Green, "Chicago Election: The Numbers and the Implications," *Illinois Issues* 9 (August 1983): 14. See *Chicago Defender*, 26 February and 3 March 1983, for other indications of post-primary euphoria among Washington's supporters.

10. *Chicago Tribune*, 4, 6, and 8 March 1983; *Chicago Sun-Times*, 27 March 1983.

11. Peter P. Peters quoted in *Chicago Sun-Times*, 27 March 1983.

12. County Commissioner John H. Stroger, 8th Ward committeeman, quoted in *Chicago Sun-Times*, 24 February 1983. City Treasurer Cecil Partee (20th Ward) was the other committeeman who endorsed Washington on election night.

13. *Chicago Tribune*, 25 February, 13 and 14 March 1983.

14. David Axelrod, "For Democratic Dissidents, the Color That Matters Is Green," *Chicago Tribune*, 13 March 1983.

15. *Chicago Tribune*, 1, 6, and 16 March 1983.

16. *Chicago Tribune*, 6, 9, 16, and 17 March 1983.

17. Both quotations are in *Chicago Tribune*, 6 March 1983. Also see Anne Keegan, "Washington Support Talk Falls on Deaf Ears," *Chicago Tribune*, 17 March 1983.

18. Among blacks, even James C. Taylor (16th Ward), Washington's long-time political enemy, endorsed him. George Dunne's (42d Ward) endorsement was the exception among white committeemen from wards with white majorities. See *Chicago Tribune*, 4 and 6 March 1983.

19. *Chicago Sun-Times* and *Chicago Tribune*, 17 March 1983.

20. *Chicago Tribune*, 17 and 18 March 1983. Also see Vernon Jarrett, "Write-In Shows Doomsday Mood," *Chicago Tribune*, 16 March 1983.

21. *Chicago Tribune*, 17 and 20 March 1983. Byrne's supporters had tried to persuade Epton to withdraw and allow her to take his place on the ballot, and they tried a similar move with the Socialist party's candidate for mayor.

22. *Chicago Tribune*, 17 and 20 March 1983.

23. Sawyer quoted in *Chicago Tribune*, 22 March 1983; see also the issues

of 24 and 27 March 1983, for the other details. Also see "In-Again, Out-Again, Gone-Again Jane," *Newsweek* (4 April 1983): 30. Just hours before Byrne's withdrawal, her lawyers had filed suit to ease the write-in requirements.

24. *Chicago Tribune,* 24 March 1983.

25. *Chicago Tribune,* 30 March 1983.

26. *Chicago Tribune,* 30 March, 9 and 10 April 1983. In addition to Damato, Dunne, Madigan, and Quigley, the other white committeemen publicly endorsing Washington were Daniel Rostenkowski (32d Ward) and Richard Mell (33rd Ward).

27. Raby quoted in *Chicago Tribune,* 24 February 1983. Also see David Axelrod, "Washington's Campaign Blunders Boon to Epton," *Chicago Tribune,* 27 March 1983; and David Moberg, "Washington Still Has Hard Row to Hoe," *In These Times,* 20–26 April 1983.

28. *Chicago Tribune,* 23 February 1983.

29. Epton quoted in Andrew Patner, "Why Bernie Epton Wants To Be Mayor," *Chicago* 32 (April 1983): 178.

30. Philip Lentz, "Epton: Independent, but Loyal to GOP," *Chicago Tribune,* 3 April 1983, provides a capsulized review of Epton's legislative career.

31. Green, "Chicago Election," pp. 13–14; *Chicago Defender,* 24 February 1983.

32. Both quotations are in *Chicago Tribune,* 13 March 1983.

33. The quotation is from David Axelrod and Douglas Franz, "Epton Maps Advertising Attack on Washington's Legal History," *Chicago Tribune,* 13 March 1983. For the other details, see Patner, "Why Bernie Epton Wants To Be Mayor," p. 178; and *Chicago Tribune,* 20 January 1983.

34. Basil Talbott, Jr., and Lynn Sweet, "GOP Gears Up for Epton Mayoral Bid," *Chicago Sun-Times,* 24 February 1983. Wallace Johnson, the Republican candidate for mayor in 1979, aided the fund-raising effort; see his comments on the receptiveness of contributors to appeals for funds, in *Chicago Tribune,* 13 March 1983.

35. *Chicago Tribune,* 24 February 1983; *Chicago Defender,* 24 February 1983.

36. Expressed as percentages of the total vote cast in all the contests, 60.2 percent of the blacks who voted supported a black candidate, and 92.0 percent of the whites voted for a white candidate. Blacks fared better among whites when running for lower-visibility offices. For example, in 1971 a black was elected city treasurer on the Democratic ticket, but he ran nearly 5 percentage points behind both Mayor Daley and the Democratic candidate for city clerk on the Northwest and Southwest Sides and 2 percentage points ahead of them in the Lake Shore wards.

37. Laurino quoted in *Chicago Tribune,* 27 March 1983; the issue of 10 April 1983 has the other quotations.

38. For assessments by the black Republican ward committeemen, see John C. White, "Black GOP Leaders Here Quietly Follow Party Line," *Chicago Tribune,* 21 March 1983.

39. *Chicago Tribune,* 24 and 26 February 1983.

40. For the Epton quotations, see *Chicago Tribune,* 24 February 1983; and Patner, "Why Bernie Epton Wants To Be Mayor," p. 177. Barr quoted in *Chi-*

cago Sun-Times, 31 October 1982. Since Washington's earlier income tax conviction and the suspension of his law license were publicized when they occurred and again when he ran for mayor in 1977, it's inconceivable that Barr and Epton had remained unaware of them.

41. The WBBM-TV (CBS) exit poll shows that 80.1 percent of the voters who made a decision during the campaign were whites. That poll was conducted by Market Shares Corporation, and the data were made available for secondary analysis by Nick Panagakis, the president of the company, and Greg Caputo, the news director of WBBM-TV. Panagakis also generously shared with me his reports on the polls conducted by Market Shares Corporation on 22, 24 March and 5 April. The WMAQ-TV (NBC) exit poll examined in Table 22 was obtained from the Roper Center for Public Opinion Research. The surveys conducted by Richard Day Research, Inc., are reported in Richard Day, Jeff Andreasen, and Kurt Becker, "Polling in the 1983 Chicago Mayoral Election," in *The Making of the Mayor: Chicago 1983*, ed. Melvin G. Holli and Paul M. Green (Grand Rapids: William B. Eerdmans, 1984), p. 87. The Gallup poll of 26–30 March is reported in *Chicago Sun-Times*, 5 April 1983.

42. *Chicago Tribune*, 6 March 1983.

43. *Chicago Tribune*, 11 and 13 March 1983.

44. Basil Talbott, Jr., "Behind the Epton Surge," *Chicago Sun-Times*, 3 April 1983; David Axelrod, "Epton Still May Be Long Shot, But Gunfight Is Far from Over," *Chicago Tribune*, 27 March 1983.

45. *Chicago Tribune*, 11 March 1983. The interview was taped on Thursday, 10 March, for broadcast on the following Sunday, but Epton did not raise the integrity issue at his campaign stops on Thursday. At an earlier press conference, Epton told reporters, "You haven't laid a glove on Harold"; *Chicago Tribune*, 5 March 1983.

46. *Chicago Tribune*, 23 March 1983. Epton claimed that Washington actually had not filed income tax returns for nineteen years, although the statute of limitations prevented prosecution for all but the last four. The prosecutor had referred to a nineteen-year gap during the sentencing, and therefore a reference did appear in the transcript. However, Washington denied the claim then, and neither side ever presented (or had to present) evidence bearing on its credibility.

47. *Chicago Tribune*, 23 March 1983. After the debate, Deardourff told reporters that getting the integrity issue out was "what we wanted to do" tonight; *Chicago Tribune*, 31 March 1983.

48. Deardourff quoted in Jeff Lyon, "Selling of a Myth: The Men Who Mold the Image," *Chicago Tribune*, 31 March 1983, and see the issue of 7 April 1983, for the sharp exchange between Deardourff and William Zimmerman, Washington's media adviser, over the charge of racial appeals.

49. Quoted in Jeff Lyon, "Selling of a Myth."

50. Mike Royko, "If Harold Loses, He'll Have Himself to Blame," *Chicago Sun-Times*, 10 April 1983; the Epton quotation is in *Chicago Tribune*, 31 March 1983. For the details of the disclosures, see *Chicago Tribune*, 6, 8, and 10 April 1983; and Green, "Chicago Election," p. 16.

51. Quoted in Moberg, "Washington Still Has Hard Row to Hoe," p. 6.

52. David Axelrod, "GOP's Epton Must Temper His Tantrums," *Chicago*

Tribune, 3 April 1983; Mike Royko, "Cut That Out, Bernie," *Chicago Sun-Times*, 5 April 1983; Vernon Jarrett, "Washington Erred, But Blacks Learned Art of Forgiving," *Chicago Tribune*, 27 March 1983; and Don Rose, "How the 1983 Mayoral Election Was Won: Reform, Racism, and Rebellion," in *The Making of the Mayor*, ed. Holli and Green, pp. 109–10.

53. See "Chicago's Ugly Election," *Newsweek* (11 April 1983): 18, for the lyric and tune; and *Chicago Tribune*, 10 April 1983, for Epton's commitment to neighborhood pride made to residents of Marquette Park on the Southwest Side.

54. Monroe Anderson, "Jeers Keep Washington from Church Services," *Chicago Tribune*, 28 March 1983; Brian J. Kelly, "How One Community's Suspicions Boiled Over," *Chicago Sun-Times*, 3 April 1983; "Chicago's Ugly Election," *Newsweek* (11 April 1983): 19; and "The Making of a Litmus Test," *Time* (11 April 1983): 15. Also see Anne Keegan, "Parish Makes News—Hard Way," *Chicago Tribune*, 2 April 1983.

55. Mitchell Locin and Douglas Frantz, "Angry Calls Follow Jeers at Washington," *Chicago Tribune*, 29 March 1983.

56. Quoted in *Chicago Tribune*, 27 March 1983.

57. Quoted in Cheryl Lavin, "A Battered Knight Surveys the Wreckage and the Dream," *Chicago Tribune*, 19 May 1983.

58. The quotation is from David Broder, "Candidates Responsible for Their 'Hired Guns,'" *Chicago Sun-Times*, 10 April 1983. For other reactions in national media, see "The Making of a Litmus Test," *Time* (11 April 1983): 15; "Chicago's Ugly Election," *Newsweek* (11 April 1983): 18–21; "Chicago's Lessons," *Nation* 236 (30 April 1983): 531; and "Racial Brush Fires," *New Republic* 188 (18 April 1983): 12–13. For Epton's critical reaction to this national coverage, see Steve Neal and Thom Shanker, "Epton Rips National Coverage of Election," *Chicago Tribune*, 8 April 1983.

59. *Chicago Tribune* editorials, 27 and 28 March 1983. In the issue of 13 March 1983, the *Chicago Tribune* had endorsed Washington for mayor. Also see *Chicago Sun-Times* editorial, 10 April 1983.

60. Quoted in Lavin, "A Battered Knight."

61. *Chicago Sun-Times*, 5 April 1983, quoting a member of the Gallup organization.

62. Copies of these were reproduced on the front page of the *Chicago Defender*, 5 and 7 March 1983; also see the story on 11 March 1983, which claimed to have traced some of the literature to the Epton camp.

63. Quoted in Lavin, "A Battered Knight."

64. The Epton quotations are in Lavin, "A Battered Knight," and *Chicago Tribune*, 6 March 1983, respectively.

65. Epton quoted in *Chicago Tribune*, 2 April 1983; Green, "Chicago Election," p. 16.

66. Washington was clearly aware of this; see his comments in William Raspbery, "On Washington's Campaign Trail," *Chicago Tribune*, 11 April 1983.

67. Axelrod, "Washington's Campaign Blunders"; Jon Margolis, "Washington a Puzzle to Democrats," *Chicago Tribune*, 3 April 1983; and Barry Cronin, "Epton Democrats Push Turnout," *Chicago Sun-Times*, 11 April 1983.

68. Moberg, "Washington Still Has a Hard Row to Hoe," pp. 6–7; Raby quoted in Lillian Williams, "Washington Campaigning on Two Fronts," *Chicago Sun-Times*, 27 March 1983.

69. Mike Royko, "If Harold Loses, He'll Have Himself to Blame," and "By Kook or Crook, We Have to Pick a Mayor," *Chicago Sun-Times*, 10 and 11 April 1983.

70. Quoted in *Chicago Tribune*, 14 and 24 March 1983; the latter issue also contains a report on the news conference Epton held to denounce Washington's remarks.

71. Both quotations are in Axelrod, "Epton Still May Be Long Shot," and the 15 March poll showed Washington with the large lead.

72. In 1919, William Hale Thompson polled 37.6 percent of the vote, winning by 3.2 percentage points over his Democratic opponent in a five-candidate field. In 1983, just over 1.33 million Chicagoans turned out on election day, but 42,381 did not cast a ballot for any of the three mayoral candidates. The Socialist party's candidate for mayor polled 3,751 votes citywide.

73. Using the precinct level voting and census data for the entire city (i.e., for 2,914 precincts), the regression of the percentage of the voting-age population for Washington on the percent black explains 87.4 percent of the variance of the vote. Using the WMAQ-TV (NBC) exit poll, education, ideology, income, party identification, religion, and sex together explain 34.9 percent of the variance of the vote for Washington. Add race to the equation as the final variable, and the proportion increases by 26.3 percentage points to a total of 61.2 percent. Moreover, in the seven-variable model, race has a partial standardized regression coefficient of .67, which is 3.5 times larger than the coefficient for education, the second-best predictor of the vote.

74. Deardourff quoted in *Chicago Sun-Times*, 10 April 1983. The subgroup analysis of the black vote used the WMAQ-TV (NBC) exit poll, and the WBBM-TV (CBS) exit poll shows the same pattern of results. Green, "Chicago Election," p. 17, incorrectly claims that white turnout was higher than black turnout. He errs in two ways. First, he measures turnout as a percentage of the registered voters. Second, and more seriously, he relies on ward data and attributes all of the turnout in predominantly white wards to white voters. But many of the predominantly white areas contained small numbers of blacks, and they often turned out at higher rates than the whites. In the white areas of the Southwest Side, for example, white turnout was 75.3 percent, and black turnout was 77.1 percent.

75. For the patterns of Hispanic support, see *Chicago Tribune*, 14 April 1983; and Midwest Voter Registration Education Project, *Final Exit Poll Report: Chicago Mayoral Election* (Columbus, Ohio: MVREP, 1983), p. 10, which indicates that 82.3 percent of the Puerto Rican respondents and 62.7 percent of the Mexicans voted for Washington. Exit polls report the vote division among those who cast ballots and ignore the nonvoters. To compare these figures with the regression estimates, add the percentages reported in the appropriate rows of Table 23 and then divide each by that sum. The resulting figure is 79.1 percent for Puerto Ricans and 54 percent for Mexicans.

76. These figures derive from a secondary analysis of the data from the exit poll conducted by the Midwest Voter Registration Education Project.

They are based on 601 Puerto Rican respondents and 249 Mexican respondents. On the importance of party identification, see the statements of Hispanic leaders quoted in James Martinez, "Mayoral Contenders Aim at Winning Hispanic Voters," *Chicago Sun-Times*, 7 April 1983. And also see Paul M. Basile, "Hispanics Buck Machine in Mayoral Race: Pave Way for Latino Political Coalition," *Heritage* 6 (Summer 1983): 3, 8–9.

77. The exit polls give Washington slightly more white support. The WBBM-TV (CBS) poll shows 23 percent of the white voters supporting Washington, and the WMAQ-TV (NBC) poll gives him 19.6 percent. However, if the regression estimates are translated into the number of votes each group cast for each candidate, they provide a closer approximation of the actual results of the election than the exit polls. For the comparative data, see Paul Kleppner, "Chicago Elects a Black Mayor: An Historical Analysis of the 1983 Election" (Chicago: American Jewish Committee, 1983), Table 3.7, p. 98.

78. In the two areas combined, only 4.1 percent of the white voting-age population supported Washington; 67.3 percent voted for Epton, and 28.4 percent didn't vote at all for mayor.

79. For example, the WMAQ-TV (NBC) exit poll shows that among whites with annual incomes of $35,000 or more, Washington received 23 percent support, but he received only 16.5 percent among whites with incomes of $8,000 or less. However, Washington's comparatively "high" support among upper-income whites was due entirely to their educational levels and ideological identifications.

80. Over half the white Catholics (52.8 percent), compared with 38.6 percent of the white non-Catholics, agreed with the statement that Chicago was not ready for a black mayor. The data in this paragraph are from a reanalysis of the WMAQ-TV (NBC) exit poll; and see Kleppner, "Chicago Elects a Black Mayor," Table 3.14, p. 120, for the patterns of support by education and sex within each of the three major religious groups.

81. These figures and those in the following paragraph derive from regression estimates (like those in Table 23) applied to the known sizes of the voting-age population in the area. For the exaggerated claims, see William C. McCready, "White Ethnic Vote for Washington: An Unsung Story That Provides Hope," *Chicago Sun-Times*, op-ed column, 27 April 1983; and "'Color Blind' Ethnics Surprise the Media in Chicago Mayoral Election," *Building Blocks* (Summer 1983): 3, quoting a study by Ed Marciniak. The publication is issued by the National Center for Urban Ethnic Affairs; Marciniak is chairman of the NCUEA board of directors and heads the Institute for Urban Life in Chicago. McCready is director of the Cultural Pluralism Center at the University of Chicago's National Opinion Research Center.

82. Technically, multiple classification analysis was used to make the adjustments, and the procedure assumes linear relationships and no significant interactions among the predictor variables. The appropriate tests show that the variables used satisfied those assumptions.

83. When all seven variables are used in tandem, only the effects of education and ideology remain statistically significant (at the .001 level). The small age differences also wiped out; and the younger age groups (eighteen to twenty-four and twenty-five to thirty-four) gave less support to Washing-

ton than the three older age categories. When blacks and whites are grouped together for analysis, a clear age pattern appears, with younger voters more heavily pro-Washington. But that simply reflects the age composition within the black group, a fact that Patrick Caddell overlooked when he referred to the comparative youth of Washington's supporters overall. For his comment, see *Chicago Sun-Times*, 14 April 1983.

84. The data for areas of the city are from regression estimates of the transition rates from the primary to the general election. The figures for the newly mobilized voters and the citywide data in the first sentence are from the WBBM-TV (CBS) exit poll. The WMAQ-TV (NBC) exit poll shows the same patterns, although the proportions of Washington support are generally a bit higher. Needless to say, the exit polls and regression estimates all show that newly mobilized blacks and those who supported Washington in the primary voted for him in the general election almost unanimously. So did the blacks who supported Byrne, but "only" 86 percent of the small number of blacks preferring Daley in the primary voted for Washington in the general election.

85. Nearly all (97.3 percent) of the votes cast for Epton came from white voters, and 11.7 percent of Washington's votes came from whites and 6.4 percent from Hispanics. The figures come from translating the regression estimates in Table 23 into the number of votes cast by each group for each of the candidates.

86. The Davis quotation and other predictions are in David Axelrod, "A Bitter Mayoral Race Goes Down to the Wire," *Chicago Tribune*, 10 April 1983.

87. See Moberg, "Washington Still Has a Hard Row to Hoe," p. 6, for the quotation. The data on contacting are from the WBBM-TV (CBS) exit poll, and those measuring how strongly blacks supported Washington are from the WMAQ-TV (NBC) exit poll. Only 12.3 percent of the blacks indicated a reservation about supporting Washington, and 3.3 percent chose him as the "least objectionable" candidate. Among whites, 55.7 percent expressed a reservation or saw Epton as the "least objectionable" choice. The polls conducted by Market Shares Corporation on 22 and 24 March showed that 70 percent and 80 percent, respectively, of the blacks were firm in their support for Washington. A Gallup poll during the first week of April showed that 74 percent of the blacks and 62 percent of the whites said there was "no chance" that anything might prevent them from voting in the election; *Chicago Sun-Times*, 8 April 1983.

88. The data in Table 27 are reported in Day, Andreasen, and Becker, "Polling in the 1983 Chicago Mayoral Election," pp. 97–98. The data for the Lake Shore wards are not confined to whites; but whites were 76.7 percent of the voting-age population of the six-ward area, while blacks made up 12.1 percent and Hispanics 11.1 percent. If one assumes that the blacks on the Lake Shore reacted as blacks elsewhere in the city (and the regression estimates show that they did on election day), then the bulk of the undecided voters there must have been whites; and most of the changes in Washington's support levels must have been due to their responses.

89. Rose, "How the 1983 Mayoral Election Was Won," p. 117, cites the 7 April 1983 poll done for Washington by Patrick Caddell.

90. The quotations are in Royko, "If Harold Loses"; and David Axelrod,

"Mayor Foes Zero in on Lakefront," *Chicago Tribune*, 3 April 1983. Gallup's interviews on 26–30 March showed 16 percent of the whites undecided; Day, Andreasen, and Becker, "Polling in the 1983 Chicago Mayoral Election," p. 95, report that on 6 April, Gallup found 12 percent of all voters undecided; and the poll by Richard Day Research, Inc., put the figure at 10 percent on 10 April.

' 91. This assumes no change in the voting patterns of blacks and Hispanics. In fact, the WMAQ-TV (NBC) exit poll gave Washington 19.6 percent support among whites and 51.9 percent of all respondents. The anomaly in Table 28 is the category of whites who attended graduate school and made their decisions two to four weeks prior to the election. That category made up 15.1 percent of all the whites who attended graduate school, while 17.1 percent made their choice in the final three days.

92. Basil Talbott, Jr., "Election May Hinge on Ethnic Turnout," *Chicago Sun-Times*, 10 April 1983, characterizes the election; Brian J. Kelly, "Epton Relies on Commercials," *Chicago Sun-Times*, 11 April 1983, quotes Epton; and David Axelrod, "Mayor Foes Zero in on Lakefront," compares the Lake Shore wards with the other areas.

93. The quotations are in Mitchell Locin and Thom Shanker, "Washington Woos Lakefront, Blacks; Epton Keeps Low Profile," *Chicago Tribune*, 10 April 1983; and Lillian Williams, "Washington Raps 'Rich' Foe," *Chicago Sun-Times*, 11 April 1983.

94. Mitchell Locin and Thom Shanker, "Epton Firm Earned $1.3 Million from Insurers, Group Says," *Chicago Tribune*, 3 April 1983; and Locin and Shanker, "Washington Woos Lakefront." The Illinois Public Action Council's political committee had endorsed Washington. In an election-day column, Mike Royko raised these and other questions bearing on Epton's integrity; see Royko, "By Kook or Crook." While not discussed publicly during the campaign, some of Epton's campaign literature inaccurately described his World War II record and his educational background; see Moberg, "Washington Still Has Hard Row to Hoe," p. 7.

95. Axelrod, "Mayor Foes Zero in on Lakefront"; and Williams, "Washington Raps 'Rich' Foe."

96. Lillian Williams and Brian J. Kelly, "Washington Blasts Democrats," *Chicago Sun-Times*, 10 April 1983; and Axelrod, "Mayor Foes Zero in on Lakefront." Also see Lochin and Shanker, "Washington Woos Lakefront"; and Moberg, "Washington Still Has Hard Row to Hoe," p. 7.

97. Washington quoted in Thom Shanker and Mitchell Locin, "Mayoral Race Hot Down to Wire," *Chicago Tribune*, 11 April 1983. Also see Lillian Williams, "Washington Alters Style, Still Revels in Campaigning," and James Martinez, "Mayoral Contenders Aim at Winning Hispanic Voters," both in *Chicago Sun-Times*, 7 April 1983.

98. Bill Zimmerman, Washington's media consultant, quoted in Ellen Warren, "Washington Advisers List Rights—and Wrongs," *Chicago Sun-Times*, 20 April 1983; and the text and description of the commercial is in Kelly, "Epton Relies on Commercials."

99. The best discussion of this background is in Rose, "How the 1983 Mayoral Election Was Won," pp. 117–18. Also see David Axelrod and Monroe An-

derson, "New Charges False, Washington Says," *Chicago Tribune*, 8 April 1983.

100. Washington quoted in Douglas Frantz and Mitchell Locin, "Don't Work Against Me, Washington Warns Vrdolyak," *Chicago Tribune*, 9 April 1983. On his failure to appear on the Wally Phillips Show and an incident with a college student, see Lillian Williams and Mark Brown, "Washington Loses Cool, Rips Questioner," *Chicago Sun-Times*, 8 April 1983.

101. Epton quoted in Frantz and Locin, "Don't Work Against Me." Deardourff expressed concern over the possible sympathy effects; see his statement quoted by Talbott, "Election May Hinge on Ethnic Turnout," which also quotes Washington's planner. For such a reaction, although not focused on the morals charge, see Roger Simon, "One Vote against Hatred and Fear," *Chicago Sun-Times*, 12 April 1983.

102. Deardourff explained what the campaign would do in its final days; see Axelrod, "Mayor Foes Zero in on Lakefront."

103. Locin and Shanker, "Washington Woos Lakefront"; and Williams and Kelly, "Washington Blasts Democrats."

104. Kelly, "Epton Relies on Commercials"; and Harry Golden, Jr., and Mark Brown, "Epton Sees Win, Gets GOP Cash," *Chicago Sun-Times*, 8 April 1983. On 10 April, the IVI criticized the commercials, saying it had not endorsed Epton when he last ran for state representative in 1980.

105. Barry Cronin, "Epton Democrats Push Turnout," *Chicago Sun-Times*, 11 April 1983; and Kelly, "Epton Relies on Commercials."

106. Williams, "Washington Raps 'Rich' Foe"; Williams and Kelly, "Washington Blasts Democrats"; Locin and Shanker, "Washington Woos Lakefront"; Shanker and Locin, "Mayor Race Hot Down to Wire"; and Golden and Brown, "Epton Sees Win."

107. David Axelrod, "Epton, Washington Tied," *Chicago Tribune*, 13 April 1983.

108. Commentators pointed to the 46th Ward as the site of Washington's best showing on the lakefront. He polled 46.8 percent of the votes cast there, which represented 23.2 percent of the ward's voting-age population. But turnout was higher in the 42d Ward, and Washington was supported by 26.5 percent of its voting-age population, but that gave him only 45.5 percent of the total number of votes cast in the ward.

109. The quotations and the assessments by both pollsters are in Brian J. Kelly and Basil Talbott, Jr., "How White Vote Spelled Victory," *Chicago Sun-Times*, 14 April 1983.

110. Quoted in Moberg, "Washington Still Has Hard Row to Hoe," p. 6 (emphasis added). The data are from the WMAQ-TV (NBC) exit poll. Among all of Washington's white voters, 58.4 percent voiced one or the other of those comments about their decision, and so did 55.7 percent of all of Epton's white supporters.

111. David Axelrod, "Party Isn't Crucial This Time," *Chicago Tribune*, 12 April 1983.

112. Anne Keegan, "Bigot Label Hung on City by a National Press with a Hang-Up," *Chicago Tribune*, 12 April 1983 (emphasis in original). Also see Basil Talbott, Jr., "Jet-Lag Journalism Bombs," *Chicago Sun-Times*, 10 April

1983; David Axelrod and Monroe Anderson, "Washington Unity Plea," *Chicago Tribune*, 14 April 1983; and Kelly and Talbott, "How White Vote Spelled Victory."

113. William J. Eaton, "U.S. Poll Cites Washington's Legal Troubles," *Chicago Sun-Times*, 12 April 1983.

114. *Chicago Tribune* editorial, 6 February 1983.

115. See Chapter 4 for the convictions of the Democrats. For the details on Scott's case, see *Chicago Tribune*, 15 and 20 March, 29 May, 4 June, and 30 July 1980; and also see Roger Simon, "Crime DOES Pay—for Bill Scott," *Chicago Sun-Times*, 9 October 1981. None of the newspaper accounts report any comments by Epton on Scott's conviction. Since Epton was then a Republican state legislator, he may have attended, or at least purchased a ticket for, the Scott dinner; but the newspapers mentioned only the higher-ranking party leaders, e.g., former Governor Richard Ogilvie, who spoke at the dinner.

116. *Chicago Tribune*, 3 March 1983. However, there was no civil or criminal prosecution involved in Vrdolyak's case.

117. Eighty-two percent of the blacks also thought Washington would win. The data are from the 22 March poll by Market Shares Corporation.

118. WMAQ-TV (NBC) exit poll. Only 10.1 percent of the blacks singled out race as the most important factor, and they voted 95.3 percent for Washington. Only 8 percent of the blacks thought Chicago wasn't ready for a black mayor, and they voted 85 percent for Washington.

119. George Will, "A Devil of a Town," *Newsweek* (13 February 1984): 92. Since virtually all of the blacks voted for Washington, the sentences could be rewritten substituting "blacks" and "Washington" for "whites" and "Epton" where appropriate. The statement of the relationships derives from a path model of voter choice, which used the WMAQ-TV (NBC) exit poll. The model used race, education, ideology, party identification, and indices of candidate and issue assessments to explain vote choices. These variables together explain 70.4 percent of the variance of the vote, and race is by far the dominant predictor. Controlled for the impact of all the other variables, the path coefficient measuring its direct effect on the vote is .362, and its indirect effect through candidate evaluations is .330. The sum of the two effects, its overall effect coefficient, is .692. For the detailed model and discussion, see Paul Kleppner and Stephen C. Baker, "Race War Chicago Style: The Election of a Black Mayor 1983" (paper presented at the annual convention of the American Political Science Association, Washington, D.C., August 1984).

120. On 10 April, Epton acknowledged that he and his staff had made a conscious decision not to campaign in black neighborhoods. See his statement, quoted in Mitchell Locin and Thom Shanker, "Washington, Epton Sound Unity Notes," *Chicago Tribune*, 12 April 1983.

Notes to Chapter 8

1. The quotations are in Douglas Frantz, "As Backers Wait, Epton Abruptly Leaves," *Chicago Tribune*, 14 April 1983. On Thursday, while vacationing in Palm Beach, Florida, Epton said: "It seems like the people voting left their brains at home." And he accused the Chicago media of "vicious, vile" reporting that unfairly depicted him as a racist. "I think the media should be thor-

oughly ashamed of itself for finding racial hatred when it was almost non-existent." For these sentiments by Epton, see *Chicago Tribune*, 16 April 1983.

2. The text of Washington's victory speech is in *Chicago Sun-Times*, 14 April 1983; I have reversed the order of the phrases but not changed the meaning of the statement.

3. David Axelrod and Monroe Anderson, "Washington Unity Plea," *Chicago Tribune*, 14 April 1983.

4. Mike Royko, "Picking Up on New Era," *Chicago Sun-Times*, 14 April 1983. For another view, see David Axelrod, "Washington Well-Equipped to Heal the City's Wounds," *Chicago Tribune*, 17 April 1983.

5. The quotations from Washington's inaugural address in this and the following paragraphs are in David Axelrod and Mitchell Locin, "Mayor Comes in Firing," *Chicago Tribune*, 30 April 1983. For Jane Byrne's reaction, see Andy Knott, "Byrne's Poker Face Finally Fades," *Chicago Tribune*, 30 April 1983.

6. Quoted in Axelrod and Locin, "Mayor Comes in Firing," *Chicago Tribune*, 30 April 1983.

7. On 11 May, Washington vetoed the resolutions, but his action was disallowed by both the Cook County Circuit Court and the Illinois Appellate Court. See *Chicago Sun-Times*, 11 June 1983, for a convenient chronology of events.

8. Rick Soll, "Vrdolyak: 'I Knew It Would Be War,'" *Chicago Sun-Times*, 8 May 1983; and Harry Golden, Jr., and Jim Merriner, "Mayor's Tough Talk Blamed for Swing to Revolt," *Chicago Sun-Times*, 4 May 1983.

9. Robert Davis, "Washington, Aldermen Talk Peace over Breakfast," *Chicago Tribune*, 20 April 1983; David Moberg, "The Man Who Wants to Break the Mold," *Chicago* 32 (October 1983): 172-77, for the meeting between Vrdolyak and Washington and its background.

10. Quoted in Moberg, "Man Who Wants to Break the Mold," p. 174.

11. The quotation is in Golden and Merriner, "Mayor's Tough Talk," *Chicago Sun-Times*, 4 May 1983. The best treatment of Vrdolyak's organizing efforts is Moberg, "Man Who Wants to Break the Mold," pp. 172-75.

12. Quoted in Moberg, "Man Who Wants to Break the Mold," p. 173.

13. David Axelrod, "'The Party's Over'—Again—for Chicago's Political Machine," *Chicago Tribune*, 17 April 1983.

14. *Chicago Sun-Times*, 24 April 1983; *Chicago Tribune*, 19 May 1983.

15. Moberg, "Man Who Wants to Break the Mold," p. 172.

16. Washington carried wards 1, 15, 22, and 37, whose aldermen have voted with the Vrdolyak bloc; and he lost wards 42, 43, 48, and 49, whose aldermen opposed the Vrdolyak group. The conviction and resignation of one of Washington's supporters reduced the effective size of his bloc to twenty. The alignment among the mass electorate is remarkably similar to that among the aldermen. A Gallup poll conducted between 5 and 18 October 1983 showed that 30 percent of the white respondents, and 82 percent of the blacks, supported Washington in the power struggle with Vrdolyak. The level of white support represented an 8-percentage-point gain from a poll on 2 August. For both sets of poll results, see *Chicago Sun-Times*, 6 November 1983.

17. Although he later denied having said it, the Vrdolyak statement was published in the Lerner newspapers. See the report by Harry Golden, Jr., and Jim Merriner, "Council Factions May Turn Scrap into 4-Year Saga," *Chicago Sun-Times*, 26 June 1983. In a 23–25 September 1983 poll by Market Shares Corporation, 43 percent of the white respondents and 72 percent of the blacks picked racism as the main reason for opposition to Washington by the Vrdolyak bloc. The results of the poll are in *Chicago Sun-Times*, 19 October 1983.

18. The quotations are in Stanley Ziemba, "Mayor Plans No Housing 'Stampede,'" *Chicago Tribune*, 17 April 1983; and Hugh Hough, "'Ethnic Distrust' of Mayor Told," *Chicago Sun-Times*, 1 February 1984. For other indications of the sensitivity of white ethnics to the location of public housing, see the reports in *Chicago Sun-Times*, 15 April and 19 June 1983; and for their all-or-nothing attitude, see Jim Keck, "CHA's Scattered-Site Program Perils Neighborhoods near Minority Areas," *Chicago Sun-Times*, 11 July 1983, op-ed essay. Keck is the consultant to the Southwest Parish and Neighborhood Federation.

19. *New York Times*, 12 April, 6, 15, and 19 May 1983; *Washington Post*, 18 April 1983. For another view of the larger impact of Chicago's results, see Joseph Clark, "Chicago Changes the Agenda," *Dissent* (Summer 1983): 281–85.

20. *New York Times*, 19 May 1983. According to the NBC exit polls, 19 percent of the whites in Chicago and 24 percent in Philadelphia voted for the black candidate. The data from both exit polls were obtained from the Roper Center for Public Opinion Research, University of Connecticut.

21. More technically, when controlled for the effects of education, ideology, income, party identification, religion, and sex, race in Chicago had a partial standardized regression coefficient of .67, and its inclusion in the model explained an additional 26.3 percent of the variance of the vote for Washington in the general election. In the same model for Philadelphia, race had a partial standardized regression coefficient of .61, and its inclusion added 16.8 percent to the explained variance of the vote for Goode. In both cities, race was by far the best predictor of voting choice, and its standardized regression coefficient was over three times larger than the second-best predictor, education.

22. *New York Times*, 20 April, 6 and 16 May 1983; *Pittsburgh Press*, 8 May 1983; and *Chicago Sun-Times*, 27 March 1983.

23. See the discussion by Stanley Lieberson, *A Piece of the Pie: Blacks and White Immigrants since 1880* (Berkeley: University of California Press, 1980), pp. 51–76; and for the process of accommodation among white elites in Atlanta and Detroit, see Peter K. Eisinger, *The Politics of Displacement: Racial and Ethnic Transition in Three American Cities* (New York: Academic Press, 1980), pp. 147–99.

24. U.S. Bureau of the Census, News Release CB83–63 (18 April 1983). The nine states were California, Illinois, Indiana, Kentucky, Louisiana, Missouri, Ohio, South Carolina, and Tennessee. If we take into account differences in the composition of the white and black groups in age, sex, income, and education, black turnout in 1982 was 9.3 percentage points higher than white turnout. In 1978, the same five-variable model showed black turnout to be

5.5 percentage points below white participation. These observations derive from a reanalysis of the data from the National Election Studies conducted by the Center for Political Studies, University of Michigan. The data were obtained from the Inter-University Consortium for Political and Social Research, University of Michigan.

25. U.S. Bureau of the Census, *Current Population Reports*, Series P-20, No. 370, *Voting and Registration in the Election of November 1980* (Washington, D.C.: Government Printing Office, 1982), Table 2, pp. 10–21; and U.S. Bureau of the Census, News Release, CB83–63 (18 April 1983), Table 2. For local reaction to the report on turnout in 1982, see *Chicago Defender*, 18 April 1982.

26. The observations derive from a reanalysis of the CBS–New York Times exit poll data, which were obtained from the Inter-University Consortium for Political and Social Research, University of Michigan. Also see Thomas E. Cavanagh, "The Reagan Referendum: The Black Vote in the 1982 Election" (paper presented at the annual meeting of the Midwest Political Science Association, Chicago, April 1983).

27. Whites also disapproved of Reagan's economic performance, but by only 53.1 percent to 44.4 percent. These data are from a reanalysis of the 1982 NBC exit poll, and the data were obtained from the Roper Center for Public Opinion Research, University of Connecticut. On both questions, I have treated an excellent or good rating as approval, and a fair or poor rating as disapproval. For similar pre-election results, see *The Gallup Report*, No. 207 (December 1982): 19–26; Cavanagh, "Reagan Referendum," pp. 2–5. The trend continued after the election. By April 1983 only 10 percent of the black respondents approved of Reagan's job performance; see the Gallup poll reported in *Chicago Sun-Times*, 1 May 1983. *The Gallup Report*, No. 212 (May 1983): 8, indicated a racial split on the question of whether blacks were being fairly or unfairly treated by the Reagan Administration: 77 percent of the blacks said unfairly, while 55 percent of the whites said fairly.

28. The information on the geographic and issue focus of movement actions was developed from data reported by Doug McAdam, *Political Process and the Development of Black Insurgency* (Chicago: University of Chicago Press, 1983), Tables 7.2 and 7.3, pp. 152–53; see pp. 146–80 for his insightful analysis of the movement's dynamics.

29. Between 1966 and 1970, only 34 percent of the actions initiated by the movement occurred in the southern and border states; see McAdam, *Political Process*, Table 8.3, p. 190, and pp. 181–229 for analysis of the factors underlying the decline of the movement.

30. Philip E. Converse et al., *American Social Attitudes Data Sourcebook, 1947–1978* (Cambridge, Mass.: Harvard University Press, 1980), Tables 1.11, 2.22, and 2.27, pp. 12, 79, and 83.

31. Warren E. Miller, Arthur H. Miller, and Edward J. Schneider, *American National Election Studies Data Sourcebook, 1952–1978* (Cambridge, Mass.: Harvard University Press, 1980), Tables 4.32, 4.38, and 4.41, pp. 269, 278, and 284. More whites gave cynical than trustful responses for the first time in 1974, which provides evidence of a Watergate effect, but the trend among blacks predated that by four years.

32. Paul Kleppner, *Who Voted? The Dynamics of Electoral Turnout, 1870–*

1980 (New York: Praeger, 1982), pp. 114–22. The off-year turnout rates were consistently lower, of course, but they display the same trend.

33. Joel D. Aberbach and Jack L. Walker, "The Meanings of Black Power: A Comparison of White and Black Interpretations of a Political Slogan," *American Political Science Review* 64 (June 1970): 367–88.

34. Vernon Jarrett, "Blacks Show Faith in the Ballot Box," *Chicago Tribune*, 9 February 1983; and Jacqueline Thomas, "Blacks Looking to New Political Horizons," *Chicago Sun-Times*, 18 April 1983.

Index